I0476758

With illustrations, charts and solved problems

FINANCIAL REPORTING

UNDER

CONSOLIDATION OF SUBSIDIARIES

ASSOCIATES AND JOINT ARRANGEMENTS

i) *Financial Reporting under Companies Act 2013*
ii) *Accounting Standards and Ind ASs on Consolidation*
iii) *Basic concepts on consolidation of financial statements*
iv) *Consolidation of holding company with one subsidiary*
v) *Chain holding including intercompany holdings*
vi) *Consolidated Profit and Loss and Consolidated Cash Flow*
vii) *Consolidation of Parent with one subsidiary and associate and / or Joint ventures or Jointly controlled entries*
viii) *Joint Arrangements*
ix) *Advanced problems on consolidation*

Written by B D Chatterjee

B.Com (Hons), ACA, ACMA, ACS, Dip IFR (ACCA - UK)

Author of books on International Financial Reporting Standards, Financial

Reporting and Accounting Standards, Indian Accounting Standards (Ind AS)

Contents	Page no

Brief profile of the author

B D Chatterjee is a Chartered Accountant with CS, CMA qualifications and a diploma holder in IFRS from ACCA UK having over 30 Years of rich experience in overall business and finance function.

He possesses expertise in CFO solutions especially in areas like, Merger & Acquisitions, financial due diligence, business strategy, business restructuring & strategic planning including development of business plan and budgetary control, implementation of global best practices, ERP- Implementation and Project Management, Audit & Change Management, Financial Analysis & Business Valuations, Enterprise Risk Management, Value added management consulting and has extensive knowledge and experience in the fields of industrial gases, chemicals, dairy and FMCG businesses.

Before launching into practice, he has held key high profile positions working as Group CFO for Mother Dairy and Director Finance India for Kelly Services, US and various other senior positions like Director Finance/ Vice-President/Finance Controller with other large global MNCs like DuPont and BOC Gases and large Indian conglomerates like Max India.

Apart from his consulting assignments, he also teaches IFRS as visiting faculty with an international institute and has authored two books on Financial Reporting and Accounting Standards for CA Final students.

Preface

In today's highly dynamic business world and intense whirlpool of competitive environment business decisions are taken at the speed of thought. In this backdrop for survival and growth corporates go through major process of consolidation and business structuring from time to time, because they know that unless they manage change well, change beyond control will take over and throw them out of business. Many of us, through our varied experience in consolidation of various businesses, have played active role in this change management process.

Keeping this in view I have thought of coming up with this work wherein I have dovetailed my decades of practical experience in financial reporting with theory and the book professes to assist the finance professionals and students of CA / CMA / CS fraternity in the following manner:
   a) comprehend the various nuances of consolidation of financial statements,
   b) delve into Indian Accounting Standards (Ind AS and AS) converged with International Financial Reporting Standards (IFRSs) related to consolidation of financial statements,
   c) explain the base concept with lucid explanation with more than hundred illustrations and solved problems
   d) Incorporate the latest statutory guidelines on Financial Reporting related to consolidation of accounts

In developing this work, references have been made from time to time from The Institute of Chartered Accountants of India and The Institute of Cost & Management Accountants of India publications related to the subject matter.

I would like to take this opportunity to mention that while considerable care has been taken to ensure that the contents of the book are accurate, a few errors and omissions might have crept in, for which I seek with all humility to my readers to bear with me.

I would like dedicate this book to my loving parents without whose constant inspiration this would not have been possible.

I would also like to thank my wife who stood by my side to ensure that the book saw the light of day.

B D Chatterjee
121/105 Silver Oaks Apartments
DLF Phase I
Gurgaon 122002
Email: bdchatterjee105@gmail.com
Website: bdc-associates.com
LinkedIn: in.linkedin.com/pub/biswajeet-chatterjee/2/5a9/b6/

Chapter 1   Financial reporting under Companies Act 2013

Learning Outcome
- **Financial reporting under Companies Act 2013**
- **Comparative analysis of Financial Reporting under Companies Act 2013 vis-à-vis Companies Act 1956**
- **Disclosure requirements under The Securities and Exchange Board of India (SEBI)**
- **Elements of financial reports published as a part of corporate reporting practice in India**
- **Abridged forms of financial statements and how are they relevant**
- **Financial reports used related to issuance of prospectus**
- **Corporate reporting requirements related to unaudited quarterly results**

1.1. Advent of financial reporting in Indian context

Corporate financial reporting in India is governed primarily by the following major legislations:

1.1.1. The Companies Act 2013

The Companies Act 2013, prescribes the detailed provisions regarding the maintenance of books of accounts and the preparation and presentation of annual accounts. Under the provisions of the Act, audit of annual accounts is compulsory for all companies registered under it. The Act prescribes the roles and responsibilities of directors and also the matters to be reported by them in the annual reports of the companies. It also deals with the qualification, appointment, rights and liabilities of the auditors and provides contents of auditors report.

1.1.1.1. Books of Account

The Companies Act requires every company to prepare and keep at its registered office

a) books of account and
b) other relevant books and papers and
c) financial statement for every financial year

which give *a true and fair view* of the state of affairs of the company including that of its branch office or offices, if any, and explain the transactions effected both at the registered office and its branches and such books are kept on *accrual basis* and according to the *double entry system of accounting.* (Section 128 (1))

As per section 2(13) *Books of account* includes records maintained in respect of:

(i)   all sums of money received and expended by a company and matters in relation to which the receipts and expenditures take place,

(ii)   all sales and purchases of goods and services by the company,

(iii)   the assets and liabilities of the company, and

(iv)   the items of cost as may be prescribed under section 148 in the case of a company which belongs to any class of companies specified under that section

As per section 2(14) *books and papers* include books of account, deeds, vouchers, writings, documents, minutes and registers maintained on paper or in electronic form,

According to section 2(40) *financial statement* in relation to a company includes,

(i)   a Balance Sheet as at the end of financial year,

(ii)   a Profit & Loss Account, or in the case of a company carrying on any activity not for profit, an income and expenditure account for the financial year,

(iii)   cash flow statement for the financial year,

(iv)   a statement of change in equity , if applicable and

(v)   any explanatory note annexed to or forming part of any document referred to in sub-clause (i) to sub-clause (iv)

Provided that the financial statement, with respect to One Person Company, small Company and dormant company, may not include the cash flow statement.

1.1.1.2. Accounting Standards

The Act provides the mechanism of issuance of accounting standards. In accordance with section 133, the Central Government may prescribe the standards of accounting or any addendum thereto, as recommended by the Institute of Chartered Accountants of India (ICAI) in consultation with and after examination of the recommendations made by the National Financial Reporting Authority.

In India, the Institute of Chartered Accountants of India (ICAI) being a premier accounting institution in the country, took upon itself the leadership role by constituting the Accounting Standards Board (ASB) in 1977. The ICAI has taken significant initiatives in the setting and issuing procedure of Accounting Standards to ensure that the standard setting process is fully consultative and transparent. The ASB considers the International Accounting Standards (IASs)/ International Financial Reporting Standards (IFRSs) while framing Indian Accounting Standards (ASs) and try to integrate them, in the light of applicable laws, customs, usages and business environment in the country. Accordingly in India this has come to be the guiding light of Indian Financial reporting norms.

Up to 1977 there was no statutory backing of accounting standards in India. In 1998, the Companies (Amendment) Ordinance, 1998 was promulgated by the President of India. This Ordinance gave statutory recognition to accounting standards and required the auditor to report on the compliance with Accounting Standards. The Ordinance also provided for the constitution of the National Advisory Committee on Accounting Standards (NACAS).

1.1.1.3. National Financial Reporting Authority (NFRA)

Under Section 132 of the Act of 2013, the name of National Advisory Committee on Accounting Standards (NACAS) has been changed to National Financial Reporting Authority (NFRA). The role of the authority has been extended to advice on matters related to Auditing Standards in addition to Accounting Standards.

The following role of National Financial Reporting Authority has been prescribed as under:
a) make recommendations to the Central Government on the formulation and laying down of accounting and auditing policies and standards for adoption by Companies or class of Companies or their auditors as the case may be,

b) monitor and enforce the compliance with accounting standards and auditing standards recommended by it in such manner as may be prescribed,

c) oversee the quality of service of the professions associated with ensuring compliance with such standards, and suggest measures required for improvement in quality of services and such other related matters as may be prescribed, and

d) perform such other functions relating to clauses (a), (b) and (c) as may be prescribed (Section 132(2))

1.1.1.4. Financial Reporting Requirements

I) Financial statements

a) The financial statements shall give a true and fair of the state of affairs of the company or companies, comply with the accounting standards notified under section 133 and shall be in the form or forms as may be provided for different class or classes of companies in Schedule III.

Provided that items contained in such financial statements shall be in accordance with the accounting standards. (Section 129(1)).

b) At every annual general meeting of a company, the Board of Directors of the company shall lay before such meeting financial statements for the financial year. (Section 129(2))

c) Where a company has one or more subsidiaries, it shall, in addition to financial statements provided under section 129(2), prepare a consolidated financial statement of the company and of all the subsidiaries in the same form and manner as that of its own which shall also be laid before the annual general meeting of the company along with the laying of its financial statement under 129(2).

Provided that the company shall also attach along with its financial statement, a separate statement containing the salient features of the financial statement of its subsidiary or subsidiaries in such form as may be prescribed. (Section 129(3))

d)The provisions of the Act of 2013 applicable to the preparation, adoption and audit of the financial statements of a holding company shall, *mutatis mutandis,* apply to the consolidated financial statements referred to in (c) above

e) Without prejudice to (a) above, where financial statements of a company do not comply with the accounting standards referred to in section 129 (1), the company shall disclose in its financial statements,

> i) the deviation from the accounting standards,

> ii) the reasons for such deviation and

> iii) the financial effects, if any, arising out of such deviation.

f) Schedule III as referred to in clause (a) above, provides general instructions for preparation of Balance Sheet and Statement of Profit and Loss of a company. These are enumerated as under:

1. Where compliance with the requirements of the Act including Accounting Standards as applicable to the companies require any change in treatment or disclosure including addition, amendment, substitution or deletion in the head or sub-head or any changes, inter se, in the financial statements or statements forming part thereof, the same shall be made and the requirements of this Schedule shall stand modified accordingly.

2. The disclosure requirements specified in this Schedule are in addition to and not in substitution of the disclosure requirements specified in the Accounting Standards prescribed under the Companies Act 2013. Additional disclosures specified in the Accounting Standards shall be made in the notes to accounts or by way of additional statement unless required to be disclosed on the face of the Financial Statements. Similarly, all other disclosures as required by the Companies Act shall be made in the notes to accounts in addition to the requirements set out in this schedule.

3. (i) Notes to Accounts shall contain information in addition to that presented in the Financial Statements and shall provide where required (a) narrative descriptions or disaggregations of items recognised in those statements; and (b) information about items that do not qualify for recognition in those statements.

   (ii) Each item on the face of the Balance Sheet and Statement of Profit and Loss shall be cross-referenced to any related information in the notes to accounts. In preparing the financial statements including the notes to accounts, a balance shall be maintained between excessive detail that may not assist users of financial statements and not providing important information as a result of too much aggregation.

4. (i) Depending upon the turnover of the company, the figures appearing in the Financial Statements may be rounded off as given below:

Turnover	Rounding off
(a)less than one hundred crore rupees	To the nearest hundreds, thousands, lakhs or millions or decimals thereof
(b)one hundred crore rupees or more	To the nearest lakhs, millions or crores or decimals thereof

(ii)Once a unit of measurement is used, it shall be used uniformly in the Financial Statements.

5. Except in the case of the first Financial Statements laid before the company (after its incorporation) the corresponding amounts (comparatives) for the immediately preceding reporting period for all items shown in the financial statements including notes shall also be given.

6. For the purpose of this Schedule, the terms used herein shall be as per the applicable Accounting Standards.

Note: The Schedule sets out minimum requirements for disclosure on the face of the Balance Sheet and the Statement of Profit and Loss (hereinafter referred to as "Financial Statements" for the purposes of this Schedule) and Notes, Line items, sub-line items and sub-totals shall be presented as an addition or substitution on the face of the Financial Statements when such presentation is relevant to an understanding of the company's financial position or performance or to cater to industry / sector-specific disclosure requirements or when required for compliance with the amendments to the Companies Act or under the Accounting Standards.

1.2. Balance Sheet: (Schedule III – Part I)
Specimen Balance Sheet format as detailed in Schedule III – Part I is reproduced below.

Name of Company............
Balance Sheet as at...........

Particulars	Note no.	Figures as at the end of current reporting period	Figures as at the end of previous reporting period
1	2	3	4
I. Equity and Liabilities			
(1)Shareholders' funds			
a) Share capital			
b) Reserve and surplus			
c) Money received against share warrants			
(2)Share application money pending allotment			
(3)Non-current liabilities			
a) Long term borrowings			
b) Deferred tax liabilities (net)			
c) Other long term liabilities and			
d) Long term provisions and			
(4)Current liabilities which covers			
a) Short term borrowings			
b) Trade payables			
c) Other current liabilities			
d) Short term provisions			
TOTAL			
II. Assets			
Non-current assets			
(I)(a) Fixed Assets			
(i) Tangible assets,			
(ii) Intangible assets,			
(iii) capital work-in-progress			
(iv)Intangibles under development			
(b) Non-current investments			
(c) Deferred tax assets (net)			
(d) Long term loans and advances and			
(e) other non-current assets and			
(2)Current assets			
(a) Current investments			
(b) Inventories			
(c) Trade receivables			
(d) Cash and cash equivalents			
(e) Short term loans and advances and			

(f) Other current assets			
TOTAL			

The format above is followed by General Instructions for preparation of Balance Sheet in Schedule III, which is summarised as under:

1. An asset shall be classified as current when it satisfies any of the following criteria:
   a) It is expected to be realized in, or is intended for sale of consumption in the company's normal operating cycle;
   b) It is held primarily for the purpose of being traded;
   c) It is expected to be realized within twelve months after the reporting date ; or
   d) It is cash or cash equivalent unless it is restricted from being exchanged or used to settle a liability for at least twelve months after the reporting date.
   All other assets shall be classified as non-current.

2. An operating cycle is the time between the acquisition of assets for processing and their realization in cash or cash equivalents. Where the normal operating cycle cannot be identified. It is assumed to have a duration of 12 months.

3. A liability shall be classified as current when it satisfies any of the following criteria
   (a) It is expected to be settled in the company's normal operating cycle
   (b) It is held primarily for the purpose of being traded
   (c) it is due to be settled within twelve months after the reporting date or
   (d) The company does not have an unconditional right to defer settlement of the liability for at least 12 months after the reporting date. The terms of a liability , that could , at the option of counter-party result in its settlement by the issue of equity instruments do not affect its classification
   All other liabilities shall be classified as non-current.

4. A receivable shall be classified as a "trade receivable" if it is in respect of the amount due on account of goods sold or services rendered in the normal course of business

5. A payable shall be classified as a "trade payable" If it is in respect of the amount due on account of goods purchased or services received in the normal course of business.

6. A company shall disclose the following in the notes to accounts

A. Share Capital
For each class of share capital (different classes of preference shares to be treated separately)
   (a) the number of amount of shares authorized
   (b) the number of shares issued, subscribed and fully paid up and subscribed and not fully paid up
   (c) par value of shares

Illustration :1 - Specimen format of Share Capital

	As at 31st March 2012	As at 31st March 2011
Authorised Share Capital: Equity shares of Rs. each Preference shares of Rs. Each	xxx xxx	xxx xxx
Total	xxx	Xxx
Issued, subscribed and paid-up: Equity shares of Rs. each Preference shares of Rs. Each Less: Calls in arrears (Rs. (Previous Year Rs.))	xxx xxx xxx	xxx xxx xxx
Total	xxx	xxx

(d) a reconciliation of number of shares outstanding at the beginning and at the end of the reporting period

Illustration 2 : Reconciliation of number of shares outstanding:

Particulars	As at 31st March 2012 No.of shares	As at 31st March 2012 Amount (Rs)	As at 31st March 2011 No.of shares	As at 31st March 2011 Amount (Rs)
Equity shares at the beginning of the year	X	X	X	X
Add: Shares issued on exercise of employee stock Option	X	X	X	X
Less: Shares cancelled on buy back of equity Shares	x	X	X	X
Equity shares at the end of the year	x	X	X	X

(e) the rights, preferences and restrictions attaching to each class of shares including restrictions on the distribution of dividend and repayment of capital

(f) shares in respect of each class in the company held by its holding company or its ultimate holding company including shares held by or by subsidiaries or associates of the holding or its ultimate holding company in aggregate

(g) shares in the company held by each shareholder holding more than 5% shares specifying the number of shares held

Illustration 3: Specimen format of details of shareholders holding more than 5% shares

Name of the shareholder	As at 31st March 2012		As at 31st March 2011	
	No. of Shares	% held	No. of Shares	% held
Share holder A	X	x	X	x
Share holder B	X	x	X	x
Share holder C	X	X	X	X

(h) shares reserved for issue under options and contracts / commitments for the sale of

shares / disinvestment including terms and amounts
(i) for the period of five years immediately preceding the date as at which the Balance Sheet is prepared :
- aggregate number and class of shares allotted as fully paid up pursuant to contracts without payment being received in cash
- aggregate number and class of shares allotted as fully paid up by way of bonus shares
- aggregate number and class of shares boughtback
(j) Terms of any securities convertible into equity / preference shares issued with the earliest date of conversion in descending order starting from the farthest such that
(k) calls unpaid (showing aggregate value of calls unpaid by directors and officers)
(l) forfeited shares (amount originally paid up)

B. Reserves and surplus

(i) Reserves and Surplus shall be classified as:

    a) Capital reserve,
    b) Capital redemption reserve,
    c) Securities premium reserve,
    d) Debenture redemption reserve
    e) Revaluation Reserve;
    f) Share Options Outstanding Account ;
    g) Other Reserves – (specify the nature and purpose of each reserve and the amount in respect thereof)
    h) Surplus i.e. balance in Statement of Profit & Loss disclosing allocations and appropriations such as dividend, bonus shares and transfer to / from reserves etc. (Additions and deductions since last balance sheet to be shown under each of the specific heads)

(ii) A reserve specifically represented by earmarked investments shall be termed as a "fund"

(iii) Debit balance of Statement of Profit and Loss shall be shown as a negative figure under the head "surplus". Similarly balance of "Reserves and surplus" after adjusting the negative balance of surplus. If any, shall be shown under the head "Reserves and surplus" even if the resulting figure is in the negative.

Illustration 4: Specimen format of Reserves and Surplus

	As at 31st March 2012	As at 31st March 2011
Revaluation Reserve		
As per last Balance Sheet	xxx	xxx
Less: Transferred to Profit and Loss Account	(xxx)	(xxx)
Less: Utilised ondemerger adjustments	(xxx)	(xxx)
Sub-total	Xxx	xxx
Capital Reserve		
As per last Balance Sheet	Xxx	xxx
Sub-total	Xxx	xxx
Capital Redemption Reserve		

As per last Balance Sheet	xxx	xxx
Add: Transferred from Profit & Loss Account on buy back of equity shares	xxx	xxx
Sub-total	xxx	xxx
Securities Premium Reserve		
As per last Balance Sheet	xxx	xxx
Add: On issue of shares	xxx	xxx
Less: Redemption of debentures / bonds	xxx	xxx
Less: Buy back of equity shares	(xxx)	(xxx)
Less: Calls in arrears – others	(xxx)	(xxx)
	(xxx)	(xxx)
Sub-total	xxx	xxx
Debenture redemption reserve		
As per last Balance Sheet	xxx	xxx
Sub-total	xxx	xxx
General Reserve		
As per last Balance Sheet	xxx	xxx
Add: Transfer from Profit and Loss Account	xxx	xxx
Sub-total	xxx	xxx
Profit & Loss Account	xxx	xxx
As per last Balance Sheet	xxx	xxx
Add: Profit for the year	xxx	xxx
Less: Appropriations		
Transfer to General Reserve	(xxx)	(xxx)
Transfer to Capital Redemption reserve on buy	(xxx)	(xxx)
Back of equity shares	(xxx)	(xxx)
Proposed dividend on equity shares	(xxx)	(xxx)
(Dividend per share Rs. (Previous Year Rs.))	(xxx)	(xxx)
Tax on dividend		
Sub-total	xxx	xxx
Total	xxx	xxx

C. Long-term borrowings

(i)   Long-term borrowings shall be classified as:
   a) Bonds / debentures
   b) Term loans
      • From banks
      • From other parties
   c) Deferred payment liabilities
   d) Deposits
   e) Loans and advances from related parties
   f) Long term maturities of finance lease obligations
   g) Other loans and advances (specify nature)

(ii)   Borrowings shall further be sub-classified as secured and unsecured. Nature of security shall be specified separately in each case.

(iii) Where loans have been guaranteed by directors and others, the aggregate amount of such loans under each head shall be disclosed.

(iv) Bonds / debentures alongwith rate of interest and particulars of redemption or conversion as the case may be) shall be stated in descending order of maturity or conversion starting from farthest date of redemption or conversion as the case may be. Where bonds/debentures are redeemable by instalments, the date of maturity for this purpose,must be reckoned as the date on which the first instalment becomes due.

(v) Particulars of any redeemed bonds / debentures which the company has the power to reissue shall be disclosed.

(vi) Terms of repayment of term loans and other loans shall be stated

(vii) Period and amount of continuing default as on the balance sheet date in repayment of loans shall be specified separately in each case

Illustration 5 : Specimen format for Long term borrowings

	As at 31st March 2012		As at 31st March 2011	
	Non-current	Current	Non-current	Current
Secured				
Non-convertible debentures	xxx	xxx	xxx	xxx
Term loans from banks	xxx	xxx	xxx	xxx
Long term maturities of finance lease obligations	xxx	xxx	xxx	xxx
Unsecured				
Bonds	xxx	xxx	xxx	xxx
Term loans from banks	xxx	xxx	xxx	xxx
Deferred payment liabililies	xxx	xxx	xxx	xxx
Total	xxx	xxx	xxx	xxx

Illustration 6: Specimen format of Maturity profile and rate of interest of Debentures and bonds

Rate of interest	2013-14	2014-15	2015-16	2016-17	2017-18
Xxx	xxx	xxx	Xxx	xxx	xxx
Xxx	xxx	xxx	Xxx	xxx	xxx
Xxx	xxx	xxx	Xxx	xxx	xxx
Xxx	xxx	xxx	Xxx	xxx	xxx

Applicable for unsecured term loans as well

D. Other long-term liabilities

Other long term liabilities to be classified as :

(a) Trade payables
(b) Others

Illustration 7 : Deferred tax Liability (net)

	As at 31st March 2012	As at 31st March 2011
Deferred tax liability Related to Fixed Assets	xxx	xxx
Deferred tax assets Disallowances under Income tax Act 1961	xxx	xxx
Total	xxx	Xxx

E. Long term provisions
The amount shall be classified as :
(a) Provision for long term benefits
(b) Others (specify nature)

F. Short-term borrowings
(i) Short term borrowings shall be classified as:
(a) loans repayable on demand
- From banks
- From other parties

(b)Loans and advances from related parties
(c)Deposits
(d)Other loans and advances (specify nature)
(ii) Borrowings shall further be sub-classified as secured and unsecured. Nature of security shall be specified separately in each case.
(iii) Where loans have been guaranteed by directors or others, the aggregate amount of such loans under each head shall be disclosed.
(iv) Period and amount of default as on the balance sheet date in repayment of loans and Interest, shall be specified separately in each case.

Illustration 8 : Specimen format of Short term borrowing

	As at 31st March 2012	As at 31st March 2011
Secured loan Working capital loan from banks	xxx	xxx
Foreign currency loans	xxx	xxx
Rupee loans	xxx	xxx
Sub-total	xxx	xxx
Unsecured loan Other loans and advances from banks	xxx	xxx

Foreign currency loans – buyers credit	xxx	xxx
Rupee loans	xxx	xxx
Sub-total	Xxx	xxx

Note:

Working capital loans are secured by hypothecation of present and future stock of raw materials, stock-in process, finished goods, stores and spares (not relating to plant and machinery), book debts, outstanding monies, receivables, claims, bills, materials in transit, etc. save and except receivables of Oil and Gas Division.

5.2 Other Loans and Advances from banks include commercial paper of 'NIL (Previous Year' NIL). Maximum balance outstanding at any time during the year being Rs. NIL (Previous Year).

G. Other current liabilities:

The amounts shall be classified as:

(a) Current maturities of long-term debt ;

    (b) Current maturities of finance lease obligations;

    (c) Interest accrued but not due on borrowings

    (d) Interest accrued and due on borrowings

    (e) Interest received in advance

    (f) Unpaid dividends

    (g) Application money received from allotment of securities and due for refund and interest accrued thereon. Share application money includes advances towards allotment of share capital. The terms and conditions including number of shares proposed to be issued, the amount of premium, if any, and the period before which shares shall be allotted should be disclosed. It shall also be disclosed whether the company has sufficient authorized capital to cover the share capital amount resulting from allotment of shares out of such share applicatio money. Further the period for which share application money has been pending beyond the period of allottment as mentioned in the document inviting application of shares along with the reason for such share application money being pending shall be disclosed.

Share application money not exceeding the issued capital and to the extent not refundable shall be shown under the head Equity and share application money to the extent refundable i.e. the amount in excess of subscription or in case the requirements of minimum subscription are not met shall be separately shown under "other current liabilities".

(h)Unpaid matured deposits and interest accrued thereon

    (i) Unpaid matured debentures and interest accrued thereon

    (j) Other payables (specify nature)

Illustration 9: Specimen format of Trade payables

	As at 31st March 2012	As at 31st March 2011
Micro, small and medium enterprises	xxx	Xxx
Others	xxx	Xxx
Total	xxx	Xxx

The details of amounts outstanding to Micro, Small and Medium Enterprises based on available information with the Company are as under:

Particulars	As at 31st March 2012	As at 31st March 2011
Principal amount due and remaining unpaid	xxx	Xxx
Interest due on above and the unpaid interest	xxx	xxx
Interest paid	xxx	xxx
Payment made beyond the appointed day during the year	xxx	xxx
Interest due and payable for the period of delay	xxx	xxx
Interest accrued and remaining unpaid	xxx	xxx
Amount of further interest remaining due and payable in succeeding years	xxx	xxx
Total	xxx	Xxx

Illustration 10: Specimen format : Other current liabilities

	As at 31st March 2012	As at 31st March 2011
Current maturities of long term debt	xxx	Xxx
Current maturities of finance lease obligations	xxx	xxx
Interest accrued but not due on borrowings	xxx	xxx
Unclaimed Dividends	xxx	xxx
Application money received and due for refund	xxx	xxx
Unpaid matured debentures and interest accrued thereon	xxx	xxx
Creditors for Capital Expenditure	xxx	xxx
Advance for Transfer of Participating Interest	xxx	xxx
Other Payables *		
Total	xxx	Xxx

* Includes statutory dues, security deposit and advance from customers.

H. Short term provisions

The amounts shall be classified as :
a) Provision for employee benefits
b) Others (specify nature)

Illustration 11: Specimen format: Short term provisions

	As at 31st March 2012	As at 31st March 2011
Provisions for Superannuation/Gratuity/Leave Encashment	xxx	xxx
Proposed Dividend	xxx	xxx
Tax on Dividend	xxx	xxx
Provision for Taxes	xxx	xxx
Other Provisions	xxx	xxx
Total	xxx	Xxx

Illustration 12: Provisions for indirect taxes

Excise Duty / Service Tax and Sales Tax / Value Added Tax
Excise duty / Service tax is accounted on the basis of both, payments made in respect of goods cleared / services provided as also provision made for goods lying in bonded warehouses. Sales tax / Value added tax paid is charged to Profit and Loss account.

I. Tangible Assets

(i)Classification shall be given as:
(a) Land
(b) Buildings

(c) Plant and Equipment
(d) Furniture and fixtures
(e) Vehicles
(f) Office equipment
(g) Others (specify nature)

(ii)Assets under lease shall be separately specified under each class of asset.

(iii)A reconciliation of the gross and net carrying amounts of each class of assets at the beginning and end of the reporting period showing additions, disposals, acquisitions through business combinations and other adjustments and the related depreciation and impairment losses / reversals shall be disclosed separately.

iv)Where sums have been written off on a reduction of capital or revaluation of assets or where sums have been added on revaluation of assets, every balance sheet subsequent to date of such write-off, or addition shall show the reduced or increased figures as applicable and shall by way of a note also show the amount of the reduction or increase as applicable together with the date thereof for the first five years subsequent to the date of such reduction or increase.

J. Intangible Assets

(i)Classification shall be given as:
a) goodwill
b) brand / trademarks
c)computer software
d)mastheads and publishing titles
e)Mining rights
f)Copyrights, patents and other intellectual property rights, services and operating rights
g)recipes, formulae, models, designs and prototypes
h)licenses and franchise
i)Others (specify nature)

ii)A reconciliation of gross and net carrying amounts of each class of assets at the beginning and the end of the reporting period showing additions, disposals, acquisitions through business combinations and other adjustments and the related amortization and impairment losses / reversals shall be disclosed separately.

iii)Where sums have been written off on a reduction of capital or revaluation of assets, every balance sheet subsequent to date of such write-off, or addition, shall show the amount of reduction or increase as applicable together with the date thereof for the first five years subsequent to the date of such reduction or increase

Illustration 13 : Specimen format : Non-current assets

Description	Gross Block				Depreciation / amortisation				Net Block	
	Op.bal	Add	Delete	Cl. bal	Op.bal	Add	Delete	Cl.bal	31.3.12	31.3. 11
TANGIBLE ASSETS : OWN ASSETS : Leasehold Land Freehold Land Buildings Plant & Machinery										

Electrical Installations Equipments Furniture & Fixtures Vehicles Ships Aircrafts & Helicopters										
Sub-total										
LEASED ASSETS : Plant & Machinery Ships										
Sub-total										
Total (A)										
INTANGIBLE ASSETS : * Technical Knowhow fees Software Development Rights Others										
Total (B)										
Total (A+B)										
Previous Year										
Capital Work-in-progress										
Intangible asset under development										

* Other than internally generated

Illustration 14: Specimen format : Fixed Assets acquired on Finance Lease

	Total minimum lease payments Outstanding as at 31st March		Future interest on outstanding lease payments		Present value of minimum lease payment as at 31st March	
	2012	2011	2012	2011	2012	2011
Within one year						
Later than one year and not later than five years						
Later than five years						
Total						

General Description of Lease terms:
(a) Lease rentals are charged on the basis of agreed terms.
(b) Assets are taken on lease over a period of 5 to 10 years.

Illustration 15: Specimen format: Capital work-in-progress

	As at 31st March 2012	As at 31st March 2011
Opening Balance	xxx	xxx
Add: Transferred from Profit and Loss Account	xxx	xxx
Interest Capitalised	xxx	xxx
Less: Project Development Expenses Capitalised during the year	xxx	xxx
Closing Balance	xxx	xxx

Illustration 16: Specimen format: Intangible asset under development

	As at 31st March 2012	As at 31st March 2011
Opening Balance	xxx	xxx
Add: Transferred from Profit and Loss Account	xxx	xxx
Interest Capitalised	xxx	xxx
Less: Intangible asset under development capitalised during the year	xxx	xxx

Closing Balance	*xxx*	*Xxx*

K.Non-current investments
(i) Non-current investments shall be classified as trade investments and other investments and further classified as:
(a) investment property ;
(b) investment in equity instruments;
(c)Investments in preference shares
(d)Investments in government or trust securities
(e)Investments in debentures or bonds ;
(f)Investments in mutual funds ;
(g)Investments in partnership firms
(h)Other non-current investments (specify nature)
Under each classification, details shall be given of names of the bodies corporate (indicating separately whether such bodies are
(i)subsidiaries,
(ii)associates,
(iii)joint ventures or
(v)controlled special purpose entities) in whom investments have been made and the nature and extent of the investment so made in such body corporate (showing separately investments which are partly paid). In regard to investments in the capital of partnership firms, the names of the firms (with the names of all their partners, the total capital and shares of each partner) shall be given.

(ii)Investments carried at other than at cost should be separately stated specifying the basis of valuation thereof.

(iii)The following shall also be disclosed:
   (a) Aggregate amount of quoted investments and market value thereof,
   (b) Aggregate amount of unquoted investments ,
   (c) Aggregate provision of dimunition in value of investments

Illustration 17: Specimen format : Non-current investments

Particulars	As at 31st March 2012	As at 31st March 2011
Trade Investments In Equity Shares - Unquoted, fully paid up In Equity Shares of Associate Companies - Unquoted, fully paid up In Preference Shares of Associate Company - Unquoted, fully paid up		
Total Trade Investments (A)		
Other Investments In Equity Shares of Associate Company - Quoted, fully paid up In Equity Shares of Associate Company - Unquoted, fully paid up In Equity Shares of Subsidiary Companies - Unquoted, fully paid up In Equity Shares of Subsidiary Companies -		

Unquoted, partly paid up		
In Preference Shares of Subsidiary Companies -		
Unquoted, fully paid up		
In Preference Shares of Subsidiary Company -		
Unquoted, partly paid up		
In Debentures of Subsidiary Companies - Unquoted, Fully paid up		
In Government Securities-Unquoted		
In Mutual Fund - Quoted fully paid up (face value Rs.)		
Total Other Investments (B)		
Total Non-Current Investments (A + B)		
Aggregate amount of quoted investments		
Market Value of quoted investments		
Aggregate amount of unquoted investments		

L. Long-term loans and advances

(i) Long-term loans and advances shall be classified as:

(a)Capital advances ;

(b)Security deposits ;

(c)Loans and advances to related parties (giving details thereof)

(d)Other loans and advances (specify nature)

(ii)The above should be separately sub-classified as:

    (a) Secured considered good

    (b) Unsecured considered good

    (c) Doubtful

(iii)Allowance for bad and doubtful loans and advances shall be disclosed under relevant heads separately

(iv)Loans and advances due by directors and other officers of the company or any of them whether severally or jointly with any other persons or amounts due by firms or private companies respectively in which any director is a partner or a director or a member should be separately stated

Illustration 18 : Specimen format : Long term loans and advances (unsecured and considered good)

Particulars	As at 31st March 2012	As at 31st March 2011
Capital Advances		
Deposits with Related parties		
Loans and Advances to Related Parties		
Advance Income Tax (Net of Provision)		
Loans and Advances in the nature of Loans given to Subsidiaries and Associates		
Other Loans and Advances*		
Total		

*Includes Loans to Employees

Illustration 19 : Specimen format : Assets given on finance lease on or after 1st April 2001:

Particulars	Total		Not later than one year		Later than one year and not later than five years		Later than five years	
	2012	2011	2012	2011	2012	2011	2012	2011
Gross Investment								
Less: Unearned Finance Income								
Present Value of Minimum								

Lease Rental				
Total				

General Description of Lease terms:
• Lease rentals are charged on the basis of agreed rate of interest.
• Assets are given on lease for a period of five years.

M. Other non-current assets
Other non-current assets shall be classified as:
(i)Long term trade receivables (including trade receivables on deferred credit terms)
(ii)others (specify nature)
(iii)Long term trade receivables, shall be sub-classified as:
  (i)(a)Secured , considered good ;
     (b) Unsecured, considered good ;
     (c)considered doubtful
  (ii)Allowance for bad and doubtful debts shall be disclosed under relevant heads
     separately
  (iii)Debts due by directors and other officers of the company or any of them whether
     severally or jointly with any other persons or amounts due by firms or private
     companies respectively in which any director is a partner or a director or a member
     should be separately stated.

N. Current Investments
(i) Current investments shall be classified as:
   (a)Investments in equity instruments ;
   (b)Investments in Preference Shares ;
   (c)Investment in government or trust securities ;
   (d)Investments in debentures or bonds ;
   (e)Investments in mutual funds ;
   (f)Investments in partnership firms ;
   (g)Other investments (specify nature)

Under each classifiation, details shall be given of names of the bodies corporate (indicating separately whether such bodies are (i)subsidiaries, (ii)associates, (iii)joint ventures, or (iv) controlled special purpose entities) in whom investments have been made and the nature and extent of the investment so made in each such body corporate (showing separately investments which are partly-paid). In regard to investments in the capital of partnership firms. The names of the firms (with the names of all their partners, total capital and the shares of each partne) shall be given;

(ii)The following shall also be disclosed:

   (a)basis of valuation of individual investments
   (b)aggregate amount of quoted investments and market value thereof
   (c)aggregate amount of unquoted investments
   (d)aggregate provision made for dimunition in the value of investments.

Illustration 20: Current Investments

Particulars	As at 31st March 2012	As at 31st March 2011
Investment in Government Securities - Quoted, Fully Paid up	xxx	xxx
Investment in Debentures or Bonds - Quoted, Fully Paid up	xxx	xxx
Investment in Mutual Fund - Quoted, Fully Paid up	xxx	xxx
Investment in Units – Quoted	xxx	xxx
Investment in Commercial Paper – Quoted	xxx	xxx
Investment in Certificate of Deposits with Scheduled Banks - Quoted	xxx	xxx
Total Current Investments	xxx	xxx

Aggregate amount of quoted investments
Market Value of quoted investments

O. Inventories

(i) Inventories shall be classified as :

(a) Raw materials

(b) Work-in-progress

(c) Finished goods

(d) Stock-in-trade (in respect of goods acquire for trading)

(e) Stores and spares

(f) Loose tools

(g) Others (specify nature)

(ii) Goods-in-transit shall be disclosed under the relevant sub-head of inventories

(iii) Mode of valuation shall be stated

Illustration 21: Specimen Format : Inventories

Particulars	As at 31st March 2012	As at 31st March 2011
Raw Materials	xxx	xxx
Raw Materials in Transit	xxx	xxx
Stock-in-Process	xxx	xxx
Finished Goods	xxx	xxx
Stores, Chemicals and Packing Materials	xxx	xxx
Stock-in-Trade	xxx	xxx
Total	*xxx*	*xxx*

P. Trade Receivables

(i) Aggregate amount of trade receivables outstanding for a period exceeding six months from the date they are due for payment should be separately stated

(ii)Trade receivables shall be sub-classified as

(a)secured, considered good

(b)unsecured considered good

(c)considered doubtful

(iii)Allowance for bad and doubtful debts shall be disclosed under the relevant heads separately (iv)Debts due by directors or other officers of the company or any of them either severally or jointly with any other person or debts due by firms or private companies respectively in which any director or partner or a director or a member should be separately stated

Illustration 22: Specimen format: Trade Receivable

Particulars	As at 31st March 2012	As at 31st March 2011
(Unsecured and Considered Good) Over six months Others	xxx xxx	xxx xxx
Total	**xxx**	**xxx**

Q. Cash and Cash equivalents

(1) Cash and cash equivalents shall be classified as:
  (a)Balances with banks ;
  (b) Cheques, drafts on hand ;
  (c)Cash in hand;
  (d)Others (speciy nature)
(2) Earmarked balances with banks (e.g. for unpaid dividend) shall be separately stated.
(3) Balances with banks to the extent held as margin money or security against borrowings, guarantees, other commitment shall be disclosed separately.
(4) Repatriation restrictions, if any, in respect of cash and bank balances shall be separately stated
(5) Bank deposits with more than 12 months maturity shall be disclosed separately.

Illustration 23: Specimen format : Cash and Cash equivalents

Particulars	As at 31st March 2012	As at 31st March 2011
Balance with Banks Cash on hand Fixed deposits with banks *	xxx xxx xxx	xxx xxx xxx
Total	**Xxx**	**xxx**

Balance with Banks includes Unclaimed Dividend of Rs. crore (Previous Year Rs. crore)
* Fixed deposits with banks include deposits of Rs. crore (Previous Year Rs. crore) with maturity of more than 12 months

R. Short-term loans and advances

(i)Short term loans and advances shall be classified as:
(a)Loans and advances to related parties (giving details thereof)
(b)Others (specify nature)
(ii)The above shall be sub-classified as:
  (a)secured, considered good
  (b)unsecured considered good
  (c)considered doubtful
(iii)Allowance for bad and doubtful loans and advances shall be disclosed under the relevant heads separately

(iv)Loans and advances due by directors or otherofficers of the company or any of them either severally or jointly with any other person or debts due by firms or private companies respectively in which any director or partner or a director or a member should be separately stated

Illustration 24: Specimen format : Short term loans and advances

Particulars	As at 31st March 2012	As at 31st March 2011
(Unsecured and Considered Good)		
Loans and Advances to Related Parties	xxx	xxx
Balance with Customs, Central Excise Authorities	xxx	xxx
Deposits	xxx	xxx
Others*#	xxx	xxx
Total	xxx	xxx

* Netted for Loans and Advances considered doubtful Rs.   crore (Previous Year Rs.   crore)
\# Includes primarily Interest Receivable on Fixed Deposits with Banks, Advance to sundry creditors and
   Forward Premium on derivative contracts.

S. Other current assets (specify nature)

This is an all-inclusive heading which incorporates current assets that do not fit into other asset categories e.g. unbilled revenue, unamortised premium on forward contracts etc.

According to Guidance Note on Revised Schedule VI issued by ICAI, in case any amount classified under this category is doubtful, it is advisable that such doubtful amount as well as any provision made against the same should be separately disclosed. It is interpreted that the Guidance Note will be applicable to Schedule III as well.

Illustration 25: Specimen format : Other Current Assets

Particulars	As at 31st March 2012	As at 31st March 2011
Interest accrued on Investment	xxx	xxx
Total	xxx	xxx

T. Contingent liabilities and commitments (to the extent not provided for)

(i)*Contingent liabilities* shall be classified as:
(a)Claims against the company not acknowledged as debt ;
(b)Guarantees ;
(c)Other money for which the company is contingently liable

(ii)*Commitments* shall be classified as:
(a)Estimated amount of contracts remaining to be executed on capital account and not provided for ;
(b)Uncalled liability on shares and otherinvestments partly paid
(c)Other commitments (specify nature)

U. The amount of dividend proposed to be distributed to equity and preference shareholders for the period and the related amount per share shall be disclosed separately.

Arrears of fixed cumulative dividends on preference shares shall also be disclosed separately.

V. Where in respect of an issue of securities made for a specific purpose, the whole or part of the amount has not been used for the specific purpose at the balance sheet date, there shall be indicated by way of a note, how such unutilised amounts have been used or invested.

W. If in the opinion of the Board, any of the assets other than fixed assets and non-current investments do not have a value on realisation in the ordinary course of business at least equal to the amount at which they are stated, the fact that the Board is of that opinion, shall be stated.

1.3. Statement of profit & loss: (Schedule III – Part II)
Specimen format of Statement of Profit & Loss as detailed in Schedule III – Part II is reproduced below.

Name of Company............

Profit & Loss statement for the year ended ....

S/No	Particulars	Note no.	Figures as at the end of current reporting period	Figures as at the end of previous reporting period
1	2	3		
I	REVENUE FROM OPERATION			
II	OTHER INCOME			
III	**(TOTAL REVENUE (I + II)**			
IV	EXPENSES:			
	(a) Cost of material consumed			
	(b) Purchase of stock-in-trade			
	(c) Changes in inventories of finished goods, work-in-progress and stock-in-trade			
	(d) Employees benefit expenses			
	(e) Finance cost			
	(f) Depreciation and amortisation expenses			
	(h) Other expenses			
	TOTAL EXPENSES			
V	PROFIT BEFORE EXCEPTIONAL AND EXTRA-ORDINARY ITEMS AND TAX (III - IV)			
VI	EXCEPTIONAL ITEMS			
VII	PROFIT BEFORE EXTRAORDINARY ITEMS AND TAX (V-VI)			
VIII	EXTRAORDINARY ITEMS			
IX	PROFIT BEFORE TAX (VII - VIII)			
X	TAX EXPENSES:			
	(a) Current tax			
	(b) Deferred tax			
XI	PROFIT/(LOSS) FOR THE PERIOD FROM			

	CONTINUING OPERATIONS (IX - X)			
XII	Profit / (loss) from discontinuing operations			
XIII	Tax expenses from discontinuing operations			
XIV	Profit / (loss) from discontinuing operations (after tax) (XII-XIII)			
XV	PROFIT/(LOSS) FOR THE PERIOD (XI + XIV)			
XVI	Earning per equity share:			
	(1) Basic			
	(2) Diluted			

The format above is followed by General Instructions for preparation of Statement of Profit & Loss in Schedule III. These are summarised as under:

1. The provisions of this Part shall apply to the Income and expenditure account referred to in sub-section (2) of Section 210 of the Act, in like manner as they apply to a statement of profit and loss.

2. (A) In respect of a company other than a finance company revenue from operations shall disclose separately in the notes revenue from
- (a) Sale of products ;
- (b) Sale of services ;
- (c) Other operating revenues ;
- (d) Less: excise duty
   (B) In respect of a finance company, revenue from operations shall include revenue from:
   (a)Interest
   (b)Other financial services
   Revenue from each of the above heads shall be disclosed separately by way of Notes to Accounts to the extent applicable.

2.1. Treatment of excise duty, sales tax, service tax, VAT etc under Schedule III

The treatment of excise duty, sales tax, service tax, VAT etc. under Schedule III (similar to Revised Schedule VI) is explained as under:

a) In accordance with *AS 9: Revenue Recognition*, the disclosure in case of excise duty needs to be shown on the face of the Statement of Profit and Loss. Since Accounting Standards override Revised Schedule VI, the presentation in respect of excise duty will have to be made on the face of the Statement of Profit and Loss.
   Accordingly, a company may choose to present the elements of revenue from sale of products, sale of services and other operating revenues also on the face of the Statement of Profit and Loss

b) According to Guidance Note of ICAI on Revised Schedule VI, indirect taxes such as sales tax, service tax, purchase tax etc. are generally collected from the customer on behalf of the government in majority of the cases. However, this may hold true in all cases and in some cases a company may act as principal rather than as agent in collecting these taxes. If the company is acting as a principal and hence responsible for paying tax on its own account, the revenue should be grossed up for the tax billed to the customer and the tax payable should be shown as an expense. However, in cases where the company is collecting tax only as an intermediary or agent i.e .simply collecting and paying tax on behalf of government, revenue should be presented net of taxes

c) As per Guidance Note on Value Added Tax (VAT), VAT is collected from customers on behalf of VAT authorities and hence is not an economic benefit for the enterprise and result in any increase in the equity of the enterprise. Accordingly VAT should not be recorded as Revenue of the enterprise. At the same time payment of VAT should not be treated as expense in the Financial Statements of the enterprise

d) Further Guidance Note states that, as per the definition of Revenue in the Guidance Note on Terms Used in Financial Statement, it excludes amounts collected on behalf of third parties such as certain taxes.

e) The Guidance Note on VAT states further that, where an enterprise has not charged VAT separately but has made a composite charge, it should segregate the portion of sales which is attributable to tax and should credit the same to VAT Payable Account at periodic intervals.

It is interpreted that the above Guidance Note will be applicable to Schedule III as well.

3. Items to be disclosed as Other Operating Revenue vis-à-vis Other Income under Schedule III

At the outset it is to be noted that Other Operating Revenue has not been defined by Schedule III. According to Guidance Note on Revised Schedule VI issued by ICAI, Other Operating Revenue would include revenue arising from a company's operating activities, but which is not part of revenue arising from the sale of products or rendering of services.

4. Whether a particular income in question would be comprised of Other Operating Revenue or Other Income would be decided based on facts of each case and detailed understanding of the company's activities. The classification of income would depend on the purpose for which the particular asset is acquired or held.

Illustration 26: Other Operating Revenue

An industrial conglomerate engaged in manufacture and sale of industrial and consumer products also has a real estate vertical. If the real estate vertical is continuously engaged in leasing of real estate properties, the rent arising from leasing of real estate is likely to be "Other Operating Revenue".

Illustration 27: Other Operating Revenue

Sale of manufacturing scrap arising out of the operations for a manufacturing company should be treated as Other Operating Revenue since the same arises on account of the company's main operating activity.

4.1. Finance costs:

Finance costs shall be classified as:

a) Interest expense

b) Other borrowing costs

Applicable net gain / loss on foreign currency transactions and translation

4.2. Other income shall be classified as:

a) Interest income (in case of a company other than a finance company);

b) Dividend income;

c) Net gain / loss on sale of investments

d) Other non-operating income (net of expenses directly attributable to such income)

Illustration 28: Other Income

A company owns a building having fifteen stories. The company uses ten stories of the building for its business and corporate use and leases out the balance five floors. The rent received from these five floors would not be a part of Other Operating Revenue but would be included under "Other Income".

Illustration 29: Other Income

Sale of fixed assets is not an operating activity of a company, and hence, profit on sales of fixed assets should be classified as Other Income and not Other Operating Revenue.

Illustration 30: Other Income

Net gain out of foreign exchange transactions should be classified as Other Income , the reason being the income has not been generated out of the business operations of the income i.e. sale of products or rendering of services but owing to fluctuation in foreign exchange rates. However, same would not be the case if the company deals in foreign exchange business.

4.3. Additional information

A Company shall disclose by way of notes additional information regarding aggregate Expenditure and income on the following items:

(i)(a) Employee benefits expense showing separately

(i)Salaries and wages

(ii)Contribution to Provident and other funds

(iii)Expense on employee stock option scheme (ESOP) and Employee Stock Purchase Plan (ESPP)

(iv)Staff welfare expenses

(b) Depreciation and amortisation expenses

(c) Any item of income or expenditure which exceeds one per cent of the revenue from operations or Rs.1,00,000 , whichever is higher,

(d) Interest income,

(e) Interest expense

(f) Dividend income

(g) Net gain / loss on sale of investments

(h) Adjustments to the carrying amount of investments

(i) Net gain or loss on foreign currency transaction and translation(other than considered as finance cost)

(j) Payments to the auditor as

- As auditor
- For Taxation matters
- For Company Law Matters
- For Management services

- For other service
- For reimbursement of expenses

(k) In case of Companies covered under section 135, amount of expenditure incurred on corporate social responsibility activities,
(l) Details of items of exceptional and extraordinary nature,
(m)Prior period items,
(ii))(a) In case of manufacturing companies :
    (1) Raw materials under broad heads
    (2) Goods purchased under broad heads

  (b)In case of trading companies, purchases in respect of goods traded in by the company under broad heads
  (c) In the case of companies rendering or supplying services, gross income derived from the services rendered or supplied under broad heads
  (d) In the case of a company, this falls under more than one of the categories mentioned in (a),(b) and (c) above, it shall be sufficient compliance with the requirements herein if purchases, sales and consumption of raw material and the gross income from services rendered is shown under broad heads
  (e) In the case of other companies, gross income derived under the broad heads
(iii)In the case of all concerns having works in progress under broad heads
(iv)(a) The aggregate, if material, of any amount set aside or proposed to be set aside, to reserve, but not including provisions made to meet any specific liability, contingency or commitment know n to exist at the date as to which the balance sheet is made up,
  (b)The aggregate, if material, of any amounts withdrawn from such reserves,
(v)(a)The aggregate, if material, of the amounts set aside to provisions made from meeting specific liabilities, contingencies or commitments
  (b)The aggregate, if material, of the amounts withdrawn from such provisions, as no longer required
(vi)Expenditure incurred on each of the following items, separately for each item:
  (a)Consumption of stores and spares,
  (b)Power and fuel
  (c)Rent
  (d)Repairs to building
  (c)Repairs to machinery
  (f)Insurance
  (g)Rates & taxes (excluding income tax)
  (h)Miscellaneous expenditure
(vii)(a)Dividends from subsidiary companies
  (b)Provisions for losses of subsidiary companies
(viii)The profit and loss account shall also contain by way of a note the following Information namely,
  (a)Value of imports calculated on C.I.F basis by the company during the Financial year in respect of:
    i) Raw materials
    ii) Components and spare parts

    iii) Capital goods
  (b) Expenditure in foreign currency during the financial year on account of royalty, know-how, professional and consultation fees, and other matters
  (c) *Total* value of all imported raw materials, spare parts and components consumed during the financial year and the *total* value of all indigenous raw materials, spare parts and components similarly consumed and the percentage of each to the total consumption
  (d) The amount remitted during the year in foreign currencies on account of dividends, with a specific mention of the *total* number of non-resident shareholders, the *total* number of shares held by them on which the dividends were due and the year to which the dividends related
  (e) Earnings in foreign exchange classified under the following heads, namely:
    I Export of goods calculated on FOB basis
    II Royalty, know-how, professional and consultation fees
    III Interest and dividends
    IV Other income, indicating the nature thereof

Illustration 31: Cost of materials consumed: Specimen format

a) Manufacturing company: Consumption (Amount in Rs.)

Particulars	For the year ended 31st March 2012	For the year ended 31st March 2011
Raw materials		
Raw materials A	XXX	XXX
Raw materials B	XXX	XXX
Others	XXX	XXX
TOTAL	XXX	XXX

b) Manufacturing company: Purchases (Amount in Rs.)

Particulars	For the year ended 31st March 2012	For the year ended 31st March 2011
Goods purchased		
Traded item A	XXX	XXX
Traded item B	XXX	XXX
Others	XXX	XXX
TOTAL	XXX	XXX

c) Manufacturing company (Amount in Rs.)

Particulars	Sales value	Closing inventory	Opening inventory

Manufactured goods			
Finished goods A	XXX	XXX	XXX
	(XXX)	(XXX)	(XXX)
	XXX	XXX	XXX
Finished goods B	(XXX)	(XXX)	(XXX)
	XXX	XXX	XXX
	(XXX)	(XXX)	(XXX)
Others			
TOTAL	XXX	XXX	XXX
	(XXX)	(XXX)	(XXX)

d) Manufacturing company: Work in progress (Amount in Rs.)

Particulars	As at 31st March 2012	As at 31st March 2011
Work in progress		
Goods A WIP	XXX	XXX
Goods B WIP	XXX	XXX
Others	XXX	XXX
TOTAL	XXX	XXX

e) Trading company: (Amount in Rs.)

Particulars	For the year ended 31st March 2012	For the year ended 31st March 2011
Traded goods		
Traded goods A	XXX	XXX
Traded goods B	XXX	XXX
Others	XXX	XXX
TOTAL	XXX	XXX

f) Service company: (Amount in Rs.)

Particulars	For the year ended 31st March 2012	For the year ended 31st March 2011
Services rendered		
Service A	XXX	XXX
Service B	XXX	XXX
Others	XXX	XXX
TOTAL	XXX	XXX

A company falling under more than one category will make the above disclosures to the extent relevant.

1.4. Narrative disclosures
A. Accounting policies

a) all significant accounting policies adopted in preparation and presentation of financial statements should be disclosed

b) disclosure of significant accounting policies should form part of the financial statements and should be disclosed in one place

c) Any change in the accounting policies which has a material effect in later periods should be disclosed in the year of such change

d) In the case of a change in accounting policies that has a material effect in the current period, the amount by which any item in the financial statements is affected by such change should also be disclosed to the extent ascertainable and where this is not possible, wholly or in part, the fact should be indicated.

B. Notes to Accounts

Some illustrative points to be covered under Notes to Accounts are:

1. Contingent liabilities and capital commitment
2. Disclosure related to Small Scale Industrial Undertaking
3. Payments to auditors
4. Value of imports etc
5. Earnings and expenditure in foreign currencies
6. Prior period items
7. Extraordinary items
8. Government grants
9. Amalgamation
10. Related party transaction
11. Leases
12. Disclosure of interest in Joint venture
13. Disclosure of earnings per share
14. Disclosure of taxes on income

1.5. Cash flow statement

According to Section 2(40) of the Companies Act 2013, financial statements include Cash flow statement except that the financial statement, with respect to One Person Company, small Company and dormant company, may not include the cash flow statement.

AS 3: Cash flow statement issued by ICAI, has been declared as a specified accounting standard for the purpose of Section 129: Financial Statement to be complied with by the companies. Also as per the requirement of clause 32 of the Listing Agreement, it is mandatory for the listed companies to prepare and present a cash flow statement in accordance with AS 3 following the indirect method. Also any enterprise having turnover more than 50 crores in a year or an enterprise that intends to issue securities is required to prepare and present cash flow statement as a principal financial statements.

AS 3 prescribes three types of activities that generate cash flows for an enterprise. These are:

a) Cash flows generated by operating activities
b) Cash flows generated by investing activities and
c) Cash flows generated by financing activities

The standard specifies two alternative methods for presentation of cash flows: direct method and indirect method mainly related to the presentation of cash flow from operating activities

1.6. Preparation of consolidated Financial Statements
1.6.1. Relevant definitions:
Definitions which are relevant and related to consolidation of accounts are highlighted as under:

1.6.1.1. Section 2(87), subsidiary company or subsidiary, in relation to any other company (that is to say the holding company) means a company in which the holding company:
(i) controls the composition of the Board of Directors; or
(ii) exercises or controls more than one-half of the total share capital
either in its own or together with one or more of its subsidiary companies:
Provided that such class or classes of holding companies as may be prescribed shall not have layers of subsidiaries beyond such numbers as may be prescribed.

Explanation – For the purposes of this clause –
(a) a company shall be deemed to be a subsidiary company of the holding company even if the control referred to in sub-clause (i) or sub-clause (ii) is of another subsidiary company of the holding company;
(b) the composition of a company's Board of Directors shall be deemed to be controlled by another company if that other company by exercise of some power exercisable by it at its discretion can appoint or remove all or a majority of the directors;
(c) the expression "company" includes any body corporate;
(d) "layer" in relation to a holding company means its subsidiary or subsidiaries

1.6.1.2. Section 2(27), control shall include the right to appoint majority of the directors or to control the management of policy decisions exercisable by a person or persons acting individually or in concert, directly or indirectly, including by virtue of their shareholding or management rights or shareholders agreements or voting agreements or in any other manner;

1.6.1.3. Section 2(89), "total voting power" in relation to any matter, means the total number of votes which may be cast in regard to that matter on a poll at a meeting of a company if all the members thereof or their proxies having a right to vote on that matter are present at the meeting and cast their votes;

1.6.1.4. Section 2(6) "associate company", in relation to another company, means a company in which that other company has a significant influence, but which is not a subsidiary company of the company having such influence, but which is not a subsidiary company of the company having such influence and includes a joint venture company.

Explanation: For the purpose of this clause, "significant influence" means control of at least twenty percent of total share capital, or of the business decisions under an agreement.

1.6.2. According to Schedule III, where a company is required to prepare Consolidated Financial Statements i.e. consolidated balance sheet and consolidated statement of profit and loss, the company shall *mutatis mutandis* follow the requirements of this Schedule as applicable to a company in the preparation of balance sheet and statement of profit & loss. In addition, the consolidated financial statements shall disclose the information as per the requirements specified in the applicable Accounting Standards including the following:

    (i)   Profit & Loss attributable to "minority interest" and to owners of the parent in the statement of profit & loss shall be presented as allocation for the period.

    (ii)   "Minority interests" in the balance sheet within equity shall be presented separately from the equity of the owners of the parent.

1.6.3. In the consolidated financial statements, the following shall be disclosed by way of additional information:

Name of the entity in the	Net Assets, i.e. total assets minus total liabilities		Share in profit or loss	
	As % of consolidated net assets	Amount	As % of consolidated profit or loss	Amount
(1)	(2)	(3)	(4)	(5)
Parent Subsidiaries Indian 1. 2. 3.				

Name of the entity in the	Net Assets, i.e. total assets minus total liabilities		Share in profit or loss	
	As % of consolidated net assets	Amount	As % of consolidated profit or loss	Amount
(1)	(2)	(3)	(4)	(5)
Foreign 1. 2. 3.				
Minority Interests in all subsidiaries				

Associates (Investment as per the equity method) Indian 1. 2. 3. Foreign 1. 2. 3.				
Joint Ventures (as per proportionate consolidation / investment as per the equity method) Indian 1. 2. 3. Foreign 1. 2. 3.				
TOTAL				

1.6.3. All subsidiaries, associates and joint ventures (whether Indian or foreign) will be covered under consolidated financial statements.

1.6.4. All entity shall disclose the list of subsidiaries or associates or joint ventures which have not been consolidated in the consolidated financial statements along with the reasons of not consolidating.

1.6.5. It needs to be clarified that, the requirement of attaching the Balance Sheet, Profit & Loss account, report of Board of Directors, Auditors Report, statement of the Holding Company's interest in the subsidiary and other reports as was required under section 212 of the Companies Act 1956 has been dispensed with.

1.7. Comparative features of Companies Act 2013 vis-a-vis Companies Act 1956

ITEM	COMPANIES ACT 2013	COMPANIES ACT 1956
a) *Books of Accounts*	Financial Statements along with books of accounts and other relevant papers are required to be prepared and maintained at the registered office	Books of Accounts and other relevant papers are required to be prepared and maintained at the registered office
	Books of Accounts may also be kept in electronic form	Books of Accounts to be maintained in physical form

	Director of the Company can inspect the Books of Accounts of the subsidiary, with the authority of the Board of Directors (Sec 128)	Director of the Company cannot inspect the books of accounts of the subsidiary company (Sec 209)
b) Period for which books of account to be kept	The companies are required to preserve books of accounts for a period of eight years In the event of any investigation which has been ordered under Chapter XIV, the Central Government may direct that the books of accounts may be kept for such period longer than eight years	The companies are required to preserve books of accounts for a period of eight years
c) Format of Balance Sheet and Profit & Loss Account	The financial statements shall a) Give a *true and fair* view of the state of affairs of the Company or companies, b) Comply with the accounting standards notified under section 133 and c) Shall be in the form as may be provided for different class or classes of Companies under Schedule III	Balance Sheet and Profit & Loss account shall a) give a true and fair view of the state of affairs of the Company or Companies and b) shall be in the form set out in Part I and Part II of Schedule VI
d) Applicability of Accounting Standards	Financial Statements shall comply with the accounting standards notified by the Central Government as recommended by the Institute of Chartered Accountants of India in consultation with and after examination of the recommendations made by the National Financial Reporting Authority	Every Balance Sheet and Profit & Loss account shall comply with the Accounting Standards recommended by ICAI prescribed by Central Government in consultation with National Advisory Committee on Accounting Standards
e) Extension of Financial Year	No such provision	Financial Year may be more or less than a calendar year but cannot exceed fifteen months, except Where Registrar has granted special permission for extension till 18 months
f) Accounts of subsidiary company	Consolidated Financial Statements of all subsidiaries and the Company shall be prepared and laid before the Annual General Meeting along with the financial statements of the Company	No such provision
g) Attaching of Accounts of subsidiary company	The Company shall attach along with its financial statements, a separate statement containing salient features of the financial statements of its Subsidiaries in such form as may be	Along with the Balance Sheet of the Holding Company, the following for the subsidiary company need to be attached: a) Balance Sheet

		prescribed The subsidiary company shall include Associate Company and Joint Venture in this regard	b) Profit & Loss Account c) Directors report d) Auditors report e) Statement of holding company interest in the subsidiary and other prescribed statements of the subsidiary company
h)	**Re-opening of Accounts**	The Act provides for re-opening or recasting of books of accounts of the Company in case of application filed by the Central Government, SEBI, Income Tax Authorities and other statutory authorities or against a specified order by a court of competent jurisdiction or tribunal	No such provision
i)	**Voluntary revision of Financial statement**	Directors of a Company may prepare revised financial statements or a revised Report in respect of any of the three preceding financial years pursuant to an approval by the Tribunal in the event of any non-compliance with regards to financial statements and board report.	No such provision
j)	**National Financial Reporting Authority**	The name of National Advisory Committee on Accounting Standards has been changed to National Financial Reporting Authority. It will be headed by chairman to be appointed by the Central Government and such other members not exceeding 15 in number, as may be prescribed. The Chairman shall be a person of eminence and having expertise in accountancy, auditing, finance and law.	The name is National Advisory Committee on Accounting Standards. The Committee shall be headed by a Chairperson and consist of 11 members nominated from different authorities and professions The Chairman shall be a person of eminence and having expertise in accountancy, auditing, business administration, business law, economics or similar disciplines.
k)	**Board of Directors' Report**	The Directors are required to include certain additional information in the Board Report like, - extract of Annual Return, - number of Board meetings in a financial year, - declaration of independent reports apart from the ones already covered under the earlier Act The following are not required to be disclosed: a)details of employees in receipt of prescribed remuneration and b) reasons for failure in completing	The Directors' Report shall contain - the details of change in Board, - Auditors' observations, - employee information, - dividend proposed, - material changes in the Company, - conservation of energy, - technology absorption, - R&D etc.

	buy-back within the time limit	
l) Corporate Social Responsibility	Every Company having a)net worth of Rs.500 crore or more or b)turnover of Rs.1000 crore or more or c)net profit of Rs.5 crore or more during any financial year, shall constitute a Corporate Social Responsibility Committee of the Board consisting of three or more Directors, out of which at least one Director shall be an Independent Director The Board of every Company referred to above, shall ensure that the Company spends at least 2% of average net profits of the company made during three immediately preceding financial years, towards its corporate social responsibility policy, If the Board fails to spend such amount, the Board shall, in its report made under clause (o) of sub-section (3) of section 134, specify the reasons of not spending such amount	No such provision
m) Internal audit	Certain class or classes of Companies as may be prescribed shall be required to appoint an Internal auditor, to conduct internal audit of the functions and activities of the company An internal auditor shall either be a Chartered Accountant or a Cost Accountant or such other professional as may be decided by the Board	No such provision

Chapter 2   Accounting Standards related to Consolidation of subsidiaries, associates and joint ventures (AS)

Learning outcomes
- **Identification of subsidiaries**
- **Formation of a subsidiary**
- **Presentation of consolidated financial statements**
- **Exclusions from consolidation**
- **Consolidation procedure**
- **Cost of control**
- **Minority interest**
- **Partial disposal of an investment in a subsidiary**
- **Disclosure requirements**

2.1 How do we identify subsidiaries

We identify subsidiaries by evaluating control. Control is presumed as under:

Control is presumed	when the parent acquires more than half of the voting rights of the entity.
	Even otherwise control may be evidenced by power: - over more than one half of the voting rights by virtue of an agreement with other investors, or - to govern the financial and operating policies of the entity under a statute or an agreement, or - to appoint or remove the majority of the members of the board of directors, or - to cast the majority vote at a meeting of the board of directors

2.2. How is a subsidiary formed

Subsidiary is formed when there is	a) direct control over another entity b) control by dominant influence by another entity c) control over potential voting rights of another entity d) indirect control over another entity
	Control signifies power to govern financial and operating policies of an entity

2.3. Circumstances Consolidated Financial Statements are prepared

AS 21 does not mandate which enterprises are required to prepare consolidated financial statements – but specifies the rules to be followed where such financial statements are prepared.

Consolidated Financial Statement will be prepared by parent company for all the companies that are controlled by the parent company either directly or indirectly, situated in India or abroad except in the following cases:

a) Control is intended to be temporary because the subsidiary is acquired and held exclusively with a view to its subsequent disposal in the near future

   (In accordance with ASI – 25, merely holding all the shares as "stock-in-trade" is not sufficient to be considered as temporary control. It is only when all the shares held as "stock-in-trade" are acquired and held exclusively with a view to their subsequent disposal in the near future, that control would be considered to be temporary)

   The term "near future" according to ASI – 8 ,is a period not exceeding twelve months

   In the normal case, at the time of making the investment, If the intention is to continue with the equity for longer period then even though it is disposed off within 12 months, investee company will still be considered a subsidiary.

   However, if the intention is to dispose of the stock at the time of purchase and the investor has not been able to do so even after 12 months, shares will continue to be held as stock.

b) Subsidiary operates under severe long-term restrictions, which would significantly impair its ability to transfer funds to its parent

2.4. How do we present consolidated financial statements?

A **parent** which presents consolidated financial statement should present these statements in addition to its separate financial statements

A **parent** which presents consolidated financial statements should consolidate all subsidiaries, domestic as well as foreign, other than those referred to in paragraph 11.

A **subsidiary** should be excluded from consolidation when:

(a) *control is intended to be temporary because the subsidiary is acquired and held exclusively with a view to its subsequent disposal in the near future; or*

(b) *it operates under severe long-term restrictions which significantly impair its ability to transfer funds to the parent.*

In consolidated financial statements, investments in such subsidiaries should be accounted for in accordance with Accounting Standard (AS) 13, Accounting for Investments. The reasons for not consolidating a subsidiary should be disclosed in the consolidated financial statement

2.5. Exclusions to Presentation of consolidated accounts

Once an entity ceases to fall within the definition of subsidiary it would fall

- under AS 23 as associate
- under AS 27 as joint venture
- under AS 13 as investment

as appropriate

However, in accordance with AS – 21 it is inappropriate to exclude subsidiaries from consolidation on the ground that their business activities are substantially dissimilar from the parent and / or rest of the group. As long as the parent retains control over such subsidiaries, they are required to be consolidated and information related to dissimilar business would be disclosed appropriately in accordance with AS 17 Segment Reporting.

2.6. When does control exist with the Parent?

Control exists with the Parent, on the following premises:

a)*One-half voting power*	The ownership, directly or indirectly through subsidiaries, of more than one-half of the voting power of an enterprise.

Illustration 1

A Ltd holds 80% shares in B Ltd
B Ltd is the subsidiary of A Ltd.
A Ltd holds 30% shares in C Ltd.
C Ltd is not a subsidiary of A Ltd
However if B Ltd holds 25% of C Ltd.
Then A Ltd holds 55% shares in C Ltd, though indirectly.
C Ltd becomes a subsidiary of A Ltd.

b)*Control of the composition of board of directors*	An enterprise is considered to control the composition of the board of directors or governing body of a company, if it has the power, without the consent of any other person, to appoint or remove all or a majority of directors of that company or members of the body and following conditions are satisfied: a) A person cannot be appointed as director / member without the exercise in his favour by that enterprise of such a power b) A person's appointment as director / member follows necessarily from his appointment to a position held by him in that enterprise or c) The director / member is nominated by that enterprise or a subsidiary thereof

In some cases however, even if the share is less than 50%, parent – subsidiary relationship can be considered as the voting power granted is greater than 50% under special circumstances.

Illustration 2

State Bank Of Mysore advanced loan of Rs.50 crores to Pinewood Ltd, whose share capital is Rs.10 crores. As per the loan agreement, in case company defaults to repay the principal or to pay the interest on due date three times, State Bank of Mysore will have right to participate in the decision making of the company and this right will come to an end with the repayment of the loan amount including interest. On the happening of this event, the bank got the voting right in its board meetings and general meetings having control on the enterprise.

2.7. Basis of consolidation procedures

Basis of consolidation procedures	In preparing consolidated financial statements, the financial statements of the parent and its subsidiaries should be combined on a line by line basis by adding together like items of assets, liabilities, income and expenses.

2.8. What are the steps involved in calculating Cost of control?

Steps involved in calculating cost of control are:	a) The cost of investment of the parent in each of the subsidiaries and the parent's share in equity of each subsidiary should be eliminated.
	b) On the date of investment if the cost of investment to the parent is more than share of equity in that particular subsidiary, the difference is taken as Goodwill in the consolidated statement
	c) On the date of investment if the cost of investment to the parent is less than the share of equity in that particular subsidiary, the difference is taken as capital reserve in the consolidated statement.
	d) Where the carrying amount of the investment in the subsidiary is different from its cost, the carrying amount is considered for the purpose of above computations
	e) Goodwill and capital reserve of different subsidiaries can be adjusted to a net figure by the parent in consolidated financial statement
	f) Goodwill of consolidated financial statement need not be written off to consolidated profit and loss account but test of impairment (AS -28) is made each time a consolidated financial statement is prepared
	g) When share application money and share allotment money is paid separately on different dates then as per AS -21 date on which investment led to acquisition to control of

	subsidiary should be taken as date of investment i.e. date of allotment h) If control is gained in the subsidiary by a series of investments, then the date of the investment which led to holding – subsidiary relationship is taken into consideration and step by step calculations are made for each of the following investments.

Illustration 3

X Ltd acquired 60% shares of B Ltd @ Rs.20 per share. Following are the extract of Balance Sheet of Y Ltd :

	Rs
1000000 Equity shares of Rs.10 each	10000000
10% debentures	1000000
Creditors	5500000
Fixed Assets	7000000
Investments	4500000
Current Assets	6800000
Loans & Advances	2200000

On the same day Y Ltd declared dividend at 20% and as agreed between both the Companies fixed assets were to be depreciated @ 10% and investment to be taken At market value of Rs.6000000. Calculate the goodwill or capital reserve to be recorded in consolidated financial statement

Solution

Calculation of goodwill / capital reserve	Rs	Rs.
Net Assets		
Fixed Assets	7000000	
Less Depreciation (7000000 x 10%)	700000	6300000
Investments at market value		6000000
Current Assets		6800000
Loans & Advances		2200000
Total Assets		21300000
Less : Total Liabilities – Creditors	5500000	
10% debentures	1000000	6500000
Equity		14800000
Majority share 60% x Rs.14800000		8880000 (A)
Cost of investment		
Equity - (1000000 x 60%) x Rs.20	12000000	
Less : Dividend (600000 x 2)	1200000	10800000 (B)
Goodwill (B – A)		1920000

Illustration 4

Alpha Ltd purchased 40% stake of Beta Ltd for Rs.12 per share. After two years Alpha Ltd decided to purchase another 40% share in Beta Ltd. Beta Ltd has 10000000 equity shares of Rs.10 each as fully paid up shares. The purchase deal was finalized in the following terms :

a) Purchase price per share to be calculated on the basis of average profit of last three years capitalized at 7.5% . Profits for last three years are Rs.35 lakhs, Rs. 65 lakhs and Rs.89 lakhs.

b) Total assets of Beta Ltd was Rs.115000000. Assets to be appreciated by Rs.40 lakhs.

C) Of the external creditors for Rs.250 lakhs one creditor to whom Rs.10 lakhs was due has expired and nothing is to be paid to settle this liability.

d) Beta Ltd will declared dividend @ 15%.

Calculate goodwill or capital reserve for Alpha Ltd in consolidated financial statement.

Solution

Calculation of purchase consideration		Rs'000	Rs'000
Profits for last three years	First	8900	
	Second	6500	
	Third	3500	
Total profits for last three years		18900	
Average profits (Rs 18900/ 3)			6300
Total value of Beta Ltd (6300 / 7.5%)			84000
Number of shares in Beta Ltd			10000
Value per share			8.40
Purchase consideration (10000000 x 40%) x 8.4			**33600**

Calculation of goodwill / capital reserve	Rs'000	Rs'000
Fixed Assets	115000	
Add: Appreciation in value	4000	119000
Less: Creditors	25000	
Less: amount written back	1000	24000
Net Asset		95000
Share in net asset (95000 x 80%)		76000 (A)
Cost of investment : Purchase consideration 33600		
Less: Dividend recd(100000000 x 40% x 15%) 6000		
27600		
Add: Investment (10000000 x 40% x 12)	48000	75600 (B)
Capital reserve (A – B)		400

2.9. What are the steps involved in calculating Minority Interest?

Steps involved in calculating Minority Interest are:	• From the net income of the subsidiary, amount proportionate to minority interest is calculated and adjusted with the group income i.e. it is deducted from the profit & loss account balance and added to minority interest , so that the income of the group belonging to

	the parent is identified separately
	• Care should be taken to adjust for the cumulative preference dividend and profits belonging to the preference shares (if any) in the minority interest for the preference shares not held by the consolidated group. This adjustment should be made irrespective of whether or not dividends have been declared
	• Minority interests in the net assets of consolidated subsidiaries should be identified and presented in the consolidated balance sheet separately from liabilities and the equity of the parent's shareholders. Minority interests in the net assets consist of :
	a) the amount of equity attributable to minorities at the date of which investment in a subsidiary is made and
	b) the minorities share of movements in equity since the date the parent-subsidiary relationship came in existence.
	• If carrying amount and cost of investment are different, carrying amount is considered

Illustration 5

Following are the Balance Sheets of Alpha Ltd and Beta Ltd: (Rs'000)

Liabilities	Alpha Ltd	Beta Ltd	Assets	Alpha Ltd	Beta Ltd
Equity shares	6000	5000	Goodwill	100	20
6% preference			Fixed Assets	3750	2750
shares	-	1000	Investments	1720	1100
General reserve	1200	800	Stock	1600	4150
Profit & Loss A/c	1020	1790	Debtors	2750	3080
Bills payable	1000	1540	Bills receivable	2050	1000
Creditors	2850	1870	Cash and bank	700	400
Proposed					
dividend	600	500			
Total	12670	12500	Total	12670	12500

Alpha Ltd purchased 3/4th interest in Beta Ltd at the beginning of the year at the premium of 25%. Other information are as follows:

a) Profit and Loss A/c of Beta Ltd includes Rs.1000 (Rs'000) bought forward from the previous year.

b) The directors of both the companies have proposed a dividend of 10% on equity share capital for the previous and current year.

From the above information calculate pre and post-acquisition profits, minority interest and cost of control.

Solution

Working Notes:

1. **Group structure**

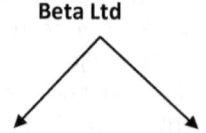

Beta Ltd

Alpha Ltd (75%)   Minority interest (25%)

2. **Statement of calculation of pre and post-acquisition profit   (Rs.)**

Particulars	Pre-acquisition profit	Post-acquisition profit
Profit and Loss Account	1000000	790000
General reserve	800000	-
Total (A)	1800000	790000
Minority interest (25% X A)	450000	197500
Cost of control (75% x A)	1350000	592500

3. **Statement of Minority Interest**

Particulars	Rs.
Paid up equity share capital (Rs.5000000 x 25%)	1250000
Paid up preference share capital	1000000
Pre-acquisition profit	450000
Post-acquisition profit	197500
Total to Consolidated Balance Sheet	2897500

4. **Statement of Cost of control / capital reserve**

Particulars	Rs.
Cost of investment in subsidiary (5000000 x 75% x 125%)	4687500
Less: Dividend received (5000000 x 75% x 10%)	375000
	4312500 (A)
	3750000
Paid up equity share capital (Rs.5000000 x 75%)	1350000
Pre-acquisition profit	5100000 (B)
Capital reserve to Consolidated Balance Sheet	787500 (A – B)

2.10. What are the other points to be kept in mind while carrying out consolidation?

Inter group transactions	The effect of unrealized profits from inter group transactions should be eliminated from consolidated financial statement. Effect of losses from inter group transactions need not be eliminated only when the cost is not recoverable.

Reporting date	As far as possible the reporting date of the financial statements should be same for parent company and all subsidiary companies. In any case not later than six months
Accounting policies	Accounting policies followed in the preparation of the financial statements of parent, subsidiaries and consolidated financial statement should be uniform for like transactions and other events in similar circumstance

2.11. What are the principles followed in disposal of investment in a subsidiary?

Disposal of investment in a subsidiary	On disposal of investment, consolidated profit and loss will include the transactions till the date the parent-subsidiary relationship ceases to exist. At this stage the difference between a) The proceeds from the disposal of investment and b) The parent's share in the net asset of the subsidiary on the basis of carrying amount on the date of the disposal is recorded in the consolidated profit and loss account. While carrying out the calculation of the share of the parent in the net asset of the subsidiary on the date of disposal, adjustment is made for the minority interest.

Please refer to the following illustration.

Illustration 6

Alpha Ltd acquired 75% share of Beta Ltd for Rs. 25 lakhs. The net assets of Beta Ltd on the day are Rs.22 lakhs. During the year Alpha Ltd sold the investment for Rs.30 lakhs and net assets of Beta Ltd on the date of disposal was Rs.35 lakhs. Calculate the profit or loss on disposal of this investment to be recognized in consolidated financial statement.

Solution

Statement of calculation of profit / loss on disposal of investment in subsidiary

Particulars		Rs.
Net assets of Beta Ltd on the date of disposal		3500000
Less: Minority interest (3500000 x 25%)		875000
Alpha Ltd's share in net assets		2625000 (A)
Proceeds from sale of investment		3000000 (B)
(B – A) = C		375000 (C)
Cost of investment by Alpha Ltd	Rs.2500000	
Less: Share of Alpha Ltd (Rs.22 lakhs x 75%)	Rs.1650000	850000 (D)
Loss on sale of investment (D – C)		475000

In the above illustration the original cost of investment plays a pivotal on the profit or loss on disposal of the investment. Let us look at the same illustration with the change in cost of investment as shown below.

Illustration 7

Alpha Ltd acquired 75% share of Beta Ltd for Rs. 18 lakhs. The net assets of Beta Ltd on the day are Rs.22 lakhs. During the year Alpha Ltd sold the investment for Rs.30 lakhs and net assets of Beta Ltd on the date of disposal was Rs.35 lakhs. Calculate the profit or loss on disposal of this investment to be recognized in consolidated financial statement.

Solution
Statement of calculation of profit / loss on disposal of investment in subsidiary

Particulars		Rs.
Net assets of Beta Ltd on the date of disposal		3500000
Less: Minority interest (3500000 x 25%)		875000
Alpha Ltd's share in net assets		2625000 (A)
Proceeds from sale of investment		3000000 (B)
(B – A) = C		375000 (C)
Cost of investment by Alpha Ltd	Rs.1800000	
Less: Share of Alpha Ltd (Rs.22 lakhs x 75%)	Rs.1650000	150000 (D)
Profit on sale of investment (C – D)		225000

2.12. What is Partial disposal of an investment in a subsidiary?

- **Partial disposal of an investment in a subsidiary while control is retained :**
  This is accounted as equity transaction with owners, and the gain or loss is not recognized
- **Partial disposal of an investment in a subsidiary that results in loss of control:** Loss of control triggers re-measurement of the residual holding to fair value. Any difference between fair value and carrying amount is a gain or loss to be recognized in profit or loss. Thereafter apply AS 23, AS 27 or AS 13, as appropriate, to the remaining holding.

2.13. ASI – 26: Accounting for taxes on income in the consolidated financial statements

While preparing consolidated financial statements, the tax expense to be shown in the consolidated financial statements should be the aggregate of the amounts of tax expense appearing in the separate financial statements of the parent and its subsidiaries.

The amounts of tax expense appearing in the separate financial statements of a parent and its subsidiaries do not require any adjustment for the purpose of consolidated financial statements. In view of this, while preparing consolidated financial statements, the tax expense to be shown in the consolidated financial statements is the aggregate of the amounts of tax expense appearing in the separate financial statements of the parent and its subsidiaries.

2.14.Disclosure requirements prescribed by the standard

In addition to disclosures required by paragraph 11 (the reason for non-consolidating a subsidiary) and 20 (uniform accounting policies), following disclosures should be made:
- (a) in consolidated financial statements a list of all subsidiaries
  including the name, country of incorporation or residence, proportion of ownership interest and, if different, proportion of voting power held;
- (b) in consolidated financial statements, where applicable:
  - (i) the nature of the relationship between the parent and a subsidiary, if the parent does not own, directly or indirectly through subsidiaries, more than one-half of the voting power of the subsidiary;
  - (ii) the effect of the acquisition and disposal of subsidiaries on the financial position at the reporting date, the results for the reporting period and on the corresponding amounts for the preceding period; and
  - (iii) the names of the subsidiary(ies) of which reporting date(s) is / are different from that of the parent and the difference in reporting dates.

2.15. Disclosures required in separate financial statements by parent that is permitted not to prepare consolidated statement

Solution

disclosures required in separate financial statements by parent that is permitted not to prepare consolidated statement	• the fact that these are separate financial statements and exemption from consolidation has been used, name and country of incorporation of the parent entity where consolidated financial statements that comply with ASs have been produced for public use and address where these are obtainable • a list of significant investments in subsidiaries, jointly controlled entities and associates including name, country of incorporation and proportion of ownership interest and voting power (if different) • a description of method used to account for foregoing investments

2.16. Illustration of Accounting Policies to the consolidated balance sheet and profit and loss account

1. **Principles of consolidation**

   The consolidated financial statements have been prepared on the following basis:

   a) The financial statements of the Company and its subsidiary companies are combined on a line-by-line basis by adding together the book values of the like items of assets, liabilities, income and expenses, after fully eliminating intra-group balances and intra-group transactions in accordance with Accounting Standard AS 21, " Consolidated Financial Statements"

   b) In case of foreign subsidiaries, being non-integral foreign operations, revenue items are consolidated at the average rate prevailing during the year. All assets and liabilities are converted at rates prevailing at the end of the year. Any exchange differences arising on consolidation is recognized in the exchange fluctuation reserve.

   c) The difference between the cost of investment in the subsidiaries, over the net assets at the time of acquisition of shares in the subsidiaries is recognized in the financial statements as Goodwill or Capital Reserve as the case may be

   d) The difference between the proceeds from disposal of investment in a subsidiary and the carrying amount of its assets less liabilities as of the date of disposal is recognized in the consolidated statement of Profit and Loss Account as exceptional item being the profit or loss on disposal of investment in subsidiary.

   e) Minority interest's share of net profit of consolidated subsidiaries for the year is identified and adjusted against the income of the group in order to arrive at the net income attributable to shareholders of the company

   f) Minority interest's share of net assets of consolidated subsidiaries is identified and presented in the consolidated balance sheet separate from liabilities and the equity of the company's shareholders.

   g) In case of associates, where the Company directly or indirectly through subsidiaries holds more than 20% of equity, investments in associates are accounted for using equity method in accordance with AS 23 " Accounting for investments in associates in consolidated financial statements".

   h) The Company accounts for its share in the change in net assets of the associates, post-acquisition, after eliminating unrealised profits and losses resulting from transactions between the Company and its associates to the extent of its share, though its profit and loss account to the extent of such change is attributable to the associates' profit and loss account and through its reserves for the balance, based on available information.

   i) The difference between the cost of investment in the associates and the share of net assets at the time of acquisition of shares in the associates is identified in the financial statements as Goodwill or Capital Reserve as the case may be

   j) As far as possible, the consolidated financial statements are prepared using uniform accounting policies for like transactions and other events in similar circumstances and are presented in the same manner as the Company's separate financial statements.

   1. Investments other than is subsidiaries and associates have been accounted as per Accounting Standard (AS) 13" Accounting for investments".

   (Source : Reliance Industries Ltd)

AS 23: Accounting for Investment in Associates in consolidated financial Statements

Learning outcomes
- **What is Significant influence**
- **Equity method and procedure**
- **Accounting of equity method**
- **Application of equity method**
- **Disclosures**

2.17. What is significant influence?

Significant influence does not extend to power to govern the financial and/or operating policies of an enterprise.

Significant influence may be gained by share ownership, statute or agreement.

As regards share ownership, if an investor holds, directly or indirectly through subsidiary (ies), 20% or more of the voting power of the investee, it is presumed that the investor has significant influence.

Conversely, if the investor holds, directly or indirectly through subsidiary (ies), less than 20% of the voting power of the investee, it is presumed that the investor does not have significant influence, unless such influence can be clearly demonstrated

Significant influence is usually evidenced by:

(a) *Representation on the board of directors or corresponding governing body of the investee;*
(b) *participation in policy making processes;*
(c) *material transactions between the investor and the investee;*
(d) *interchange of managerial personnel; or*
(e) *provision of essential technical information.*

What is significant influence is explained in the chart below.

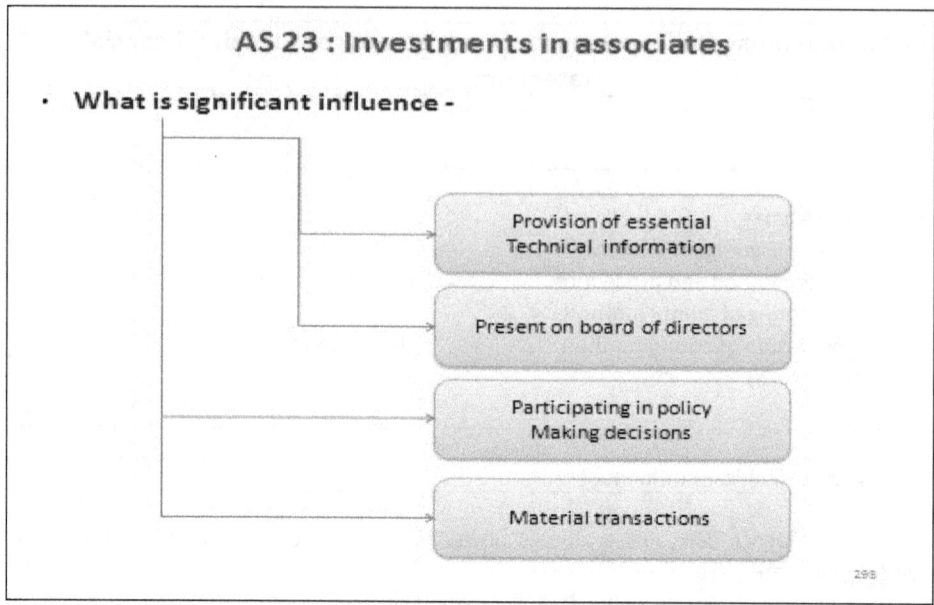

Investing Company would have significant influence when the following points are satisfied:

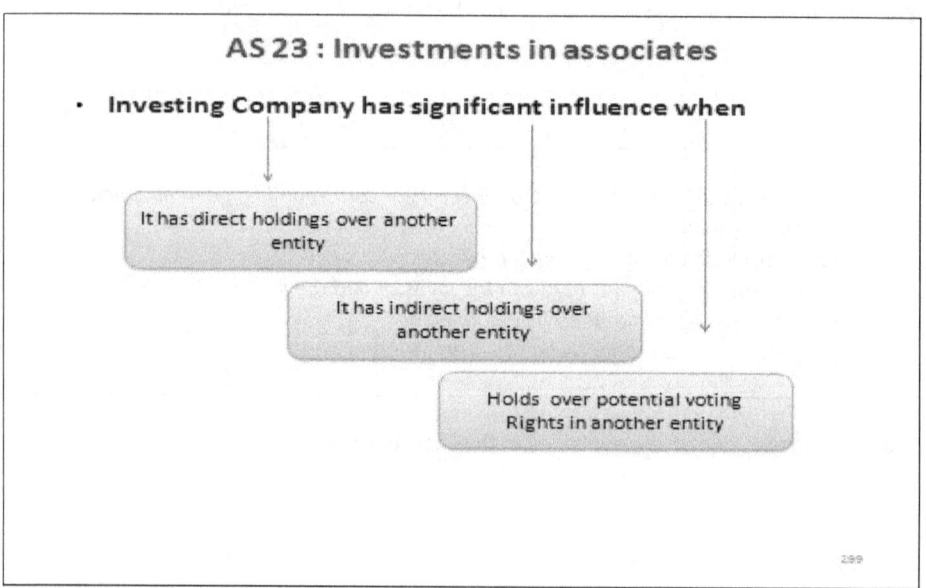

2.18. What is Equity method?

2.18.1. Equity method	It is a method of accounting whereby a) the investment is initially recorded at cost, b) any surplus or deficit in cost and net asset to be recorded as goodwill or capital reserve arising at the time of acquisition. c) The carrying amount is adjusted for the post-acquisition change in the investor's share of - net assets of the associate share of profit or loss included in income statement and - the share of other changes included in equity

2.18.2. Procedure for the equity method is:

- Eliminating intra group profits and losses arising from transactions between investor and investee
  - identifying the goodwill portion of the purchase price
  - amortization of goodwill
  - adjustments for depreciation of depreciable assets , based on their fair values
  - adjustments for the effect of cross holdings
  - using uniform accounting policies

2.18.3. Circumstances under which Equity method is followed

An investment in an associate should be accounted for in consolidated financial statements under the equity method except when:

> (a) the investment is acquired and held exclusively with a view to its subsequent disposal in the near future; or
> (b) the associate operates under severe long-term restrictions that significantly impair its ability to transfer funds to the investor.

Investments in such associates should be accounted for in accordance with Accounting Standard (AS) 13, Accounting for Investments. The reasons for not applying the equity method in accounting for investments in an associate should be disclosed in the consolidated financial statements.

An investor should discontinue the use of the equity method from the date that:

> (a) it ceases to have significant influence in an associate but retains, either in whole or in part, its investment; or
> (b) the use of the equity method is no longer appropriate because the associate operates under severe long-term restrictions that significantly impair its ability to transfer funds to the investor.

From the date of discontinuing the use of the equity method, investments in such associates should be accounted for in accordance with Accounting Standard (AS) 13, Accounting for Investments. For this purpose, the carrying amount of the investment at that date should be regarded as cost thereafter.

2.18.4. Disclosure requirements prescribed by this Standard

> An appropriate listing and description of associates including the proportion of ownership interest and, if different, the proportion of voting power held should be disclosed in the consolidated financial statements.

> Investments in associates accounted for using the equity method should be classified as long-term investments and disclosed separately in the consolidated balance sheet. The investor's share of the profits or losses of such investments should be disclosed separately in the consolidated statement of profit and loss. The investor's share of any extraordinary or prior period items should also be separately disclosed.

> The name(s) of the associate(s) of which reporting date(s) is/are different from that of the financial statements of an investor and the differences in reporting dates should be disclosed in the consolidated financial statements.

> In case an associate uses accounting policies other than those adopted for the consolidated financial statements for like transactions and events in similar circumstances and it is not practicable to make appropriate adjustments to the associate's financial statements, the fact should be disclosed along with a brief description of the differences in the accounting policies.

2.18.5. Relevant accounting standard interpretations prescribed by ICAI	
ASI 16	**Treatment of proposed dividend in Associates in consolidated financial statements** In case an associate has made a provision for proposed dividend in its financial statements, the investor's share of the results of operations of the associate should be computed without taking into consideration the proposed dividend
ASI 18	**Consideration of potential equity shares for determining whether an investee is an associate. Accounting for investments in Associates in consolidated financial statements:** The potential equity shares of the investee held by the investor should not be taken into account for determining the voting power of the investor.

Q.2.1.
Alpha Ltd acquire 40% of Beta Ltd shares on April 01 2010, the price paid was RS.15 Lakhs. Following are the extract of Balance Sheet of Beta Ltd: Paid up equity share capital   Rs.1000000 Securities premium   Rs.100000 Reserves and surplus   Rs.500000 Beta Ltd has reported net profits of Rs.300000 and paid dividends of Rs. 100000. Calculate the amount at which the investment in Beta Ltd should be shown in the consolidated Balance Sheet

of Alpha Ltd as on March 31st 2011. (*CA Final study material adapted*)

Solution

Calculation of carrying amount of investment under equity method	Rs
Equity share capital	1000000
Securities premium	100000
Reserves and surplus	500000
Net assets	1600000
40% of net asset	640000
Add: 40% of profits for the year (40% x Rs.300000)	120000
Less: 40% of dividend	(40000)
	720000
Less: Cost of investment	1500000
Goodwill	780000

Consolidated Balance Sheet (extract)	Rs.
Investment in Beta Ltd	720000
Goodwill	780000
Total cost of investment in B ltd	1500000

Q.2.2.

Delta Ltd acquire 40% of Gamma Ltd shares on April 2 2010, the price paid being R.150000. Gamma Ltd information are as follows:

	Rs
Equity shares (paid up)	50000
Share premium	150000
Retained earnings	100000
	300000

Further Gamma Ltd reported a net income of Rs.30000 and paid dividends of Rs.10000. Delta Ltd has subsidiary on 31.3.2011. Calculate the amount at which the investment in Gamma Ltd would be shown in the consolidated balance sheet of Delta Ltd as on 31.3.11.

Solution

As per AS 23, the investment in associate shall be carried by equity method and goodwill / capital reserve to be calculated and disclosed.

Statement of extract of Balance Sheet of Delta Ltd as on 31.3.2011

Liabilities	Rs.	Assets		Rs.
		Investment in Gamma Ltd	Rs.128000	
		Add: Goodwill	Rs.20000	148000

Working Notes

1. **Statement of value of investment as per equity method:**

Particulars	Rs

Price paid to acquire Gamma Ltd	140000
Add: Delta's share of net income in Gamma Ltd(Rs.30000 x 40%)	12000
Less: Delta's share of dividend in Gamma Ltd (Rs.10000 x 40%)	(4000)
Value of investment	148000

2. **Statement of calculation of goodwill**

Particulars	Rs
Price paid to acquire Gamma Ltd	140000 (A)
Equity shares + Share premium + retained earnings (50000 + 150000+ 100000) = Rs.300000 x 40%	120000 (B)
Goodwill (A – B)	20000

Q.2.3.

A Ltd holds 22% share of B Ltd on 1st April of the year and following are the relevant Information as available on the date are cost of investment Rs.33000 and total equity on the date of acquisition Rs.200000. What will the treatment if cost of investment is Rs.55000.(*CA Final adapted*)

Solution

Case I

A Ltd's share in equity (200000 x 22%)	Rs.44000
Less: cost of investment	Rs.33000
Capital reserve	Rs.11000

Extract of Balance Sheet of A Ltd

Investment in B Ltd	Rs.44000	
Less: Goodwill	Rs. 11000	Rs.33000

Case II

A Ltd's share in equity (200000 x 22%)	Rs.44000
Less: cost of investment	Rs.55000
Goodwill	Rs.11000

Extract of Balance Sheet of A Ltd

Investment in B Ltd	Rs.44000	
Add: Goodwill	Rs. 11000	Rs.55000

Q.2.4.

Sandstone Ltd purchased 30% equity shares of Limestone Ltd on 1.4.2009 at a cost of Rs.5 lakhs. On that date Limestone Ltd equity was as under:

Equity share capital	Rs.10.0 lakhs
Reserves and surplus	Rs.3.0 lakhs

During the years 2009-10 and 2010-11 Limestone Ltd incurred a loss of Rs.10 lakhs and Rs.15 lakhs respectively. Sandstone Ltd has a subsidiary and is required to prepare consolidated financial statements, how the investments in associates will be shown in consolidated financial statements of Sandstone Ltd.

Solution

As per AS 23, the investment in associate shall be carried by equity method and goodwill / capital reserve to be calculated and disclosed.

As at 31.3.2010			
Statement of extract of Balance Sheet of Sandstone Ltd and its subsidiaries as on 31.3.2011			
Liabilities	Rs.	Assets	Rs.
		Investment in	
		Gamma Ltd Rs. 90000	
		Add: Goodwill Rs.110000	200000

Working Notes

1. **Statement of value of investment as per equity method**:

Particulars	Rs
As at 31.3.2010	500000
Price paid to acquire Limestone Ltd	
Less: Sandstone's share of loss in Limestone Ltd (Rs.1000000 x 30%)	300000
Value of investment as on 31.3.2010	200000
As at 31.3.2011	
Value of investment as above	200000
Less: Sandstone's share of loss in Limestone Ltd (Rs.1500000 x 30%)	450000
Value of investment as on 31.3.2011	(250000)

2. **Statement of calculation of goodwill**

Particulars	Rs
Price paid to acquire Limestone Ltd	500000 (A)
Equity shares + Reserves and surplus (1000000 + 300000) = Rs.1300000 x 30%	390000 (B)
Goodwill (A – B)	110000

As at 31.3.2011

Statement of extract of Balance Sheet of Sandstone Ltd and its subsidiaries as on 31.3.2011			
Liabilities	Rs.	Assets	Rs.
		Investment in associate	Nil

Note: Since the carrying value of the investment as per equity method is (-) Rs.250000 investment will be reported at nil value in the consolidated balance sheet. Also going forward if there are continuing losses in the associate, it will not be recognized by Sandstone Ltd.

Q.2.5.
A Ltd acquired 35% of the capital of B Ltd on 1.7.2010 at Rs.120000, when the opening balance of reserve and surplus stood at Rs.40000. On 31.3.2011 the reserve and surplus stood at Rs.250000

with revaluation reserve created after 1st July for Rs.90000. Equity share capital of B Ltd is Rs.250000. Give the extract of investment in B Ltd in the consolidated financial statement to be prepared by A Ltd as on 31.3.2011, when B Ltd proposed dividend to the extent of Rs.60000 for the year 2010-11 adjusted in the books.(*CA Final RTP Nov 2011*)

Solution

Statement of extract of Consolidated Balance Sheet

Particulars	Rs.
Assets	
Net worth of Investment	120000
(include goodwill Rs.2750)	
Add: share of revenue	
profit Rs.47250	
revaluation	
reserve Rs.31500	78750
	198750

Working Notes
1. **Analysis of profit of B Ltd**

Particulars	Rs.	Capital Profit Rs.	Revenue Reserve Rs.	Revenue Profit Rs.
Reserves and surplus (Rs.250000 – Rs.90000)	160000			
Add: Proposed dividend	60000*			
	220000			
Less: Opening balance	40000	40000		
	180000			
Less: For 3 months	45000	45000		
	135000			135000
Revaluation reserve			90000	
Total		85000	90000	135000
Share of associates (35%)		29750	31500	47250

Note (*)As per Accounting standard interpretation no. 16 (at present added as an explanation (b) to para 6 of AS 23, proposed dividend if any deducted from profit and loss account of Associates shall be reversed before the share of the investor is computed.

2.Statement of calculation of goodwill

Particulars		Rs
Investments		120000 (A)
Nominal value of share capital (250000 x 35%)	Rs.87500	
Capital profit (WN1)	Rs. 29750	117250 (B)

Goodwill (A – B)	2750	

Q.2.6.
A Ltd acquired 25% shares in B Ltd as on 31.3.2002 for Rs.3 lakhs. The Balance Sheet of B Ltd as on 31.3.2002 is given below:

	Rs.
Share capital	5,00,000
Reserves and surplus	5,00,000
	10,00,000
Fixed Assets	5,00,000
Investments	2,00,000
Current Assets	3,00,000
	10,00,000

During the year ended 31.3.2003 the following are the additional information available:
I)   A Ltd received dividend from B Ltd for the year ended 31.3.2002 at 40% from the reserves.
II) B Ltd made a profit after tax of Rs.7 lakhs for the year ended 31.3.2003
III) B Ltd declared a dividend @ 50% for the year ended 31.3.2003 on 30.4.2003.

A Ltd is preparing consolidated financial statements in accordance with AS 21 for its various subsidiaries.

Calculate:
a) Goodwill if any on acquisition of B Ltd's shares
b) How A Ltd will reflect the value of investment in B Ltd in the consolidated financial statements?
c) How the dividend received from B Ltd will be shown in the consolidated financial statements?

Solution
In terms of AS 23 B Ltd will be considered as an associate company of A Ltd as share acquired represent more than 20%.

a) **Calculation of goodwill**   Rs Lakhs
Cost of investment   3.00
Less: Share in the value of equity of B Ltd as at the
Date of investment
(25% of Rs.10 lakhs (Rs.5 lakhs + Rs.5 lakhs))   2.50
Goodwill   0.50

b)   **A Ltd**
Extract of Consolidated Profit and Loss Account for the year ended 31st March 2003

	Rs Lakhs	Rs Lakhs
By Share of profit in B Ltd		1.75
By Dividend received from B Ltd	0.50	
Transfer to investment A/c	0.50	nil

c)

A Ltd

Extract of Consolidated Balance Sheet as on 31st March 2003

	Rs Lakhs
Investment in B Ltd	
Share in B Ltd's equity	2.50
Less: Dividend received	0.50
	2.00
Share of profit for year 2002-03	1.75
	3.75
Add: Goodwill	0.50
	4.25

Working Notes

1. Dividend received from B Ltd amounting to Rs.0.50 lakhs will be reduced from Investment value in the books of A Ltd. However goodwill will not change.

2. B Ltd made a profit of Rs.7 lakhs for the year ended 31st March 2003. A Ltd's share in the profits of Rs.7 lakhs is Rs.1.75 lakhs. Investment in B Ltd will be increased by Rs.1.75 lakhs and consolidated profit and loss account of A Ltd will be credited with Rs.1.75 lakhs in the consolidated financial statement of A Ltd.

3. Dividend declared on 30th April 2003 will not be recognized in the consolidated financial statements of A Ltd

Q.2.7.

Bright Ltd acquired 30% of East India Ltd Shares for Rs.2,00,000 on 01–06–09. By such an acquisition, Bright can exercise significant influence over East India Ltd. During the financial year ending on 31–03–09, East India Ltd earned profits Rs.80,000 and declared a dividend of Rs.50,000 on 12–08–09. East India reported earnings of Rs.3,00,000 for the financial year ending on 31-3–10 and declared dividends of Rs.60,000 on 12–06–2010.

a. Calculate the carrying amount of investment in
Separate Financial Statement of Bright Ltd as on 31–03–10,
Consolidated Financial Statement of Bright Ltd as on 31–03–10,
b. What will be the Carrying Amount as on 30–06–2010 in Consolidated Financial Statements?

Solution

1. Separate Financial Statements of Bright Ltd as at 31.03.2010:
   To be disclosed in accordance with AS 13 - Accounting for Investments, i.e. at Cost as follows:

Particulars	Rs.
Cost of Acquisition	200000
Less: Pre Acquisition Period Dividend (Rs.50,000 × Bright Ltd's Share 30%)	(15,000)
Net Cost = To be disclosed in Separate Financial Statements	1,85,000

2. Consolidated Financial Statements of Bright Ltd as at 31.03.2010:

To be disclosed in accordance with AS 23 Accounting for Investment in Associates, i.e. as per Equity Method as follows:

Particulars		Rs.
Net Cost as per Separate Financial Statements		185000
Less: Pre Acquisition Period Reserves		
(Rs.30,000 × Bright Ltd's Share 30%)	(9000)	
Add: Share of post-acquisition Period Reserves		
(Rs.3,00,000 × Bright Ltd's Share 30%)	90000	
Carrying Amount in Consolidated Balance sheet		2,66,000

Note: Dividends actually received before the date of Balance Sheet should be considered. Dividends after the Balance Sheet date, 31.03.2010 should not be considered.

3. Consolidated Financial Statements of Bright Ltd as at 30.06.2010:

   To be disclosed in accordance with AS 23 Accounting for Investment in Associates, i.e. as per Equity Method as follows:

Particulars	Rs.
Net Cost as per Separate Financial Statements	185000
Less: Pre Acquisition Period Reserves (Rs.30,000 × Bright Ltd's Share 30%)	(9000)
Add: Share of post-acquisition Period Reserves	
(Rs.2,40,000 × Bright Ltd's Share 30%)	72000
Carrying Amount in Consolidated Balance sheet	2,48,000

Note: Dividends actually received is accounted as per AS 13 – Accounting for Investments. It is assumed that the Dividend Declared on 30.06.2010 is out of profits for the year ended 31.03.2010. Hence the same will be credited to the Profit and Loss Account.

Note to Point 2 and Point 3 above:

It is assumed that East India Ltd did not have any other Reserves other than those earned during Financial Year 2008–09 and 2009–10.

The amount of Goodwill / Capital Reserve on Consolidation is not ascertainable, since the Amount of Net Assets attributable to Bright Ltd is not given.

AS 27: Financial reporting of interests in joint ventures

Learning outcomes
- **Characteristics of a JV**
- **Jointly controlled operations (JCO)**
- **Jointly controlled Asset (JCA)**
- **Jointly controlled entities (JCE)**
- **Consolidated Financial Statements of a Venturer**
- **Proportionate consolidation method**
- **Transactions between a Venturer and Joint Venture**
- **Disclosures**

2.19. What are the characteristics of a JV?

The characteristics of a JV are:	• Where two or more parties undertake an economic activity that is subject to joint control under a contractual arrangement is termed as joint venture • The existence of a contract which would contain ➢ the activity , duration and reporting obligations of the joint venture ➢ the appointment of the board of directors ➢ the voting rights of the venturers ➢ capital contribution by the venturers ➢ the sharing of the venturers of the output, income, expenses or results of the joint venture • The parties undertake an economic activity The economic activity is subject to joint control

2.20.Types of JVs

- *jointly controlled operations*
- *jointly controlled assets*
- *jointly controlled entities*

Joint control exists only when the strategic, financial and operating decisions related to economic activity require the undisputed consent of the parties sharing control.

A venturer recognizes its interest in a jointly controlled operation by recognizing in its financial statements the assets that it controls, the liabilities and expenses it incurs and its share of income from the sale of goods and services of the joint venture.

A venturer recognizes its interest in jointly controlled assets on a proportional basis

The venturer also recognizes any liabilities or expenses it incurs, its share of liabilities or expenses incurred jointly, and any income from the sale or use of its share of the output of the joint venture.

A venturer recognizes its interest in a jointly controlled entity using either

> - *the equity method in accordance with AS 23 on investment in associates*
>
>   *or*
>
> - *proportionate consolidation.*

This is not applicable when

> a) *the investment is classified as held for sale under AS 24 on " discontinued operations "*
>
> *or*
>
> b) *the venturer itself is a subsidiary, its owners do not object to proportionate consolidation or the equity method not being applied and its debt and equity securities are not publicly traded. In this case the venture's parent must present consolidated financial statements that comply with IFRSs.*

A venturer discontinues proportionate consolidation or the equity method from the date it ceases to have joint control over a jointly controlled entity.

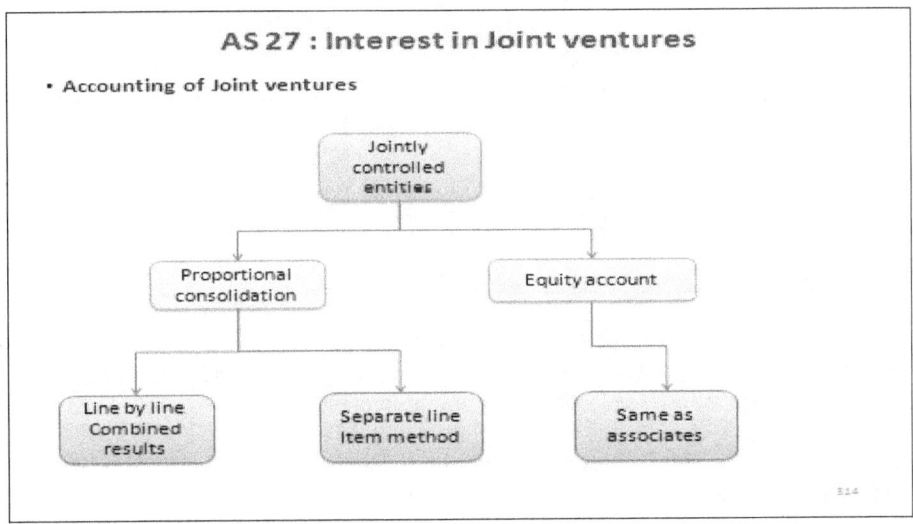

AS 27 : Interest in Joint ventures

- Accounting of Joint ventures

2.21. What are the general accounting considerations that apply?

General accounting considerations	Transactions between a venturer and joint venture are treated as follows: - the venturer's share of unrealized profits on sales or contribution of assets to a joint venture is eliminated - full unrealized loss on sale or contribution of assets to a joint venture is eliminated - the venturer's share of profits or losses on sales of assets by a joint venture to the venturer is eliminated - An investor in a joint venture that does not have joint control should report its interest in a joint venture in the consolidated financial statements under AS 13 or it has significant influence in terms of AS 23. - Operators or managers of a joint venture should account for any fees as revenue in terms of AS 9

2.22. How do we evidence Contractual obligations?

The contractual arrangement may be evidenced in a number of ways, for example by a contract between the venturers or minutes of discussions between the venturers. In some cases, the arrangement is incorporated in the articles or other by-laws of the joint venture. Whatever its form, the contractual arrangement is normally in writing and deals with such matters as:

> (a) the activity, duration and reporting obligations of the joint venture;
> (b) the appointment of the board of directors or equivalent governing body of the joint venture and the voting rights of the venturers;
> (c) capital contributions by the venturers; and
> (d) the sharing by the venturers of the output, income, expenses or results of the joint venture.

2.23. Key features of Jointly controlled operations (JCO)

The operation of some joint ventures involves the use of the assets and other resources of the venturers rather than the establishment of a corporation, partnership or other entity, or a financial structure that is separate from the venturers themselves.

Each venturer uses its own fixed assets and carries its own inventories. It also incurs its own expenses and liabilities and raises its own finance, which represent its own obligations

In respect of its interests in jointly controlled operations, a venturer should recognise in its separate financial statements and consequently in its consolidated financial statements

---

(a) the assets that it controls and the liabilities that it incurs; and

(b) the expenses that it incurs and its share of the income that it earns from the joint venture

---

Jointly controlled operations (JCO)	• each venturer has his own separate business • there is no separate entity for joint venture business • all venturers are creating their own assets and maintain them • each venturer record only his own transactions without any separate set of books maintained for the joint venture business • there is a common agreement between all of them • venturers use their assets for the joint venture business • venturers meet the liabilities created by them for the joint venture business • venturers meet the expenses of the joint venture business from their funds • any revenue generated or income earned from the joint venture is shared by the venturers as per the contract

Illustration 8: Jointly controlled operations (JCO)

Mr.X , Mr Y and Mr. Z entered into a joint venture to purchase a land, construct and sell flats. Mr. X purchased a land for Rs.6000000 on 1.1.2010 and for the purpose he took loan from a bank for Rs.5000000 @ 8% interest p.a. He also paid registering fees Rs.60000 on the same day. Mr. Y supplied the materials for R.450000 from his go-down and further he purchased materials for Rs.500000 for the joint venture. Mr C met all other expenses of advertising, labour and other incidental expenses which turn out to be Rs.900000. On 30th June 2010 each of the venturers agreed to take away one flat each to be valued at Rs.10 lakhs each and rest were sold by them as follows:

Mr X : Rs.40 lakhs

Mr.Y : Rs.20 lakhs

Mr. Z : Rs.10 lakhs

Loan was repaid on the same day by Mr. X along with interest and net proceeds were shared by the partners equally.

Required: Prepare the consolidated profit and loss account and joint venture account in the books of each venturer. *(Adapted: CA Final : study material)*

Solution

Extract of Consolidated Profit and Loss Account

Particulars	Rs.	Rs.
I. Income		
Sale of flats		
Mr. X	4000000	
Mr. Y	2000000	
Mr. Z	1000000	7000000
Flats taken by venturers		
Mr. X		
Mr. Y	1000000	
Mr. Z	1000000	
	1000000	3000000
		10000000
II. Expenses		
Purchase of land		6000000
Mr.X		
Registration fees		60000
Mr X		
Materials		950000
Mr. Y		
Other expenses		900000
Mr. Z		
Bank Interest:		200000
Mr. X		
Profits:	630000	
Mr. X	630000	
Mr. Y	630000	1890000
Mr. Z		
		10000000

In the books of Mr.X
Joint Venture Account

Particulars	Rs.	Particulars	Rs.
To Bank loan (purchase of land)	5000000	By bank (sale of flats)	4000000
To Bank (purchase of land)	1000000	By Land & building	1000000
To Bank (registration fees)	60000	By Bank (paid to Mr. Y)	1420000
To Bank (Bank interest)	200000	By Bank (Paid to Mr. Z)	470000
To Profit on JV	630000		
Total	6890000		6890000

In the books of Mr.Y
Joint Venture Account

Particulars	Rs.	Particulars	Rs.
To Bank loan (material supplied)	450000	By bank (sale of flats)	2000000

To Bank (materials)	500000	By Land & building	1000000
To Bank (recd from Mr.X)	1420000		
To Profit on JV	630000		
Total	3000000		3000000

In the books of Mr. Z
Joint Venture Account

Particulars	Rs.	Particulars	Rs.
To Bank loan (misc. expenses)	900000	By bank (sale of flats)	1000000
To Bank (received from Mr.X)	470000	By Land & building	1000000
To Profit on JV	630000		
Total	2000000		2000000

2.24. Key features of Jointly controlled assets (JCA)

Jointly controlled Assets(JCA)	• There is no separate legal entity • There is a common control over the joint assets • Venturers use these assets to derive some economic benefit to themselves • Each venturer incurs separate expenses for their transactions • Expenses on jointly held assets are shared by the venturers as per the contract • In their financial statement, venturer shows only their share of the asset and total income earned by them along with total expenses incurred by them • As the assets, liabilities, income and expenses are already recognized in the separate financial statements of the venturer and consequently in its consolidated financial statements, no adjustments or other consolidation procedures are required in respect of these items when the venturer presents consolidated financial statements • Financial statements may not be prepared for the joint venture although the venturers may prepare the accounts for internal use so that they may evaluate the performance of the joint venture.

Illustration 9: Jointly controlled assets

X Ltd, Y Ltd and Z Ltd decided to jointly construct a pipeline to transport gas from one place to another, that was manufactured by them. For the purpose following expenditure was incurred by them : buildings: Rs.12 lakhs to be depreciated @ 5% p.a., pipeline for Rs.60 lakhs to be depreciated @ 15% p.a., computers and other appliances for Rs.300000 to be depreciated @ 40% p.a. and various vehicles of Rs.900000 to be depreciated @ 20% p.a.

They also decided to equally bear the total expenditure incurred on the maintenance of the pipeline that comes to Rs.600000 each year.

Required: show the consolidated financial balance sheet and the extract of profit and loss account and balance sheet for each venturer. (*CA Final study material*)

Solution

Extract of Consolidated Balance Sheet

Particulars	Note	Rs.
I.Equity and liabilities		
(1)Shareholders' funds		
(a)Share capital	1	7740000
Total		7740000
II.Assets		
(1)Non-current assets		
(a)Tangible assets	2	7740000
Total		7740000

Notes on Accounts

S/L No	Particulars	Amount (Rs)	Amount (Rs)
1.	Share capital		
	Capital of venturers		
	A Ltd	2580000	
	B Ltd	2580000	
	C Ltd	2580000	**7740000**
2.	Tangible assets		
	Land & Building		
	A Ltd	380000	
	B Ltd	380000	
	C Ltd	380000	1140000
	Plant & Machinery		
	A Ltd	1900000	
	B Ltd	1900000	
	C Ltd 1900000		5700000
	Computers		
	A Ltd	60000	
	B Ltd	60000	
	C Ltd 60000		180000
	Vehicles		
	A Ltd	240000	
	B Ltd	240000	
	C Ltd 240000		720000	**7740000**

Extract of Profit & Loss Account (in the books of the venturers)

Particulars	A Ltd	B Ltd	C Ltd
To Depreciation			
Land and building	20000	20000	20000
Plant and Machinery	300000	300000	300000
Computers	40000	40000	40000
Vehicles	60000	60000	60000
	420000	420000	420000
To Pipeline expenses	200000	200000	200000

Extract of Balance Sheet (in the books of the venturers)

Particulars	A Ltd	B Ltd	C Ltd
Land and building	400000	400000	400000
Less: Depreciation	20000	20000	20000
Net book value	380000	380000	380000
Plant and Machinery	2000000	2000000	2000000
Less: Depreciation	300000	300000	300000
Net book value	1700000	1700000	1700000
Computers	100000	100000	100000
Less: Depreciation	40000	40000	40000
Net book value	60000	60000	60000
Vehicles	300000	300000	300000
Less: Depreciation	60000	60000	60000
Net book value	240000	240000	240000

2.25. Key features of Jointly controlled entity (JCE)

Jointly controlled entity (JCE)	• A jointly controlled entity is a joint venture which involves the establishment of a corporation, partnership or other entity in which each venturer has an interest. The entity operates in the same way as other enterprises, except that a contractual arrangement between the venturers establishes joint control over the economic activity of the entity.
	• A jointly controlled entity controls the assets of the joint venture, incurs liabilities and expenses and earns income. It may enter into contracts in its own name and raise finance for the purposes of the joint venture activity.
	Each venturer is entitled to a share of the results of the jointly controlled entity, although some jointly controlled entities also involve a sharing of the

	output of the joint venture. • An example of a jointly controlled entity is when two enterprises combine their activities in a particular line of business by transferring the relevant assets and liabilities into a jointly controlled entity. Another example is when an enterprise commences a business in a foreign country in conjunction with the government or other agency in that country, by establishing a separate entity which is jointly controlled by the enterprise

Illustration 10: Jointly Controlled Entities (JCE)

X Ltd a UK based company entered into a joint venture with Y Ltd, in India, wherein Y Ltd will import the goods manufactured by X Ltd on account of joint venture and sell them in India. X Ltd and Y Ltd agreed to share the expenses and revenues in the ratio of 5 : 4 respectively whereas profits are distributed equally. X Ltd invested 49% of total capital but has equal share in all the assets and is equally liable for all the liabilities of the joint venture. Following is the trial balance of the joint venture at the end of the first year:

Particulars	Dr	Cr.
Purchases	900000	
Other expenses	306000	
Sales		1305000
Fixed assets	600000	
Current assets	200000	
Unsecured loans		200000
Current liabilities		100000
Capital		401000

Closing stock was valued at Rs.100000.
Required: prepare the consolidated financial statement

Solution

Extract of Consolidated Profit & Loss Account

Particulars	Rs.	Rs.
I. Income		
Sales		
X Ltd	725000	
Y Ltd	580000	
		1305000
Closing stock		
X Ltd	50000	
Y Ltd	50000	100000
Total		1405000
II.Expenses		
Purchases		
X Ltd	500000	

Y Ltd		<u>400000</u>	900000
Other expenses			
X Ltd		170000	
Y Ltd		<u>136000</u>	306000
To Net Profits			
X Ltd		99500	
Y Ltd		<u>99500</u>	199000
	Total		1405000

Extract of Consolidated Balance Sheet

Particulars		Rs.	Rs.
I. Equity and Liabilities			
(1) Shareholders' funds			
(a) Share capital			
X Ltd		196490	
Y Ltd		<u>204510</u>	401000
(b)Reserves and surplus			
Profit & Loss A/c			
X Ltd		99500	
Y Ltd		<u>99500</u>	199000
(2)Non-current liabilities			
(a)Long term borrowings (assumed)			
Unsecured loans			
X Ltd		100000	
Y Ltd		<u>100000</u>	200000
(3)Current liabilities			
(a)Trade Payables (assumed)			
X Ltd		50000	
Y Ltd		<u>50000</u>	100000
	Total		900000
II. Assets			
(1)Non-current Assets			
(a)Tangible assets			
X Ltd		300000	
Y Ltd		<u>300000</u>	600000
(2)Current Assets			
(a) Inventories			
Closing stock			
X Ltd		50000	
Y Ltd		<u>50000</u>	100000
(b) Other current assets			
X Ltd		100000	
Y Ltd		<u>100000</u>	200000

Total	900000	

2.26. What the Consolidated Financial Statements of a Venturer should report?

In its consolidated financial statements, a venturer should report its interest in a jointly controlled entity using proportionate consolidation except

> (a) *an interest in a jointly controlled entity which is acquired and held exclusively with a view to its subsequent disposal in the near future; and*
> (b) *an interest in a jointly controlled entity which operates under severe long-term restrictions that significantly impair its ability to transfer funds to the venturer.*

Interest in such a jointly controlled entity should be accounted for as an investment in accordance with Accounting Standard (AS) 13, Accounting for Investments.

2.27. What are the features of Proportionate consolidation method?

Features of proportionate consolidation method	- Stress is given on substance over form i.e. more importance is given to the share of venturers in the profit or loss of the venture from the share of assets and liabilities rather than the nature and form of joint venture - Venturers' share of joint assets, liabilities, expenses and income are shown on the separate lines in the consolidated financial statement - Most of the provisions of proportionate consolidation method are similar to the provision of AS 21 - As far as possible the reporting date of the financial statements of JCE and venturers should be the same (the difference not more than 6 months) - Accounting policies followed by the JCE and the venturers need to be uniform - otherwise adjustments need to be made to bring it inline. - Any asset or liability should not be adjusted by another liability or asset. Similarly any income or expense cannot be adjusted by another expense or income. Such adjustments are made only when it is legally allowed to adjust them and such items lead to settlement of obligation or writing off of assets - On the date when interest in joint entity is acquired if the interest in venturer in net assets of the entity is less than the cost of investment in joint entity, the difference will be recognized as goodwill in the consolidated statement, and if the net asset is

<table>
<tr>
<td></td>
<td>higher than cost of investment, the difference is taken to capital reserve

- An investor who doesn't have joint control in the entity is like an associate as per AS 23, therefore the treatment of losses will be similar to AS 23.</td>
</tr>
</table>

2.28. When do we discontinue a proportionate consolidation method?

A venturer should discontinue the use of proportionate consolidation from the date that

(a) it ceases to have joint control over a jointly controlled entity but retains, either in whole or in part, its interest in the entity; or
(b) the use of the proportionate consolidation is no longer appropriate because the jointly controlled entity operates under severe long-term restrictions that significantly impair its ability to transfer funds to the venturer

From the date of discontinuing the use of the proportionate consolidation interest in a jointly controlled entity should be accounted for:

(a) in accordance with Accounting Standard (AS) 21, Consolidated Financial Statements, if the venturer acquires unilateral control over the entity and becomes parent within the meaning of that Standard; and
(b) in all other cases, as an investment in accordance with Accounting Standard (AS) 13, Accounting for Investments, or in accordance with Accounting Standard (AS) 23, Accounting for Investments in Associate in Consolidated Financial statement as appropriate

2.29. What are the kinds of transactions between a Venturer and Joint Venture?

- When a venturer contributes or sells assets to a joint venture, recognition of any portion of a gain or loss from the transaction should reflect the substance of the transaction.
- While the assets are retained by the joint venture, and provided the venturer has transferred the significant risks and rewards of ownership, the venturer should recognise only that portion of the gain or loss which is attributable to the interests of the other venturers.
- The venturer should recognise the full amount of any loss when the contribution or sale provides evidence of a reduction in the net realisable value of current assets or an impairment loss.
- When a venturer purchases assets from a joint venture, the venturer should not recognise its share of the profits of the joint venture from the transaction until it resells the assets to an independent party. A venturer should recognise its share of the losses resulting from these transactions in the same way as profits except that

losses should be recognised immediately when they represent a reduction in the net realisable value

2.30. Disclosure requirements prescribed by the standard

Disclosure requirements	A venturer should disclose the aggregate amount of the following contingent liabilities, unless the probability of loss is remote, separately from the amount of other contingent liabilities: (a) any contingent liabilities that the venturer has incurred in relation to its interests in joint ventures and its share in each of the contingent liabilities which have been incurred jointly with other venturers; (b) its share of the contingent liabilities of the joint ventures themselves for which it is contingently liable; and (c) those contingent liabilities that arise because the venturer is contingently liable for the liabilities of the other venturers of a joint venture. A venturer should disclose the aggregate amount of the following commitments in respect of its interests in joint ventures separately from other commitments: (a) any capital commitments of the venturer in relation to its interests in joint ventures and its share in the capital commitments that have been incurred jointly with other venturers; and (b) its share of the capital commitments of the joint ventures themselves. A venturer should disclose a list of all joint ventures and description of interests in significant joint ventures. In respect of jointly controlled entities, the venturer should also disclose the proportion of ownership interest, name and country of incorporation or residence.

Illustration 11: Proportionate consolidation method

X Ltd floated a joint venture with Y Ltd a new venture Z Ltd on 1: 1 basis. Balance Sheet of three companies as on 31.03.11 are given below: (Rs.)

	X Ltd	Y Ltd	Z Ltd
Share capital	14000	10000	4000
Reserve and surplus	24000	26000	2000
Loan funds	14000	10000	8000
	52000	46000	14000
Fixed Assets – net	36000	40000	10000
Investment in Joint venture	2000	2000	-
Net current asset	14000	4000	4000
	52000	46000	14000

Prepare the balance sheet of X Ltd and Y Ltd under proportionate consolidation method.

Solution

Extract of Balance Sheet under proportionate consolidation method

Particulars	X Ltd Rs.	Particulars	Y Ltd Rs.
I. **Equity and Liabilities**		I. **Equity and Liabilities**	
(1)Shareholders' funds		**(1)Shareholders' funds**	
(a)Share capital	14000	(a)Share capital	10000
(b)Reserves & surplus		(b)Reserves & surplus	
(24000+1000)	25000	(26000+1000)	27000
(2)Non-current liabilities		**(2)Non-current liabilities**	
(a)Long term borrowings		(a)Long term borrowings	
(14000 + 4000)	18000	(10000 + 4000)	14000
Total	57000	Total	51000
II.Assets		**II.Assets**	
(1)Non-current assets		**(1)Non-current assets**	
(a)Tangible assets		(a)Tangible assets	
(36000 + 5000)	41000	(40000 + 5000)	45000
(2)Net current assets*		**(2)Net current assets***	
(14000 + 2000)	16000	(4000 + 2000)	6000
Total	57000	Total	51000

*In the absence of availability of information on current liabilities, net current assets have been shown under Assets side of the Balance Sheet to adjust to the Revised Schedule VI format.

Illustration 12: Proportionate consolidation method

A Ltd floated a joint venture with B Ltd a new venture Z Ltd in the ratio of 40% and 60% respectively. Balance Sheet of three companies as on 31.03.11 are given below: (Rs.)

	A Ltd	B Ltd	Z Ltd
Share capital	500000	300000	100000
Reserve and surplus	300000	100000	50000
Loan funds	200000	100000	30000
	1000000	500000	180000
Fixed Assets – net	800000	350000	120000
Investment in Joint venture	40000	60000	-
Net current assets	160000	90000	4000
	1000000	500000	180000

Prepare the balance sheet of A Ltd and B Ltd under proportionate consolidation method.

Solution

Extract of Balance Sheet under proportionate consolidation method

Particulars	A Ltd Rs.	Particulars	B Ltd Rs.
I. **Equity and Liabilities**		I. **Equity and Liabilities**	
(1)Shareholders' funds		**(1)Shareholders' funds**	
(a)Share capital	500000	(a)Share capital	300000
(b)Reserves & surplus		(b)Reserves & surplus	
(300000+20000)	320000	(100000+30000)	130000
(2)Non-current liabilities		**(2)Non-current liabilities**	
Long term borrowings		Long term borrowings	
(200000 + 12000)	212000	(100000 + 18000)	118000
Total	1032000	Total	548000
II.Assets		**II.Assets**	
(1)Non-current assets		**(1)Non-current assets**	
(a)Tangible assets		(a)Tangible assets	
(800000 + 48000)	848000	(350000 + 72000)	422000
(2)Net current assets*		**(2)Net current assets***	
(160000 + 24000)	184000	(90000 + 36000)	126000
Total	1032000	Total	548000

*In the absence of availability of information on current liabilities, net current assets have been shown under Assets side of the Balance Sheet to adjust to the Revised Schedule VI format.

Chapter 3   Indian Accounting Standards (Ind AS) on consolidation of subsidiaries, associates and joint arrangements converged with IFRS

3.1. Introduction

Ministry of Corporate Affairs has notified Companies (Indian Accounting Standards) Rules, 2015 which shall come into effect from 1 April 2015. The said rules require adoption for Indian Accounting Standards (Ind AS):-

3.1.1. From FY 15-16: Any company can voluntary adopt Indian Accounting Standards from Financial year 15-16 with comparatives to be given for the period ending on 31 March 2015 or thereafter.

3.1.2. From FY 16-17: Following companies to mandatorily adopt Ind AS from FY 16-17 onwards with comparatives for period ending 31 March 2016 or thereafter:-

- Companies with net worth of Rs 500 crores or more and whose equity or debt securities are either listed or in the process of listing in any Indian stock exchange.
- Companies other than above and whose net worth is Rs 500 crores or more.
- Holding, subsidiary, joint venture and associate of above companies.

3.1.3. From FY 17-18: Following companies to mandatorily adopt Ind AS from FY 17-18 onwards with comparatives for period ending 31 March 2017 or thereafter:-

- Companies with net worth less than Rs 500 crores and whose equity or debt securities are either listed or in the process of listing in any Indian stock exchange.
- Companies other than above and whose net worth is Rs 250 crores or more but less than Rs 500 crores.
- Holding, subsidiary, joint venture and associate of above companies.
- Provided that nothing stated above, except companies adopting Ind AS voluntarily, shall apply to companies whose securities are listed or are in the process of being listed on SME exchange as referred to in Chapter XB or on the Institutional Trading Platform without Initial public offering in accordance with the provisions of Chapter XC of the Securities and Exchange Board of India (Issue of Capital and Disclosure Requirements) Regulations, 2009.

Note 1:- 'Net worth' shall have the meaning assigned to it in clause (57) of section 2 of the Companies Act, 2013. The net worth shall be calculated in accordance with the stand-alone financial statements of the company as on 31st March, 2014 or the first audited financial statements for accounting period which ends after that date.

For companies which are not in existence on 31st March, 2014 or an existing company falling under any of thresholds specified above for the first time after 31st March, 2014, the net worth shall be calculated on the basis of the first audited financial statements ending after that date in respect of which it meets the thresholds specified above. Such companies should adopt Ind AS for immediately next year. For e.g. The companies meeting threshold for the first time as on 31st March, 2018shall apply Ind AS for the financial year 2018-19 onwards and so on.

Note 2:- MCA has notified 39 Ind AS. The Ind AS should be adopted for standalone financial statements as well as consolidated financial statements.

Note 3:- Overseas subsidiary, associate, joint venture and other similar entities of an Indian company may prepare its standalone financial statements in accordance with the requirements of the specific jurisdiction. Provided that such Indian company shall prepare its consolidated financial statements in accordance with the Indian Accounting Standards (Ind AS) either voluntarily or mandatorily if it meets the criteria as specified above.

Note 4:- Indian company which is a subsidiary, associate, joint venture and other similar entities of a foreign company shall prepare its financial statements in accordance with the Indian Accounting Standards (Ind AS) either voluntarily or mandatorily if it meets the criteria as specified above.

Note 5:- Once the option for applying Ind AS is applied then company should keep on applying Ind AS consistently.

Note 6:- The insurance companies, banking companies and non-banking finance companies shall not be required to apply Indian Accounting Standards (Ind AS) for preparation of their financial statements either voluntarily or mandatorily.

Note 7:- For the companies on which Ind AS is not applicable as per the rules mentioned above, such companies can continue to apply Accounting Standards as notified by Companies (Accounting Standards) Rules, 2006.

3.2. Consolidated Financial statements (Ind AS 110)

3.2.1. Objective

The objective of this Indian Accounting Standard (Ind AS) is to establish principles for the presentation and preparation of consolidated financial statements when an entity controls one or more other entities. To meet the above objective, this Ind AS:

(a) requires an entity (the *parent*) that controls one or more other entities (*subsidiaries*) to present consolidated financial statements;

(b) defines the principle of *control*, and establishes control as the basis for consolidation;

(c) sets out how to apply the principle of control to identify whether an investor controls an investee and therefore must consolidate the investee;

(d) sets out the accounting requirements for the preparation of consolidated financial statements; and

(e) defines an investment entity and sets out an exception to consolidating particular subsidiaries of an investment entity.

This Ind AS does not deal with the accounting requirements for business combinations and their effect on consolidation, including goodwill arising on a business combination (see Ind AS 103, *Business Combinations*).

3.2.2. Scope

An entity that is a parent shall present consolidated financial statements. This Ind AS applies to all entities, except as follows:

(a) A parent need not present consolidated financial statements if it meets all the following conditions:

    (i) it is a wholly-owned subsidiary or is a partially-owned subsidiary of another entity and all its other owners, including those not otherwise entitled to vote, have been informed about, and do not object to, the parent not presenting consolidated financial statements;

    (ii) its debt or equity instruments are not traded in a public market (a domestic or foreign stock exchange or an over-the-counter market, including local and regional markets);

    (iii) it did not file, nor is it in the process of filing, its financial statements with a securities commission or other regulatory organisation for the purpose of issuing any class of instruments in a public market; and

    (iv) its ultimate or any intermediate parent produces consolidated financial Statements that are available for public use and comply with Ind ASs.

(b) post-employment benefit plans or other long-term employee benefit plans to which Ind AS19, *Employee Benefits,* applies.

(c) an investment entity need not present consolidated financial statements if it is required, in accordance with paragraph 31 of this Ind AS, to measure all of its subsidiaries at fair value through profit or loss.

3.2.3. Concept of group

In today's global economy, most companies operate as a group, in which one main company controls the operations of many other entities. In such situations, it becomes imperative for the shareholders, directors, employees, suppliers, customers, government departments and other stakeholders to know the financial standing of the group as a whole. This is the genesis of consolidated financial statements for a group.

Ind AS 10 specifies that consolidated financial statements have to be prepared where a group of entities are controlled by a parent.
Consolidated financial statements are prepared by combining the financial statements of all the group entities, with a view to determine the financial status of the group as if it were one single entity.

However, it should be understood that,
a) Merely preparing consolidated financial statements do not establish a single operating unit,
b) A group does not have any legal existence, except for accounting purposes.

Hence,

Group is a parent with all its subsidiaries
Parent is an entity that controls one or more entities
Subsidiary is an entity that is controlled by another entity

(Ind AS 10, Appendix A)

3.2.4. Concept of control
In accordance with Para 7 of Ind AS 110, an investor controls an investee if an only if the investor has ALL of the following characteristics:
a) Power over the investee
b) Exposure, or rights, to variable returns from its involvement with the investee and
c) Ability to use its power over the investee to affect the amount of the investor's returns.
Hence control is:

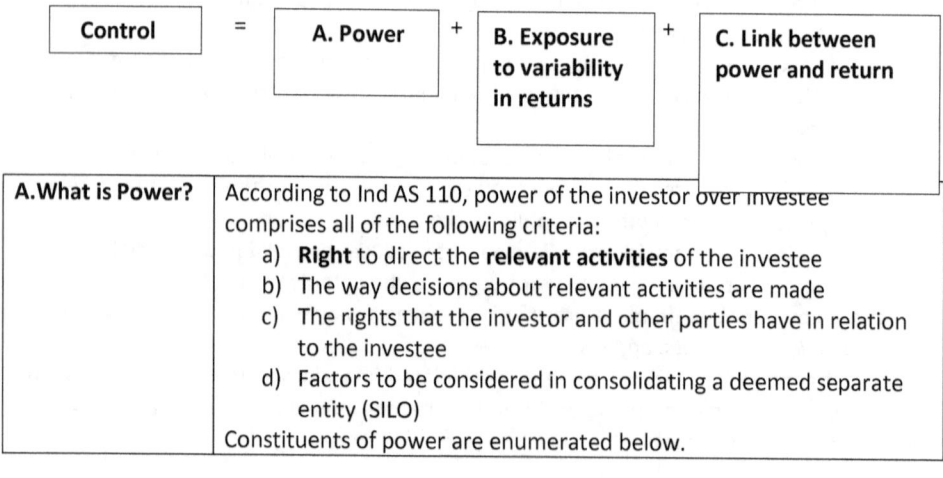

A.What is Power?	According to Ind AS 110, power of the investor over investee comprises all of the following criteria:	
	a) **Right** to direct the **relevant activities** of the investee	
	b) The way decisions about relevant activities are made	
	c) The rights that the investor and other parties have in relation to the investee	
	d) Factors to be considered in consolidating a deemed separate entity (SILO)	
	Constituents of power are enumerated below.	

1. Existing rights	To have power over an investee, an investor must have
	a) *Existing rights* that
	b) Give the investor *current ability* to
	c) Direct the *relevant activities*.
Examples of	a)rights in the form of voting rights or potential voting rights of an investee

existing rights	b)rights to appoint, reassign or remove members of an investee's key management personnel who have the right to direct the relevant activities c)rights to appoint or remove another entity that directs the relevant activities d)rights to direct the investee to enter into, or veto any changes to, transactions for the benefit of the investor and e)other rights (such as decision making rights specified in a management contract) that give the holder the ability to direct the relevant activities In order to assess power, only ***substantive rights*** should be considered.
2. substantive rights	Substantive rights are determined as under: a)Whether there are any barriers (economic or otherwise) that prevent holders from exercising rights b)when the exercise of rights requires the agreement of more than one party, or when the rights are held by more than one party, whether a mechanism is in place that provides those parties with the practical ability to exercise their rights collectively if they choose to do so c)whether the party or parties that hold the rights would benefit from the exercise of those rights However ***Protective rights*** do not contribute to power under IFRS 10.
3. Protective rights	Protective rights are designed to protect the interest of their holder, but do not give that party power over the investee. Protective rights give the holder protection in exceptional circumstances or prevent fundamental changes from being made to the activities of the investee. *Examples of protective rights include*: a)a lender's right to restrict the borrower from undertaking activities that could significantly change the credit risk of the borrower to the detriment of the lender b)the right of a party holding a non-controlling interest in an investee to approve capital expenditure greater than that required in the ordinary course of business, or to approve the issue of debt or equity instruments c)the right of a lender to seize assets of a borrower if the borrower fail to meet specified loan repayment conditions
4. Relevant activities	Relevant activities are activities of the investee that significantly affect the investor's returns. While assessing control over an investee, an investor shall consider the purpose and design of the investee in order to identify the relevant activities. *Examples of relevant activities are:* a)selling and purchasing of goods and services b)managing financial assets during their life (including upon default) c)selecting, acquiring or disposing of assets, d)researching and developing new products or processes and e)determining a funding structure or obtaining funding
5.Voting rights	a) **Power with a majority of the voting rights** – Control arises when an Investor owns over 50% of the voting rights of an investee. However, Voting rights need to be substantive and not protective. Non-controlling interest – is the equity in a subsidiary not attributable, Directly or indirectly to a parent. b)**Majority of the voting rights but no power** – Voting rights may be designed in a manner such that they are not the dominant factor in deciding control over an investee. This is possible if the investor cannot direct the relevant activities of the investee or the rights may not be substantive. In such cases the investor does not control the investee c)**Power without a majority of the voting rights** – This could be due to

	- contractual arrangement between the investor and other vote holders - rights arising from other contractual arrangements - the investor's voting rights, referred to as de-facto control (e.g. when the investor holds significantly greater voting rights than any other vote holder or organised group of vote holders -potential voting rights only when they are substantive and not protective, - a combination of above.
6. Control over specified assets	An investor shall consider whether it treats a portion of an investee as a deemed separate entity and, if so, whether it controls the deemed separate entity. The deemed separate entity or the "silo" is a new concept compared to IAS 27, which dealt with only the legal entities. This opens up possibility that only a part of the entity represented by this "silo" may be considered. The conditions are: a)specified assets of the investee (and related credit enhancements, if any) are the only source of payment for specified liabilities of or specified other interests in, the investee b)parties other than those with the specified liability do not have rights or obligations related to the specified assets or to residual cash flows from those assets, c)In substance, none of the returns from the specified assets can be used by the remaining investee and none of the liabilities of the deemed separate entity are payable from the assets of the remaining investee Thus, all the assets, liabilities and equity of that deemed separate entity is "ring fenced" from the overall investee. Such a deemed separate entity is often called "silo".
7.Design of an investee	While assessing control of an investee, an investor need to consider the purpose and design of the investee in order to identify: - The relevant activities - How decisions about the relevant activities are made - Who has the current ability to direct those activities and - Who receives returns from those activities.

To simplify the concept of power over an investee, please refer to the chart below:

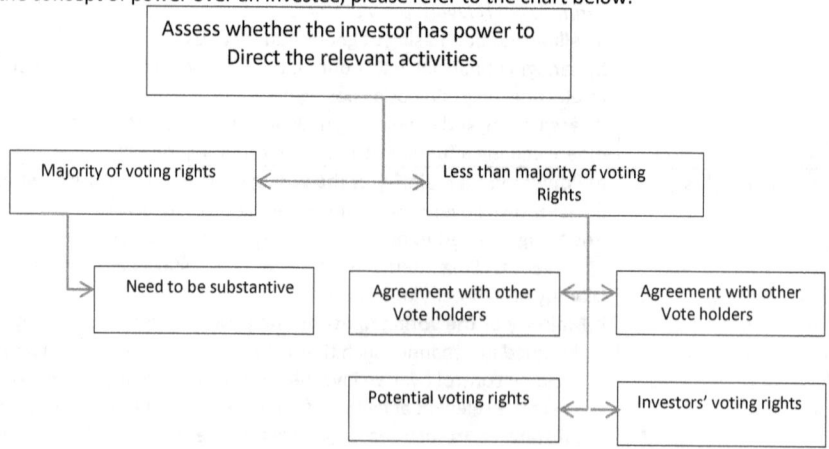

B.Exposure to Variability in returns	To control an investee, an investor must be exposed, or have rights to variable returns from its involvement with the investee. This occurs when the investor's returns from its involvement have the potential to vary as a result of the investee's performance. Although only one investor can control an investee, more than one party can share the returns of an investee, e.g. holders of non-controlling interest can share the profits or distributions of an investee, but cannot control the investee.

C.Link between power and returns	The investor does not control the investee in the following circumstances: a)an investor has power over an investee, but cannot benefit from that power b)an investor receives return from an investee, but cannot use its power to direct the activities that significantly affect the returns of that investee. Therefore it becomes necessary that the investor should have the ability to use its power over the investee to affect its returns. Hence, a)when an investor with decision making rights (a decision maker) assesses whether it controls an investee, it shall determine whether it is a principal or an agent. b)an investor shall also determine whether another entity with decision making rights is acting as an agent for the investor c)an agent is a party primarily engaged to act on behalf of and for the benefit of another party or parties (i.e. the principals) and therefore does not control the investee when it exercises its decision-making authority.

3.2.5. Consolidated financial statements

According to Ind AS 110, consolidated financial statements have to be prepared where a group of entities are controlled by a parent (barring a few exceptional cases highlighted by the standard). So consolidated financial statements are the financial statements of a group presented as those of a single economic entity.

3.2.6. Objectives of preparing consolidated financial statements

The objectives of preparing consolidated financial statements are:
a) Determine financial status of group as one single entity   b) Safeguard interests of ordinary shareholders of parent company   c) Show full earnings on parent's investments   d) Show where group as a whole stands   e) Assist in prevention of malpractices and manipulations in financial statements

3.2.7. Circumstances when subsidiaries should be excluded from consolidated financial statements

Ind AS 110 specifies that consolidated financial statements shall include the accounts of ALL the subsidiaries of the parent – both domestic and foreign. The standard has been very strict about exclusions from consolidated financial statements because otherwise companies will indulge in manipulation of their results.

There are *no specific exemptions* for the following subsidiaries:	1. Subsidiaries whose business activities are dissimilar from those of the other entities within the group 2. Subsidiaries of venture capital organisation, mutual funds, unit trust or any other similar entity 3. Subsidiaries held for sale, i.e. investments by a parent in an entity only for the purpose of selling it. In case of such subsidiaries measurement and accounting is done as per Ind AS 105.

***Exemption* from preparing consolidated financial statements if all the four conditions are fulfilled:**	1. The parent itself is a wholly or partially owned subsidiary of another entity and its owners have been informed and do not object to the parent not presenting consolidated financial statements 2. The ultimate or any intermediate parent of the parent produces consolidated financial statements available for public use that comply with IFRSs 3. The parent's debt or equity instruments are not traded in a public market (e.g. a domestic or foreign stock exchange or an over-the-counter market, including local and regional markets 4. The parent has not filed, nor in the process of filing, its financial instruments with a securities commission or other regulatory organisation for the purpose of issuing any class of instruments in a public market.

3.2.8. Need for using coterminous year-ends and uniform accounting policies when preparing consolidated financial statements and how is it achieved in practical world

Co-terminus year-ends	Means that the financial year ends of two or more entities are identical. It signifies that the financial year used for recording financial statements by two or more entities is the same. If the parent and all its subsidiaries do not have the same year-end, the consolidated financial statements will not reflect a correct picture of the financial status of the group. Hence Ind AS 110 specifies that the financial statements of the parent and its subsidiaries used in the preparation of the consolidated financial statements shall be prepared as of the same date. However, if it is not practicable, then a) adjustments should be made for the effects of significant transactions or events that occur between the reporting dates of the subsidiary and parent b) a gap of not more than three months between the reporting date of the parent and subsidiary is allowed. This means if the gap is more than 3 months apart, the subsidiary would need to prepare full financial statements at the parent company's year-end date, to be used for consolidation purposes.
Uniform accounting policies	According to IAS 8 Para 5, Accounting policies are the specific principles, bases, conventions, rules and practices applied by an entity in preparing and presenting financial statements (e.g. valuation of inventories – FIFO or weighted average cost, valuation of Properties, Plant & Equipment – historical cost or revaluation method, valuation of investments – fair value, amortised cost method etc) Ind AS 110 prescribes that consolidated financial statements shall be prepared using uniform accounting policies for similar transactions and

	events having occurred in similar circumstances.
	If uniform accounting policies are not followed for all the group entities, the consolidated financial statements will not reflect a correct portrayal of the financial status of the group.

3.2.9. Process followed in summary for consolidation of parent with subsidiaries

The consolidation process is summarised as under:

Step I	Add all items like assets, liabilities, income and expenditure of the parent and the subsidiary line by line
Step II	Cancel parent's investment in subsidiary (in parent's books), with parent's portion in subsidiary's ordinary shares (in subsidiary books) Dr. Ordinary share capital (in subsidiary books) Cr. Investment (in parent books
Step III	Eliminate all intra-group balances, transactions, income and expenses in full from both parent as well as subsidiary books. Some examples are: - Intra group revenue - Intra group inventories - Unrealised profit on intra group inventories (including treatment of deferred tax) - Intra group purchase / sale of tangible assets - Unrealised profit on intra group tangible assets (including treatment of deferred tax) - Intra group loan - Intra group dividends
Step IV	Make required adjustments for part cancellations
Step V	Split profit / loss of subsidiary between pre and post-acquisition portions based on acquisition date
Step VI	Calculate fair value of assets of subsidiary if any on acquisition date
Step VII	Determine deferred tax on increase in fair value of assets
Step VIII	Calculate value of Non-controlling interest (NCI) as on acquisition date
Step IX	Calculate goodwill / bargain purchase on the date of acquisition
Step X	Calculate parents share in subsidiary's profit = Profit of subsidiary – share of non-controlling interest

Step XI	Calculate parent's reserve
Step XII	Calculate NCI on SOFP date and show it in consolidated SOFP under Equity

3.2.10. Purchase consideration

Consideration	Consideration is the amount an investor pays to acquire holding in investee company. The consideration transferred in a business combination is to be measured at fair value. The possible variants of considerations may be as under: a) Cash b) Share exchange c) Contingent consideration d) Deferred consideration
Cash	When consideration is paid in cash it is accounted as under: Dr. Investment x Cr. Cash x

Share exchange	In this case consideration may be in the form of share exchange.
	Example:
	On 1st Jan 2012, P Co acquired 27000 shares in S Co by way of exchange of two shares in P Co for every three shares in S Co. The face value of P Co's share is Rs 1 each and its market price is Rs 3 each.
	Hence the consideration in S Co will work to:
	(27000 x 2/3) x Rs. 3 = Rs. 54000
	
	Dr .Investment Rs. 54000
	     Cr. Share capital (27000 x 2/3) x Re.1 Rs. 18000
	     Cr. Share Premium (27000 x 2/3) x Re. 2 Rs. 36000

Contingent consideration	This is a consideration that an acquirer commits to the acquiree in cash or additional equity interests or other assets after the acquisition date on the fulfilment of a certain specified event or condition in the future. We need to bear in mind that subsequent measurement of contingent consideration does not affect goodwill. On the date of acquisition, contingent consideration is valued at acquisition date fair value. Subsequent changes in fair value of contingent consideration (post acquisition date) are accounted for as under: a)If the contingent consideration is classified as equity then it is not remeasured and is accounted for in equity itself b)if the contingent consideration is classified as a financial instrument in accordance with Ind AS 109 Financial Instruments: Recognition and Measurement, it is measured at fair value and change in the value is recognised either in profit or loss or equity in accordance with the requirements of Ind AS 109 c)if the contingent consideration is not classified as a financial instrument in accordance with Ind AS 109 and is recognised in line with Ind AS 37 Provisions, contingent liabilities and contingent assets or any other applicable standard, then the change in the value is recognised in the profit or loss. d)Goodwill is not impacted by the actual outcome of the contingent consideration
Deferred	Deferred consideration is the one which is not payable immediately but is payable

consideration	in the future and which is not contingent is called a deferred consideration. Such consideration is valued at present value of the amount payable. For this, amount payable in future should be multiplied by the present value factor (conventional practice is to use cost of capital of the parent to calculate the present value factor)

	Example:
	On 1st January 2011 S Co acquired 60% Re. 1 shares in S Co out of 100 m shares. It agreed to pay Rs. 5 per share in cash immediately and Rs. 120 m after 31st December 2012. Present value factor for P Co is 10%.
	a)Hence the consideration is calculated as under:
	Immediate (100 m x 60% x Rs. 5) = Rs. 300 m
	Deferred Rs. 120 m x (1/(1.10)2) = Rs. 99 m
	Total consideration = Rs.399 m
	This amount would be used for valuation of goodwill.
	
	b)Cash entry would be:
	   Dr. Consideration Rs. 300 m
	      Cr. Cash Rs. 300 m
	(Being part consideration paid in cash)
	c)On 31st December 2011, the following entry would be passed:
	Dr. Finance cost (Rs.99 m x 10%) Rs. 10 m
	     Cr. Provision for deferred consideration Rs. 10 m
	(Being unwinding of discount on deferred consideration)
	Accordingly as on 31st December 2011 the deferred consideration would be valued at (Rs. 99 + Rs. 10) = Rs. 109 m (rounded off)
	d)As on 31st December 2012 the deferred consideration would be valued at Rs. 11 (Rs. 109 m x 10%) by further unwinding and the entry will be:
	Dr. Finance cost (Rs. 109 m x 10%) Rs. 11 m
	     Cr. Provision for deferred consideration Rs. 11 m
	(Being unwinding of discount on deferred consideration)
	Hence the final deferred consideration will become (Rs. 109 m + Rs. 11 m) = Rs.120 m
	e)Deferred consideration paid on or after 31st December 2012 will have the following entry:
	Dr. Provision for deferred consideration Rs.21 m
	     Cr. Cash Rs. 21 m
	(Being deferred consideration paid in cash)

3.2.11. Non-controlling Interest (NCI)

When a subsidiary is not wholly owned (i.e. owned 100% by the parent), a part of the net assets belong to the minority shareholders. This is called the non-controlling interest (NCI) earlier known as Minority Interest.
Ind AS 103 allows an accounting policy choice, available on a transaction by transaction basis, to measure NCI either at:
   a) Fair value (sometimes called the full goodwill method) or
   b) The NCI's proportionate share of net assets of the acquiree (option is available on a transaction by transaction basis)
Further,
   a) Management must elect, for each acquisition, the option to measure the NCI
   b) If NCI is measured at fair value, it can be determined by referring to the market price of

shares held by non-controlling shareholders just before the acquisition by the parent. According to new requirements of Ind AS 103, for each business combination, the acquirer shall measure at the acquisition date components of any non-controlling interests in the acquiree that are present ownership interests and entitle their holders to a proportionate share of the entity's net assets in the event of liquidation at their:

a) Fair value or
b) The present ownership instruments' proportionate share in the recognised amounts of the acquiree's identifiable net assets

All other components of non-controlling interests shall be measured at their acquisition date fair values, unless another measurement basis is required by Ind AS.

Thus the choice to measure NCI using any of the two methods will not be available and these components of non-controlling interests shall be measured at their acquisition date fair values. However, if any other Ind AS requires another basis of measurement it will be measured in accordance with that Ind AS. For example, if a share based transaction is classified as equity, an entity will be expected to measure it in accordance with Ind AS 2.

Hence non-controlling share is calculated on

a) **Acquisition date for calculation of goodwill and**
b) **Reporting date and shown in the consolidated statement of financial position within equity but separately from the parent entity's share in the equity.**

This is further clarified by the chart below:

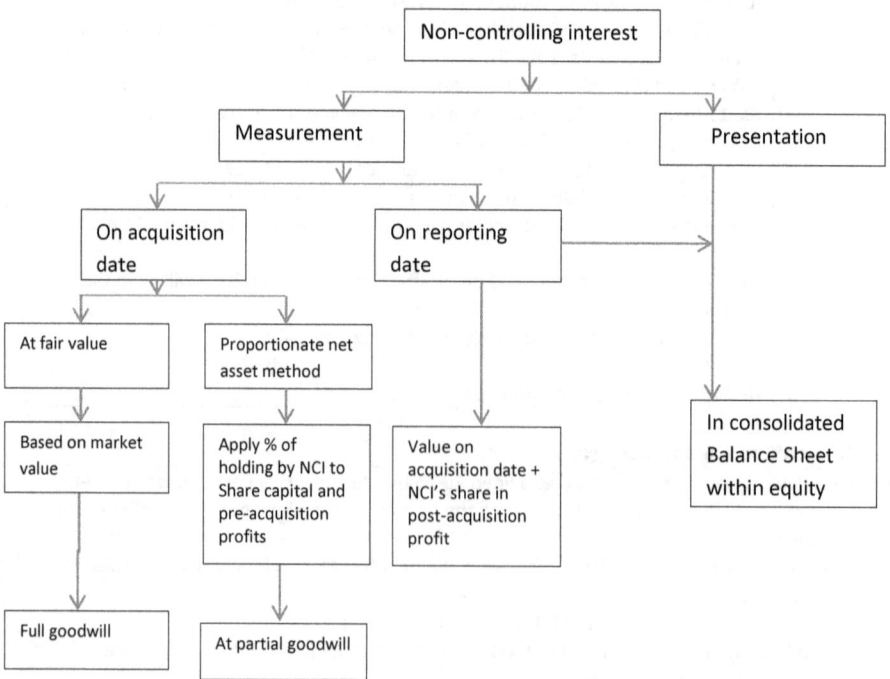

3.2.12. Measurement and recognition of goodwill in consolidated financial statements

Here we revisit the concept of recognition of goodwill in consolidated financial statements. According to Ind AS 103 Appendix A, Goodwill is an asset representing the future economic benefits arising from other assets acquired in a business combination that are not individually identified and separately recognised.

In accordance with Ind AS 103, the acquirer shall recognise goodwill as of the acquisition date measured as the excess of:

a) Aggregate of i)the consideration transferred measured in accordance with this IFRS, which generally requires acquisition date fair value	X
ii)the amount of non-controlling interest in the acquiree measured in accordance with this IFRS and	X
iii)in case of business combination achieved in stages, the acquisition date fair value of the acquirer's previously held equity interest in the acquiree	X
TOTAL (A)	X
b) The net of acquisition date amounts of the identifiable assets acquired and the liabilities assumed measured in terms of this IFRS	X
TOTAL (B)	X
Goodwill (A- B)	X
Bargain purchase (B – A)	X *

Note: There are two ways of calculating goodwill viz:
   a) Full goodwill method, based on fair value of NCI
   b) Partial goodwill method based on share of NCI in the value of net assets of the company acquired. In this case goodwill shows only the acquirer's share (as the share of non-controlling interest appears in both the sides i.e. value of NCI as well as net assets of subsidiary and therefore does not affect goodwill)

The US standard on business combinations requires goodwill to be calculated on "full" basis. The underlying principle in IFRS 3 and in Ind AS 103 is that all components of the business acquired are to be recognised at their fair value. This effectively means that the consideration paid, the assets and liabilities of the acquiree as well as the equity attributable to NCI are measured at fair value. This basis was proposed in the exposure draft which preceded the revised standard. However, in view of strong disagreement on the proposed revision regarding recognising NCI at fair value, the IASB introduced a choice as to how NCI is to be measured. Hence this allows goodwill to be measured in the same way as depicted in the old standard.

Logically, allowing a choice as to the valuation of NCI is driven by the future intentions to acquire the NCI. If such intention is perceived, determining goodwill at "full basis" is likely to be the adopted choice. Standards are supposed to usher in consistency in approach, which unfortunately has been obviated in the IFRS 3.

*In case of bargain purchase the resulting gain has to be recognised by the acquirer in capital reserve on the acquisition date and the gain has to be attributed to the acquirer. This is different from the treatment in IFRS, wherein resulting gain arising out of bargain purchase is credited to Statement of Profit & loss.

3.2.13. Treatment for acquisition related costs

These are costs the acquirer incurs to effect a business combination. Those costs include finder's fees, advisory, legal, accounting, valuation and other professional or consulting fees, general administrative costs, including the costs of maintaining an internal acquisitions departments, and costs of registering and issuing debt and equity securities.

According to Ind AS 103, the acquirer is required to recognise acquisition related costs as expenses in the periods in which the costs are incurred and the services are received.

3.2.14. Measurement of contingent liabilities in business combination

Treatment as on acquisition date	A contingent liability as at the acquisition date is assumed in a business combination should be recognised if: a) It is a present obligation that arises from past events and b) Its fair value can be measured reliably. Hence, even if it is not probable that an outflow of resources embodying economic benefits will be required to settle the obligation, a contingent liability will be recognised at the acquisition date fair value.
Subsequent measurement of contingent liabilities	After initial recognition and until liability is settled, cancelled or expired, the acquirer shall measure a contingent liability recognised in a business combination at the higher of: a)the amount that would be recognised in accordance with Ind AS 37, and b)the amount initially recognised, less, if appropriate, cumulative amortisation recognised in accordance with IAS 18 Revenue. This requirement does not apply to contracts accounted for in accordance with Ind AS 109.

3.2.15. Accounting treatment of pre-acquisition and post-acquisition profit

Pre-acquisition profit	Pre-acquisition profits are made by the subsidiary prior to the date of acquisition by the parent. Formula: Pre-acquisition profit = All the brought forward reserves of the subsidiary + profit for the year in which the subsidiary is acquired, up to acquisition date Pre-acquisition profits are to be deducted from the consideration in the subsidiary when calculating goodwill.
Post-acquisition profit	Post-acquisition profits include profit reflected in the retained earnings in the subsidiary's accounts after the acquisition date. Post-acquisition profits are added to parent entity's retained earnings in the consolidated Balance Sheet

	Post-acquisition profits of subsidiary = Reserves at the year-end *minus* Pre-acquisition profits.

The Accounting treatment may be summarised through a chart below:

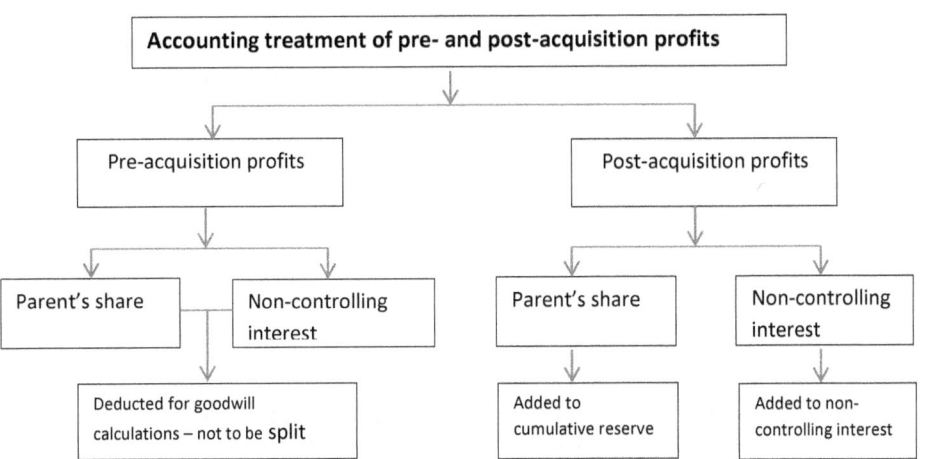

ILLUSTRATION 3

As at 31st December 2012	P Co		S Co	
The Balance Sheets of P Co and S Co as on 31st December 2012 are as under:				
	Rs	Rs	Rs	Rs
Assets				
Non-current assets				
Tangible assets		50000		25000
Investments		25000		
Loan stock of S Co		10000		
Current assets				
Inventories	24000		4000	
Receivables	12000		10000	
Cash at bank	4000	40000	2000	16000
Total assets		125000		41000
Equity and Liabilities				
Capital and reserves				
Ordinary shares (Re.1)	75000		15000	
Retained earnings	25000	100000	7500	22500
Non-current liabilities				

Loan stock				10000
Current liabilities				
Payables	25000			8500
Total Liabilities	125000			41000

Additional information:
1. P Co acquired 11250 shares in S Co on 1st July 2012 by issuing 2 shares for every 3 shares in S Co. The market price of P Co's shares was Rs.3. P Co has not accounted for this investment yet.
2. Payables of P Co include Rs. 7000 payable to S Co
3. Receivables in S Co comprise receivables from P Co only.
4. The retained earnings of S Co on acquisition date were Rs. 3500.
5. Fair value of the non-controlling interest is Rs. 7000.

Required :
Prepare a consolidated Balance Sheet for the group.

Solution
Steps

Step I	Determine percentage holding of Parent Co and non-controlling interest
Step II	Determine purchase consideration based on exchange ratio
Step III	Calculate pre-acquisition reserves
Step IV	Calculate goodwill
Step V	Calculate post-acquisition reserves
Step VI	Calculate non-controlling interest
Step VII	Cancel out intra-group transactions and if there is any balance on receivables , treat this as goods-in-transit
Step VIII	Cancel out intra-group loan stock
Step IX	Consolidate all items of assets and liabilities line by line.

P Co – Consolidated Balance Sheet as at 31st December 2012

	Rs	Rs
Assets		
Non-current assets		
Intangible assets		
Goodwill (WN2)		11000
Tangible assets (50000 + 25000)		75000
Investments		25000
Current assets		
Inventories (24000 + 4000 + 3000)	31000	
Receivables (12000 + 10000 – 10000)	12000	
Cash at bank (4000 + 2000)	6000	49000
Total assets		160000
Equity and Liabilities		
Capital and reserves		
Ordinary shares (75000 + 7500)		
Retained earnings (WN3)	82500	110500
Share Premium	28000	

Non-controlling interest (WN4)		15000
Current liabilities		8000
Payables (25000 + 8500 – 7000)		
		26500
Total Liabilities		160000

Workings:
Working Note 1
Computation of group share

Item	% Holding
Total value of shares	15000
Par value of shares acquired by P Co	11250
Percentage holding	75%
Non-controlling interest	25%

Working Note 2
Computation of consideration

Item	Rs	Rs
Purchase consideration: two shares of P Co against 3 shares of S Co, market price of P Co shares were Rs. 3. Hence:		
(2/3 x 11250 shares x Rs. 3)		22500
Since this transaction has not been given effect in books, the entry would be as under:		
Dr Investment	22500	
Cr Share Capital		7500
Cr Share Premium		15000

Working Note 3
Computation of Goodwill (on acquisition date of 30th June 2012) (Rs)

Item	P Co	S Co
Consideration		22500
Fair value of non-controlling interest		7000
		29500
Ordinary shares in S Co books	15000	
Retained earnings (pre-acquisition)	3500	18500
Goodwill on purchase of shares of S Co		11000

Working Note 4
Post-acquisition reserves (Rs)

Item	P Co	S Co
Retained earnings as on 31.12.2012	25000	7500
Less: Pre-acquisition reserves		(3500)
		4000
Share	3000 (75%)	1000(25%)
To consolidated Balance Sheet	**28000**	

Working Note 5
Non-controlling interest

Item	Rs
Fair value of non-controlling interest	7000
Post-acquisition reserves	1000
Total to consolidated Balance Sheet	**8000**

Working Note 6
Intra company receivables and payables cancel out to the extent of Rs. 7000.
Balance amount of Rs. 3000 is treated as goods-in-transit and included under inventories.

Working Note 7
Intra-company loan stock of Rs. 10000 gets cancelled out in Balance Sheet.

3.2.16. Consolidated income statement

a)If income consists of post-acquisition profits only (i.e. the subsidiary has been acquired for over one year) and no non-controlling interest exists - add all the items in individual income statement line by line for consolidation up-to the line " profit after tax for the year"

b) If income consists of post-acquisition profits only (i.e. the subsidiary has been acquired for over one year) and non-controlling interest exists –

i)add all the items in individual income statement line by line for consolidation up-to the line " profit after tax for the year"
ii)then show NCI share in subsidiary profit after tax separately as NCI interest in the income statement
iii)parent share is shown below NCI share and is calculated as (i)less (ii)above

c)If the subsidiary is acquired during the year:

i)The profits for the year of the subsidiary are split to ascertain pre and post-acquisition profits by splitting the income statement
ii)Pre-acquisition profits- total net assets including pre-acquisition profits are deducted from the total of the consideration, the value of NCI and acquisition date fair value of the previously held equity interests for calculating goodwill.
iii)Post-acquisition profits – Parent's share added to parent's income for the year and reflected in consolidated statement of comprehensive income
iv)Post-acquisition profits – NCI share added to non-controlling interest and included in consolidated Balance Sheet

The steps in preparation of consolidated income statement are as under:

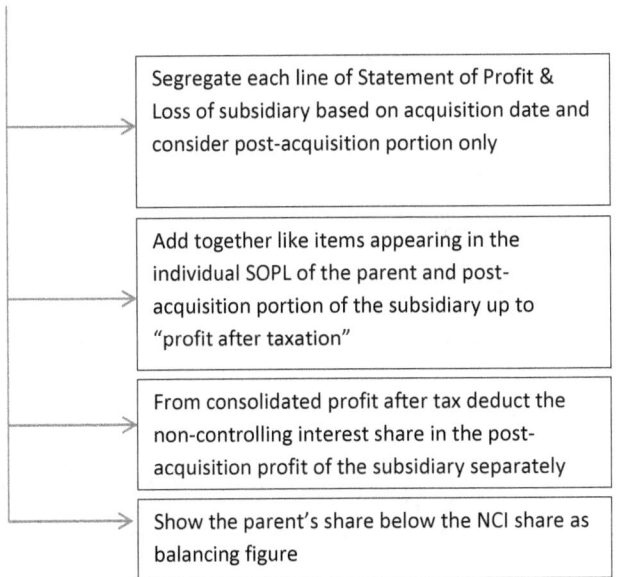

ILLUSTRATION 4: STATEMENT OF PROFIT & LOSS

P Co acquired 80% shares of S Co on 30 June 2012. SOPL of P Co and S Co for the year ended 31st December 2012 are: (Rs)

Item	P Co	S Co
Turnover	150000	75000
Cost of sales	(75000)	(37500)
Gross Profit	75000	37500
Administrative expenses	(25000)	(12500)
Profit before taxation	50000	25000
Taxation	(15000)	(7500)
Profit after taxation	35000	17500

On 31st December 2012, S Co's property was revalued from Rs 150000 to Rs 200000.
Required:
Prepare a consolidated SOPL for the group.
Solution
P Co – SOPL for the year ended 31st December 2012

Item	Rs
Turnover (150000 + ½ x75000)	187500
Cost of sales (75000 + 1/2 x 37500)	(93750)
Gross Profit	93750
Administration expenses (25000 + ½ x 12500)	(31250)
Profit before taxation	62500
Taxation (15000 + ½ x 7500)	(18750)
Profit for the year	43750

Other comprehensive income – not reclassified subsequently	
Gain on property revaluation	50000
Total comprehensive income for the year	93750
Profit attributable to:	
Owners of parent	42000
Non-controlling interest (20% of 17500 x ½)	1750
	43750
Total comprehensive income attributable to:	
Owners of parent	82000
Non-controlling interest (20% of ((50000 +17500) x ½))	11750
	93750

3.2.17. Consolidated statement of changes in equity

Steps are as under:
a) In parent's equity its share in the subsidiaries' post acquisition equity should be added.
b)NCI's share in equity needs to be shown separately
c)Parent's share in the dividend paid by subsidiary should be cancelled out in preparing
  Consolidated SOPL
d) NCI's share in the dividend should be shown under the NCI category.

ILLUSTRATION 5

The summarised statements of changes in equity of P Co and S Co for the year ended 31st December 2012 are as under:

Summarised statement of changes in equity	P Co	S Co
	Rs	Rs
Balance as at 01.01.2012	120000	85000
Net profit for the period	20000	5000
Dividend paid	(8000)	(6000)
Balance as at 31.12.2012	132000	84000

On 1st July 2010, P Co acquired 80% equity shareholding in Beta. The equity of Beta as shown in its own financial statements at that date was Rs.30 million. The fair value of non-controlling interest at the acquisition date was Rs. 9 million.
Prepare consolidated statement of changes in equity.

Solution
Working Notes
WN 1
Statement of consolidated equity at 01.01.2012 (Parent's share)

Item	P Co
	Rs
P CO	120000
Add: S Co (Rs. 85000 – Rs. 30000) x 80%	44000
	164000

WN 2

Statement of consolidated equity at 01.01.2012 (NCI)

Item	P Co Rs.
Fair value of NCI	9000
Add: Consolidated post acquisition increase Rs.85000 x 80%	17000
	26000

WN 3

Statement of share of net profit

Item	P Co Rs	NCI Rs
Fair value of NCI	20000	
Add: Share of profit	4000	1000
	24000	1000

Consolidated statement of changes in equity for the year ended 31st December 2012

Item	P Co	NCI	Total
Balance as at 1st January 2012 (WN1 & WN2)	164000	26000	190000
Net profit for the period (WN3)	24000	1000	25000
Dividend paid	(8000)	(1200)	(9200)
	180000	25800	205800

3.2.18. Treatment of unrealised profit related to inventories in preparation of consolidated financial statements

Consolidated financial statements are prepared with the assumption that all group entities are one economic unit. As one economic unit cannot make a profit or a loss from a sale to itself it is imperative to remove the impact of unrealised profit (URP) from inventory as well as from the parent's profit in the consolidated statement of financial position.

The treatment of URP on inventories is twofold:

Sale by parent to its subsidiary	Sale by subsidiary to its parent
URP lies in a) Inventory in subsidiary books b) Profit in Parent books	URP lies in a) Inventory in parent books b) Profit in subsidiary books
Effect: a) Deduct from inventory b) Deduct from SOPL of parent	Effect: c) Deduct from inventory d) Deduct from SOPL of subsidiary
Since profit is in parent books – NCI will not be impacted	Since profit is in subsidiary books, in case of partly owned subsidiary – NCI will be impacted

Entry:	Entry:	
Dr. Group retained earnings x	Dr. Group retained earnings	
Cr. Inventories x	(parent share)	x
	Dr. NCI (NCI's share)	x
	Cr. Inventories	x
Tax effect:	Tax effect:	
Dr. Deferred tax asset x	Dr. Deferred tax asset x	
Cr. Group retained earnings x	Cr. Group retained earnings	x
	(parent share)	
	Cr. Non-controlling interest	x
	(NCI share)	

ILLUSTRATION 6: CONSOLIDATION WITH DOWN STREAM TRANSACTION (INVENTORIES)

The Balance Sheets of P Co and S Co as on 31st December 2012 are as under:

As at 31st December 2012	P Co		S Co	
	Rs	Rs	Rs	Rs
Assets				
Non-current assets				
Tangible assets		50000		25000
Investments		25000		
Loan stock of S Co		10000		
Current assets				
Inventories	24000		6000	
Receivables	12000		10000	
Cash at bank	4000	40000	2000	18000
Total assets		125000		43000
Equity and Liabilities				
Capital and reserves				
Ordinary shares (Re.1)	75000		15000	
Retained earnings	25000	100000	7500	22500
Non-current liabilities				
Loan stock				10000
Current liabilities				
Payables		25000		10500
Total Liabilities		125000		43000

Additional information:
1. P Co acquired 11250 shares in S Co on 1st July 2012 by issuing 2 shares for every 3 shares in S Co. The market price of P Co's shares was Rs. 3. P Co has not accounted for this investment yet.
2. Payables of P Co include Rs. 7000 payable to S Co
3. Receivables in S Co comprise receivables from P Co only.
4. The retained earnings of S Co on acquisition date were Rs. 3500.
5. Fair value of the non-controlling interest is Rs. 7000.

6. Inventory of S Co consists entirely of purchases made from P Co on 29 December 2012. P Co sells goods at a mark-up of 20% over cost.

Required :
Prepare a consolidated Balance Sheet for the group.

Solution
Tutorial note:

Step I	Determine percentage holding of Parent Co and non-controlling interest
Step II	Determine purchase consideration based on exchange ratio
Step III	Calculate pre-acquisition reserves
Step IV	Calculate goodwill
Step V	Calculate and eliminate unrealised profit on inventories. Since this is a downstream transaction, inventory of S Co is reduced and at the same time the retained earnings of P Co is reduced. Entry: Dr. Retained Earnings in P Co Cr. Inventories in S Co
Step VI	Calculate post-acquisition reserves
Step VII	Calculate non-controlling interest
Step VIII	Cancel out intra-group transactions and if there is any balance on receivables , treat this as goods-in-transit
Step IX	Cancel out intra-group loan stock
Step X	Consolidate all items of assets and liabilities line by line.

P Co – Consolidated Statement of Financial Position as at 31st December 2012

	Rs	Rs
Assets		
Non-current assets		
Intangible assets		
Goodwill (WN3)		11000
Tangible assets (50000 + 25000)		75000
Investments		25000
Current assets		
Inventories (**WN4**)	32000	
Receivables (12000 + 10000 – 10000)	12000	
Cash at bank (4000 + 2000)	6000	50000
Total assets		161000
Equity and Liabilities		
Capital and reserves		
Ordinary shares (75000 + 7500)	82500	
Retained earnings (WN5)	27000	109500
Share Premium		15000
Non-controlling interest (WN6)		8000
Loan stock (10000 – 10000)		-
Current liabilities		
Payables (25000 + 10500 – 7000)		28500
Total Liabilities		161000

Workings:
Working Note 1
Computation of group share

Item	% Holding
Total value of shares	15000
Par value of shares acquired by P Co	11250
Percentage holding	75%
Non-controlling interest	25%

Working Note 2
Computation of consideration

Item	Rs	Rs
Purchase consideration: two shares of P Co against 3 shares of S Co, market price of P Co shares were Rs. 3. Hence: (2/3 x 11250 shares x Rs. 3) Since this transaction has not been given effect in books, the entry would be as under:		22500
Dr Investment	22500	
Cr Share Capital		7500
Cr Share Premium		15000

Working Note 3
Computation of Goodwill (on acquisition date of 30th June 2012) (Rs)

Item	P Co	S Co
Consideration		22500
Fair value of non-controlling interest		7000
		29500
Ordinary shares in S Co books	15000	
Retained earnings (pre-acquisition)	3500	18500
Goodwill on purchase of shares of S Co		11000

Working Note 4
Inventory (Rs)

Item	P Co	S Co
Per question	24000	6000
Less: URP (20/120 X Rs. 6000)		1000
		5000
Add: Inventory of S Co	5000	
Add: Goods in transit (10000 – 7000)	3000	
	32000	

Working Note 5

Post-acquisition reserves (Rs.)

Item	P Co	S Co
Retained earnings as on 31.12.2012	25000	7500
Less: Pre-acquisition reserves		(3500)
Less: URP in inventory (*)	(1000)	4000
Share		
	3000 (75%)	1000(25%)
To consolidated Balance Sheet	**27000**	

(*) Since the inventory of S Co was purchased entirely from P Co, the margin is included in P Co books, hence adjusted fully from the retained earnings of P Co.

Working Note 6

Non-controlling interest

Item	Rs
Fair value of non-controlling interest	7000
Post-acquisition reserves	1000
Total to consolidated Balance Sheet	**8000**

Working Note 7

Intra company receivables and payables cancel out to the extent of Rs. 7000.
Balance amount of Rs. 3000 is treated as goods-in-transit and included under inventories.

Working Note 8

Intra-company loan stock of Rs. 10000 gets cancelled out in Balance Sheet

ILLUSTRATION 7: CONSOLIDATION WITH UPSTREAM TRANSACTION (INVENTORIES)

The Balance Sheets of P Co and S Co as on 31st December 2012 are as under:

As at 31st December 2012	P Co		S Co	
	Rs	Rs	Rs	Rs
Assets				
Non-current assets				
Tangible assets		50000		25000
Investments		25000		
Loan stock of S Co		10000		
Current assets				
Inventories	24000		6000	
Receivables	12000		10000	
Cash at bank	4000	40000	2000	18000
Total assets		125000		43000
Equity and Liabilities				
Capital and reserves				
Ordinary shares (Re.1)	75000		15000	
Retained earnings	25000	100000	7500	22500

Non-current liabilities				
Loan stock				10000
Current liabilities				
Payables		25000		10500
Total Liabilities		125000		43000

Additional information:
1. P Co acquired 11250 shares in S Co on 1st July 2012 by issuing 2 shares for every 3 shares in S Co. The market price of P Co's shares was Rs. 3. P Co has not accounted for this investment yet.
2. Payables of P Co include Rs. 7000 payable to S Co
3. Receivables in S Co comprise receivables from P Co only.
4. The retained earnings of S Co on acquisition date were Rs. 3500.
5. Fair value of the non-controlling interest is Rs. 7000.
6. 50% of Inventory of P Co consists of purchases made from S Co on 1st October 2012. S Co sells goods at a mark-up of 25% over cost. Ignore deferred tax.

Required :
Prepare a consolidated Balance Sheet for the group.

Solution
Steps:

Step I	Determine percentage holding of Parent Co and non-controlling interest
Step II	Determine purchase consideration based on exchange ratio
Step III	Calculate pre-acquisition reserves
Step IV	Calculate goodwill
Step V	Calculate and eliminate unrealised profit on inventories. Since this is an upstream transaction, 50% inventory of P Co is reduced and at the same time the retained earnings of S Co is reduced. Entry: Dr. Retained Earnings in S Co (parent share) Dr. NCI (NCI share) Cr. Inventories in P Co
Step VI	Calculate post-acquisition reserves
Step VII	Calculate non-controlling interest
Step VIII	Cancel out intra-group transactions and if there is any balance on receivables , treat this as goods-in-transit
Step IX	Cancel out intra-group loan stock
Step X	Consolidate all items of assets and liabilities line by line.

P Co – Consolidated Balance Sheet as at 31st December 2012

	Rs	Rs
Assets		
Non-current assets		
Intangible assets		
Goodwill (WN3)		11000
Tangible assets (50000 + 25000)		75000
Investments		25000
Current assets		

Inventories (**WN4**)	30600	
Receivables (12000 + 10000 – 10000)	12000	
Cash at bank (4000 + 2000)	6000	48600
Total assets		159600
Equity and Liabilities		
Capital and reserves		
Ordinary shares (75000 + 7500)	82500	
Retained earnings (WN5)	26200	108700
Share Premium		15000
Non-controlling interest (WN6)		7400
Loan stock (10000 – 10000)		-
Current liabilities		
Payables (25000 + 10500 – 7000)		28500
Total Liabilities		159600

Workings:
Working Note 1
Computation of group share

Item	% Holding
Total value of shares	15000
Par value of shares acquired by P Co	11250
Percentage holding	75%
Non-controlling interest	25%

Working Note 2
Computation of consideration

Item	Rs	Rs
Purchase consideration: two shares of P Co against 3 shares of S Co, market price of P Co shares were Re. 3. Hence:		
(2/3 x 11250 shares x Re. 3)		22500
Since this transaction has not been given effect in books, the entry would be as under:		
Dr Investment	22500	
Cr Share Capital		7500
Cr Share Premium		15000

Working Note 3
Computation of Goodwill (on acquisition date of 30th June 2012) (Rs)

Item	P Co	S Co
Consideration		22500
Fair value of non-controlling interest		7000
		29500
Ordinary shares in S Co books	15000	
Retained earnings (pre-acquisition)	3500	18500
Goodwill on purchase of shares of S Co		11000

Working Note 4
Inventory (Rs)

Item	P Co	S Co
Per question	24000	6000
Less: URP((25/125 X Rs.24000)*0.5)	2400	
	21600	6000
Add: Inventory of S Co	6000	
Add: Goods in transit (10000 – 7000)	3000	
	30600	

Working Note 5
Post-acquisition reserves (Rs)

Item	P Co	S Co
Retained earnings as on 31.12.2012	25000	7500
Less: Pre-acquisition reserves		(3500)
Less: URP in inventory (*)		(2400)
		1600
Group share	1200 (75%)	400 (NCI – 25%)
To consolidated Balance Sheet	**26200**	

(*) Since 50% of the inventory of P Co was purchased from S Co, the margin is included in S Co books, hence adjusted fully from the retained earnings of S Co.

Working Note 6
Non-controlling interest

Item	Rs
Fair value of non-controlling interest	7000
Post-acquisition reserves (WN5)	400
Total to consolidated Balance Sheet	**7400**

Working Note 7
Intra company receivables and payables cancel out to the extent of Rs. 7000.
Balance amount of Rs. 3000 is treated as goods-in-transit and included under inventories.

Working Note 8
Intra-company loan stock of Rs. 10000 gets cancelled out in Balance Sheet

3.2.19. Treatment of unrealised profit related to sale of non-current assets in preparation of consolidated financial statements

Similar to the treatment of unrealised profit in inventories, it is imperative to remove the impact of unrealised profit (URP) from sale of non-current assets in preparation of the consolidated statement of financial position.

The treatment of URP on sale of non-current assets is twofold:

Sale by parent to its subsidiary	Sale by subsidiary to its parent
URP lies in	URP lies in
a) Non-current asset in subsidiary books	a) Non-current asset in parent books

b) Effect of depreciation if non-current asset is sold at a profit c) Profit in Parent books	b) Effect of depreciation if non-current asset is sold at a profit c) Profit in subsidiary books
Effect: a) Deduct from non-current asset b) Adjust depreciation c) Deduct from SOCI of parent	Effect: a) Deduct from non-current asset b) Adjust depreciation c) Deduct from SOCI of subsidiary
Since profit is in parent books – NCI will not be impacted	Since profit is in subsidiary books, in case of partly owned subsidiary – NCI will be impacted

Entry on URP on non-current asset reversal
Dr. Group retained earnings   x
   Cr. Group Non-current asset   x
	Entry on URP of non-current asset reversal
	Dr. Group retained earnings
	(parent share) x
	Dr. NCI (NCI's share) x
	   Cr. Group Non-current asset x

Tax effect:
Dr. Deferred tax asset   x
   Cr. Group retained earnings   x
	Tax effect:
	Dr. Deferred tax asset x
	   Cr. Group retained earnings x
	     (parent share)
	   Cr. Non-controlling interest x
	     (NCI share)

Entry on additional depreciation charged by subsidiary: (NCI is impacted)
Dr. Group Non-current asset   x
   Cr. Group retained earnings   x
   Cr. Non-controlling interest   x
	Entry on additional depreciation charged by parent: (NCI not impacted)
	Dr. Group Non-current asset x
	   Cr. Group retained earnings x

Tax effect:
Dr. Group retained earnings   x
Dr. Non-controlling interest   x
   Cr. Deferred tax asset   x
	Tax effect:
	Dr. Group retained earnings x
	   Cr. Deferred tax asset x

3.2.20. Treatment of intra-group interest expense

In SOPL the amount of interest expense of one group company is cancelled against the amount of interest income of another group company.

3.2.21. Treatment of intra-group dividends

The treatment of intra-group dividends is as under:

Dividends payable out of post-acquisition profit	Dividend paid out of pre-acquisition profit
In the consolidated Balance Sheet: - Dividend payable to parent is not reflected separately. It is cancelled out with the dividend receivable - Dividend payable to the non-controlling interest is reflected as a current liability (This is because the entire profit of subsidiary has been consolidated. If the dividend received by the parent company was also included, this	In the consolidated Balance Sheet : - Dividend payable by the parent is reflected as a liability in the consolidated SOFP - Dividend payable by the subsidiary is: a) NCI's share of dividend is reflected as current liability in the consolidated B/S. b) Parent's share in subsidiary's dividend is deducted from the cost of investment in

would lead to double counting)	the subsidiary.
	c) This would result in reducing the amount of goodwill.
	d) If the subsidiary is acquired during the year then we have to determine how much dividend is paid out of pre-acquisition profits. In the absence of any specific information, the dividend is assumed to have accrued evenly throughout the year.
In the consolidated statement of changes in equity: - Dividend payable to NCI is reflected under NCI equity - Under controlling equity, only the amount of dividend by the parent is shown - Dividend payable to parent is not shown	No impact

ILLUSTRATION 8: TREATMENT OF INTRA-GROUP DIVIDEND

P Co acquired 60% in S Co on 1st July 2012. The balance in retained earnings of S Co on 1.1.2012 was nil. The fair value of the non-controlling interest at the date of acquisition is Rs. 12000.

Statement of Profit & Loss of P Co and S Co for the year ended 31st December 2012 are:

	P Co	S Co
	Rs	Rs
Turnover	100000	54000
Cost of sales	(49000)	(28500)
Gross Profit	51000	25500
Administrative expense	(20000)	(9500)
Profit before taxation	31000	16000
Taxation	(5400)	(4000)
Profit after taxation	25600	12000

Out of the profit above, P Co paid a dividend of Rs.10000 and S Co of Rs.6000
The Balance Sheet of P Co and S Co as at 31st December 1012 are:

As at 31st December 2012	P Co		S Co	
	Rs	Rs	Rs	Rs
Assets				
Non-current assets				
Tangible assets		58250		29000
Investments : shares in S Co		21000		
Current assets				
Inventories	7750		4000	
Receivables	8000		6000	
Others	4000	19750	3000	13000
Total assets		99000		42000
Equity and Liabilities				
Equity				

Ordinary shares	59400		25000	
Retained earnings	15600	75000	6000	31000
Current liabilities				
Payables	14000		5000	
Dividend payable	10000	24000	6000	11000
Total Liabilities		99000		42000

Required:
Prepare the consolidated financial statements for the year ended 31st December 2012

Solution

Steps

Step I	Determine percentage holding of Parent Co and non-controlling interest
Step II	Determine purchase consideration
Step III	Calculate pre-acquisition reserves
Step IV	Calculate goodwill
Step V	Segregate dividend of subsidiary payable out of pre-acquisition and post-acquisition profits
Step VI	Deduct parent's share of pre-acquisition dividend from cost of investment in calculating goodwill
Step VII	Add patent's share of post-acquisition dividend to retained earnings.
Step VIII	Calculate post-acquisition reserves
Step IX	Calculate non-controlling interest
Step X	Consolidate all items of assets and liabilities line by line.

P Co acquired S co on 1st July 2012. Therefore, half the dividends ($ 6000 x ½) =Rs. 3000 are out of post-acquisition profits and the balance half of Rs. 3000 are out of pre-acquisition profits.

P Co – Consolidated SOPL for the year ended 31st December 2012

Item	Rs
Turnover (100000 + 54000 x ½)	127000
Cost of sales (49000 + 28500 x ½)	(63250)
Gross Profit	63750
Administrative expenses (including depreciation (20000 + 9500 x ½)	(24750)
Profit before taxation	39000
Taxation (5400 + 4000 x ½)	(7400)
Profit after taxation	31600
Profit attributable to:	
Non-controlling interest (WN1)	2400
Owners of parent	29200
	31600

P Co - Consolidated Balance Sheet as at 31st December 2012

	Rs	Rs
Assets		
Non-current assets		
Goodwill (WN2)		3200

Tangible assets (58250+29000)		87250
Current assets		
Inventories (7750 + 4000)	11750	
Receivables (8000 + 6000)	14000	
Others (4000+3000)	<u>7000</u>	32750
Total assets		123200
Equity and Liabilities		
Equity		
Ordinary shares	59400	
Retained earnings (WN4)	<u>19200</u>	78600
Non-controlling interest (WN3)		13200
Current liabilities		
Payables (14000 + 5000)	19000	
Dividends payable (WN5)	12400	31400
Total Liabilities		123200

Working Notes

WN1: Share on non-controlling interest on S Co profit:

Item	Rs
Post-acquisition profit of S Co	**6000**
Non-controlling interest at 40%	**2400**

WN2: Statement of calculation of goodwill:

Item	Rs	Rs
Investment in S Co by P Co		21000
Less: Share in pre-acquisition dividend (60% of Rs. 3000)		(1800)
Add: Fair value of non-controlling interest		<u>12000</u>
		31200
Less: net assets represented by:		
Ordinary shares	(25000)	
Pre-acquisition retained earnings (50% of Rs. 6000)	<u>(3000)</u>	(28000)
Goodwill to Balance Sheet		3200

WN3: Statement of non-controlling interest

Item	Rs	Rs
Fair value of Non-controlling interest		12000
Post-acquisition profits (WN4)		1200
Non-controlling interest to Balance Sheet		13200

WN4: Statement of retained earnings

Item	P Co Rs	S Co Rs
Per question	25600	12000
Less: Dividend paid	(10000)	(6000)

Less: Pre-acquisition retained earnings (WN2 above)		(3000)
Post-acquisition retained earnings		3000
Dividend receivable (60% of Rs 3000)	1800	
Add: Group share in S Co (60% x Rs. 3000)	1800	
Total	19200	1200 (NCI)

WN5: Statement of dividend payable

Item	Rs.
Per question - S Co	10000
Payable to non-controlling interest (40% of $ 6000)	2400
	12400

3.2.22. Treatment of fair value in the consideration paid for a subsidiary as well as in determining subsidiary's identifiable assets and liabilities when preparing consolidated financial statements

We know that conceptual *framework* related to financial statements fulfil two purposes:
a) the assessment of stewardship or accountability of management and
b) the provision of information for economic decision making
The assets, liabilities and equity may be recorded at historical cost in the individual Balance Sheet of the acquirer and acquiree.

However, according to Ind AS 103 all business combinations shall be accounted for by applying the acquisition method which states that fair values are to be used while measuring the cost of the business combination (purchase consideration).
The standard goes on to state that acquirer should measure the identifiable assets acquired and the liabilities assumed at their acquisition date fair value and also permits measurement of non-controlling interest at the acquisition date fair value.

This signifies that in any business combination, fair value will be used for the following:

a) Cost of investment (purchase consideration)
b) Identifiable assets and liabilities
c) Non-controlling interest and
d) Acquirer's previously held investment in acquiree, in the case of step acquisition.

Hence the acquirer shall measure the cost of a business combination as the aggregate of the fair values, at the date of acquisition, of all the above items in exchange of control of the entity.
Accordingly, applying the **acquisition method** to business combinations would mean that the cost is viewed from the acquirer's perspective and valued at fair value.

The effect of fair value adjustments to assets are as under:

Increase in fair value	Decrease in fair value

a)Dr. Group non-current asset   x
   Cr. Goodwill   x
 (Being non-current asset brought to fair value and the effect considered in goodwill calculation)
	a)Dr. Goodwill x
	   Cr. Group non-current asset x
	 (Being non-current asset brought to fair value and the effect considered in goodwill calculation)

Difference between carrying value and fair value will be adjusted in calculating goodwill. NCI's share of fair value adjustments to individual assets / liabilities will be relevant only for calculation of NCI value using proportionate net asset method. If fair value method is used for NCI valuation, this need not be separately considered	Difference between carrying value and fair value will be adjusted in calculating goodwill. NCI's share of fair value adjustments to individual assets / liabilities will be relevant only for calculation of NCI value using proportionate net asset method. If fair value method is used for NCI valuation, this need not be separately considered

b)Increase in depreciation – subsequent to increase in value of assets owing to fair value adjustment on acquisition date:
 Dr. Group retained earning   X
   (parent share)
 Dr.Non-controlling interest
   (NCI share)   x
   Cr. Group non-current asset   x
 (Being additional depreciation accounted For)
	b)decrease in depreciation – subsequent to decrease in value of assets owing to fair value adjustment on acquisition date:
	 Dr. Group non-current asset x
	   Cr. Group retained earning X
	   (parent share)
	   Cr. Non-controlling interest
	   (NCI share) x
	 (Being excess depreciation charged earlier written back)

c)Impact on valuation of goodwill: - Increase in fair value of asset = value of goodwill decreases - Increase in fair value of liabilities = value of goodwill increases	c)Impact on valuation of goodwill: - Decrease in fair value of asset = value of goodwill increases - Decrease in fair value of liabilities = value of goodwill decreases

d)Impact on deferred tax
 An increase in fair value of asset and decrease in fair value of liabilities would lead to carrying value of net asset being more than tax base. As a result in future taxable profit will be greater than accounting profits and would create a taxable temporary difference and hence a deferred tax liability as under:
 Dr. Group retained earnings   x
   Cr. Deferred tax liability   x
 (Being deferred tax liability recognised owing to fair value adjustments)
	d)Impact on deferred tax
	 A decrease in fair value of asset and increase in fair value of liabilities would lead to carrying value of net asset being less than tax base. As a result in future taxable profit will be lower than accounting profits and would create a deductible temporary difference and hence a deferred tax asset as under:
	 Dr. Deferred tax asset x
	   Cr. Group retained earnings x
	 (Being deferred tax asset recognised owing to fair value adjustments)

ILLUSTRATION 9: FAIR VALUE ADJUSTMENTS TO ASSETS

As at 31st December 2012	P Co		S Co	
P Co acquired 60% share in S Co on 1st January 2012. The retained earnings on the date of acquisition were nil. The fair value of the non-controlling interest on the date of acquisition was Rs. 20000. The Balance Sheets of P Co and S Co as at 31st December 2012 are:				
	Rs	Rs	Rs	Rs
Assets				

Non-current assets				
Tangible assets				
Land	-		10000	
Property, Plant & Equipment	33000	33000	15000	25000
Investments : shares in S Co		27000		
Current assets				
Inventories	10500		9000	
Receivables	3000		10000	
Cash at bank	1000	14500	3000	22000
Total assets		74500		47000
Equity and Liabilities				
Equity				
Ordinary shares	42000		25000	
Retained earnings	18500	60500	17000	42000
Current liabilities				
Payables	14000	14000	5000	5000
Total Liabilities		74500		47000

The directors of P Co carried out a fair value exercise on the net assets of S Co on the date of acquisition. The following matters arose from the exercise:

1. On the date of acquisition, the fair value of S Co's land was Rs 5000 more than its carrying amount and that of its plant was Rs 10000 more than its carrying value of Rs 5000. S Co charges depreciation at 10% SLM.

2. Inventories were included at cost to S Co of Rs 7000. The selling price of the inventories was estimated to be Rs 9000 and a reasonable allowance for profit on sale was Rs 1400. All the inventories as at 1 January 2012 had been sold by 31st December 2012.

3. On 1st January 2012, S Co had a brand name that was protected legally, but was not included in the Balance Sheet because S Co's directors considered that it did not meet the recognition criteria for internally developed intangible assets. The directors of P Co considered that the brand name had a market value of Rs 4000 on 1st January 2012 and that it would give competitive advantage for 5 years from that date.

4. Fair value adjustments give rise to temporary differences. The rate of taxation to apply to temporary differences is 20%.

Required:
Prepare the consolidated financial statements for the group.

Solution
Steps

Step I	Determine percentage holding of Parent Co and non-controlling interest
Step II	Determine purchase consideration
Step III	Calculate pre-acquisition reserves
Step IV	Calculate fair value of assets on acquisition date.
Step V	Calculate deferred tax on fair value changes on acquisition date.
Step VI	Calculate goodwill
Step VII	Calculate post-acquisition retained earnings.
Step VIII	Calculate deferred tax reversal if any on post-acquisition retained earnings on fair value changes e.g. additional depreciation on fair value changes on assets
Step IX	Calculate non-controlling interest

Step X	Consolidate all items of assets and liabilities line by line.

Working Notes:

WN1 Statement of fair value changes during the year

Item	Carrying value (Rs) 1.1.2012 (A)	Change to goodwill (Rs) 1.1.2012 ((B-A)= C)	Fair value (Rs) 1.1.2012 (B)	Change (Rs) 2012 (D)	Change to B/S date(Rs) 31.12.2012 ((C –D) = E)
Land	10000	5000	15000	-	5000
Plant & Equipment	5000	10000	15000	1000	9000
Inventories	7000	600	7600	600	-
Brand name	-	4000	4000	800	3200
Total	22000	19600	41600	2400	17200
Deferred tax 20%		3920		(480)	3440

WN2 Statement of goodwill

Item	Rs	Rs
Investment in S Co		27000
Fair value of NCI (40%)		20000
		47000
Less: Net assets represented by:		
Ordinary shares	(25000)	
Fair value adjustments (WN1)	(19600)	
Deferred tax adjustment	3920	40680
Goodwill		6320

WN3 Statement of retained earnings

Item	P Co Rs	S Co Rs
Per question above	18500	17000
Less: Fair value adjustments		(2400)
Deferred tax reversal		480
		15080
Share of parent (P Co) – 60%	9048	
To NCI below – 40%		6032
Total	27548	6032

WN4 Statement of Non-controlling interest

Item	Rs	Rs
NCI – Fair value		20000
From retained earnings - NCI above – 40%		6032
Total		26032

Consolidated Balance Sheet as at 31st December 2012		
	Rs	Rs
Assets		
Non-current assets		
Goodwill (WN2)		6320
Tangible assets		
Land (10000 + 5000)	15000	
Property,Plant & Equipment(33000+15000+9000)	57000	72000
Intangible assets		3200
Current assets		
Inventories (10500+9000)	19500	
Receivables (3000 + 10000)	13000	
Cash at bank (1000+3000)	4000	36500
Total assets		118020
Equity and Liabilities		
Equity		
Ordinary shares	42000	
Retained earnings (WN3)	27548	69548
Non-controlling interest (WN4)		26032
Non-current liabilities		
Deferred tax		3440
Current liabilities		
Payables (14000 + 5000)		19000
Total Liabilities		118020

3.2.23. Partial disposal of an investment in a subsidiary

a) **Partial disposal of an investment in a subsidiary while control is retained:** This is accounted as equity transaction with owners, and the gain or loss is not recognized

b) **Partial disposal of an investment in a subsidiary that results in loss of control:** Loss of control triggers re-measurement of the residual holding to fair value. Any difference between fair value and carrying amount is a gain or loss to be recognized in profit or loss . Thereafter apply Ind AS 28, Ind AS 111 or IND AS 109, as appropriate, to the remaining holding.

ILLUSTRATION 10: Power – relevant activities

Two investors form an investee to develop and market a medical product. One investor is responsible for developing and obtaining regulatory approval of the medical product—that responsibility includes having the unilateral ability to make all decisions relating to the development of the product and to obtaining regulatory approval. Once the regulator has approved the product, the other investor will manufacture and market it—this investor has the unilateral ability to make all decisions about the manufacture and marketing of the project. If all the activities—developing and obtaining regulatory approval as well as manufacturing and marketing of the medical product—are relevant activities, each investor needs to determine whether it is able to direct the activities that *most* significantly affect the investee's returns. Accordingly, each investor needs to consider whether developing and obtaining regulatory approval or the manufacturing and marketing of the medical product is the activity that *most* significantly affects the investee's returns and whether it is able to direct that activity. In determining which investor has power, the investors would consider:

(a) the purpose and design of the investee;

(b) the factors that determine the profit margin, revenue and value of the investee as well as the value of the medical product;

(c) the effect on the investee's returns resulting from each investor's decision-making authority with respect to the factors in (b); and

(d) the investors' exposure to variability of returns.

In this particular example, the investors would also consider:

(e) the uncertainty of, and effort required in, obtaining regulatory approval (considering the investor's record of successfully developing and obtaining regulatory approval of medical products); and

(f) which investor controls the medical product once the development phase is successful.

ILLUSTRATION 11 – Power- exposure to variability of returns

An investment vehicle (the investee) is created and financed with a debt instrument held by an investor (the debt investor) and equity instruments held by a number of other investors. The equity tranche is designed to absorb the first losses and to receive any residual return from the investee. One of the equity investors who holds 30 per cent of the equity is also the asset manager. The investee uses its proceeds to purchase a portfolio of financial assets, exposing the investee to the credit risk associated with the possible default of principal and interest payments of the assets. The transaction is marketed to the debt investor as an investment with minimal exposure to the credit risk associated with the possible default of the assets in the portfolio because of the nature of these assets and because the equity tranche is designed to absorb the first losses of the investee. The returns of the investee are significantly affected by the management of the investee's asset portfolio, which includes decisions about the selection, acquisition and disposal of the assets within portfolio guidelines and the management upon default of any portfolio assets. All those activities are managed by the asset manager until defaults reach a specified proportion of the portfolio value (i.e. when the value of the portfolio is such that the equity tranche of the investee has been consumed). From that time, a third-party trustee manages the assets according to the instructions of the debt investor. Managing the investee's asset portfolio is the relevant activity of the investee. The asset manager has the ability to direct the relevant activities until defaulted assets reach the specified proportion of the portfolio value; the debt investor has the ability to direct the relevant activities when the value of defaulted assets surpasses that specified proportion of the portfolio value. The asset manager and the debt investor each need to determine whether they are able to direct the activities that *most* significantly affect the investee's returns, including considering the purpose and design of the investee as well as each party's exposure to variability of returns.

ILLUSTRATION 12: Power – Substantive rights

The investee has annual shareholder meetings at which decisions to direct the relevant activities are made. The next scheduled shareholders' meeting is in eight months. However, shareholders that individually or collectively hold at least 5 per cent of the voting rights can call a special meeting to change the existing policies over the relevant activities, but a requirement to give notice to the other shareholders means that such a meeting cannot be held for at least 30 days. Policies over the relevant activities can be changed only at special or scheduled shareholders' meetings. This includes the approval of material sales of assets as well as the making or disposing of significant investments. The above fact applies to examples described below. Each example is considered in isolation.

12.1.
An investor holds a majority of the voting rights in the investee. The investor's voting rights are substantive because the investor is able to make decisions about the direction of the relevant activities when they need to be made. The fact that it takes 30 days before the investor can exercise its voting rights does not stop the investor from having the current ability to direct the relevant activities from the moment the investor acquires the shareholding.

12.2.
An investor is party to a forward contract to acquire the majority of shares in the investee. The forward contract's settlement date is in 25 days. The existing shareholders are unable to change the existing policies over the relevant activities because a special meeting cannot be held for at least 30 days, at which point the forward contract will have been settled. Thus, the investor has rights that are essentially equivalent to the majority shareholder in example 3A above (i.e. the investor holding the forward contract can make decisions about the direction of the relevant activities when they need to be made). The investor's forward contract is a substantive right that gives the investor the current ability to direct the relevant activities even before the forward contract is settled.

12.3.
An investor holds a substantive option to acquire the majority of shares in the investee that is exercisable in 25 days and is deeply in the money. The same conclusion would be reached as above.

12.4.
An investor is party to a forward contract to acquire the majority of shares in the investee, with no other related rights over the investee. The forward contract's settlement date is in six months. In contrast to the examples above, the investor does not have the current ability to direct the relevant activities. The existing shareholders have the current ability to direct the relevant activities because they can change the existing policies over the relevant activities before the forward contract is settled.

ILLUSTRATION 13: Protective rights

Examples of protective rights include but are not limited to:
  (a) a lender's right to restrict a borrower from undertaking activities that could significantly change the credit risk of the borrower to the detriment of the lender.
  (b) the right of a party holding a non-controlling interest in an investee to approve capital expenditure greater than that required in the ordinary course of business, or to approve the issue of equity or debt instruments.
  (c) the right of a lender to seize the assets of a borrower if the borrower fails to meet specified loan repayment conditions.

ILLUSTRATION 14: Voting rights

An investor acquires 48 per cent of the voting rights of an investee. The remaining voting rights are held by thousands of shareholders, none individually holding more than 1 per cent of the voting rights. None of the shareholders has any arrangements to consult any of the others or make collective decisions. When assessing the proportion of voting rights to acquire, on the basis of the relative size of the other shareholdings, the investor determined that a 48 per cent interest would be sufficient to give it control. In this case, on the basis of the absolute size of its holding and the relative size of the other shareholdings, the investor concludes that it has a sufficiently dominant voting interest to meet the power criterion without the need to consider any other evidence of power.

ILLUSTRATION 15: Voting rights

Investor A holds 40 per cent of the voting rights of an investee and twelve other investors each hold 5 per cent of the voting rights of the investee. A shareholder agreement grants investor A the right to appoint, remove and set the remuneration of management responsible for directing the relevant activities. To change the agreement, a two-thirds majority vote of the shareholders is required. In this case, investor A concludes that the absolute size of the investor's holding and the relative size of the other shareholdings alone are not conclusive in determining whether the investor has rights sufficient to give it power. However, investor A determines that its contractual right to appoint, remove and set the remuneration of management is sufficient to conclude that it has power over the investee. The fact that investor A might not have exercised this right or the likelihood of investor A exercising its right to select, appoint or remove management shall not be considered when assessing whether investor A has power.

ILLUSTRATON 16: Voting rights

Investor A holds 45 per cent of the voting rights of an investee. Two other investors each hold 26 per cent of the voting rights of the investee. The remaining voting rights are held by three other shareholders, each holding 1 per cent. There are no other arrangements that affect decision-making. In this case, the size of investor A's voting interest and its size relative to the other shareholdings are sufficient to conclude that investor A does not have power. Only two other investors would need to co-operate to be able to prevent investor A from directing the relevant activities of the investee.

ILLUSTRATION 17: Voting rights

An investor holds 45 per cent of the voting rights of an investee. Eleven other shareholders each hold 5 per cent of the voting rights of the investee. None of the shareholders has contractual arrangements to consult any of the others or make collective decisions. In this case, the absolute size of the investor's holding and the relative size of the other shareholdings alone are not conclusive in determining whether the investor has rights sufficient to give it power over the investee. Additional facts and circumstances that may provide evidence that the investor has, or does not have, power shall be considered.

ILLUSTRATION 18: Voting rights

An investor holds 35 per cent of the voting rights of an investee. Three other shareholders each hold 5 per cent of the voting rights of the investee. The remaining voting rights are held by numerous other shareholders, none individually holding more than 1 per cent of the voting rights. None of the shareholders has arrangements to consult any of the others or make collective decisions. Decisions about the relevant activities of the investee require the approval of a majority of votes cast at relevant shareholders' meetings—75 per cent of the voting rights of the investee have been cast at recent relevant shareholders' meetings. In this case, the active participation of the other shareholders at recent shareholders' meetings indicates that the investor would not have the practical ability to direct the relevant activities unilaterally, regardless of whether the investor has directed the relevant activities because a sufficient number of other shareholders voted in the same way as the investor.

ILLUSTRATION 19: Voting rights

Investor A holds 70 per cent of the voting rights of an investee. Investor B has 30 per cent of the voting rights of the investee as well as an option to acquire half of investor A's voting rights. The option is exercisable for the next two years at a fixed price that is deeply out of the money (and is expected to remain so for that two-year period). Investor A has been exercising its votes and is actively directing the relevant activities of the investee. In such a case, investor A is likely to meet the power criterion because it appears to have the current ability to direct the relevant activities. Although investor B has currently exercisable options to purchase additional voting rights (that, if exercised, would give it a majority of the voting rights in the investee), the terms and conditions associated with those options are such that the options are not considered substantive.

ILLUSTRATION 20: Voting rights

Investor A and two other investors each hold a third of the voting rights of an investee. The investee's business activity is closely related to investor A. In addition to its equity instruments, investor A also holds debt instruments that are convertible into ordinary shares of the investee at any time for a fixed price that is out of the money (but not deeply out of the money). If the debt were converted, investor A would hold 60 per cent of the voting rights of the investee. Investor A would benefit from realising synergies if the debt instruments were converted into ordinary shares. Investor A has power over the investee because it holds voting rights of the investee together with substantive potential voting rights that give it the current ability to direct the relevant activities.

ILLUSTRATION 21

An investee's only business activity, as specified in its founding documents, is to purchase receivables and service them on a day-to-day basis for its investors. The servicing on a day-today basis includes the collection and passing on of principal and interest payments as they fall due. Upon default of a receivable the investee automatically puts the receivable to an investor as agreed separately in a put agreement between the investor and the investee. The only relevant activity is managing the receivables upon default because it is the only activity that can significantly affect the investee's returns. Managing the receivables before default is not a relevant activity because it does not require substantive decisions to be made that could significantly affect the investee's returns—the activities before default are predetermined and amount only to collecting cash flows as they fall due and passing them on to investors.

Therefore, only the investor's right to manage the assets upon default should be considered when assessing the overall activities of the investee that significantly affect the investee's returns.

In this example, the design of the investee ensures that the investor has decision-making authority over the activities that significantly affect the returns at the only time that such decision-making authority is required. The terms of the put agreement are integral to the overall transaction and the establishment of the investee. Therefore, the terms of the put agreement together with the founding documents of the investee lead to the conclusion that the investor has power over the investee even though the investor takes ownership of the receivables only upon default and manages the defaulted receivables outside the legal boundaries of the investee.

ILLUSTRATION 22: Exposure to variability of returns from other interests

A decision maker (fund manager) establishes, markets and manages a publicly traded, regulated fund according to narrowly defined parameters set out in the investment mandate as required by its local laws and regulations. The fund was marketed to investors as an investment in a diversified portfolio of equity securities of publicly traded entities. Within the defined parameters, the fund manager has discretion about the assets in which to invest. The fund manager has made a 10 per cent pro rata investment in the fund and receives a market based fee for its services equal to 1 per cent of the net asset value of the fund. The fees are commensurate with the services provided. The fund manager does not have any obligation to fund losses beyond its 10 per cent investment. The fund is not required to establish, and has not established, an independent board of directors. The investors do not hold any substantive rights that would affect the decision-making authority of the fund manager, but can redeem their interests within particular limits set by the fund.

Although operating within the parameters set out in the investment mandate and in accordance with the regulatory requirements, the fund manager has decision-making rights that give it the current ability to direct the relevant activities of the fund—the investors do not hold substantive rights that could affect the fund manager's decision-making authority. The fund manager receives a market-based fee for its services that is commensurate with the services provided and has also made a pro rata investment in the fund. The remuneration and its investment expose the fund manager to variability of returns from the activities of the fund without creating exposure that is of such significance that it indicates that the fund manager is a principal.

In this example, consideration of the fund manager's exposure to variability of returns from the fund together with its decision-making authority within restricted parameters indicates that the fund manager is an agent. Thus, the fund manager concludes that it does not control the fund.

ILLUSTRATION 23: Exposure to variability of returns from other interests

A decision maker establishes, markets and manages a fund that provides investment opportunities to a number of investors. The decision maker (fund manager) must make decisions in the best interests of all investors and in accordance with the fund's governing agreements. Nonetheless, the fund manager has wide decision-making discretion. The fund manager receives a market-based fee for its services equal to 1 per cent of assets under management and 20 per cent of all the fund's profits if a specified profit level is achieved. The fees are commensurate with the services provided.

Although it must make decisions in the best interests of all investors, the fund manager has extensive decision-making authority to direct the relevant activities of the fund. The fund manager is paid fixed and performance-related fees that are commensurate with the services provided. In addition, the remuneration aligns the interests of the fund manager with those of the other investors to increase the value of the fund, without creating exposure to variability of returns from the activities of the fund that is of such significance that the remuneration, when considered in isolation, indicates that the fund manager is a principal.

The above facts and analysis and talk about other variants as well.

ILLUSTRATION 24

The fund manager also has a 2 per cent investment in the fund that aligns its interests with those of the other investors. The fund manager does not have any obligation to fund losses beyond its 2 per cent investment. The investors can remove the fund manager by a simple majority vote, but only for breach of contract.

The fund manager's 2 per cent investment increases its exposure to variability of returns from the activities of the fund without creating exposure that is of such significance that it indicates that the fund manager is a principal. The other investors' rights to remove the fund manager are considered to be protective rights because they are exercisable only for breach of contract.

In this example, although the fund manager has extensive decision-making authority and is exposed to variability of returns from its interest and remuneration, the fund manager's exposure indicates that the fund manager is an agent. Thus, the fund manager concludes that it does not control the fund.

ILLUSTRATION 25

The fund manager has a more substantial pro rata investment in the fund, but does not have any obligation to fund losses beyond that investment. The investors can remove the fund manager by a simple majority vote, but only for breach of contract.

In this example, the other investors' rights to remove the fund manager are considered to be protective rights because they are exercisable only for breach of contract. Although the fund manager is paid fixed and performance-related fees that are commensurate with the services provided, the combination of the fund manager's investment together with its remuneration could create exposure to variability of returns from the activities of the fund that is of such significance that it indicates that the fund manager is a principal. The greater the magnitude of, and variability associated with, the fund manager's economic interests (considering its remuneration and other interests in aggregate), the more emphasis the fund manager would place on those economic interests in the analysis, and the more likely the fund manager is a principal.

For example, having considered its remuneration and the other factors, the fund manager might consider a 20 per cent investment to be sufficient to conclude that it controls the fund.

However, in different circumstances (i.e. if the remuneration or other factors are different), control may arise when the level of investment is different.

ILLUSTRATION 26

The fund manager has a 20 per cent pro rata investment in the fund, but does not have any obligation to fund losses beyond its 20 per cent investment. The fund has a board of directors, all of whose members are independent of the fund manager and are appointed by the other investors. The board appoints the fund manager annually. If the board decided not to renew the fund manager's contract, the services performed by the fund manager could be performed by other managers in the industry.

Although the fund manager is paid fixed and performance-related fees that are commensurate with the services provided, the combination of the fund manager's 20 per cent investment together with its remuneration creates exposure to variability of returns from the activities of the fund that is of such significance that it indicates that the fund manager is a principal.

However, the investors have substantive rights to remove the fund manager—the board of directors provide a mechanism to ensure that the investors can remove the fund manager if they decide to do so.

In this example, the fund manager places greater emphasis on the substantive removal rights in the analysis. Thus, although the fund manager has extensive decision-making authority and is exposed to variability of returns of the fund from its remuneration and investment, the substantive rights held by the other investors indicate that the fund manager is an agent. Thus, the fund manager concludes that it does not control the fund.

ILLUSTRATION 27

An investee is created to purchase a portfolio of fixed rate asset-backed securities, funded by fixed rate debt instruments and equity instruments. The equity instruments are designed to provide first loss protection to the debt investors and receive any residual returns of the investee. The transaction was marketed to potential debt investors as an investment in a portfolio of asset-backed securities with exposure to the credit risk associated with the possible default of the issuers of the asset-backed securities in the portfolio and to the interest rate risk associated with the management of the portfolio. On formation, the equity instruments represent 10 per cent of the value of the assets purchased. A decision maker (the asset manager) manages the active asset portfolio by making investment decisions within the parameters set out in the investee's prospectus. For those services, the asset manager receives a market-based fixed fee (ie 1 per cent of assets under management) and performance-related fees (i.e. 10 per cent of profits) if the investee's profits exceed a specified level. The fees are commensurate with the services provided. The asset manager holds 35 per cent of the equity in the investee. The remaining 65 per cent of the equity, and all the debt instruments, are held by a large number of widely dispersed unrelated third party investors. The asset manager can be removed, without cause, by a simple majority decision of the other investors.

The asset manager is paid fixed and performance-related fees that are commensurate with the services provided. The remuneration aligns the interests of the fund manager with those of the other investors to increase the value of the fund. The asset manager has exposure to variability of returns from the activities of the fund because it holds 35 per cent of the equity and from its remuneration.

Although operating within the parameters set out in the investee's prospectus, the asset manager has the current ability to make investment decisions that significantly affect the investee's returns—the removal rights held by the other investors receive little weighting in the analysis because those rights are held by a large number of widely dispersed investors. In this example, the asset manager places greater emphasis on its exposure to variability of returns of the fund from its equity interest, which is subordinate to the debt instruments.

Holding 35 per cent of the equity creates subordinated exposure to losses and rights to returns of the investee, which are of such significance that it indicates that the asset manager is a principal. Thus, the asset manager concludes that it controls the investee.

ILLUSTRATION 28

A decision maker (the sponsor) sponsors a multi-seller conduit, which issues short-term debt instruments to unrelated third party investors. The transaction was marketed to potential investors as an investment in a portfolio of highly rated medium-term assets with minimal exposure to the credit risk associated with the possible default by the issuers of the assets in the portfolio. Various transferors sell high quality medium-term asset portfolios to the conduit.

Each transferor services the portfolio of assets that it sells to the conduit and manages receivables on default for a market-based servicing fee. Each transferor also provides first loss protection against credit losses from its asset portfolio through over-collateralisation of the assets transferred to the conduit. The sponsor establishes the terms of the conduit and manages the operations of the conduit for a market-based fee. The fee is commensurate with the services provided. The sponsor approves the sellers permitted to sell to the conduit, approves the assets to be purchased by the conduit and makes decisions about the funding of the conduit. The sponsor must act in the best interests of all investors.

The sponsor is entitled to any residual return of the conduit and also provides credit enhancement and liquidity facilities to the conduit. The credit enhancement provided by the sponsor absorbs losses of up to 5 per cent of all of the conduit's assets, after losses are absorbed by the transferors. The liquidity facilities are not advanced against defaulted assets.

The investors do not hold substantive rights that could affect the decision-making authority of the sponsor.

Even though the sponsor is paid a market-based fee for its services that is commensurate with the services provided, the sponsor has exposure to variability of returns from the activities of the conduit because of its rights to any residual returns of the conduit and the provision of credit enhancement and liquidity facilities (ie the conduit is exposed to liquidity risk by using short-term debt instruments to fund medium-term assets). Even though each of the transferors has decision-making rights that affect the value of the assets of the conduit, the sponsor has extensive decision-making authority that gives it the current ability to direct the activities that *most* significantly affect the conduit's returns (ie the sponsor established the terms of the conduit, has the right to make decisions about the assets (approving the assets purchased and the transferors of those assets) and the funding of the conduit (for which new investment must be found on a regular basis)). The right to residual returns of the conduit and the provision of credit enhancement and liquidity facilities expose the sponsor to variability of returns from the activities of the conduit that is different from that of the other investors. Accordingly, that exposure indicates that the sponsor is a principal and thus the sponsor concludes that it controls the conduit. The sponsor's obligation to act in the best interest of all investors does not prevent the sponsor from being a principal.

3.2.24. Convergence with IFRS (Comparison with IFRS 10)

a) IFRS 10 requires all investments to be measured at fair value to qualify for the exemption from consolidation available to an investment entity. Since, Ind AS 40, *Investment*

Properties requires all investment properties to be measured at cost initially and cost less depreciation subsequently, relevant section has been deleted as this deal with investment property measured at fair value which is not relevant in the Indian context.

b) Different terminology is used, as used in existing laws e.g, the term 'balance sheet' is used instead of 'Statement of financial position' and 'Statement of profit and loss' is used instead of 'Statement of comprehensive income'.

c) Appendix C of IFRS 10 dealing with effective date, transition and withdrawal of other IFRSs have not been included in Ind AS 10, due to the following reasons:

(i) Effective date is not relevant as the date of application will be notified under the Companies Act.

(ii) Transitional provisions related to Ind ASs, wherever considered appropriate have been included in Ind AS 101, *First-time Adoption of Indian Accounting Standards,* corresponding to IFRS 1, *First-time Adoption of International Financial Reporting Standards.*

(iii) Paragraphs dealing with withdrawal of other IFRSs are not relevant.

3.3. Ind AS 27: Separate Financial statements

3.3.1. Objective
The objective of this Standard is to prescribe the accounting and disclosure requirements for investments in subsidiaries, joint ventures and associates when an entity prepares separate financial statements.

3.3.2. Scope
This Standard shall be applied in accounting for investments in subsidiaries, joint ventures and associates when an entity elects, or is required by law, to present separate financial statements.

This Standard does not mandate which entities produce separate financial statements. It applies when an entity prepares separate financial statements that comply with Indian Accounting Standards.

3.3.3. Definitions
The following terms are used in this Standard with the meanings specified:

Consolidated financial statements are the financial statements of a group in which the assets, liabilities, equity, income, expenses and cash flows of the parent and its subsidiaries are presented as those of a single economic entity.

Separate financial statements are those presented by a parent (i.e an investor with control of a subsidiary) or an investor with joint control of, or significant influence over, an investee, in which the investments are accounted for at cost or in accordance with Ind AS 109, *Financial Instruments*.

The following terms are defined in Appendix A of Ind AS 110, *Consolidated Financial Statements*, Appendix A of Ind AS 111, *Joint Arrangements*, and paragraph 3 of Ind AS 28, *Investments in Associates and Joint Ventures*:
- Associate
- control of an investee
- group
- Investment Entity
- joint control
- joint venture
- joint venturer
- parent
- significant influence
- subsidiary.

According to Para 6 Separate financial statements are those presented in addition to consolidated financial statements or in addition to financial statements in which investments in associates or joint ventures are accounted for using the equity method, other than in the circumstances set out in paragraphs 8-8A. Separate financial statements need not be appended to, or accompany, those statements.

Financial statements in which the equity method is applied are not separate financial statements. These may be termed as 'consolidated financial statements'. Similarly, the financial statements of an entity that does not have a subsidiary, associate or joint venturer's interest in a joint venture are not separate financial statements. (Para 7)

In accordance with Para 8, an entity that is exempted in accordance with paragraph 4(a) of Ind AS 110 from consolidation or paragraph 17 of Ind AS 28 from applying the equity method may present separate financial statements as its only financial statements.

According to Para 8A An investment entity that is required, throughout the current period and all comparative periods presented, to apply the exception to consolidation for all of its subsidiaries in accordance with paragraph 31 of Ind AS 110 presents separate financial statements as its only financial statements.

3.3.4. Preparation of separate financial statements
i) Separate financial statements shall be prepared in accordance with all applicable Ind AS, except as provided in paragraph 10.
ii) When an entity prepares separate financial statements, it shall account for investments in subsidiaries, joint ventures and associates either:
(a) at cost, or
(b) in accordance with Ind AS 109.
The entity shall apply the same accounting for each category of investments. Investments accounted for at cost shall be accounted for in accordance with Ind AS 105, *Non-current Assets Held for Sale and Discontinued Operations,* when they are classified as held for sale (or included in a disposal group that is classified as held for sale). The measurement of investments accounted for in accordance with Ind AS 109 is not changed in such circumstances.
iii) According to Para 11 If an entity elects, in accordance with paragraph 18 of Ind AS 28, to measure its investments in associates or joint ventures at fair value through profit or loss in accordance with Ind AS 109, it shall also account for those investments in the same way in its separate financial statements.
iv) Para 11A - If a parent is required, in accordance with paragraph 31 of Ind AS 110, to measure its investment in a subsidiary at fair value through profit or loss in accordance with Ind AS 109, it shall also account for its investment in a subsidiary in the same way in its separate financial statements.
v) 11B When a parent ceases to be an investment entity, or becomes an investment entity, it shall account for the change from the date when the change in status occurred, as follows:
  (a) when an entity ceases to be an investment entity, the entity shall, in accordance with paragraph 10, either:
    (i)account for an investment in a subsidiary at cost. The fair value of the subsidiary at the date of the change of status shall be used as the deemed cost at that date; or
    (ii) continue to account for an investment in a subsidiary in accordance with Ind AS 109.

(b) when an entity becomes an investment entity, it shall account for an investment in a subsidiary at fair value through profit or loss in accordance with Ind AS 109. The difference between the previous carrying amount of the subsidiary and its fair value at the date of the change of status of the investor shall be recognised as a gain or loss in profit or loss. The cumulative amount of any fair value adjustment previously recognised in other comprehensive income in respect of those subsidiaries shall be treated as if the investment entity had disposed of those subsidiaries at the date of change in status.

vi) An entity shall recognise a dividend from a subsidiary, a joint venture or an associate in profit or loss in its separate financial statements when its right to receive the dividend is established.

vii) Para 13 - When a parent reorganises the structure of its group by establishing a new entity as its parent in a manner that satisfies the following criteria:

(a) the new parent obtains control of the original parent by issuing equity instruments in exchange for existing equity instruments of the original parent;

(b) the assets and liabilities of the new group and the original group are the same immediately before and after the reorganisation; and

(c) the owners of the original parent before the reorganisation have the same absolute and relative interests in the net assets of the original group and the new group immediately before and after the reorganisation,

and the new parent accounts for its investment in the original parent in accordance with paragraph 10(a) in its separate financial statements, the new parent shall measure cost at the carrying amount of its share of the equity items shown in the separate financial statements of the original parent at the date of the reorganisation.

Similarly, an entity that is not a parent might establish a new entity as its parent in a manner that satisfies the criteria in paragraph 13. The requirements in paragraph 13 apply equally to such reorganisations. In such cases, references to 'original parent' and 'original group' are to the 'original entity'.(Para 14)

3.3.5. Disclosure

16.5.1. Para – 15. An entity shall apply all applicable Ind ASs when providing disclosures in its separate financial statements, including the requirements in paragraphs 16 and 17.

16.5.2. When a parent, in accordance with paragraph 4(a) of Ind AS 110, elects not to prepare consolidated financial statements and instead prepares separate financial statements, it shall disclose in those separate financial statements:

(a) the fact that the financial statements are separate financial statements; that the exemption from consolidation has been used; the name and principal place of business (and country of incorporation, if different) of the entity whose consolidated financial statements that comply with Ind ASs have been produced for public use; and the address where those consolidated financial statements are obtainable.

(b) a list of significant investments in subsidiaries, joint ventures and associates, including:

   (i) the name of those investees.

   (ii) the principal place of business (and country of incorporation, if different) of those investees.

   (iii) its proportion of the ownership interest (and its proportion of the voting rights, if different) held in those investees.

(c) a description of the method used to account for the investments listed under (b).

16.5.3. When an investment entity that is a parent prepares, in accordance with paragraph 8A, separate financial statements as its only financial statements, it shall disclose that fact. The investment entity shall also present the disclosures relating to investment entities required by Ind AS 112, *Disclosure of Interests in Other Entities*. (Para 16A)

16.5.4. When a parent (other than a parent covered by paragraphs 16-16A) or an investor with joint control of, or significant influence over, an investee prepares separate financial statements, the parent or investor shall identify the financial statements prepared in accordance with Ind AS 110, Ind AS 111 or Ind AS 28 to which they relate. The parent or investor shall also disclose in its separate financial statements:
(a) the fact that the statements are separate financial statements
(b) a list of significant investments in subsidiaries, joint ventures and associates, including:
> (i) the name of those investees.
> (ii) the principal place of business (and country of incorporation, if different) of those investees.
> (iii) its proportion of the ownership interest (and its proportion of the voting rights, if different) held in those investees.
(c) a description of the method used to account for the investments listed under (b).(Para 17)

3.3.6. Convergence with IFRS (Comparison with IAS 27 Separate Financial Statements)
3.2.6.1. Paragraph 17 (a) of IAS 27 requires to disclose the reason for preparing separate financial statements if not required by law. As the Companies Act mandates preparation of separate financial statements, paragraph 17 (a) has been modified to remove such requirement.
3.2.6.2. IAS 27 allows the entities to use the equity method to account for investment in subsidiaries, joint ventures and associates in their Separate Financial Statements (SFS). Such option is not given in Ind AS 27, as the equity method is not a measurement basis like cost and fair value but is a manner of consolidation and therefore would lead to inconsistent accounting conceptually.

3.4: Ind AS 28: Investment in associates and Joint Ventures

3.4.1. Objective
The objective of this Standard is to prescribe the accounting for investments in associates and to set out the requirements for the application of the equity method when accounting for investments in associates and joint ventures.

3.4.2. Scope
This Standard shall be applied by all entities that are investors with joint control of, or significant influence over, an investee.

3.4.3. Definitions
3.4.3.1. The following terms are used in this Standard with the meanings specified:

An *associate* is an entity over which the investor has significant influence.

Consolidated financial statements are the financial statements of a group in which assets, liabilities, equity, income, expenses and cash flows of the parent and its subsidiaries are presented as those of a single economic entity.

The equity method is a method of accounting whereby the investment is initially recognised at cost and adjusted thereafter for the post-acquisition change in the investor's share of the investee's net assets. The investor's profit or loss includes its share of the investee's profit or loss and the investor's other comprehensive income includes its share of the investee's other comprehensive income.

A joint arrangement is an arrangement of which two or more parties have joint control.

Joint control is the contractually agreed sharing of control of an arrangement, and exists only when the decisions about the relevant activities require the unanimous consent of the parties sharing control.

A joint venture is a joint arrangement whereby the parties that have joint control of the arrangement have rights to the net assets of the arrangement.

A joint venturer is a party to a joint venture that has joint control of that joint venture

Significant influence is the power to participate in the financial and operating policy decisions of the investee but is not control or joint control of those policies.

3.4.3.2. The following terms are defined in paragraph 4 of Ind AS 27, *Separate Financial Statements,* and in Appendix A of Ind AS 110, *Consolidated Financial Statements,* and are used in this Standard with the meanings specified in the Ind ASs in which they are defined:
- control of an investee
- group
- parent
- separate financial statements
- subsidiary.

3.4.4. Significant influence
3.4.4.1. if an entity holds, directly or indirectly (e.g. through subsidiaries), 20% or more of the voting power of the investee, it is presumed that the entity has significant influence unless it can be clearly demonstrated that this is not the case.

Conversely, if the entity holds, directly or indirectly (e.g. through subsidiaries), less than 20% of the voting power of the investee, it is presumed that the entity does not have significant influence, unless such influence can be clearly demonstrated. A substantial or majority ownership by another investor does not necessarily preclude an entity from having significant influence. (Para 5)

3.4.4.2. According to Para 6, the existence of significant influence by an entity is usually evidenced by:
   (a) Representation on the board of directors or corresponding governing body of the investee;
   (b) participation in policy making processes;
   (c) material transactions between the investor and the investee;
   (d) interchange of managerial personnel; or
   (e) provision of essential technical information.

3.4.4.3. According to Para 7, The existence and effect of potential voting rights that are currently exercisable or convertible, including potential voting rights held by other entities, are considered when assessing whether an entity has significant influence. Potential voting rights are not currently exercisable or convertible when, for example, they cannot be exercised or converted until a future date or until the occurrence of a future event.

3.4.4.4. In assessing whether potential voting rights contribute to significant influence, the entity examines all facts and circumstances (including the terms of exercise of the potential voting rights and any other contractual arrangements whether considered individually or in combination) that affect potential rights, except the intentions of management and the financial ability to exercise or convert those potential rights.

3.4.4.5. Para 9 stipulates that an entity loses significant influence over an investee when it loses the power to participate in the financial and operating policy decisions of that investee. The loss of significant influence can occur with or without a change in absolute or relative ownership levels. It could occur, for example, when an associate becomes subject to the control of a government, court, administrator or regulator. It could also occur as a result of a contractual arrangement.

3.4.5. Equity method
3.4.5.1. Under the equity method, on initial recognition the investment in an associate or a joint venture is recognised at cost, and the carrying amount is increased or decreased to recognise the investor's share of the profit or loss of the investee after the date of acquisition. The investor's share of the investee's profit or loss is recognised in the investor's profit or loss. Hence initial recognition and measurement is applied at cost.

3.4.5.2. Because the investor has joint control of, or significant influence over, the investee, the investor has an interest in the associate's or joint venture's performance and, as a result, the return on its investment. The investor accounts for this interest by extending the scope of its financial statements to include its share of the profit or loss of such an investee. As a result, application of the equity method provides more informative reporting of the investor's net assets and profit or loss.

3.4.5.3. When potential voting rights or other derivatives containing potential voting rights exist, an entity's interest in an associate or a joint venture is determined solely on the basis of existing ownership interests and does not reflect the possible exercise or conversion of potential voting rights and other derivative instruments, unless paragraph 13 applies.

3.4.5.4. Para 13 stipulates that in some circumstances, an entity has, in substance, an existing ownership as a result of a transaction that currently gives it access to the returns associated with an ownership interest.
In such circumstances, the proportion allocated to the entity is determined by taking into account the eventual exercise of those potential voting rights and other derivative instruments that currently give the entity access to the returns.

3.4.5.5. According to Para 14, Ind AS 109, *Financial Instruments,* does not apply to interests in associates and joint ventures that are accounted for using the equity method. When instruments containing potential voting rights in substance currently give access to the returns associated with an ownership interest in an associate or a joint venture, the instruments are not subject to Ind AS 109. In all other cases, instruments containing potential voting rights in an associate or a joint venture are accounted for in accordance with Ind AS 109.

3.4.5.6. Unless an investment, or a portion of an investment, in an associate or a joint venture is classified as held for sale in accordance with Ind AS 105, *Non-current Assets Held for Sale and Discontinued Operations*, the investment, or any retained interest in the investment not classified as held for sale, shall be classified as a non-current asset. (Para 15)

3.4.6. Exemptions to Equity method
3.4.6.1. According to Para 17 an entity need not apply the equity method to its investment in an associate or a joint venture if the entity is a parent that is exempt from preparing consolidated financial statements by the scope exception in paragraph 4(a) of Ind AS 110 or if all the following apply:

    (a) The entity is a wholly-owned subsidiary, or is a partially-owned subsidiary of another entity and its other owners, including those not otherwise entitled to vote, have been informed about, and do not object to, the entity not applying the equity method.

    (b) The entity's debt or equity instruments are not traded in a public market (a domestic or foreign stock exchange or an over-the-counter market, including local and regional markets).

    (c) The entity did not file, nor is it in the process of filing, its financial statements with a securities commission or other regulatory organisation, for the purpose of issuing any class of instruments in a public market.

    (d) The ultimate or any intermediate parent of the entity produces consolidated financial statements available for public use that comply with Ind ASs.

3.4.6.2. When an investment in an associate or a joint venture is held by, or is held indirectly through, an entity that is a venture capital organisation, or a mutual fund, unit trust and similar entities including investment-linked insurance funds, the entity may elect to measure investments in those associates and joint ventures at fair value through profit or loss in accordance with Ind AS 109.(Para 18)

3.4.6.3. When an entity has an investment in an associate, a portion of which is held indirectly through a venture capital organisation, or a mutual fund, unit trust and similar entities including investment-linked insurance funds, the entity may elect to measure that portion of the investment in the associate at fair value through profit or loss in accordance with Ind AS 109 regardless of whether the venture capital organisation has significant influence over that portion of the investment. If the entity makes that election, the entity shall apply the equity method to any remaining portion of its investment in an associate that is not held through a venture capital organisation.(Para 19)

3.4.7. Procedure for the equity method:

In the consolidated Balance Sheet	*On date of acquisition:*
	 The investment in the associate company is stated at cost
	 On reporting date:
	 The investment in associate company will be reflected in the consolidated Balance Sheet after making the following adjustments:
	    a) If the associate makes a profit : group share of profit will be added to investment
	    b) If the associate incurs a loss : group share of loss will be deducted from the investment
	 The procedures used for determining the profit / loss under the equity method are similar to those used for determining profit / loss under the full consolidation method

In the consolidated Statement of Profit & Loss	*On the date of acquisition:* The pre-acquisition profits have to be revised, to incorporate all fair value adjustments. The group's share in the revised profit will be deducted from consideration in arriving at goodwill. *On reporting date:* The group's share in the post-acquisition profits of the associate company is included in the consolidated SOPL

The Steps for equity method is summarised below:

- Eliminating intra group profits and losses arising from transactions between investor and investee
- identifying the goodwill portion of the purchase price
- amortization of goodwill
- adjustments for depreciation of depreciable assets , based on their fair values
- adjustments for the effect of cross holdings
- using uniform accounting policies

ILLUSTRATION 29: Equity Method of Accounting

Day Ltd acquired 40% interest in the ordinary shares of Kay Inc on the date of incorporation Jan 1 2006 for an amount of Rs. 22000. This enabled Day Ltd to exercise significant influence over Kay Inc. On Dec 2009 the shareholders equity of Kay Inc was as follows:

	Rs
Ordinary issued share capital	55000
Reserves	18000
Accumulated profit	65000
TOTAL	138000

Extract of Income statement and statement of changes in equity:

Income statement

PAT	22800
Extraordinary items	(1200)
Net profit for the period	21600
Statement of change in equity	
Accumulated profit (beginning of the year)	65000
Net profit for the period	21600
Dividend paid	(8000)
Accumulated profit at the end of the year	78600

In Nov 2010 Day Ltd sold inventories to Kay Ltd for the first time at Rs. 5000 and earned a profit of Rs. 1000. None of the inventories were sold by Dec 31. IT rate 30%

Solution

Calculation of equity method	Rs
Ordinary cost (Rs.55000 X 40%)	22000
Post-acquisition profit beginning of the year <(18000+65000)X40%>	33200
Carrying amount (Jan 1 2010)	**55200**
Attributable portion of net profit (Schedule I)	8360
Dividend received (8000 X 40%)	(3200)
	60360

Schedule I

Attributable portion of net profit	
Net profit (21600 X 40%)	8640
After tax effect of unrealized profit <40%X(70%X1000)>	(280)
Total (as above)	**8360**

3.4.8. Treatment of unrealised intra-group profits related to associates

Gains and losses resulting from 'upstream' and 'downstream' transactions between an entity (including its consolidated subsidiaries) and its associate or joint venture are recognised in the entity's financial statements only to the extent of unrelated investors' interests in the associate or joint venture. 'Upstream' transactions are, for example, sales of assets from an associate or a joint venture to the investor. 'Downstream' transactions are, for example, sales or contributions of assets from the investor to its associate or its joint venture. The investor's share in the associate's or joint venture's gains or losses resulting from these transactions is eliminated. (Para 28)

Treatment of elimination of unrealised intra-group profits related to associates is shown as under:

Downstream transactions	Upstream transactions
If the sale of goods / assets at profit is made by the investor to the associate, it is known as a downstream transaction.	If the sale of goods / assets at profit is made by the associate to the investor, it is known as upstream transaction.

The entry is as under:
Dr. Cost of sales (CSOPL)
    Cr. Investment in associate   (CBS)
(Being the elimination of group's share in unrealised intra-group profits)
	The entry is as under:
	Dr. Cost of sales (CSOPL)
	    Cr. Inventory (CBS)
	(Being elimination of URP on inventory owing to upstream transactions)

Rationale: In this case, URP is included in the associate's inventory, but associate's inventory is not shown in the investor's financial statements as it does not consolidate the accounts of the associate. Hence URP needs to be eliminated from the investment and not from inventory.	Rationale: In this case, URP is included in the investor's inventory which is included in consolidated financial statements. Hence, URP needs to be eliminated from the inventory and corresponding effect will always go to cost of sales / retained earnings

3.4.9. Accounting treatment of goodwill, bargain purchases and losses with respect to associates

According to Para 32 An investment is accounted for using the equity method from the date on which it becomes an associate or a joint venture. On acquisition of the investment, any difference between the cost of the investment and the entity's share of the net fair value of the investee's identifiable assets and liabilities is accounted for as follows:
(a) Goodwill relating to an associate or a joint venture is included in the carrying amount of the investment. Amortisation of that goodwill is not permitted.
(b) Any excess of the entity's share of the net fair value of the investee's identifiable assets and liabilities over the cost of the investment is recognised directly in equity as capital reserve in the period in which the investment is acquired.

Accounting treatment of goodwill and bargain purchases with respect to associates is shown in table below:

Goodwill		Capital reserve	
Cost of investment	x (A)	Cost of investment	x (A)

Less: Investor's share of net fair
    Value of associate's
    Identifiable net assets
	<u>x (B)</u>	Less: Investor's share of net fair
		    Value of associate's
		    Identifiable net assets
			<u>x (B)</u>

Goodwill (A – B)	X	Capital Reserve (B – A)	X
Positive goodwill is already included in the cost of investment and so needs no further accounting treatment		The gain on bargain purchase will be recognised directly in equity as capital reserve in the period in which the investment is acquired.	

> All adjustments made for goodwill impairment and fair value changes in accounting for subsidiaries are also made in accounting for associates
>
> If the group's share of losses pertaining to the associate exceeds its investment in the associate, then the investor has to stop accounting for further losses. Hence the cost of investment will be recorded as nil in the consolidated financial statements.
>
> After the entity's interest is reduced to zero, additional losses are provided for, and a liability is recognised, only to the extent that the entity has incurred legal or constructive obligations or made payments on behalf of the associate or joint venture. If the associate or joint venture subsequently reports profits, the entity resumes recognising its share of those profits only after its share of the profits equals the share of losses not recognised.(Para 39)

3.4.10. Financial statements are prepared at different dates

When, in accordance with paragraph 33, the financial statements of an associate or a joint venture used in applying the equity method are prepared as of a date different from that used by the entity, adjustments shall be made for the effects of significant transactions or events that occur between that date and the date of the entity's financial statements. In any case, the difference between the end of the reporting period of the associate or joint venture and that of the entity shall be no more than three months. The length of the reporting periods and any difference between the ends of the reporting periods shall be the same from period to period.

3.4.11. Classification as held for sale

According to para 20, An entity shall apply Ind AS 105 to an investment, or a portion of an investment, in an associate or a joint venture that meets the criteria to be classified as held for sale. Any retained portion of an investment in an associate or a joint venture that has not been classified as held for sale shall be accounted for using the equity method until disposal of the portion that is classified as held for sale takes place. After the disposal takes place, an entity shall account for any retained interest in the associate or joint venture in accordance with Ind AS 109 unless the retained interest continues to be an associate or a joint venture, in which case the entity uses the equity method.

In accordance with Para 21, when an investment, or a portion of an investment, in an associate or a joint venture previously classified as held for sale no longer meets the criteria to be so classified, it shall be accounted for using the equity method retrospectively as from the date of its classification as held for sale. Financial statements for the periods since classification as held for sale shall be amended accordingly.

3.4.12. Discontinuing the use of Equity method

According to Para 22 An entity shall discontinue the use of the equity method from the date when its investment ceases to be an associate or a joint venture as follows:
(a) If the investment becomes a subsidiary, the entity shall account for its investment
    in accordance with Ind AS 103, *Business Combinations,* and Ind AS 110.
(b) If the retained interest in the former associate or joint venture is a financial asset,
the entity shall measure the retained interest at fair value. The fair value of the retained interest shall be regarded as its fair value on initial recognition as a financial asset in

accordance with Ind AS 109. The entity shall recognise in profit or loss any difference between:

(i) the fair value of any retained interest and any proceeds from disposing of a part interest in the associate or joint venture; and

(ii) the carrying amount of the investment at the date the equity method was discontinued.

(c) When an entity discontinues the use of the equity method, the entity shall account for all amounts previously recognised in other comprehensive income in relation to that investment on the same basis as would have been required if the investee had directly disposed of the related assets or liabilities.

Therefore, if a gain or loss previously recognised in other comprehensive income by the investee would be reclassified to profit or loss on the disposal of the related assets or liabilities, the entity reclassifies the gain or loss from equity to profit or loss (as a reclassification adjustment) when the equity method is discontinued.

> For example, if an associate or a joint venture has cumulative exchange differences relating to a foreign operation and the entity discontinues the use of the equity method, the entity shall reclassify to profit or loss the gain or loss that had previously been recognised in other comprehensive income in relation to the foreign operation. (Para 23)

The Standard clarifies that, if an investment in an associate becomes an investment in a joint venture or an investment in a joint venture becomes an investment in an associate, the entity continues to apply the equity method and does not re-measure the retained interest.

3.4.13. Change in ownership interest

According to Para 25 If an entity's ownership interest in an associate or a joint venture is reduced, but the entity continues to apply the equity method, the entity shall reclassify to profit or loss the proportion of the gain or loss that had previously been recognised in other comprehensive income relating to that reduction in ownership interest if that gain or loss would be required to be reclassified to profit or loss on the disposal of the related assets or liabilities.

3.4.14. Impairment losses

3.4.14.1. According to Para 41A, the net investment in an associate or joint venture is impaired and impairment losses are incurred if, and only if, there is objective evidence of impairment as a result of one or more events that occurred after the initial recognition of the net investment (a 'loss event') and that loss event (or events) has an impact on the estimated future cash flows from the net investment that can be reliably estimated. It may not be possible to identify a single, discrete event that caused the impairment. Rather the combined effect of several events may have caused the impairment. Losses expected as a result of future events, no matter how likely, are not recognised. Objective evidence that the net investment is impaired

includes observable data that comes to the attention of the entity about the following loss events:

(a) significant financial difficulty of the associate or joint venture;

(b) a breach of contract, such as a default or delinquency in payments by the associate or joint venture;

(c) the entity, for economic or legal reasons relating to its associate's or joint venture's financial difficulty, granting to the associate or joint venture a concession that the entity would not otherwise consider;

(d) it becoming probable that the associate or joint venture will enter bankruptcy or other financial reorganisation; or

(e) the disappearance of an active market for the net investment because of financial difficulties of the associate or joint venture.

3.4.14.2. According to Para 41B, the disappearance of an active market because the associate's or joint venture's equity or financial instruments are no longer publicly traded is not evidence of impairment. A downgrade of an associate's or joint venture's credit rating or a decline in the fair value of the associate or joint venture, is not of itself, evidence of impairment, although it may be evidence of impairment when considered with other available information.

3.4.14.3. Para 41C stipulates that, In addition to the types of events in paragraph 41A, objective evidence of impairment for the net investment in the equity instruments of the associate or joint venture includes information about significant changes with an adverse effect that have taken place in the technological, market, economic or legal environment in which the associate or joint venture operates, and indicates that the cost of the investment in the equity instrument may not be recovered. A significant or prolonged decline in the fair value of an investment in an equity instrument below its cost is also objective evidence of impairment.

3.4.14.4. The carrying amount of the investment is tested for impairment in accordance with Ind AS 36 as a single asset, by comparing its recoverable amount (higher of value in use and fair value less costs to sell) with its carrying amount, whenever application of paragraphs 41A-41C indicates that the net investment may be impaired.

3.4.14.5. An impairment loss recognised in those circumstances is not allocated to any asset, including goodwill, that forms part of the carrying amount of the net investment in the associate or joint venture. Accordingly, any reversal of that impairment loss is recognised in accordance with Ind AS 36 to the extent that the recoverable amount of the net investment subsequently increases. In determining the value in use of the net investment, an entity estimates:

(a) its share of the present value of the estimated future cash flows expected to be generated by the associate or joint venture, including the cash flows from the operations of the associate or joint venture and the proceeds from the ultimate disposal of the investment;

or

(b) the present value of the estimated future cash flows expected to arise from dividends to be received from the investment and from its ultimate disposal.

Using appropriate assumptions, both methods give the same result.

3.4.14.6. Para 43 stipulates that the recoverable amount of an investment in an associate or a joint venture shall be assessed for each associate or joint venture, unless the associate or joint venture does not generate cash inflows from continuing use that are largely independent of those from other assets of the entity.

3.4.15. Separate financial statements

An investment in an associate or a joint venture shall be accounted for in the entity's separate financial statements in accordance with paragraph 10 of Ind AS 27.(Para 44).

3.4.16. Major differences between Ind AS 28 and AS 23

S/L No	Ind AS 28	AS 23
1	Defines control as the power to govern the financial and operating policies of an entity so as to obtain benefits from its activities	Defines control as ownership either directly or indirectly, through subsidiaries holding more than half of the voting power of an enterprise ; or control of the composition of board of directors in the case of a company or of the composition of corresponding governing body in case of any other entity so as to obtain economic benefits from its activities
2	Defines significant influence "as power to participate in the financial and operating policy decisions of the investee but is not control or joint control over those policies	Defines significant influence as "power to participate in the financial and / or operating policy decisions of the investee but is not control over those policies"
3	Existence and effect of potential voting rights that are currently exercisable or convertible are considered when assessing whether an entity has significant influence or not	For the purpose of considering share ownership for significant influence, potential equity shares of the investee held by investor are not taken into account by the current standard
4	Length of difference in reporting dates should not be more than three months unless it is impracticable	There is no limit on the length of difference in the reporting dates of the investor and the associate
5	The standard does not permit any exemption in this regard	Provides that similar accounting policies should be used for preparation of investor's financial statements and in case of an associate uses a different accounting policy for similar transactions, appropriate adjustments need to be made to the accounting policies of the associate. However, if that is not possible, then the fact shall be appropriately disclosed with a brief description of the differences in accounting policies.
6	On acquisition of the investment of the associate, any difference between the cost of the acquisition and investor's share of the net fair value of the associate's identifiable	On acquisition of the investment in an associate any difference between the cost of acquisition and investor's share of equity of the associate is described as goodwill / capital reserve and the same is included in

	assets and liabilities is accounted for as follows: • Goodwill related to an associate is included in the carrying amount of the investment. Amortization of the goodwill is not permitted • Any excess of the investor's share of the net fair value of the associate's assets and liabilities over the cost of the investment is included as income in the determination of the investor's share of the associate's profit or loss in the period in which the investment is acquired	the carrying amount of investment in the associate but disclosed separately For calculating goodwill / capital reserve , equity of the associate is determined on the basis of carrying amounts of assets and liabilities on the date of acquisition
7	For recognition of investor's share of losses in the associate, carrying amount of investment in the associate as well as its other long term interests in the associate, which in substance, form part of the investor's net investment in the associate shall be considered	Investors share of losses in the associate is recognized to the extent of carrying amount of investment in the associate

3.4.17. Convergence with IFRS (Comparison with IAS 28)

1. Paragraph 35 of Ind AS 28 requires use of uniform accounting policies, unless, in case of an associate, it is impracticable, which IAS 28 does not provide. This change has been made because the investor does not have 'control' over the associate, it may not be able to influence the associate to prepare additional financial statements or to follow the accounting policies that are followed by the investor.

2. Paragraph 32 (b) has been modified on the lines of Ind AS 103, *Business Combinations,* to transfer excess of the investor's share of the net fair value of the investee's identifiable assets and liabilities over the cost of investment in capital reserve whereas in IAS 28, it is recognised in profit or loss.

3. Different terminology is used, as used in existing laws, e.g. the term 'balance sheet' is used instead of 'Statement of financial position'.

3.5. Ind AS 103: Business Combinations

3.5.1. Objective

The objective of the Standard is to improve the relevance, reliability and comparability of the information that a reporting entity provides in its financial statements about a business combination and its effects. To accomplish that, the Standard establishes principles and requirements for how the acquirer:

a) recognizes and measure in its financial statements the identifiable assets acquired, the liabilities assumed and any non-controlling interest in the acquiree,

b) recognizes and measures the goodwill acquired in the business combination or a gain from a bargain purchase and

c) determines what information to disclose to enable users of the financial statements to evaluate the nature and financial effects of the business combination

3.5.2. Scope and exclusion

3.5.2.1. According to para 2, this Standard applies to a transaction or other event that meets the definition of a business combination.

3.5.2.2. This Ind AS does not apply to:

(a) the accounting for the formation of a joint arrangement in the financial statements of the joint arrangement itself.

(b) the acquisition of an asset or a group of assets that does not constitute a business. In such cases the acquirer shall identify and recognise the individual identifiable assets acquired (including those assets that meet the definition of, and recognition criteria for, intangible assets in Ind AS 38, Intangible Assets) and liabilities assumed. The cost of the group shall be allocated to the individual identifiable assets and liabilities on the basis of their relative fair values at the date of purchase. Such a transaction or event does not give rise to goodwill.

3.5.2.3. Para 2A The requirements of this Standard do not apply to the acquisition by an investment entity, as defined in Ind AS 110, Consolidated Financial Statements, of an investment in a subsidiary that is required to be measured at fair value through profit or loss.

3.5.2.4. Para 2B - Appendix C deals with accounting for combination of entities or businesses under common control.

3.5.3. Identifying a business combination

Para 3 - An entity shall determine whether a transaction or other event is a business combination by applying the definition in this Ind AS, which requires that the assets acquired and liabilities assumed constitute a business. If the assets acquired are not a business, the reporting entity shall account for the transaction or other event as an asset acquisition. Paragraphs B5–B12 of the Standard provide guidance on identifying a business combination and the definition of a business.

3.5.4. The acquisition method

3.5.4.1. According to Para 4 An entity shall account for each business combination by applying the acquisition method.

Para 5 prescribes the steps related to acquisition method:

(a) identifying the acquirer;
(b) determining the *acquisition date;*
(c) recognising and measuring the identifiable assets acquired, the liabilities assumed and any non-controlling interest in the acquiree; and
(d) recognising and measuring goodwill or a gain from a bargain purchase.

3.5.4.2. Identifying the acquirer

a) For each business combination, one of the combining entities shall be identified as the acquirer.

b)Para 7 stipulates that the guidance in Ind AS 110 shall be used to identify the acquirer— the entity that obtains *control* of another entity, i.e. the acquiree. If a business combination has occurred but applying the guidance in Ind AS 110 does not clearly indicate which of the combining entities is the acquirer, the factors in paragraphs B14– B18 shall be considered in making that determination.

3.5.4.3. Determining the acquisition date

a)The acquirer shall identify the acquisition date, which is the date on which it obtains control of the acquiree.(Para 8)

b)The date on which the acquirer obtains control of the acquiree is generally the date on which the acquirer legally transfers the consideration, acquires the assets and assumes the liabilities of the acquiree—the closing date. However, the acquirer might obtain control on a date that is either earlier or later than the closing date. For example, the acquisition date precedes the closing date if a written agreement provides that the acquirer obtains control of the acquiree on a date before the closing date. An acquirer shall consider all pertinent facts and circumstances in identifying the acquisition date.(Para 9)

3.5.4.4. Recognising and measuring the identifiable assets acquired, the liabilities assumed and any non-controlling interest in the acquiree
3.5.4.4.1. Recognition principle

As of the acquisition date, the acquirer shall recognise, separately from goodwill, the identifiable assets acquired, the liabilities assumed and any non-controlling interest in the acquiree. Recognition of identifiable assets acquired and liabilities assumed is subject to the conditions specified in paragraphs 11 and 12.(Para 10)

According to Para 15 At the acquisition date, the acquirer shall classify or designate the identifiable assets acquired and liabilities assumed as necessary to apply other Ind ASs subsequently.

The acquirer shall make those classifications or designations on the basis of the contractual terms, economic conditions, its operating or accounting policies and other pertinent conditions as they exist at the acquisition date.

3.5.4.4.2. Recognition condition

a) the identifiable assets acquired and liabilities assumed must meet the definitions of assets and liabilities in the *Framework for the Preparation and Presentation of Financial Statements in accordance with Indian Accounting Standards* issued by the Institute of Chartered Accountants of India at the acquisition date.

ILLUSTRATION 30

Costs the acquirer expects but is not obliged to incur in the future to effect its plan to exit an activity of an acquiree or to terminate the employment of or relocate an acquiree's employees are not liabilities at the acquisition date. Therefore, the acquirer does not recognise those costs as part of applying the acquisition method. Instead, the acquirer recognises those costs in its post combination financial statements in accordance with other Ind AS.

b) the identifiable assets acquired and liabilities assumed must be part of what the acquirer and the acquiree (or its former *owners*) exchanged in the business combination transaction rather than the result of separate transactions.

3.5.5. Measurement principle

a) Para 18 The acquirer shall measure the identifiable assets acquired and the liabilities assumed at their acquisition-date fair values.

b)Para 19 For each business combination, the acquirer shall measure at the acquisition date components of non-controlling interest in the acquiree that are present ownership interests and entitle their holders to a proportionate share of the entity's net assets in the event of liquidation at either:

(a) fair value; or

(b) The present ownership instruments' proportionate share in the recognised amounts of the acquiree's identifiable net assets

All other components of non-controlling interests shall be measured at their acquisition date fair values, unless another measurement basis is required by Ind AS.

Any non-controlling interest in an acquiree is measured at fair value or as the non-controlling interest's proportionate share of the acquirers net identifiable assets.

3.5.6. Limited exceptions

- ➢ leases and insurance contracts are required to be classified on the basis of contractual terms and other factors at the inception of the contract (or when the terms have changed) rather than the factors existing on acquisition date
- ➢ only those contingent liabilities assumed in business combination that are a present obligation and can be measured reliably are recognized
- ➢ Some assets and liabilities are required to be recognized or measured in accordance with other Ind ASs , rather than at fair value. The assets and liabilities fall within the scope of Ind AS 12
- ➢ There are special requirements for measuring a reacquired right
- ➢ Indemnification of assets are recognized and measured on the basis that is consistent with the item that is subject to the indemnification, even if that measure is not fair value.

3.5.7. Goodwill

Para 32 of this Standard prescribes that, the acquirer shall recognise goodwill as of the acquisition date measured as the excess of (a) over (b) below:

(a) the aggregate of:

(i) the consideration transferred measured in accordance with this Ind AS, which generally requires acquisition-date fair value (see paragraph 37);

  (ii) the amount of any non-controlling interest in the acquiree measured
  in accordance with this Ind AS; and

  (iii) in a business combination achieved in stages (see paragraphs 41 and 42), the
  acquisition-date fair value of the acquirer's previously held equity interest in the
  acquiree.

(b) the net of the acquisition-date amounts of the identifiable assets acquired and
the liabilities assumed measured in accordance with this Ind AS.

3.5.8. Bargain purchase

In extremely rare circumstances where the fair value of net assets exceeds acquirer's interest, the resultant gain called " bargain purchase" shall be recognised by the acquirer in other comprehensive income on the acquisition date and accumulate the same in equity as capital reserve. The gain shall be attributed to the acquirer.

3.5.9. Consideration transferred

3.5.9.1. According to Para 37 The consideration transferred in a business combination shall be measured at fair value, which shall be calculated as the sum of the acquisition-date fair values of the assets transferred by the acquirer, the liabilities incurred by the acquirer to former owners of the acquiree and the equity interests issued by the acquirer.

Examples of potential forms of consideration include cash, other assets, a business or a subsidiary of the acquirer, *contingent consideration*, ordinary or preference equity instruments, options, warrants and member interests of *mutual entities*.

3.5.9.2. Contingent consideration

a) The consideration the acquirer transfers in exchange for the acquiree includes any asset or liability resulting from a contingent consideration arrangement (see paragraph 37). The acquirer shall recognise the acquisition-date fair value of contingent consideration as part of the consideration transferred in exchange for the acquiree.(Para 39)

b) The acquirer shall classify an obligation to pay contingent consideration that meets the definition of a financial instrument as a financial liability or as equity on the basis of the definitions of an equity instrument and a financial liability in paragraph 11 of Ind AS 32, *Financial Instruments: Presentation*. The acquirer shall classify as an asset a right to the return of previously transferred consideration if specified conditions are met. Paragraph 58 provides guidance on the subsequent accounting for contingent consideration.(Para 40)

c) According to Para 58 some changes in the fair value of contingent consideration that the acquirer recognises after the acquisition date may be the result of additional information that the acquirer obtained after that date about facts and circumstances that existed at the acquisition date.

Such changes are measurement period adjustments in accordance with paragraphs 45–49. However, changes resulting from events after the acquisition date, such as meeting an earnings target, reaching a specified share price or reaching a milestone on a research and development project, are not measurement period adjustments. The acquirer shall account for changes in the fair value of contingent consideration that are not measurement period adjustments as follows:

(a) Contingent consideration classified as equity shall not be remeasured and its subsequent settlement shall be accounted for within equity.

(b) Other contingent consideration that:

    (i) is within the scope of Ind AS 109 shall be measured at fair value at each reporting date and changes in fair value shall be recognised in profit or loss in accordance with Ind AS 109.

    (ii) is not within the scope of Ind AS 109 shall be measured at fair value at each reporting date and changes in fair value shall be recognised in profit or loss .

3.5.10. Additional guidance for applying the acquisition method to particular types of business combinations

The Standard additional guidance for applying acquisition method in the following types of business combinations:

a) A business combination achieved in stages

An acquirer sometimes obtains control of an acquiree in which it held an equity interest immediately before the acquisition date. For example, on 31 December 20X1, Entity A holds a 35 per cent non-controlling equity interest in Entity B. On that date, Entity A purchases an additional 40 per cent interest in Entity B, which gives it control of Entity B. This Ind AS refers to such a transaction as a business combination achieved in stages, sometimes also referred to as a step acquisition. (Para 41)

In a business combination achieved in stages, the acquirer shall re-measure its previously held equity interest in the acquiree at its acquisition-date fair value and recognise the resulting gain or loss, if any, in profit or loss or other comprehensive income, as appropriate (Para 42)

b) A business combination achieved without the transfer of consideration

An acquirer sometimes obtains control of an acquiree without transferring consideration. The acquisition method of accounting for a business combination applies to those combinations. Such circumstances include:

    (a) The acquiree repurchases a sufficient number of its own shares for an existing investor (the acquirer) to obtain control.

    (b) Minority veto rights lapse that previously kept the acquirer from controlling an acquiree in which the acquirer held the majority voting rights.

    (c) The acquirer and acquiree agree to combine their businesses by contract alone. The acquirer transfers no consideration in exchange for control of an acquiree and holds no equity interests in the acquiree, either on the acquisition date or previously. Examples of business combinations achieved by contract alone include bringing two businesses together in a stapling arrangement or forming a dual listed corporation.(Para 43)

In a business combination achieved by contract alone, the acquirer shall attribute to the owners of the acquiree the amount of the acquiree's net assets recognised in accordance with this Ind AS. In other words, the equity interests in the acquiree held by parties other than the acquirer are a non-controlling interest in the acquirer's post-combination financial statements even if the result is that all of the equity interests in the acquiree are attributed to the non-controlling interest.(Para 44)

3.5.11. Measurement period

a)If the initial accounting for a business combination is incomplete by the end of the reporting period in which the combination occurs, the acquirer shall report in its financial statements provisional amounts for the items for which the accounting is incomplete.

b)During the measurement period, the acquirer shall retrospectively adjust the provisional amounts recognised at the acquisition date to reflect new information obtained about facts and circumstances that existed as of the acquisition date and, if known, would have affected the measurement of the amounts recognised as of that date.

c)During the measurement period, the acquirer shall also recognise additional assets or liabilities if new information is obtained about facts and circumstances that existed as of the acquisition date and, if known, would have resulted in the recognition of those assets and liabilities as of that date.

d)The measurement period ends as soon as the acquirer receives the information it was seeking about facts and circumstances that existed as of the acquisition date or learns that more information is not obtainable. However, the measurement period shall not exceed one year from the acquisition date.

e) The measurement period provides the acquirer with a reasonable time to obtain the information necessary to identify and measure the following as of the acquisition date in accordance with the requirements of this Ind AS:

(a) the identifiable assets acquired, liabilities assumed and any non-controlling interest in the acquiree;

(b) the consideration transferred for the acquiree (or the other amount used in measuring goodwill);

(c) in a business combination achieved in stages, the equity interest in the acquiree previously held by the acquirer; and

(d) the resulting goodwill or gain on a bargain purchase.

3.5.12. Subsequent measurement and accounting

In general, an acquirer shall subsequently measure and account for assets acquired, liabilities assumed or incurred and equity instruments issued in a business combination in accordance with other applicable Ind ASs for those items, depending on their nature. However, this Ind AS provides guidance on subsequently measuring and accounting for the following assets acquired, liabilities assumed or incurred and equity instruments issued in a business combination:

(a) reacquired rights;

(b) contingent liabilities recognised as of the acquisition date;

(c) indemnification assets; and

(d) contingent consideration.

Paragraph B63 provides related application guidance as reproduced below:

Examples of other Ind ASs that provide guidance on subsequently measuring and accounting for assets acquired and liabilities assumed or incurred in a business combination include:

(a) Ind AS 38 prescribes the accounting for identifiable intangible assets acquired in a business combination. The acquirer measures goodwill at the amount recognised at the acquisition date less any accumulated impairment losses. Ind AS 36, *Impairment of Assets,* prescribes the accounting for impairment losses.

(b) Ind AS 104, *Insurance Contracts,* provides guidance on the subsequent accounting for an insurance contract acquired in a business combination.

(c) Ind AS 12 prescribes the subsequent accounting for deferred tax assets (including unrecognised deferred tax assets) and liabilities acquired in a business combination.

(d) Ind AS 102 provides guidance on subsequent measurement and accounting for the portion of replacement share-based payment awards issued by an acquirer that is attributable to employees' future services.

(e) Ind AS110 provides guidance on accounting for changes in a parent's ownership interest in a subsidiary after control is obtained.

3.5.13. Disclosure

i) The standard requires the acquirer to disclose information that enables users of its financial statements to evaluate the nature and financial effect of business combinations that occurred either:
   a) during the current reporting period or
   b) after the reporting date but before the financial statements are approved for issue.(Para 59)

   To meet the objective in paragraph 59, the acquirer shall disclose the information specified in paragraphs B64—B66 under Application guidance.

ii) The acquirer shall disclose information that enables users of its financial statements to evaluate the financial effects of adjustments recognised in the current reporting period that relate to business combinations that occurred in the period or previous reporting periods. (Para 61) Disclosure requirements of Para 61 are highlighted in Para B67 under Application guidance

3.5.14. Business combinations of entities under common control (Appendix C to Ind AS 103)

3.5.14.1. Scope

This appendix deals with accounting for business combinations of entities or businesses under common control.

3.5.14.2. Definitions

The following terms are used in this Appendix with the meaning specified:

Transferor means an entity or business which is combined into another entity as a result of a business combination.

Transferee means an entity in which the transferor entity is combined.

Reserve means the portion of earnings, receipts or other surplus of an entity (whether capital or revenue) appropriated by the management for a general or a specific purpose other than provision for depreciation.

Common control business combination means a business combination involving entities or businesses in which all the combining entities or businesses are ultimately controlled by the same party or parties both before and after the business combination, and that control is not transitory.

3.5.14.3. Common control Business Combinations

a) Common control business combinations will include transactions, such as transfer of subsidiaries or businesses, between entities within a group.

b)The extent of non-controlling interests in each of the combining entities before and after the business combination is not relevant to determining whether the combination involves entities under common control. This is because a partially-owned subsidiary is nevertheless under the control of the parent entity.

c)The fact that one of the combining entities is a subsidiary that has been excluded from the consolidated financial statements of the group in accordance with Ind AS 27 is not relevant to determining whether a combination involves entities under common control.

d)An entity can be controlled by an individual, or by a group of individuals acting together under a contractual arrangement, and that individual or group of individuals may not be subject to the financial reporting requirements of Ind ASs. Therefore, it is not necessary for combining entities to be included as part of the same consolidated financial statements for a business combination to be regarded as one having entities under common control.

e) A group of individuals are regarded as controlling an entity when, as a result of contractual arrangements, they collectively have the power to govern its financial and operating policies so as to obtain benefits from its activities, and that ultimate collective power is not transitory.

3.5.14.4. Method of accounting for common control business combinations

a) Business combinations involving entities or businesses under common control shall be accounted for using the pooling of interests method.

b) The pooling of interest method is considered to involve the following:

(i) The assets and liabilities of the combining entities are reflected at their carrying amounts.

(ii) No adjustments are made to reflect fair values, or recognise any new assets or liabilities. The only adjustments that are made are to harmonise accounting policies.

(iii) The financial information in the financial statements in respect of prior periods should be restated as if the business combination had occurred from the beginning of the preceding period in the financial statements, irrespective of the actual date of the combination. However, if business combination had occurred after that date, the prior period information shall be restated only from that date.

c) The consideration for the business combination may consist of securities, cash or other assets. Securities shall be recorded at nominal value. In determining the value of the consideration, assets other than cash shall be considered at their fair values.

d) The balance of the retained earnings appearing in the financial statements of the transferor is aggregated with the corresponding balance appearing in the financial statements of the transferee. Alternatively, it is transferred to General Reserve, if any.

e) The identity of the reserves shall be preserved and shall appear in the financial statements of the transferee in the same form in which they appeared in the financial statements of the transferor.

Thus, for example, the General Reserve of the transferor entity becomes the General Reserve of the transferee, the Capital Reserve of the transferor becomes the Capital Reserve of the transferee and the Revaluation Reserve of the transferor becomes the Revaluation Reserve of the transferee. As a result of preserving the identity, reserves which are available for distribution as dividend before the business combination would also be available for distribution as dividend after the business combination.

The difference, if any, between the amount recorded as share capital issued plus any additional consideration in the form of cash or other assets and the amount of share capital of the transferor shall be transferred to capital reserve and should be presented separately from other capital reserves with disclosure of its nature and purpose in the notes.

3.5.14.5. Disclosure
i) The following disclosures shall be made in the first financial statements following the business combination:
(a) names and general nature of business of the combining entities;
(b) the date on which the transferor obtains control of the transferee;
(c) description and number of shares issued, together with the percentage of each entity's equity shares exchanged to effect the business combination; and
(d) the amount of any difference between the consideration and the value of net identifiable assets acquired, and the treatment thereof.

3.5.14.6. Business combination after the balance sheet date
When a business combination is effected after the balance sheet but before the approval of the financial statements for issue by either party to the business combination, disclosure is made in accordance with Ind AS 10 *Events after the Reporting Period*, but the business combination is not incorporated in the financial statements. In certain circumstances, the business combination may also provide additional information affecting the financial statements themselves, for instance, by allowing the going concern assumption to be maintained.

3.5.14.7. Convergence with IFRS (Comparison with IFRS 3)
a) IFRS 3 excludes from its scope business combinations of entities under common control. Ind AS 103 (Appendix C) gives the guidance in this regard. Consequently, paragraph 2 has been modified and paragraph 2B has been added in Ind AS 103. Ind AS 103 (Appendix C) gives the guidance in this regard. Consequently, paragraph 2 has been modified and paragraph 2B has been added in Ind AS 103.

b) The transitional provisions given in IFRS 3 have not been given in Ind AS 103, since all transitional provisions related to Ind ASs, wherever considered appropriate have been included in Ind AS101, *First-time Adoption of Indian Accounting Standards,* corresponding to IFRS 1, *First-time Adoption of International Financial Reporting Standards*, will deal with the same.

c) IFRS 3 requires bargain purchase gain arising on business combination to be recognised in profit or loss. Ind AS 103 requires the same to be recognised in other comprehensive income and accumulated in equity as capital reserve, unless there is no clear evidence for the underlying reason for classification of the business combination as a bargain purchase, in which case, it shall be recognised directly in equity as capital reserve. This has some consequential changes such as change in wording of paragraphs 34, 36 and 48, additional disclosure in paragraph B64(n) and addition of new paragraph 36A. Cross-reference to the new paragraph 36A has been added in paragraphs B46, B64(n).

3.5.14.8. Case studies: Business Combinations
1. On 1 October 2007 Omega purchased 8 million of Target's 12 million equity shares. The acquisition was financed as follows:
A cash payment of Rs.2·00 per share, Rs.1·20 per share being payable on 1 October 2007

and Rs.0·80 being payable on 30 September 2008. Any discounting calculations should be performed using a cost of capital of 8% per annum.

A share exchange of 1 equity share in Omega for every 2 shares acquired in Target. The market value of a Target share was Rs.3·90 on 1 October 2007. The market values of an Omega share were Rs.4 on 1 October 2007 and Rs.4·20 on 31 March 2008.

A further share issue by Omega on 30 September 2008 of 1 share for every 8 shares acquired in Target provided the profits after tax of Target exceeded a given figure. Estimates indicate that this share issue is likely to be made.

Omega incurred acquisition costs of Rs.600,000. Rs.350,000 of these costs were external due diligence costs, Rs.100,000 were Omega's best estimate of management time spent in negotiating the acquisition, and Rs.150,000 were costs incurred in connection with the issue of Omega's shares.

The directors of Omega carried out a fair value exercise on 1 October 2007 and the following matters emerged:

The net assets of Target that were recognised in Target's own financial statements were Rs.30 million based on their carrying values in the individual financial statements of Target.

On 1 October 2007 the carrying value of Target's freehold property was Rs.15 million. The property had been purchased on 1 October 1997 for Rs.17·5 million and the buildings element of the property (allocated cost Rs.10 million) was being depreciated over its estimated useful economic life of 40 years. On 1 October 2007 the market value of the property was Rs.22 million, of which Rs.12 million related to the buildings element. The original estimate of the useful economic life of the buildings is still considered valid.

On 1 October 2007 Target was engaged in contracts with three different customers under which they supplied each customer for a five year period from 1 October 2007. The directors of Omega believe that this creates an intangible asset with a fair value of Rs.7·5 million. In addition the directors of Omega believe that the fair value of the assembled workforce of Target creates an intangible asset with a fair value of Rs.15 million. The average remaining working life of the employees of Target at 1 October 2007 is 15 years. Neither of these intangible assets has been recognised in the individual financial statements of Target.

At 1 October 2007 Target was engaged in a legal dispute with a customer. The directors of Target consider that the case can be successfully defended and have made no provision for legal costs in its financial statements. The directors of Omega estimated that the fair value of the claim at 1 October 2007 was Rs.600,000. Events since 1 October 2007 have reduced this estimate to Rs.500,000 by 31 March 2008 (these events do not affect the fair value of the claim at 1 October 2007).

Due to the acquisition of Target the directors of Omega intend to reorganise the group, starting in June 2009.

The estimated cost of this reorganisation is Rs.20 million.

In the year ended 31 March 2008 Target reported a post-tax profit of Rs.6 million (accruing evenly over the period) and paid a dividend of Rs.1·5 million on 31 December 2007 out of post-acquisition profits. The retained earnings of Omega at 31 March 2008 were Rs.18 million. This figure includes the dividend received from Target but does not include any other adjustments to its own earnings that are required as a result of the acquisition of Target.

The acquisition costs of Rs.600,000 referred to above have been charged to retained earnings by Omega. Omega has no subsidiaries other than Target and no associates or joint venture entities.

The goodwill on acquisition of Target had not suffered any impairment at 31 March 2008.

Required:

(i) Compute the goodwill on acquisition of Target as initially measured at 1 October 2007.

(ii) Compute the balance of retained earnings that will be shown in the consolidated statement of financial position of Omega at 31 March 2008.

Note: your figures should be supported by appropriate explanations, both for amounts you include and for amounts you exclude. (*ACCA UK – Adapted*)

Solution

All values in Rs'000

(i) computation of original goodwill on acquisition of Target

Fair value of consideration given (W1)	35,876
8/12 of fair value of net assets acquired (W2)	(29,267)
So goodwill equals	6,609

Working 1 – fair value of consideration given

		Explanation
Immediate cash payment	9,600	Actual amount paid
Deferred cash payment	5,926	Present value of actual amount payable
Share exchange	16,000	4 million shares issued at a market value of Rs.4 per share 1
Contingent consideration	4,000	Include as share issue probable. Present value is implied in the share price
Acquisition costs	350	Direct costs of the acquisition other than the costs of issuing shares
	35,876	

Working 2 – fair value of net assets acquired

		Explanation
As per financial statements of Target	30,000	
Adjustment for property	7,000	Market value exceeds carrying value by 7,000
Adjustment for customer relationships	7,500	An identifiable intangible asset with a measurable fair value
Adjustment for workforce	Nil	Per Ind AS 38 – *intangible assets* – assembled workforce fails the 'control test'
Adjustment for re-organisation	Nil	per Ind AS 103 – *business combinations* – must treat as post-acquisition items
Adjustment for contingency	(600)	Per Ind AS 103 include at fair value
	43,900	

(ii) computation of consolidated retained earnings at 31 March 2008

		Explanation
Omega – as given	18,000	
Interest charge on deferred cash consideration	(237)	5,926 x 8% x 6/12 1
Re organisation provision	Nil	Per Ind AS 37 – *provisions, contingent liabilities and contingent assets* – an intention is not an obligation
Adjustment acquisition costs	500	Per Ind AS 103 350 included in cost of investment and 150 deducted from share premium
	18,263	
Target (6,000 x 6/12)	3,000	Only post-acquisition earnings included
Dividend	(1,500)	Paid out of post-acquisition profits
Extra depreciation on building (W1)	(75)	
Amortisation of customer relationship asset	(750)	7,500 x 1/5 x 6/12
Reduction in fair value of contingency	100	A post-acquisition item
	775	
775 x 8/12 equals	517	
So total consolidated retained earnings equals	**18,780**	

ii) computation of consolidated retained earnings at 31 March 2008
Working 1 – extra depreciation on building

New annual depreciation charge 12,000 x 1/30	400
Previous annual depreciation charge 10,000 x 1/40	(250)
So excess annual charge equals	150
150 x 6/12 equals	75

2. On 1 October 2006 Omega acquired a new subsidiary, Sigma, purchasing all 150 million shares of Sigma. The terms of the sale agreement included the exchange of four shares in Omega for every three shares acquired in Sigma. On 1 October 2006 the market value of a share in Omega was Rs.10 and the market value of a share in Sigma Rs.12·00.

The terms of the share purchase included the issue of one additional share in Omega for every five acquired Sigma if the profits of Sigma for the two years ending 30 September 2008 exceeded a target figure. Current estimates are that it is 80% probable that the management of Sigma will achieve this target.

Legal and professional fees associated with the acquisition of Sigma shares were Rs.1, 200,000, including Rs.200,000 relating to the cost of issuing shares. The senior management of Omega estimate that the cost of their time that can be fairly allocated to the acquisition is Rs.200,000. This figure of Rs.200,000 is not included in the legal and professional fees of $1,200,000 mentioned above.

The individual balance sheet of Sigma at 1 October 2006 comprised net assets that had a fair value at that date of Rs.1,200 million. Additionally Omega considered Sigma possessed certain intangible assets that were not recognised in its individual balance sheet:

Customer relationships – reliable estimate of value Rs.100 million. This value has been derived from the sale of customer databases in the past.

An in process research and development project that had not been recognised by Sigma since the necessary conditions laid down in International Financial Reporting Standards for capitalisation were only just satisfied at 30 September 2007. However, the fair value of the whole project (including the research phase) is estimated at Rs.50 million.

Employee expertise – directors' estimate of value Rs.80 million. The market value of a share in Omega on 30 September 2007 was Rs.11.

Required:

Compute the goodwill on consolidation of Sigma that will appear in the consolidated balance sheet of Omega at 30 September 2007. (ACCA – UK Adapted)

Solution

Cost of investment (Values in Rs'000)

Market value of shares issued (150 million x 4/3 x Rs.10)	2,000,000
Initial estimate of market value of shares to be issued (150 million x 1/5 x Rs.10)	300,000
Subsequent adjustment to contingent consideration (30 million x (Rs.11 – Rs.10))	30,000
Incremental acquisition costs other than the issue cost of shares	1,000
Total	2,331,000

Comments – all refer to Ind AS 103 – *Business combinations*

Shares issued are recorded at their market value at the date of issue. Contingent consideration is recognised in full if payment is probable.

Where material, future consideration is measured at the present value of the amount payable. In the case of shares to be issued, this is represented by the share price. Where the estimated value of contingent consideration changes then this is recorded as an adjustment to goodwill.

Incremental costs associated with the acquisition, other than the issue costs of financial instruments, can be included in the cost of the investment.

Fair value of identifiable net assets at the date of acquisition	
As per Sigma's balance sheet	1,200,000
Fair value of customer relationships	100,000
Fair value of research and development project	50,000
Total	1,350,000

Comments

Under Ind AS 38 – *Intangible assets* – intangible assets can be recognised separately from *goodwill provided they* are identifiable, are under the control of the acquiring entity, and their fair value can be measured reliably.

Customer relationships that are similar in nature to those previously traded pass these tests but employee relationships fail the 'control' test. Both the research and development phases of an in process project can be capitalised provided their fair value can be measured reliably.

Calculation of goodwill

Fair value of consideration given	2,331,000
Fair value of net assets acquired	(1,350,000)

So goodwill on acquisition equals	981,000

Comments
Under Ind AS 103 goodwill is not written down unless impairment is evident.

3. Epsilon has an 80% subsidiary that it acquired on 31 March 2005 for a cash payment of Rs.80 million. The fair value exercise revealed that the fair value of the identifiable net assets of the subsidiary at that date was Rs.90 million. The fair value adjustments were incorporated into the individual financial statements of the subsidiary at 31 March 2005.
The summarised balance sheet of the subsidiary at 31 March 2007 showed the following balances:

	Rs'000
Non-current assets	100,000
Current assets	30,000
	130,000
Equity	85,000
Non-current liabilities	35,000
Current liabilities	10,000
	130,000

Your assistant is aware that the goodwill of the subsidiary had not suffered any impairment loss when it was tested for impairment at 31 March 2006. However he is unsure what this means. He also provides you with the information that the value in use of the non-current assets of the subsidiary (a single cash-generating unit) is Rs.97 million, and that one of the non-current assets (included in the above balance sheet at a carrying value of Rs.4 million) has been destroyed and is in fact worthless.

Solution
The consolidated balance sheet at 31 March will include the assets and liabilities of the subsidiary and the consolidated income statement will include its income and expenses. However the non-current assets of the subsidiary will need to be reduced by Rs.4 million to reflect the destruction and consequent loss of value. This will lead to a charge of Rs.4 million in the consolidated income statement.
The original goodwill on acquisition of the subsidiary was Rs.8 million (Rs.80 million – 80% x Rs.90 million). Ind AS 103 – *Business combinations* – requires that purchased goodwill be reviewed annually for impairment using the principles of Ind IAS 36 – *Impairment of assets*. This involves computing the recoverable amount of the asset. This is the higher of the net selling price of the asset (not applicable in the case of goodwill since it cannot be sold separately) and its value in use – the present value of the future cash flows derivable from the asset. For many assets – including goodwill – it is not possible to attribute cash flows to individual assets but rather to groups of assets – referred to in Ind AS 36 as cash generating units. In this case the goodwill is located in a cash generating unit together with the non-current assets. The calculation of the impairment loss is as follows:

Rs.m

Carrying value of non-current assets	100
Related goodwill – group share	8
Notionally allocated to minority interest	2
	110
Value-in-use	(97)
So total impairment	13

Rs.4 million of this impairment is allocated to the specifically impaired non-current asset and the balance of Rs.9 million to goodwill. Since the goodwill relates to an 80% share the impairment will be 80% x Rs.9 million = Rs.7·2 million. This means that the new carrying value of the goodwill will be Rs.0·8 million (Rs.8 million – Rs.7·2 million).

4. Kappa is an entity that regularly purchases subsidiaries. Kappa prepares financial statements to 30 September each year. In its year ended 30 September 2003 Kappa purchased a new subsidiary, Omega, and began to amortise the goodwill on consolidation of Omega over an estimated useful economic life of 20 years.

On 30 June 2005 the entity acquired all the 100 million equity shares of Lambda by issuing one share in Kappa for every two shares acquired in Lambda. On 30 June 2005 the market value of a Kappa share was Rs.5·40 and the market value of Lambda share Rs.2·40.

The directors of Lambda prepared a balance sheet as at 30 June 2005 and the net assets of Lambda that were included were measured at Rs.180 million (their fair values at that date). The directors of Kappa noted that the following assets of Lambda had not been included in the draft balance sheet prepared by the directors:

(i) Internally developed brands having an identifiable fair value of Rs.10 million at 30 June 2005.

(ii) The value of future services of existing employees that was estimated to have a value of Rs.15 million at 30 June 2005.

Required:

(a) Calculate the goodwill arising on initial consolidation of Lambda at 30 June 2005 and explain (without performing any calculations) how its carrying amount at 30 September 2005 would be measured. You should refer to relevant International Financial Reporting Standards to support your conclusions. (ACCA UK – Adapted)

Solution

a) The goodwill on consolidation is the difference between the fair value of the consideration given and the fair value of the identifiable net assets acquired. The fair value of the consideration given is Rs.270m (50m x Rs.5·40).

The fair value of the identifiable net assets acquired is Rs.190m (Rs.180m + Rs.10m). Ind AS 38 – *Intangible Assets* – *states that* most intangibles that satisfy the definition of assets will be regarded as identifiable when acquired as part of the acquisition of a business. This would certainly apply to brands which, from the perspective of Kappa, have been acquired as part of the acquisition of Lambda. However the estimated value of future services of employees could not be regarded as an identifiable asset because enterprises do not normally have sufficient control over the potential benefits derivable from those services – the employees can normally leave.

Therefore the goodwill on consolidation is Rs.80m (Rs.270m – Rs.190m). Under the provisions of Ind AS 103 – *Business Combinations* – *the goodwill is not amortised but reviewed annually for impairment. Thus at 30 September 2005 goodwill* will be measured at its cost of Rs.80m less any necessary impairment. It can never be revalued.

5.On 1st April 20X1, S acquired 100% of ordinary share capital in two subsidiary companies, H and M in separate acquisitions. Consolidated goodwill is as under:

	H (Rs'000)	M (Rs'000)
Purchase consideration	12000	4500
Estimated fair value of net assets	(8000)	(3000)
Consolidated goodwill	4000	1500

A review of fair value of each subsidiary's net assets was undertaken in March 20X2. Unfortunately both co's net assets declined in value. Estimated value of its net assets as At 1.4.20X1 was only Rs.7 m. M's net assets were estimated to have a fair value of Rs. 500000 less than the carrying value. The fall is due to some physical damage occurring to its Plant & Machinery. Comment.

Solution
Under Ind AS 103 Business Combination, on acquisition of a subsidiary, purchase consideration should be allocated to fair value of net assets and the balance should go to goodwill (or negative goodwill if assets have a greater fair value than purchase consideration). Ind AS 103 recognizes that it is always not possible to assess the value of assets accurately during date of acquisition. Therefore provisional accounting can be made within 12 months of acquisition. Hence in case of H , estimated fair value would be Rs.7 m and goodwill at Rs.5 m respectively, the fall of Rs.1 m is not an impairment loss and should not be charged to Income statement.
In the case of M, since fair value of assets have reduced by Rs.500000, the carrying value owing to some physical damage of the Plant. Plant & Machinery should be written down to Recoverable value and impairment loss charged to Income statement. However, since the Recoverable value of the Company has not fallen, goodwill will not be impaired.

3.6. Ind AS 111 Joint Arrangements

Learning Outcomes
- **Objective**
- **Scope**
- **Definitions**
- **Major changes highlighted in Ind AS 111 related to Joint venture accounting**
- **Joint arrangements**
- **Types of joint arrangement**
- **Financial statements of parties to a joint arrangement**
- **Joint operation**
- **Joint ventures**

3.6.1. Objective

The objective of this Indian Accounting Standard (Ind AS) is to establish principles for financial reporting by entities that have an interest in arrangements that are controlled jointly (i.e. *joint arrangements*).

This Standard defines *joint control* and requires an entity that is a *party to a joint arrangement* to determine the type of joint arrangement in which it is involved by assessing its rights and obligations and to account for those rights and obligations in accordance with that type of joint arrangement.

3.6.2. Scope

This Ind AS shall be applied by all entities that are a party to a joint arrangement.

3.6.3. Definitions (Appendix A to Ind AS 111)

Item	Description
joint arrangement	An arrangement of which two or more parties have **joint control.**
joint control	The contractually agreed sharing of control of an arrangement, which exists only when decisions about the relevant activities require the unanimous consent of the parties sharing control.
joint operation	A **joint arrangement** whereby the parties that have **joint control** of the arrangement have rights to the assets, and obligations for the liabilities, relating to the arrangement
joint operator	A party to a **joint operation** that has **joint control** of that joint operation.
joint venture	A **joint arrangement** whereby the parties that have **joint control** of the arrangement have rights to the net assets of the arrangement.
joint venturer	A party to a **joint venture** that has **joint control** of that joint venture.
party to a joint arrangement	An entity that participates in a **joint arrangement**, regardless of whether that entity has **joint control** of the arrangement.
Separate vehicle	A separately identifiable financial structure, including separate legal entities or entities recognised by statute, regardless of whether those entities have a legal personality.

3.6.4. Major changes highlighted in Ind AS 111 related to Joint venture accounting

a)Reason for new standard	According to previous standard -Ind AS 31, the classification of entity (as jointly controlled entity) was dependent on existence of separate vehicle, substance of the arrangement was not considered.
	Jointly controlled entity allowed both proportionate consolidation and equity accounting. Often co-venturers did not have direct rights over assets and obligations for liabilities, proportional consolidation not appropriate
	Common belief: little difference between investment in joint ventures and investment in associates

b)Major changes to joint venture accounting	Joint ventures will no longer be classified as jointly controlled operations, jointly controlled assets and jointly controlled entities
	Joint arrangements are classified as either joint operations or joint ventures, the accounting treatment will depend on classification
	Proportionate consolidation is not permitted for joint ventures as defined by the new standard
	Joint ventures that are accounted for using proportionate consolidation method under the earlier Ind AS will be accounted for using the equity method under Ind AS 111
	A joint operator is required to recognise certain items in relation to its interest in a joint operation as under: - Its assets, including its share of any assets held jointly - Its liabilities, including its share of any liabilities incurred jointly - Its revenue from sale of its share of the output of the joint operation - Its share of the revenue from the sale of the output by the joint operation - Its expenses, including its share of any expenses incurred jointly

3.6.5. Joint Arrangement
As defined above, joint arrangement is an arrangement of which two or more parties have joint control.
A joint arrangement has the following characteristics:
(a) The parties are bound by a contractual arrangement
(b) The contractual arrangement gives two or more of those parties joint control of the arrangement

3.6.6. Types of Joint arrangement
a) **A joint arrangement** is either a *joint operation* or a *joint venture*.
b)An entity shall determine the type of joint arrangement in which it is involved. The classification of a joint arrangement as a joint operation or a joint venture depends upon the rights and obligations of the parties to the arrangement.
c) *A joint operation* is a joint arrangement whereby the parties that have joint control of the arrangement have rights to the assets, and obligations for the liabilities, relating to the arrangement. Those parties are called joint operators.

d) **A joint venture** is a joint arrangement whereby the parties that have joint control of the arrangement have rights to the net assets of the arrangement. Those parties are called joint venturers.

3.6.7. Comparative Accounting treatment related to types of joint arrangements

The accounting treatment related to types of **joint arrangements** is shown in the table below as per classification prescribed under Ind AS 111:

Joint operations	Joint venture
Characteristic	**Characteristic**
Each joint operator may: a)use its own property, plant and equipment b)carry its own inventories c)incur own expenses and liabilities d)raise its own finance, which represents its own obligations Alternatively, each joint operator may have joint control and often joint ownership of one or more assets: a)contributed to or acquired for the purpose of the joint arrangement, and b)dedicated to the purposes of the arrangement According to joint venture agreement, each joint operator may take a share of the output from the assets and each bears an agreed share of the revenues earned and expenses incurred	In this type of joint arrangements, the venturers establish a corporation, partnership or other separate entity in order to undertake an economic activity The entities operate in the same way as other entities. The only distinguishing feature is that there exists contract between the venturers in order to establish joint control over the financial and operating decisions related to the activity.
Accounting treatment A joint operator would recognise in its books: a)its assets, including its share of assets held jointly, b) its liabilities, including its share of assets held jointly, c)its revenues from the sale of its share of the output of the joint operation, d)its share of the revenue from the sale of the output by the joint operation , and e)its expenses, including its share of any expenses incurred jointly A joint operator accounts for the assets, liabilities, revenues and expenses related to its involvement in joint operation in accordance with the relevant IFRSs. A joint arrangement which is not in the form of a separate vehicle –e.g. a separate legal entity, would compulsorily be treated as joint operation.	**Accounting treatment** Joint venture has to maintain its own accounting records and prepare and present financial statements in the same way as other entities according to the requirements of the IFRSs. Each venturer usually contributes cash or other resources to the joint venture. These contributions are included in the accounting records of the venturer and recognised in its financial statements as an investment in the joint venture. A venturer needs to recognise its interest in a joint venture using the equity method.
Legal form If in accordance with the legal form, parties are conferred direct rights to assets and obligation to its liabilities, then it is a joint operation	**Legal form** If the arrangement is structured through a separate vehicle it becomes a joint venture

Contractual arrangement	Contractual arrangement
If in accordance with the contractual arrangement, parties have rights to assets and obligation for liabilities – and not the entity – then the arrangement is a joint operation	If no such contractual arrangement is there, but is covered by a separate legal entity it is a joint venture

ILLUSTRATION 31

Assume that three parties establish an arrangement: A has 50 per cent of the voting rights in the arrangement, B has 30 per cent and C has 20 per cent. The contractual arrangement between A, B and C specifies that at least 75 per cent of the voting rights are required to make decisions about the relevant activities of the arrangement. Even though A can block any decision, it does not control the arrangement because it needs the agreement of B. The terms of their contractual arrangement requiring at least 75 per cent of the voting rights to make decisions about the relevant activities imply that A and B have joint control of the arrangement because decisions about the relevant activities of the arrangement cannot be made without both A and B agreeing.

ILLUSTRATION 32

Assume an arrangement has three parties: A has 50 per cent of the voting rights in the arrangement and B and C each have 25 per cent. The contractual arrangement between A, B and C specifies that at least 75 per cent of the voting rights are required to make decisions about the relevant activities of the arrangement. Even though A can block any decision, it does not control the arrangement because it needs the agreement of either B or C. In this example, A, B and C collectively control the arrangement. However, there is more than one combination of parties that can agree to reach 75 per cent of the voting rights (ie either A and B or A and C). In such a situation, to be a joint arrangement the contractual arrangement between the parties would need to specify which combination of the parties is required to agree unanimously to decisions about the relevant activities of the arrangement.

ILLUSTRATION 33

Assume an arrangement in which A and B each have 35 per cent of the voting rights in the arrangement with the remaining 30 per cent being widely dispersed. Decisions about the relevant activities require approval by a majority of the voting rights. A and B have joint control of the arrangement only if the contractual arrangement specifies that decisions about the relevant activities of the arrangement require both A and B agreeing.

3.6.8. Decision tree on assessing Joint control

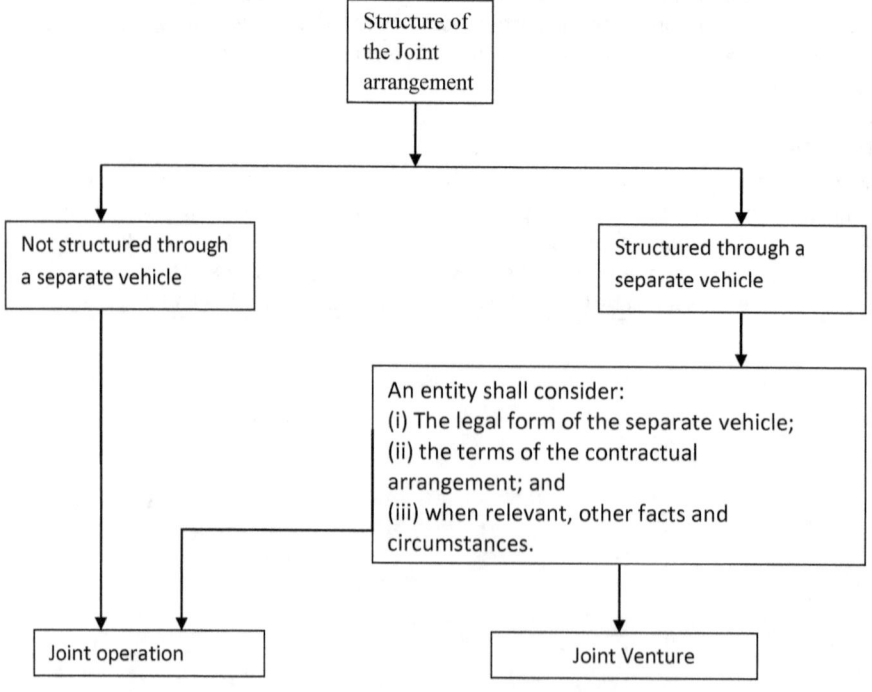

When an arrangement is outside the scope of Ind AS 111, an entity accounts for its interest in the arrangement in accordance with relevant Ind ASs, such as Ind AS 110, Ind AS 28 or Ind AS 109.

3.6.9. Classification of a joint arrangement: assessment of the parties' rights and obligations arising from the arrangement

The legal form and structure of joint arrangement would like as follows:

ILLUSTRATION 34

Let us assume that two parties structure a joint arrangement in an incorporated entity. Each party has a 50 per cent ownership interest in the incorporated entity. The incorporation enables the separation of the entity from its owners and as a consequence the assets and liabilities held in the entity are the assets and liabilities of the incorporated entity. In such a case, the assessment of the rights and obligations conferred upon the parties by the legal form of the separate vehicle indicates that the parties have rights to the net assets of the arrangement.

However, the parties modify the features of the corporation through their contractual arrangement so that each has an interest in the assets of the incorporated entity and each is liable for the liabilities of the incorporated entity in a specified proportion. Such contractual modifications to the features of a corporation can cause an arrangement to be a joint operation.

ILLUSTRATION 35: Joint Operation

Two parties structure a joint arrangement in an incorporated entity (entity C) in which each party has a 50 per cent ownership interest. The purpose of the arrangement is to manufacture materials required by the parties for their own, individual manufacturing processes. The arrangement ensures that the parties operate the facility that produces the materials to the quantity and quality specifications of the parties.

The legal form of entity C (an incorporated entity) through which the activities are conducted initially indicates that the assets and liabilities held in entity C are the assets and liabilities of entity C. The contractual arrangement between the parties does not specify that the parties have rights to the assets or obligations for the liabilities of entity C. Accordingly, the legal form of entity C and the terms of the contractual arrangement indicate that the arrangement is a joint venture.

However, the parties also consider the following aspects of the arrangement:

a) The parties agreed to purchase all the output produced by entity C in a ratio of 50:50. Entity C cannot sell any of the output to third parties, unless this is approved by the two parties to the arrangement. Because the purpose of the arrangement is to provide the parties with output they require, such sales to third parties are expected to be uncommon and not material.

b) The price of the output sold to the parties is set by both parties at a level that is designed to cover the costs of production and administrative expenses incurred by entity C. On the basis of this operating model, the arrangement is intended to operate at a break-even level.

From the fact pattern above, the following facts and circumstances are relevant:

a) The obligation of the parties to purchase all the output produced by entity C reflects the exclusive dependence of entity C upon the parties for the generation of cash flows and, thus, the parties have an obligation to fund the settlement of the liabilities of entity C.

b)The fact that the parties have rights to all the output produced by entity C means that the parties are consuming, and therefore have rights to, all the economic benefits of the assets of entity C.

These facts and circumstances indicate that the arrangement is a joint operation. The conclusion about the classification of the joint arrangement in these circumstances would not change if, instead of the parties using their share of the output themselves in a subsequent manufacturing process, the parties sold their share of the output to third parties.

If the parties changed the terms of the contractual arrangement so that the arrangement was able to sell output to third parties, this would result in entity C assuming demand, inventory and credit risks. In that scenario, such a change in the facts and circumstances would require reassessment of the classification of the joint arrangement. Such facts and circumstances would indicate that the arrangement is a joint venture.

3.6.10. Comparative analysis of the various entities in consolidation of financial statements

Investment	Nature	Accounting treatment
Investment > 50% control	Subsidiary	Full consolidation – line by line
Significant influence – between > 20% and < 50%	Associate	Equity method
In case of joint control	Joint venture	Equity method
In case of joint control	Joint operation	Share of assets, liabilities, income and expenses in a joint operation
< 20% investment and not a joint venture	None of the above	Treatment in accordance with Ind AS 109

3.6.11. Convergence with IFRS (Comparison with IFRS 11)

1. Appendix C of IFRS 11 dealing with effective date, transition and withdrawal of other IFRSs has not been included in Ind AS 111, due to the following reasons:

   (i) Effective date is not relevant as the date of application will be notified under the Companies Act.

   (ii) Transitional provisions related to Ind ASs, wherever considered appropriate have been included in Ind AS 101, *First-time Adoption of Indian Accounting Standards,* corresponding to IFRS 1, *First-time Adoption of International Financial Reporting Standards.*

   (iii) The paragraph which relate to withdrawal of other IFRSs is not relevant.

2 Paragraph B33D refers to the accounting specified in Appendix C 'Business Combinations under Common Control' of Ind AS 103 for the acquisition of an interest in a joint operation when the parties sharing joint control, including the entity acquiring the interest in the joint operation, are under the common control of the same ultimate controlling party or parties both before and after the acquisition, and that control is not transitory. IFRS 11 scopes out the same as IFRS 3, *Business Combinations,* does not deal with business combinations under common control.

3.7. Ind AS 112: *Disclosure of Interests in Other Entities*

Learning Outcomes
- **Objective**
- **Scope**
- **Significant judgement and assumptions**
- **Interest in subsidiaries**
- **Interests in unconsolidated subsidiaries (investment entities)**
- **Interests in joint arrangements and associates**
- **Interests in unconsolidated structured entities**

3.7.1. Objective
The objective of this Indian Accounting Standard (Ind AS) is to require an entity to disclose information that enables users of its financial statements to evaluate:
(a) the nature of, and risks associated with, its *interests in other entities*; and
(b) the effects of those interests on its financial position, financial performance and cash flows.
To achieve the objective of this Standard the entity would disclose the following:
(a) the significant judgements and assumptions it has made in determining:
      (i) the nature of its interest in another entity or arrangement;
      (ii) the type of joint arrangement in which it has an interest;
      (iii) that it meets the definition of an investment entity, if applicable; and
(b) information about its interests in:
      (i) subsidiaries;
      (ii) arrangements and associates; and
      (iii) *structured entities* that are not controlled by the entity (unconsolidated structured entities).

3.7.2. Scope
This Ind AS will be applied to an entity that has interest in any one of the following:
      (a) subsidiaries
      (b) joint arrangements (ie joint operations or joint ventures)
      (c) associates
      (d) unconsolidated structured entities.
This Ind AS does not apply to:
(a) post-employment benefit plans or other long-term employee benefit plans to which Ind AS 19, *Employee Benefits,* applies.
(b) an entity's separate financial statements to which Ind AS 27, *Separate Financial Statements,* applies. However, if an entity has interests in unconsolidated structured entities and prepares separate financial statements as its only financial statements, it shall apply the requirements of this Standard when preparing those separate financial statements.
(c) an interest held by an entity that participates in, but does not have joint control of, a joint arrangement unless that interest results in significant influence over the arrangement or is an interest in a structured entity.
(d) an interest in another entity that is accounted for in accordance with Ind AS 109, *Financial Instruments.* However, an entity shall apply this Ind AS:

(i) when that interest is an interest in an associate or a joint venture that, in accordance with Ind AS 28, *Investments in Associates and Joint Ventures*, is measured at fair value through profit or loss; or

(ii) when that interest is an interest in an unconsolidated structured entity.

3.7.3. Definitions (Appendix A to Ind AS 112)

Item	Description
income from a structured entity	Includes, but is not limited to, recurring and non-recurring fees, interest, dividends, gains or losses on the re-measurement or derecognition of interests in structured entities and gains or losses from the transfer of assets and liabilities to the structured entity.
interest in another entity	An interest in another entity refers to contractual and non-contractual involvement that exposes an entity to variability of returns from the performance of the other entity.
	An interest in another entity can be evidenced by, but is not limited to, the holding of equity or debt instruments as well as other forms of involvement such as the provision of funding, liquidity support, credit enhancement and guarantees.
	It includes the means by which an entity has control or joint control of, or significant influence over, another entity. An entity does not necessarily have an interest in another entity solely because of a typical customer supplier relationship.
structured entity	An entity that has been designed so that voting or similar rights are not the dominant factor in deciding who controls the entity, such as when any voting rights relate to administrative tasks only and the relevant activities are directed by means of contractual arrangements.
Associate **Consolidated financial statements** **Control of an entity** **Equity method** **Group** **Investment entity** **Joint arrangement** **Joint control** **Joint operation** **Joint venture** **Non-controlling interest** **Parent** **Protective rights** **Relevant activities** **Separate financial statements**	These terms are defined in Ind AS 27 , Ind AS 28 , Ind AS 110 and Ind AS 111, *Joint Arrangements,* and are used in this Ind AS with the meanings specified in those Ind ASs

Separate vehicle Significant influence Subsidiary.	

3.7.4. Significant judgement and assumptions

An entity shall disclose information about significant judgements and assumptions it has made (and changes to those judgements and assumptions) in determining:
- (a) that it has control of another entity, I.e. an investee as described in Ind AS 110, *Consolidated Financial Statements*;
- (b) that it has joint control of an arrangement or significant influence over another entity; and
- (c) the type of joint arrangement (i.e. joint operation or joint venture) when the arrangement has been structured through a separate vehicle.

3.7.5. Interest in subsidiaries by Parent

An entity shall disclose information that enables users of its consolidated financial statements
(a) to understand:
    (i) the composition of the group; and
    (ii) the interest that non-controlling interests have in the group's activities and cash flows and
(b) to evaluate:
(i) the nature and extent of significant restrictions on its ability to access or use assets, and settle liabilities, of the group;
(ii) the nature of, and changes in, the risks associated with its interests in consolidated structured entities;
(iii) the consequences of changes in its ownership interest in a subsidiary that do not result in a loss of control; and
(iv) the consequences of losing control of a subsidiary during the reporting period

3.7.6. The interest that non-controlling interests have in the group's activities and cash Flows

An entity shall disclose for each of its subsidiaries that have non-controlling interests that are material to the reporting entity:
(a) the name of the subsidiary.
(b) the principal place of business (and country of incorporation if different from the principal place of business) of the subsidiary.
(c) the proportion of ownership interests held by non-controlling interests.
(d) the proportion of voting rights held by non-controlling interests, if different from the proportion of ownership interests held.
(e) the profit or loss allocated to non-controlling interests of the subsidiary during the reporting period.
(f) accumulated non-controlling interests of the subsidiary at the end of the reporting period.
(g) summarised financial information about the subsidiary

3.7.7. Consequences of changes in a parent's ownership interest in a subsidiary during reporting period

that do not result in a loss of control	Results in losing control
An entity shall present a schedule that shows the effects on the equity attributable to owners of the parent of any changes in its ownership interest in a subsidiary that do not result in a loss of control.	An entity shall disclose the gain or loss, if any, calculated in accordance with Ind AS 110, and: (a) the portion of that gain or loss attributable to measuring any investment retained in the former subsidiary at its fair value at the date when control is lost; and (b) the line item(s) in profit or loss in which the gain or loss is recognised (if not presented separately).

3.7.8. Interests in unconsolidated subsidiaries (investment entities)

i)For each unconsolidated subsidiary, an investment entity shall disclose:
(a) the subsidiary's name;
(b) the principal place of business (and country of incorporation if different from the principal place of business) of the subsidiary; and
(c) the proportion of ownership interest held by the investment entity and, if different, the proportion of voting rights held.
ii)If an investment entity is the parent of another investment entity, the parent shall also provide the disclosures for investments that are controlled by its investment entity subsidiary.
iii)The disclosure may be provided by including, in the financial statements of the parent, the financial statements of the subsidiary (or subsidiaries) that contain the above information.
iv)An investment entity shall disclose:
(a) the nature and extent of any significant restrictions (e.g. resulting from borrowing arrangements, regulatory requirements or contractual arrangements) on the ability of an unconsolidated subsidiary to
    a)   transfer funds to the investment entity in the form of cash dividends or
    ii)   to repay loans or advances made to the unconsolidated subsidiary by the investment entity; and
(b) any current commitments or intentions to provide financial or other support to an unconsolidated subsidiary, including commitments or intentions to assist the subsidiary in obtaining financial support.

(c) If, during the reporting period, an investment entity or its subsidiaries has, without having a contractual obligation to do so, provided financial or other support to an unconsolidated subsidiary (e.g. purchasing assets of, or instruments issued by, the subsidiary or assisting the subsidiary in obtaining financial support), the entity shall disclose:
(i) the type and amount of support provided to each unconsolidated subsidiary; and
(ii) the reasons for providing the support.

(d)An investment entity shall disclose the terms of any contractual arrangements that could require the entity or its unconsolidated subsidiaries to provide financial support to an unconsolidated, controlled, structured entity, including events or circumstances that could expose the reporting entity to a loss

(e) If during the reporting period an investment entity or any of its unconsolidated subsidiaries has, without having a contractual obligation to do so, provided financial or other support to an unconsolidated, structured entity that the investment entity did not control, and if that provision of support resulted in the investment entity controlling the structured entity, the investment entity shall disclose an explanation of the relevant factors in reaching the decision to provide that support.

3.7.9. Interests in joint arrangements and associates

An entity shall disclose information that enables users of its financial statements to evaluate:

(a) the nature, extent and financial effects of its interests in joint arrangements and associates, including the nature and effects of its contractual relationship with the other investors with joint control of, or significant influence over, joint arrangements and associates and

(b) the nature of, and changes in, the risks associated with its interests in joint ventures and associates.

3.7.9.1. Nature, extent and financial effects of an entity's interests in joint arrangements and associates

An entity shall disclose:

(a) for each joint arrangement and associate that is material to the reporting entity:
- (i) the name of the joint arrangement or associate.
- (ii) the nature of the entity's relationship with the joint arrangement or associate
- (iii) the principal place of business (and country of incorporation, if applicable and different from the principal place of business) of the joint arrangement or associate.
- (iv) the proportion of ownership interest or participating share held by the entity and, if different, the proportion of voting rights held (if applicable).

(b) for each joint venture and associate that is material to the reporting entity:
- (i) whether the investment in the joint venture or associate is measured using the Equity method or at fair value.
- (ii) summarised financial information about the joint venture or associate
- (iii) if the joint venture or associate is accounted for using the equity method, the fair value of its investment in the joint venture or associate, if there is a quoted market price for the investment.

(c) financial information as specified in paragraph B16 about the entity's investments in joint ventures and associates that are not individually material:
- (i) in aggregate for all individually immaterial joint ventures and, separately,
- (ii) in aggregate for all individually immaterial associates.

3.7.9.2. Risks associated with an entity's interests in joint ventures and associates

An entity shall disclose:

(a) commitments that it has relating to its joint ventures separately from the amount of other commitments

(b) in accordance with Ind AS 37, *Provisions, Contingent Liabilities and Contingent Assets*, unless the probability of loss is remote, contingent liabilities incurred relating to its interests in joint ventures or associates (including its share of contingent liabilities incurred jointly with other investors with joint control of, or significant influence over, the joint ventures or associates), separately from the amount of other contingent liabilities.

3.7.10. Interests in unconsolidated structured entities

An entity shall disclose information that enables users of its financial statements:
    (a) to understand the nature and extent of its interests in unconsolidated structured entities and
    (b) to evaluate the nature of, and changes in, the risks associated with its interests in unconsolidated structured entities

3.7.10.1. Disclosure requirements related to interests in unconsolidated structured entities are summarised below:

Nature of interest	Nature of risk
a) An entity shall disclose qualitative and quantitative information about its interests in unconsolidated structured entities, including, the nature, purpose, size and activities of the structured entity and how the structured entity is financed. b) If an entity has sponsored an unconsolidated structured entity for which it does not provide information required (e.g. because it does not have an interest in the entity at the reporting date), the entity shall disclose: (i) how it has determined which structured entities it has sponsored; (ii) *income from those structured entities* during the reporting period, including a description of the types of income presented; and (iii) the carrying amount (at the time of transfer) of all assets transferred to those structured entities during the reporting period.	An entity shall disclose in tabular format, unless another format is more appropriate, a summary of: (a) the carrying amounts of the assets and liabilities recognised in its financial statements relating to its interests in unconsolidated structured entities. (b) the line items in the balance sheet in which those assets and liabilities are recognised.

3.7.11. Comparison of Consolidation of Financial Statements with other GAAPs (Ind AS 110, Ind AS 28, Ind AS 111)

Accounting Standards (AS)	IFRS	US GAAP	Ind AS
Definition of subsidiary Based on voting control or control over the composition of the board of directors. The existence of currently exercisable potential voting right is not taken into consideration	Control is presumed exist when parent owns directly or indirectly through subsidiaries more than one half of an entity's voting power. Control is defined as combination of power, exposure to returns and link between power and returns. Power arises from rights to direct the relevant activities. Voting rights include substantive voting rights as well as currently exercisable potential voting rights, based on which a parent could have control over an entity in circumstances where it holds less than 50% of the voting rights of an entity	Similar to IFRS. However, a bipolar consolidation model is used which distinguishes between a variable interest model and a voting interest model. Control may be direct or indirect and may exist with a lesser percentage age of ownership voting rights.	Control is presumed exist when parent owns directly or indirectly through subsidiaries more than one half of an entity's voting power. Control is defined as combination of power, exposure to returns and link between power and returns. Power arises from rights to direct the relevant activities. Voting rights include substantive voting rights as well as currently exercisable potential voting rights, based on which a parent could have control over an entity in circumstances where it holds less than 50% of the voting rights of an entity
Definition of associates Based on significant influence, presumed if 20% or greater interest or participation in entity's affairs	Based on significant influence, presumed if 20% or greater interest or participation in entity's affairs	Similar to IFRS, although the term equity investment is used instead of associate.	Similar to IFRS
Presentation of associate results In consolidated financial statements equity method is	In consolidated financial statements equity	In consolidated financial statements similar to IFRS	In consolidated financial statements equity method is used. Share of

used. Share of post-tax results is shown. In stand-alone financials ; at cost less impairment	method is used. Share of post-tax results is shown. In stand-alone financials ; at cost or fair value in accordance with IFRS 9		post-tax results is shown. In stand-alone financials ; at cost or fair value in accordance with Ind AS 109
Joint venture definition Contractual arrangement whereby two or more parties undertake an economic activity which is subject to joint control Exclusion if it meets the definition of a subsidiary	Contractual arrangement whereby two or more parties are bound by joint control of the arrangement. Exclusion if investment is held for sale. Joint arrangement can be either a Joint operation or Joint venture. Joint control is the contractually agreed sharing of control of an arrangement, which exists only when decisions about the relevant activities require the unanimous consent of the parties sharing control.	A corporation owned and operated by small group of businesses as a separate and specific business or project for the mutual benefit of the members of the group.	Contractual arrangement whereby two or more parties are bound by joint control of the arrangement. Exclusion if investment is held for sale. Joint arrangement can be either a Joint operation or Joint venture. Joint control is the contractually agreed sharing of control of an arrangement, which exists only when decisions about the relevant activities require the unanimous consent of the parties sharing control.
Presentation In consolidated financial statements proportional consolidation is used; In stand-alone financials; at cost less impairment	In consolidated financial statements A joint operator shall account for the assets, liabilities, revenues and expenses relating to its interest in a joint operation in accordance with		In consolidated financial statements A joint operator shall account for the assets, liabilities, revenues and expenses relating to its interest in a joint operation in accordance with the Ind ASs applicable to the particular assets,

	the IFRSs applicable to the particular assets, liabilities, revenues and expenses. A joint venturer shall recognise its interest in a joint venture as an investment and shall account for that investment using the equity method in accordance with IAS 28, *Investments in Associates and Joint Ventures*		liabilities, revenues and expenses. A joint venturer shall recognise its interest in a joint venture as an investment and shall account for that investment using the equity method in accordance with Ind AS 28, *Investments in Associates and Joint Ventures*

3.7.12. General illustrations
Illustration 36. Ind AS 103, Calculation of goodwill on acquisition

Kampa Ltd acquired al the 5,00,000 shares of Cola Ltd as at 1st January 2012 for Rs.25 per share. Just before the acquisition date, Cola's Balance Sheet reported net assets of Rs. 10 million. Kampa did a financial due diligence and determined the fair value of Cola's property and equipment at Rs. 1 million higher than the amount reported by Cola. What would be the amount of goodwill calculated by Kampa Ltd on acquisition of Cola?

A. Rs. 5,00,000
B. Rs. 15,00,000
C. Rs.0

Solution
Statement of calculation of goodwill:

		Amount Rs.
Cost of acquisition (5,00,000 x Rs. 15/-)	(A)	125,00,000
Fair value of net assets (Rs.100,00,000 + Rs.10,00,000)	(B)	110,00,000
Goodwill	(A – B)	15,00,000

Hence correct answer is **B.**

Illustration 37. Ind AS 103: Business Combination: Computation of goodwill

Parent Ltd paid Rs.600 million for the outstanding share of Partner Ltd. At the acquisition date Partner Ltd reported the following condensed balance sheet.

Condensed balance sheet of Partner Ltd

	Amount (Rs million)
Plant & Equipment(net)	760
Current assets	80
Goodwill	30
Liabilities	400
Shareholders' equity	470

The fair value of plant and equipment was Rs.120 million more than its recorded book value. The fair values of all other identifiable assets and liabilities were equal to their recorded book values. Calculate the amount of goodwill Parent Ltd should report on its consolidated Balance Sheet.

Solution

Statement of calculation of purchased goodwill:

	Amount (Rs million)	Amount (Rs million)
Cost of investment		600.00(A)
Less: Fair value of net assets		
Plant & Equipment (net)	880	
Current assets	80	
Liabilities	(400)	560(B)
Purchased goodwill (A-B)		40

Goodwill reported in Partner Ltd's balance sheet is an identifiable asset and hence not an intangible asset under IAS 38 and hence ignored in calculation of Parent's goodwill amount.

Illustration 38. Ind AS 110, Adjustment of intra-company receivables and payables in consolidation

Alpha controls another entity Beta, owning 60% of its ordinary share capital. At the group's year end, 31st December 2012, Beta included Rs.6000 in its receivables in respect of goods supplied to Alpha. However, the payables of Alpha included only Rs.4000 in respect of amounts due to Beta. The difference arose because, on 31st December 2012, Alpha sent a cheque of Rs.2000, which was not received by Beta until 3rd January 2013.

Which one of the following sets of consolidation adjustments to current assets and current liabilities is correct?

A. Deduct Rs.6000 from both consolidated receivables and consolidated payables
B. Deduct Rs.3600 from both consolidated receivables and consolidated payables
C. Deduct Rs.6000 from consolidated receivables and Rs.4000 from consolidated payables and include Rs.2000 as cash-in-transit
D. Deduce Rs.6000 from consolidated receivables and Rs. 4000 from consolidated payables and include inventory in transit of Rs.2000.

Solution

Correct answer is C

Deduct Rs.6000 from consolidated receivables and Rs.4000 from consolidated payables and include Rs.2000 as cash-in-transit

Illustration 39: Ind AS 28: Adjustment of unrealised profit on goods sold by Associate to Parent in Consolidated financial statements.

P Ltd held 25% of the shares of A Ltd and exerts significant influence over it. A Ltd sells goods to P Ltd during the year for Rs.100,000. The cost of goods to A Ltd was Rs.80,000. At the year-end, P Ltd's inventories include Rs.16000 of goods purchased from A Ltd.

Calculate the adjustment required in respect of unrealised profit, and describe the accounting treatment of the adjustment in the consolidated income statement and the consolidated balance sheet.

Solution

Calculation of unrealised profit included in P Ltd's inventories:

= (100,000 - 80,000)/100000 x 16000

= Rs.3200.

P Ltd's share of unrealised profit = 25% x Rs.3200 = Rs.800.

Hence in the consolidated balance sheet, consolidated inventories would be reduced by Rs.800. In the consolidated income statement, this amount would be deducted from Share of profits of associates.

Tutorial note:

If A Ltd would have been a subsidiary then the entire amount of unrealised profit of Rs.3200 would have been deducted from consolidated inventories and debited to consolidated retained earnings.

Illustration 40. Ind AS 110: Calculation of consolidate profit before tax on disposal of shares

At 1st April 2012, AB Ltd held 80000 of the 1, 00, 000 issued ordinary shares of XY Ltd. The acquisition of XY Ltd took place on 1st April; 2011 and goodwill on acquisition was recorded at Rs.1, 20,000. The directors of AB Ltd decided to amortise the goodwill on acquisition on the straight line basis at the rate of 20% each year. On 1st October 20122, AB Ltd disposes of 20,000 shares in XY Ltd for Rs.1, 25,000. At that date, XY Ltd's total net assets are Rs.4, 00,000.

Calculate the consolidated profit or loss before tax on disposal of the shares.

Solution

Statement of consolidated profit before tax on disposal of shares

Particulars	Rs'000
Disposal proceeds	125
Share of net assets (20% x Rs.4,00,000)	(80)
Less: Unamortised goodwill: Rs.1,20,000 x 3.5/5 x 20/80	(21)
Consolidated profit on disposal	24

Illustration 41. Ind AS 110: Calculation of carrying amount of investment in consolidated balance sheet

On 1st January 2011, Alpha Ltd purchased 40% of the ordinary shares capital of Beta Ltd for Rs.280,000, which provided it a significant influence over Beta Ltd's activities. In the financial year ended 31st December 2011, Beta Ltd reported pre-tax profit of Rs.62,000. The tax charge was Rs.20,000. During the financial year ended 31st December 2012, Beta Ltd paid a total dividend of Rs.5,000 to its shareholders.

In the year ended 31st December 2012, Beta Ltd made a pre-tax loss of Rs.18,000, with a tax credit of Rs.4,000. A review of Alpha Ltd's investment in Beta Ltd at 31st December 2012 concluded that impairment had taken place. An impairment loss of Rs.45,000 was charged in Alpha Ltd's

consolidated financial statements for the year.
The carrying amount of the investment in Beta Ltd to be included in Alpha Ltd'S consolidated
Balance Sheet at 31st December 2012 was :

   A. Rs.2,44,200
   B. Rs.2,43,400
   C. Rs.2,46,700
   D. Rs.2,58,000

Solution

The carrying amount of investment in Beta Ltd included in Alpha Ltd's consolidated balance sheet at 31st December 2012:

Particulars		Rs'000	Rs'000
Cost of investment			280
2011 profit before tax		62	
2011 tax charge		(20)	
2011 profit after tax		42	
2011 Dividend paid		(5)	
2011 Net available profit	(A)	37	
2012 pre-tax loss		(18)	
2011 tax credit		4	
2011 after-tax loss	(B)	(14)	
Total net available profit (2011 + 2012)	(A + B)	23	
Share of Alpha (40% of 23)			9.2
Total cost of investment			289.2
Less: Impairment			(45.0)
			244.2

Hence answer is (A).

Illustration 42. Ind AS 110, Calculation of effective interest by Parent entity

XYZ owns 60% of the issued ordinary share capital of ABC. ABC owns 60% of the issued capital of KBC. Which one of the following statements is correct?
The effective interest of XYZ in KBC is:

   A. 24%
   B. 36%
   C. 20%
   D. 60%

Solution

The effective interest of XYZ in KBC would be 60% x 60% = 36%.
Hence correct answer is **B**.

Illustration 43. Ind AS 111, Treatment of consolidated revenue with a joint venture entity

On 31st December 2012, LMN set up a joint venture entity PQR with two partners. Each partner owns exactly 1/3 rd of the issued share capital of PQR and all business decisions are taken jointly.
Throughout its financial year ended 31st March 2013, LMN held 80% of the share capital of its subsidiary XYZ.
Revenue for the period ended 31st March 2013 recorded in the books of three entities was as under:

Entities	Rs.
LMN	23,500
PQR	5,400
XYZ	14,600

LMN's directors have decided to adopt proportionate method of consolidation. During the year, XYZ supplied LMN with goods with a sales value of Rs.1,400. The cost to XYZ of these goods was Rs.1,200.

What is the amount of consolidated revenue for inclusion in LMN group's income statement for the year ended 31st March 2013?

    A. 37,150
    B. 38,500
    C. 31,980
    D. 37,700.

Solution

Statement of consolidated revenue is as under:

Entities	Rs.
LMN	23,500
PQR (1/3 x 5400)	1,800
XYZ	14,600
Less: Intra-group sales	(1,400)
Consolidated revenue	38,500

Illustration 44. Ind AS 110, Calculation of minority interest

Alpha owns 75% of the issued ordinary share capital and 25% of the issued irredeemable preference shares in Delta. The share capital and accumulated profits of Delta at 31st March 2013, the Alpha group's year-end, were,

Ordinary share capital	Rs.60,000	
7% Preference share capital	Rs.20,000	Rs.80,000
Accumulated profits		Rs.2,15,000
		Rs.2,95,000

Upon acquisition of Alpha's interest in Delta, which took place on 30th September 2012, the fair values of Delta's net assets were the same as book values, with the exception of an item of Plant. The carrying value of the Plant at 30th September 2012 was Rs.10,200 and its fair value was Rs.15,600. Its estimated remaining useful life at that date was 4 years. Depreciation is charged for each month of ownership. No adjustment was made in Delta's own accounting records for the increase in fair value.

Calculate the minority interest in Delta at 31st March 2013 for inclusion in the group's consolidated balance sheet to the nearest rupee.

Solution

Particulars	Rs.	Rs.	Rs.
Minority share of preferred share capital Rs.20000 x 75%			15,000
Ordinary share capital and reserves: Rs.60,000 +Rs.2,15,000		2,75,000	
Fair value of Plant (Rs.15,600 – Rs.10,200)	5,400		

Less: Depreciation for 6 months (Rs.5,400/4 x 6/12) Total	(675)	4,725 2,79,725	
Minority share: 25%			69,931
Total minority share			84,931

Illustration 45: Ind AS 28: Treatment of unrealised profit in intra-group transaction with Associates

AB owns a controlling interest in another entity CD and exerts significant influence over EF, an entity in which it holds 40% of the ordinary share capital.

During the financial year ended 30th April 2013, EF sold goods to AB valued at Rs.80,000. The cost of the goods to EF was Rs.60,000. 25% of the goods remained in AB's inventory at 30th April 2013.

Which one of the following is the correct consolidation adjustment in respect of the inventory?

    A. Dr. Consolidated reserves Rs.5,000 Cr. Inventory   Rs.5,000

    B. Dr. Consolidated reserves Rs.2,000 Cr. Inventory   Rs.2,000

    C. Dr. Consolidated reserves Rs.5,000 Cr. Investment in associates Rs.5,000

    D. Dr. Consolidated reserves Rs.2,000 Cr. Investment in associates Rs.2,000

Solution

Calculation of unrealised profit = (Rs.80, 000 – Rs.60, 000) x 25% = Rs.5, 000

The group share is 40% in EF, hence the calculation of unrealised profit would be = Rs.5000 x 40% = Rs.2, 000. Since EF sold goods to AB it is an UPSTREAM transaction, hence the correct answer is **B**.

Illustration 46: Ind AS 28: Treatment of unrealised profit in intra-group transaction with Associates

AB owns a controlling interest in another entity CD and exerts significant influence over EF, an entity in which it holds 40% of the ordinary share capital.

During the financial year ended 30th April 2013, AB sold goods to EF valued at Rs.80,000. The cost of the goods to EF was Rs.60,000. 25% of the goods remained in AB's inventory at 30th April 2013.

Which one of the following is the correct consolidation adjustment in respect of the inventory?

    A. Dr. Consolidated reserves Rs.5,000 Cr. Inventory   Rs.5,000

    B. Dr. Consolidated reserves Rs.2,000 Cr. Inventory   Rs.2,000

    C. Dr. Consolidated reserves Rs.5,000 Cr. Investment in associates Rs.5,000

    D. Dr. Consolidated reserves Rs.2,000 Cr. Investment in associates Rs.2,000

Solution

Calculation of unrealised profit = (Rs.80, 000 – Rs.60, 000) x 25% = Rs.5, 000

The group share is 40% in EF, hence the calculation of unrealised profit would be = Rs.5000 x 40% = Rs.2, 000. Since AB sold goods to EF it is a DOWNSTREAM transaction,

hence the correct answer is **D**.

Illustration 47: Ind AS 107 and Ind AS 110: consolidated cash flow

On 1st of March 2012, Alpha Ltd acquired 30% of the shares of Beta Ltd. The investment was accounted for as an associate in Alpha's consolidated financial statements. Both Alpha and Beta have an accounting year end of 31st October. Alpha has no other investments in associates.

Net profit for the year in Beta's income statement for the year ended 31st October 2012 was Rs.230000. It declared and paid dividend of Rs.100,000 on 1st July 2012. No other dividends were paid in the year.

What amount will be shown as an inflow in respect of earnings from the associate in the consolidated cash flow statement of Alpha for the year ended 31st October 2012?
- A. Rs. 20,000
- B. Rs. 26,000
- C. Rs. 30,000
- D. Rs. 46,000

Solution

Dividend paid by Associate Beta Ltd   = Rs.1, 00,000

Alpha's share of dividend 30% x Rs.1, 00,000 = Rs. 30, 000

This is the amount that should appear in the cash flow statement of Alpha as this is the share of Alpha's dividend from the Associate.

Hence correct answer is C

Illustration 48: Ind AS 7 and Ind AS 110: Reconciliation of purchases in consolidated cash flow statement

Kaka Ltd is preparing its consolidated cash flow statement for the year ended 31st October 2012; its consolidated opening balance at net book value for property, plant and equipment was Rs.207000. During the year the Kaka group disposed of plant for proceeds of Rs.8500 that had cost Rs.62000 several years ago and which was fully written down at 1st November 2011. There were no other disposals. The depreciation charge for the year ended 31st October 2012 was Rs.32, 000. The consolidated closing book value for property, plant and equipment was RS.228000.

Calculate the cash outflow in respect of purchases of property, plant and equipment for inclusion in the consolidated cash flow statement of Kaka group for the year ended 31st October 2012.
- A. Rs.11,000
- B. Rs.44,500
- C. Rs.53,000
- D. Rs.115,000

Solution

Statement of calculation of purchases of property, plant and equipment for the year ended 31st October 2012

Particulars	Amount Rs.
Opening balance of property , plant and equipment	207000
Less: Depreciation	32000
Add: Purchases (balancing figure)	53000
Closing balance of property, plant and equipment	228000

Hence correct answer is C

Illustration 49: Ind AS 7 & Ind AS 110: Reconciliation of minority interest in consolidated cash flow statement

On 31st August 2011, the consolidated balance sheet of Messi Ltd included minority interests of Rs.77, 600. One year later, on 31st August 2012, the balance of minority interest was Rs.64,700. During the year ended 31st August 2012, Messi Ltd had disposed off of its holding of 75% of the ordinary share capital of its subsidiary Rooney Ltd. At the date of disposal the net assets of Rooney Ltd totalled Rs.64, 000. The minority interests in the Messi group's profit for the year ended 31st August 2012 was Rs.6, 500.

What amount would be included in the consolidated cash flow statement as a dividend paid to the minority interests during the year ended 31st August 2012?

A. Rs.3100
B. Rs.3400
C. Rs.19400
D. Rs.22400

Solution

Statement of reconciliation of minority interest in consolidated cash flow statement

Particulars	Amount Rs.
Balance brought forward	77600
Disposal (25% x Rs.64000)	(16000)
Share of profit for the period ended 31st August 2012	6500
Dividend paid (balancing figure)	(3400)
Balance carried forward	64700

Hence correct answer is B

Illustration 50: Ind AS 7 & Ind AS 28: Investment in associates in consolidated cash flow statement

Beckham Ltd's financial statements included an investment in associate at Rs.66, 00,000 in its consolidated balance sheet at 30th September 2011. At 30th September 2012, the investment in associate had increased to Rs.67, 50,000. Beckham Ltd's pre-tax share of profit in the associate was Rs.4, 20,000, with a related tax charge of Rs.1, 80,000. The net amount of Rs.2, 40,000 was included in the consolidated income statement for the year ended 30th September 2012.

There were no impairments to the investment in associate, or acquisitions or disposals of shares during the financial year.

What is the amount of the cash flow related to this investment for inclusion in the consolidated cash flow statement for the year ended 30th September 2012?

A. Rs.90,000
B. Rs.240,000
C. Rs.390,000
D. Rs.420,000

Solution

Statement of reconciliation of investment in associates

Particulars	Amount Rs
Opening balance of investment in Associate	66,00,000
Add: Share of profit in Associate	2,40,000
Less: Cash flow (dividend paid) balancing figure	(90,000)
Closing balance of investment in Associate	67,50,000

Hence correct answer is A.

Illustration 51. Ind AS 7 & Ind AS 110 Reconciliation of minority interest in consolidated cash flow statement.

The consolidated financial statements of Parent Ltd for the year ended 31st March 2013 showed the following balances:

Minority interest in the consolidated balance sheet at 31st March 2013 is Rs.6 million (Rs.3.6 million at 31st March 2012)

Minority interest in the consolidated income statement for the year ended 31st March 2013 is Rs.2 million.

During the year ended 31st March 2013, the group acquired a new 75% subsidiary, whose net assets at the date acquisition were Rs.6.4 million. On 31st March 2013, the group revalued all its properties and the minority interest and the revaluation surplus was Rs.1.5 million. There were no dividends payable to minority shareholders at the beginning or end of the year.

Required:

What is the dividend paid to minority shareholders that will be shown in the consolidated cash flow statement of Parent Ltd for the year ended 31st March 2013?

Solution

Reconciliation of minority interest in consolidated cash flow statement

Particulars	Amount Rs.Mil
Opening balance of minority interest	3.6
Profit for the year	2.0
Acquisition (Rs.6.4 million x 25%)	1.6
Revaluation of property	1.5
Dividend (balancing figure)	(2.7)
Closing balance of minority interest	6.0

Chapter 4 : Miscellaneous adjustments on consolidation of financial statements (advanced)

Learning Outcomes
- **Principles of consolidation**
- **Inter-company transactions.**
- **Miscellaneous adjustments**

4.1. What is the procedure followed for consolidation?

As we have seen in the previous chapters, in preparing consolidated financial statements, the financial statements of the parent and its subsidiaries should be combined on a line by line basis by adding together like items of assets, liabilities, income and expenses.

4.1.1.Calculation of cost of control (steps revisited)

Cost of control	Steps involved in calculating cost of control are:
	b) The cost of investment of the parent in each of the subsidiaries and the parent's share in equity of each subsidiary should be eliminated.
	c) On the date of investment if the cost of investment to the parent is more than share of equity in that particular subsidiary, the difference is taken as Goodwill in the consolidated statement
	d) On the date of investment if the cost of investment to the parent is less than the share of equity in that particular subsidiary, the difference is taken as capital reserve in the consolidated statement.
	i) Where the carrying amount of the investment in the subsidiary is different from its cost, the carrying amount is considered for the purpose of above computations
	j) Goodwill and capital reserve of different subsidiaries can be adjusted to a net figure by the parent in consolidated financial statement
	k) Goodwill of consolidated financial statement need not be written off to consolidated profit and loss account but test of impairment (AS-28) is made each time a consolidated financial statement is prepared
	l) When share application money and share allotment money is paid separately on different dates then as per AS -21 date on which investment led to acquisition to control of subsidiary should be taken as date of investment i.e. date of allotment
	m) If control is gained in the subsidiary by a series of investments, then the date of the investment which led to holding – subsidiary relationship is taken into consideration

	and step by step calculations are made for each of the following investments.

4.1.2.Calculation of Minority Interest (steps revisited)

Minority Interest	• From the net income of the subsidiary, amount proportionate to minority interest is calculated and adjusted with the group income i.e. it is deducted from the profit & loss account balance and added to minority interest , so that the income of the group belonging to the parent is identified separately
	• Care should be taken to adjust for the cumulative preference dividend and profits belonging to the preference shares (if any) in the minority interest for the preference shares not held by the consolidated group. This adjustment should be made irrespective of whether or not dividends have been declared
	• Minority interests in the net assets of consolidated subsidiaries should be identified and presented in the consolidated balance sheet separately from liabilities and the equity of the parent's shareholders. Minority interests in the net assets consist of :
	  a) the amount of equity attributable to minorities at the date on which investment in a subsidiary is made and
	  b) the minorities share of movements in equity since the date the parent-subsidiary relationship came in existence.
	• If carrying amount and cost of investment are different, carrying amount is considered

4.1.3.Consolidation of Profit and Loss Account (steps revisited)

Steps involved in consolidation of Profit and Loss Account	a) all the revenue items are to be added line by line basis and from the consolidated revenue items inter-company transactions should be eliminated b) with respect to any unrealized profit in the stock of goods, of any of the group company, such unrealized profit is to be eliminated from the value of stock to arrive at the consolidated profit. c) Also it is necessary to eliminate the share of holding company in the proposed dividend of the subsidiary.

4.1.4.Consolidation of Cash Flow statement (steps revisited)

All the items of cash flow from operating activities, investing activities and financing activities are to be added on line by line basis and from the consolidated items, inter-company transactions should be eliminated.

4.2.Principles of consolidation with respect to consolidated financial statements

The basic principles of consolidation are to aggregate the assets and liabilities of both holding and subsidiary company or companies after adjusting and eliminating the following:
  a) Inter-co investment account
  b) Inter-co balances
  c) Unrealized inter-co profits.

The steps related to consolidation are as under: (revisited)	Step 1 - Elimination of investment account Step 2 – Calculation of Goodwill / cost of control or capital reserve Step 3 – Calculation of Minority interest Step 4 – Calculation of Capital profit / pre-acquisition profit and Step 5 - revenue profit / post-acquisition profit / current profit Step 6 - Inter-company transactions. Step 7 - Miscellaneous adjustments

The above steps are briefly explained with illustrations below.

4.2.1. Step I: Elimination of investment account	• The equity shares of subsidiary company which are acquired by the holding company is shown in the asset side of the Balance Sheet of holding company under the head "*investment*" and • the same is shown in the liability side of the Balance Sheet of subsidiary company under the head "*Share capital*". • If the holding company acquires the whole of the equity shares of subsidiary company i.e. in the cases of wholly owned subsidiary, say , at par, in that case, for the purpose of consolidation, - the investment accounts from the Balance Sheet of the holding company and - the share capital from the Balance Sheet of the subsidiary company are *squared off*.

Please refer to the following example:

Illustration 1

Balance Sheet as at 31st December 2010

Liabilities	A Ltd	B Ltd	Assets	A Ltd	B Ltd
Share capital of Rs.10 each	100000	50000	Sundry assets Investments:	150000	80000

| Sundry creditors | 100000 | 30000 | 5000 shares at par | 50000 | - |
| | 200000 | 80000 | | 200000 | 80000 |

Prepare a consolidated Balance Sheet.

Solution

Consolidated Balance Sheet of A Ltd and its
Subsidiary B Ltd as on 31st December 2010

Particulars	Note no.	Amount

I.   **Equity and Liabilities**
    (1)Shareholder's funds
    (a) Share capital
      (b) Reserves and surplus
    (2)Non-current liabilities
      Long-term borrowing
    (3)Current liabilities
      Trade payables
	
	1
	
	2
		
		100000
		-
		
		-
		
		130000

Total		230000

II.   **Assets**
    (1)Non-current assets
      (a)Fixed Assets
        Tangible assets
      (b)Non-current investments
    (2)Current assets
      (a)Inventories
      (b)Trade receivables
      (c)Cash and cash equivalents
	
	3
	
		230000
		
		-

Total		230000

Notes on Accounts

S/L No	Particulars	Amount (Rs)	Amount (Rs)
1.	Share capital Issued, subscribed and paid up 10000 equity shares of Rs.10 each fully paid up		100000
2.	Current liabilities Trade Payable A Ltd B Ltd	 100000 30000	 130000
3.	Tangible assets Sundry assets A Ltd B Ltd	 150000 80000	 230000

> Hence it is evident from the above consolidation exercise that, investment which is made by the holding company in the form of equity capital of the subsidiary is replaced with subsidiary company's assets and liabilities post consolidation.

4.2.2. **Step 2 :** **Goodwill / cost of control or capital reserve**	In the above illustration the problem was very simple and straightforward where the holding company acquires the shares of the subsidiary at par and net assets of the subsidiary are exactly equal to share capital. In real life, however, - Subsidiary company may have some accumulated profit or loss at the date of acquisition and the shares which are acquired by holding company may be taken either at a premium or at a discount. - The profit if any is credited to capital reserve account and loss if any is debited to goodwill account. - At the same time if the shares are acquired at a premium there would be a *goodwill* and - on the other hand if the shares are acquired at a discount, there will be *capital reserve*.

Please see a specimen format below.

Calculation of Goodwill / cost of control or Capital reserve

S/L No	Particulars	Amount Rs.	Amount Rs.
A.	Net cost of investments : - Amount paid for purchase of equity and preference shares of subsidiary Less: Dividend received out of pre-acquisition profits (Equity / Preference dividend) Less: Share of Holding co in proposed pref. Dividend of subsidiary	xxx (xxx) (xxx)	 xxx
B.	Holding Company's share in net assets of subsidiary : - Paid-up value of equity shares (including bonus shares) held currently - Paid-up value of preference shares held - Holding company's share of capital profits of subsidiary	xxx xxx xxx	 Xxx
C.	Goodwill (A > B)/Capital reserve (B > A)		Xxx

Please check out the next illustration.

Illustration 2

Balance Sheet as at 31st December 2010

Liabilities	A Ltd	B Ltd	Assets	A Ltd	B Ltd
Share capital of Rs.10 each	100000	50000	Sundry assets	65000	60000
			Investments		
Profit and Loss A/c	20000	5000	5000 shares in B Ltd	75000	
General reserve A/c	10000	4000			
Sundry liabilities	10000	1000			
	140000	60000		140000	60000

A Ltd acquired the share of B Ltd on 31st December 2010. Prepare a Consolidated Balance Sheet.

Solution
Statement of cost of control / goodwill

	Rs.	Rs.
Cost of investment		75000
Less: Face value of shares held	50000	
Profit and loss A/c	5000	
General reserve A/c	4000	59000
Cost of control / goodwill		16000

Conversely, if the net assets are higher than cost of investment then it would result in capital reserve.

Consolidated Balance Sheet of A Ltd and its Subsidiary B Ltd as on 31st December 2010

Particulars	Note no.	Amount
I. **Equity and Liabilities**		
(1)Shareholder's funds		
(a) Share capital	1	100000
(b) Reserves and surplus	2	30000
(2)Non-current liabilities		
Long-term borrowing		-
(3)Current liabilities		
Trade payables	3	11000
Total		141000
II. **Assets**		
(1)Non-current assets		
(a)Fixed Assets		
Tangible assets	4	125000
Intangible assets (goodwill)		16000
(b)Non-current investments		-
(2)Current assets		-

(a)Inventories			
(b)Trade receivables			
(c)Cash and cash equivalents			
	Total		**141000**

Notes on Accounts

S/L No	Particulars	Amount (Rs)	Amount (Rs)
1.	**Share capital** **Issued, subscribed and paid up** 10000 equity shares of Rs.10 each fully paid up		100000
2.	**Reserves & surplus** Profit & Loss A/c General reserve	20000 10000	30000
3.	**Current liabilities** Trade Payable A Ltd B Ltd	10000 1000	11000
4.	**Tangible assets** Sundry assets A Ltd B Ltd	65000 60000	125000

4.2.3. *Step 3 :* *Calculation of Minority interest*	• In cases where the holding company does not own the whole of the share capital of the subsidiary, there arises the question of *minority interest*, i.e. the proportion of net assets applicable to the shares held outside the group. • In other words, the amount of minority interest would comprise a)the nominal amount of shares held by the outside shareholders b)plus the proportionate capital or revenue profits and / or reserves or c) minus proportionate capital and revenue losses. This is shown as a liability in the consolidated Balance Sheet. Please refer the following example for further clarity.

Please see a specimen format below.

Calculation of minority interest

S/L No	Particulars	Amount Rs.	Amount Rs.
A.	Paid-up value of equity shares (including bonus shares) held by minority	xxx	
B.	Paid-up value of preference shares presently held by minority	xxx	
C.	Capital profit in subsidiary – share of minority	xxx	
D.	Reserve profit in subsidiary – share of minority	xxx	
E.	Revenue reserve in subsidiary – share of minority	xxx	
F.	Proposed Preference Dividend of subsidiary – share of minority	xxx	Xxx
G.	Minority interest (A + B + C + D + E + F)		Xxx

Illustration 3

A Ltd acquired 4000 shares of B Ltd on 31st December 2010. On that date their Balance Sheet stood as under:

Liabilities	A Ltd	B Ltd	Assets	A Ltd	B Ltd
Share capital of			Sundry assets	80000	60000
Rs.10 each	100000	50000	Investments:		
Profit and Loss A/c	10000	5000	4000 shares of B Ltd	40000	
Sundry liabilities	10000	5000			
	120000	60000		120000	60000

Solution

In this case, A Ltd acquired only 4/5th share of B Ltd and 1/5th share held by outside shareholders.

Therefore, proportion of holding shares:

A Ltd's share in B Ltd = 4000 / 5000 = 4/5th

Minority share = 1000 / 5000 = 1/5th

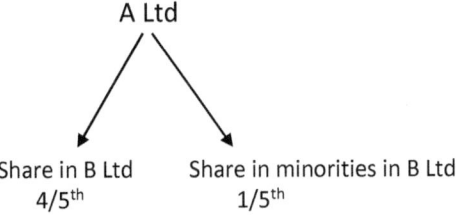

A Ltd

Share in B Ltd 4/5th Share in minorities in B Ltd 1/5th

Statement of Minority interest:

			Rs.
Share capital: Rs.50000 x 1/5th		=	10000
Profit & Loss A/c Rs.5000 x 1/5th		=	1000
			11000

Statement of Capital reserve:

	Rs.	Rs.
Cost of investment		40000
Less: Nominal value of shares held	40000	
Capital profit (Rs.5000 x 4/5th)	4000	44000
Capital reserve		4000

Consolidated Balance Sheet of A Ltd and its Subsidiary B Ltd as on 31st December 2010

Particulars	Note no.	Amount
I. Equity and Liabilities		
(1)Shareholder's funds		
(a) Share capital	1	100000
(b) Reserves and surplus	2	14000
(2)Minority Interest		11000
(3)Non-current liabilities		
Long-term borrowing		
(4)Current liabilities	3	15000
Trade payables		
Total		140000
II. Assets		
(1)Non-current assets		
(a)Fixed Assets		
Tangible assets	4	140000
Intangible assets (goodwill)		-
(b)Non-current investments		-
(2)Current assets		
(a)Inventories		
(b)Trade receivables		
(c)Cash and cash equivalents		
Total		140000

Notes on Accounts

S/L	Particulars	Amount	Amount

No		(Rs)	(Rs)
1.	Share capital		
	Issued, subscribed and paid up		
	10000 equity shares of Rs.10 each fully paid up		<u>100000</u>
2.	Reserves & surplus		
	Profit & Loss A/c	10000	
	Capital reserve	<u>4000</u>	<u>14000</u>
3.	Current liabilities		
	Trade Payable		
	A Ltd	10000	
	B Ltd	<u>5000</u>	<u>15000</u>
4.	Tangible assets		
	Sundry assets		
	A Ltd	80000	
	B Ltd	<u>60000</u>	<u>140000</u>

4.2.4.	• Profit and loss Account balance (including reserves) of the subsidiary company must be allocated between
Step 4 and Step 5	a) pre-acquisition and
Capital profit / pre-acquisition profit and revenue profit / post-acquisition profit / current profit	b) post-acquisition periods i.e. prior to acquisition and post-acquisition. In other words, the date of acquisition of the shares in the subsidiary company is the primary factor in order to distribute profits between capital and revenue.
	• The profit (including reserves) standing in the Balance Sheet at the time of acquisition of shares is known as *capital profit*. Similarly, profits (including reserves) earned subsequent to the date of purchase are treated as *revenue profit*.
	• Capital profits (to the extent of holding company's share) are to be adjusted only against cost of control / goodwill.
	• Current profit (to the extent of holding company's share) is to be shown in the liability side of the consolidated Balance Sheet

The specimen format is as under:

S/L No	Particulars	Capital Profit	Revenue Profit	Revenue Reserve

		Rs.	Rs.	Rs.
1.	Opening balance of General reserve	xxx		
2.	Opening balance of Profit and Loss A/c	xxx		
3.	Reserve (in the ratio of pre-acquisition and post-acquisition period)	xxx		xxx
4.	Profit earned (in the ratio of pre-acquisition and post-acquisition period)	xxx	xxx	
5.	Less: Reserve created (in the ratio of pre-acquisition and post-acquisition period)	(xxx)	(xxx)	
6.	Less: Final dividend (equity) previous year	(xxx)		
7.	Less: Proposed Preference dividend (in the ratio of pre-acquisition and post-acquisition period)	(xxx)	(xxx)	
	Total	Xxx	xxx	xxx
	Share of minority			
	Share of holding company			

The following illustration will seek to explain the above concept.

Illustration 4

Balance Sheet as at 31st December 2010

Liabilities	A Ltd	B Ltd	Assets	A Ltd	B Ltd
Share capital of Rs.10 each	100000	50000	Sundry assets	60000	63000
			Investments:		
Reserve	10000	5000	4000 shares in B Ltd	65000	
Profit & Loss A/c	10000	4000			
Sundry liabilities	5000	4000			
	125000	63000		125000	63000

A Ltd acquired the shares of B Ltd on 1st January 2010. On that date the Profit and Loss Account of S Ltd had a credit balance of Rs.1000 and in Reserve Rs.3000.

Prepare a consolidated Balance Sheet.

Solution

1. **Statement of proportion of holding shares:**

   A Ltd's share in B Ltd   = 4000 / 5000   = 4/5th
   Minority interest   = 1000 / 5000   = 1/5th

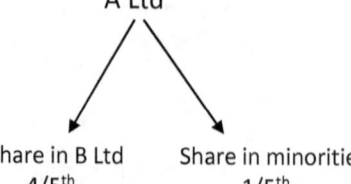

A Ltd

Share in B Ltd
4/5th

Share in minorities in B Ltd
1/5th

2. Statement of profit

Particulars	Capital profit 1.1.2010	Revenue profit 31.12.2010	Total profit
	Rs.	Rs.	Rs.
Reserve	3000	2000	5000
Profit & Loss A/c	1000	3000	4000
	4000	5000	9000
A Ltd share of profit 4/5th	3200	4000	7200
Minority interest 1/5th	800	1000	1800

3. Minority interest

	Rs.	Rs.
Share capital (Rs.50000 x 1/5th)		10000
Capital profit (as above)	800	
Revenue profit (as above)	1000	1800
		11800

4. Statement of cost of control / goodwill

	Rs.	Rs
Cost of investment		65000
Less: Nominal value of shares held 4/5x 5000	40000	
Capital profit	3200	43200
Goodwill		21800

Consolidated Balance Sheet of A Ltd and its Subsidiary B Ltd as on 31st December 2010

Particulars	Note no.	Amount
I. Equity and Liabilities		
(1)Shareholder's funds		
(a) Share capital	1	100000
(b) Reserves and surplus	2	24000
(2)Minority Interest		11800
(3)Non-current liabilities		-
Long-term borrowing		
(4)Current liabilities	3	9000
Trade payables		
Total		144800
II. Assets		
(1)Non-current assets		
(a)Fixed Assets		
Tangible assets	4	123000
Intangible assets (goodwill)		21800

(b)Non-current investments			-
(2)Current assets			
(a)Inventories			
(b)Trade receivables			
(c)Cash and cash equivalents			
Total			144800

Notes on Accounts

S/L No	Particulars		Amount (Rs)	Amount (Rs)
1.	Share capital			
	Issued, subscribed and paid up			
	10000 equity shares of Rs.10 each fully paid up			100000
2.	Reserves & surplus			
	Reserve			
	A Ltd	10000		
	B Ltd (2000 x 4/5)	1600	11600	
	Profit & Loss			
	A Ltd	10000		
	B Ltd (4000 - 1600)	2400	12400	24000
3.	Current liabilities			
	Trade Payable		5000	
	A Ltd		4000	9000
	B Ltd			
4.	Tangible assets			
	Sundry assets			
	A Ltd		60000	
	B Ltd		63000	123000

4.2.5.
Step 6: Inter-company transactions
	• It is possible that the holding company would have business dealings with the subsidiary company before the consolidation. Since a consolidated Balance Sheet is being prepared those inter-company transactions have to be adjusted.
	• Usually the inter-company transactions include the following:
	   - Building
	   - Machinery
	   - Inventories
	   - Sundry debtors and creditors
	   - Bills receivable and bills payable

		- Loans and advances - Current account - Contingent liabilities			

The treatment is shown in the following illustration:

Illustration 5

The Balance Sheets of A Ltd and B Ltd as at 31.12.2010 were as follows: (Rs)

Liabilities	A Ltd	B Ltd	Assets	A Ltd	B Ltd
Share capital:			Fixed Assets	350000	145000
50000 equity shares			Investments:		
of Rs.10 each fully	500000	-	15000 equity shares of		
paid			Rs.10 each	150000	-
20000 equity shares	-	200000	Bills receivable	40000	20000
of Rs.10 each fully	50000	30000	Debtors	100000	80000
paid	100000	40000	Cash and bank	20000	10000
Bills payable			Current Account:		
Sundry creditors	10000	-	A Ltd	-	15000
Current Account:					
B Ltd					
	660000	270000		660000	270000

Contingent liabilities for bills discounted	4000	6000

Additional information:
a) Sundry creditors of B Ltd include Rs.10000 due to A Ltd
b) Bills Receivables of A Ltd include Rs. 8000 accepted by B Ltd
c) Bills Receivables of B Ltd include Rs.10000 accepted by A Ltd
d) The difference in Current Account of the companies is due to the fact that a cheque for Rs.5000
   was sent by A Ltd but it has not reached B Ltd as yet.
e) Contingent liability of Rs.4000 for bills discounted as shown in the Balance Sheet of A Ltd
   relates to a bill accepted by B Ltd

Prepare a consolidated Balance Sheet as at 31.12.2010.

Solution

Consolidated Balance Sheet of A Ltd and its Subsidiary B Ltd as on 31st December 2010

Particulars	Note no.	Amount
I. Equity and Liabilities		
(1)Shareholder's funds		
(a) Share capital	1	500000
(b) Reserves and surplus		-

	(2)Minority Interest	2	50000
	(3)Non-current liabilities Long-term borrowing		-
	(4)Current liabilities Trade payables	3	192000
	Total		742000
II.	Assets		
	(1)Non-current assets (a)Fixed Assets		
	Tangible assets	4	495000
	Intangible assets (goodwill)		-
	(b)Non-current investments		-
	(2)Current assets	5	247000
	Total		742000

Notes on Accounts

S/L No	Particulars	Amount (Rs)	Amount (Rs)
1.	**Share capital** **Issued, subscribed and paid up** 50000 equity shares of Rs.10 each fully paid up		500000
2.	**Minority interest** (5000 shares x Rs.10 each)		50000
3.	**Current liabilities**		

Trade Payable
Bills payable:
A Ltd 50000
B Ltd 30000
80000

Less: Mutual acceptance
Per contra
Held by A Ltd 8000
B Ltd 10000 18000
62000

Sundry creditors
A Ltd 100000
B Ltd 40000
140000
Less: Mutual indebtedness
Per contra 10000 130000

Current Account:
A Ltd 10000
Less: Common indebtedness
per contra 10000 Nil 192000

4.	Tangible assets			
	Sundry assets			
	A Ltd		350000	
	B Ltd		145000	495000
5.	**Current assets**			
	Bills receivables			
	A Ltd	40000		
	B Ltd	20000		
		60000		
	Less: Mutual acceptance			
	Per contra			
	Held by A Ltd	10000		42000
	B Ltd	8000	18000	
	Sundry debtors			
	A Ltd	100000		
	B Ltd	80000		
		180000		
	Less: Mutual			
	Indebtedness			
	Per contra		10000	170000
	Cash and cash equivalent			
	A Ltd	20000		
	B Ltd	10000		
	Cash in transit	5000		35000
	Current Account:			
	B Ltd	15000		
	Less: cash in transit	5000		
		10000		
	Less: Common			
	indebtedness			nil
	per contra	10000		247000

4.2.6. Step 7: Miscellaneous adjustments

a)Unrealised inter-company profits	An *unrealized inter-company profit* exists only when - there is a sale of goods by one company in the group to another at a profit and the same goods remain unsold and appear as an asset in the Balance Sheet. - This unrealized profit made by the selling company is to be eliminated at the time of preparing a consolidated Balance Sheet. The following principles should be followed:

	i) Ascertain the amount of profit on unsold stock supplied by the company in the group, ii) Share of minority interest should be deducted from such unrealized profit so calculated, and iii) The balance of unrealized profit (i.e. Holding Company's share or after deducting minority interest) is to be deducted from the profit of the company which is selling the goods and from the books of the company receiving those goods as well

In other words, the holding company's share of unrealized profit shall be deducted from

- a) the consolidated stock in the assets side of the Consolidated Balance Sheet and
- b) the same amount shall also be deducted from the Profit and Loss Account in the Consolidated Balance Sheet.

Specimen format for interco adjustments and unrealised profit would be as under:

Item	Building	Machinery	Inventories	Debtors	Bills receivable	Cash & bank	Debentures	Creditors	Bills payable
H Ltd	Xxx	Xxx	Xxx	Xxx	Xxx	Xxx	Xxx	Xxx	Xxx
S Ltd	xxx	Xxx	xxx	xxx	xxx	xxx	xxx	xxx	xxx
Total									
Less Unrealised profit	(xxx)	(xxx)	(xxx)						
Less Mutual owings				(xxx)	(xxx)		(xxx)	(xxx)	(xxx)
Cash in transit						xxx			
Depreciation adjustment	xxx	Xxx							
Balances to consolidated Balance Sheet									

Please refer illustration explaining this as under:

Illustration 6

A Ltd acquired 4000 shares of B Ltd on 1.1.2010. Their Balance Sheets as at 31.12.2010 stood as follows:

Balance Sheet as at 31st December 2010

Liabilities	A Ltd	B Ltd	Assets	A Ltd	B Ltd
Share capital:			Fixed assets	80000	45000
10000 equity shares of			Investments:		
Rs.10 each fully paid up	100000	-	4000 shares in B Ltd		
5000 equity shares of			at par	40000	-
Rs.10 each fully paid up	-	50000	Stock	20000	10000
General Reserve(1.1.10)	40000	10000	Debtors	25000	10000
Profit & Loss A/c	20000	10000	Cash and bank	5000	10000
Sundry creditors	10000	5000			

	170000	75000			170000	75000

On 1.1.2010 the Profit and Loss Account of B Ltd showed a credit balance of Rs.4000. Stock of A Ltd includes Rs.2500 for goods at invoice price from B Ltd on which the latter company made a profit of 25% on cost.
Prepare a consolidated Balance Sheet.

Solution
1. **Statement of proportion of holding shares:**

   A Ltd's share in B Ltd   = 4000 / 5000   = $4/5^{th}$

   Minority interest   = 1000 / 5000   = $1/5^{th}$

A Ltd

Share in B Ltd   Share in minorities in B Ltd

$4/5^{th}$ $1/5^{th}$

2. **Statement of profit**

Particulars	Capital profit 1.1.2010	Revenue profit 31.12.2010	Total profit
	Rs.	Rs.	Rs.
General Reserve	10000	-	10000
Profit & Loss A/c	4000	6000	10000
	14000	6000	20000
A Ltd share of profit $4/5^{th}$	11200	4800	16000
Minority interest $1/5^{th}$	2800	1200	4000

3. **Statement of Minority interest**

		Rs.
Share capital (Rs.50000 x $1/5^{th}$)		10000
Capital profit (as above)	2800	
Revenue profit (as above)	1200	4000
		14000

4. **Statement of capital reserve**

	Rs.	Rs
Cost of investment		40000
Less: Nominal value of shares held 4/5x 5000	40000	
Capital profit	11200	51200
Capital reserve		
(11200)		

5. **Statement of unrealized profit on stock**

Invoice value of goods taken from B Ltd = Rs.2500
= Rs.2500 x 25/125
= Rs.500
A Ltd's share = Rs.500 x 4/5 = Rs.400

Consolidated Balance Sheet of A Ltd and its Subsidiary B Ltd as on 31ˢᵗ December 2010

Particulars	Note no.	Amount
I. **Equity and Liabilities**		
(1)Shareholder's funds		
(a) Share capital	1	100000
(b) Reserves and surplus	2	75600
(2)Minority Interest		14000
(3)Non-current liabilities		-
Long-term borrowing		
(4)Current liabilities	3	15000
Trade payables		
Total		**204600**
II. **Assets**		
(1)Non-current assets		
(a)Fixed Assets		
Tangible assets	4	125000
Intangible assets (goodwill)		-
(b)Non-current investments		-
(2)Current assets		
(a)Inventories	5	29600
(b)Trade receivables	6	35000
(c)Cash and cash equivalents	7	15000
Total		**204600**

Notes on Accounts

S/L No	Particulars	Amount (Rs)	Amount (Rs)
1.	**Share capital**		
	Issued, subscribed and paid up		
	10000 equity shares of Rs.10 each fully paid up		100000
2.	**Reserves & surplus**		
	Capital reserve	11200	
	General reserve	40000	
	Profit & Loss A/c		

	A Ltd	20000		
	B Ltd	4800		
		24800		
	Less: unrealized profit on stock	400	24400	75600
3.	**Current liabilities** Trade Payable Sundry creditors			
	A Ltd		10000	
	B Ltd		5000	15000
4.	**Tangible assets** Sundry assets			
	A Ltd		80000	
	B Ltd		45000	125000
5.	**Inventories** Stock		20000	
	A Ltd		10000	
	B Ltd		30000	
	Less: unrealized profit on stock		400	29600
6.	**Trade receivable** Sundry debtors			
	A Ltd		25000	
	B Ltd		10000	35000
7.	**Cash and cash equivalents**			
	A Ltd		5000	
	B Ltd		10000	15000

b)Issue of bonus shares	When a subsidiary company issues *bonus shares*,
	- the same will increase only the number of shares in the hands of the holding company.
	- The treatment would depend on the sources from which such bonuses are issued i.e. whether the bonus shares are issued out of the
	- pre-acquisition profit / capital profit or out of the
	- post-acquisition profit / revenue profit.
	i)If bonus shares are issued out of capital profit
	- There will be no effect in cost of control or goodwill account and minority interest for this purpose
	- since pre-acquisition profit is reduced on one hand and paid up value of share held will increase on the other.
	- As a result there will be no effect for the purpose of issuing bonus shares out of capital profit in goodwill

	account or capital reserve or minority interest.

Illustration 7

A Ltd acquired 6000 equity shares of Rs.10 each in B Ltd on 31st December 2010. The summarized Balance Sheets of A Ltd and B Ltd as on that date were: (Rs)

Liabilities	A Ltd	B Ltd	Assets	A Ltd	B Ltd
Capital: Authorised	400000	120000	Fixed Assets	253000	128000
Issued and Paid up: 60000 shares of Rs 5 each	300000		Investments in Subsidiary Ltd at cost,6000 shares of Rs 10 each	100000	
8000 shares of Rs 10 each		80000	Stock in hand	30000	10000
Capital reserve		34000	Bill receivable (including Rs 1000 from B ltd)	2000	
General reserve	20000	10000	Debtors and balance at bank	20000	17000
Profit & Loss A/c	50000	10000			
Bills payable (including Rs 1000/- to A Ltd)		3500			
Creditors	35000	17500			
	405000	155000		405000	155000

Note: Balance Sheet of A Ltd: Contingent liability for the bill discounted Rs 1200/-

On 1.1.2010 Subsidiary Ltd utilized part of its capital reserve to make a bonus issue of one share for every four shares held. You are required to prepare the consolidated Balance Sheet as on 31.12.2010 and show how your figures are made up.

Solution:

1) **Proportion of holding shares:**   Rs

   A Ltd's share in B ltd   = 6000/8000 = 3/4

   Minority interest   = 2000/8000 = 1/4

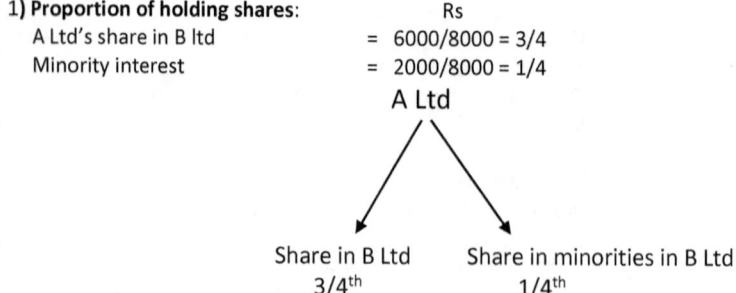

2) Statement of Capital reserve:

	Rs.
Cost of shares	100000
Less: Face value of shares held 60000	
Capital profits 25500	
FV of bonus shares 15000	100500
Capital Reserve	500

3) There shall be no current profits since the shares were acquired at 31.12.2010 i.e at the time of preparing final accounts

4) Statement of Capital Profits:

	Rs.	Rs.
Capital reserve	34000	
Less bonus shares	20000	14000
Revenue reserve		10000
Profit & loss		10000
34000		
Parent Ltd	Rs 34000 X ¾ =25500	
Minority interest	Rs 34000 X ¼ = 8500	

5) Statement of Minority Interest:

		Rs.
Share Capital (2000 x Rs 10)	20000	
Capital Profit	8500	
FV of bonus shares (20000 x ¼)	5000	
		33500

Consolidated Balance Sheet of A Ltd and its subsidiary
B Ltd as at 1ˢᵗ January 2011 (Rs)

Particulars	Note no.	Amount
I. **Equity and Liabilities**		
(1)Shareholder's funds		
(a) Share capital	1	300000
(b) Reserves and surplus	2	70500
(2)Minority Interest		33500
(3)Non-current liabilities		-
Long-term borrowing		
(4)Current liabilities	3	55000
Trade payables		
Total		459000
II. **Assets**		
(1)Non-current assets		
(a)Fixed Assets		

	Tangible assets	4	381000
	Intangible assets (goodwill)		-
	(b)Non-current investments		-
	(2)Current assets		
	(a)Inventories	5	40000
	(b)Trade receivables	6	38000
	(c)Cash and cash equivalents		
	Total		459000

Notes on Accounts

S/L No	Particulars	Amount (Rs)	Amount (Rs)
1.	**Share capital**		
	Authorised, Issued and paid up		
	60000 equity shares of Rs.5 each		300000
2.	**Reserves & surplus**		
	Capital reserve	500	
	General reserve	20000	
	Profit & Loss A/c	50000	70500
3.	**Current liabilities**		
	Trade Payable		
	Sundry creditors		
	A Ltd	35000	
	B Ltd	17500	52500
	Bills payable		
	B Ltd	3500	
	Less: Bills held by A Ltd		
	Per contra	1000	2500	55000
4.	**Tangible assets**		
	Sundry assets		
	A Ltd	253000	
	B Ltd	128000	381000
5.	**Inventories**		
	Stock		
	A Ltd	30000	
	B Ltd	10000	40000
6.	**Trade receivable**		
	Debtors		
	A Ltd	20000	
	B Ltd	17000	37000
	Bills receivable		
	A Ltd	2000	

	Less: Acceptance by B Ltd			
	Per contra	1000	**1000**	**38000**

b)Issue of bonus shares	ii)If bonus shares are issued out of current profit: In such cases, - holding company's shares in current profit shall be calculated only after making the proper adjustment for bonus issue from the said current profits, which will ultimately reduce the amount of holding company's share in current profits - Thus, cost of goodwill will be reduced by the amount of increased value of paid-up shares.

An illustration on this is shown as under:

Illustration 8
The summarized Balance Sheets of A Ltd and B Ltd as on 31.12.2010 were:

Liabilities	A Ltd	B Ltd	Assets	A Ltd	B Ltd
Share capital: (Rs.10 each)	400000	100000	Fixed Assets	350000	100000
General Reserve	100000	40000	Investments in B Ltd at cost,8000 shares	100000	
Profit & Loss A/c	50000	30000	Current Assets	150000	80000
Creditors	50000	10000			
	600000	180000		600000	180000

B Ltd had a credit balance of Rs.40000 in the general reserve when A Ltd acquired shares in B Ltd, capitalized Rs.20000 out of profits earned after the acquisition of its shares by A Ltd by making a bonus issue of one share for every five shares held.
Prepare a consolidated Balance Sheet as at 31.12.2010.

Solution
1) Proportion of holding shares: Rs

    A Ltd's share in B ltd   = 8000/10000 = 4/5
    Minority interest   = 2000/10000 = 1/5

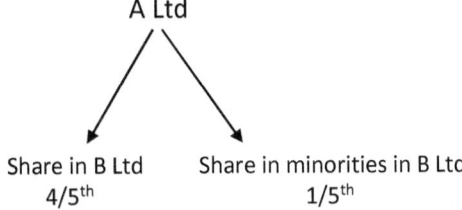

A Ltd

Share in B Ltd   Share in minorities in B Ltd
    4/5th   1/5th

2) Statement of Capital reserve:

		Rs.
Cost of shares		100000
Less: Face value of shares held	80000	
Capital profits	32000	
FV of bonus shares	16000	128000
Capital Reserve		28000

3) Statement of Capital Profits:

	Rs.
General reserve	40000
	40000
A Ltd	Rs 40000 X 4/5 = 32000
Minority interest	Rs 40000 X 1/5 = 8000

4) Statement of Current Profits:

	Rs.
Profit & Loss A/c	30000
Less: bonus issue	20000
	10000
A Ltd	Rs 10000 X 4/5 = 8000
Minority interest	Rs 10000 X 1/5 = 2000

5) Statement of Minority Interest:

	Rs.
Share Capital (2000 x Rs 10)	20000
Capital Profit	8000
Current profit	2000
FV of bonus shares (20000 x 1/5)	4000
	34000

Consolidated Balance Sheet of A Ltd and its subsidiary B Ltd as at 31st December 2010 (Rs)

Particulars	Note no.	Amount
I. **Equity and Liabilities**		
(1)Shareholder's funds		
(a) Share capital	1	400000
(b) Reserves and surplus	2	186000
(2)Minority Interest		34000
(3)Non-current liabilities		-
Long-term borrowing		
(4)Current liabilities	3	60000

	Trade payables		
	Total		680000
II.	**Assets**		
	(1)Non-current assets		
	(a)Fixed Assets		
	Tangible assets	4	450000
	Intangible assets (goodwill)		-
	(b)Non-current investments		-
	(2)Current assets	5	230000
	Total		680000

Notes on Accounts

S/L No	Particulars	Amount (Rs)	Amount (Rs)
1.	**Share capital**		
	Authorised, Issued and paid up		
	40000 equity shares of Rs.10 each fully paid up		400000
2.	**Reserves & surplus**		
	Capital reserve	28000	
	General reserve	100000	
	Profit & Loss A/-balance 50000		
	Add: current profit from B Ltd 8000	58000	186000
3.	**Current liabilities**		
	Trade Payable		
	Sundry creditors		
	A Ltd	50000	
	B Ltd	10000	60000
4.	**Tangible assets**		
	Sundry assets		
	A Ltd	350000	
	B Ltd	100000	450000
5.	**Current Assets**		
	A Ltd	150000	
	B Ltd	80000	230000

c)Preference shares of subsidiary company	**i)when preference shares are held by outsiders:** When preference shares are held by outsiders, - the same will be included with minority interest by the amount paid up on shares held (including the arrear dividend if any). - But a proper provision should be made against existing

	reserves which is to be added with minority interest if the profit of the subsidiary company becomes insufficient to pay cumulative dividend on preference shares.

Illustration 9

The summarized Balance Sheets of A Ltd and B Ltd as on 31.12.2010 were:

Liabilities	A Ltd	B Ltd	Assets	A Ltd	B Ltd
Share capital: (Rs.100 each) 10000 equity shares of Rs.10 each fully paid up 5000 8% preference shares of Rs.10 each fully paid up	1000000	100000 50000	Fixed Assets	800000	120000
General Reserve	100000	20000	Investments in B Ltd at cost,8000 shares	100000	
Creditors	50000	10000	Current Assets	250000	65000
Dividend due on preference shares		5000			
	1150000	185000		1150000	185000

B Ltd had a credit balance of Rs.15000 in the general reserve as on 1.12010. No dividend has been declared by B Ltd in 2010.
Prepare a consolidated Balance Sheet as at 31.12.2010.

Solution

1) Proportion of holding shares:

		Rs
A Ltd's share in B ltd	=	8000/10000 = 4/5
Minority interest	=	2000/10000 = 1/5

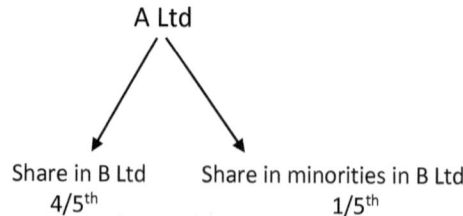

A Ltd

Share in B Ltd   Share in minorities in B Ltd
4/5th   1/5th

2) Statement of Goodwill:

	Rs.
Cost of shares	100000
Less: Face value of shares held 80000	
Capital profits 12000	
	92000
Capital Reserve	8000

3) Statement of Capital Profits:

	Rs.	Rs.
General reserve	15000	
		15000
-		
A Ltd	Rs 15000 X 4/5 = 12000	
Minority interest	Rs 15000 X 1/5 = 3000	

4) Statement of Current Profits:

		Rs.
General reserve (Rs.20000 – Rs.15000)		5000
A Ltd	Rs 5000 X 4/5 = 4000	
Minority interest	Rs 1000 X 1/5 = 1000	

5) Statement of Minority Interest:

	Rs.
Share Capital (2000 x Rs 10)	20000
Preference share capital	50000
Capital Profit	3000
Current profit	1000
Dividend due on preference shares	5000
	79000

Consolidated Balance Sheet of A Ltd and its subsidiary B Ltd as at 31st December 2010 (Rs)

Particulars	Note no.	Amount
I. **Equity and Liabilities**		
(1)Shareholder's funds		
(a) Share capital	1	1000000
(b) Reserves and surplus	2	104000
(2)Minority Interest		79000
(3)Non-current liabilities		-
Long-term borrowing		
(4)Current liabilities	3	60000
Trade payables		
Total		1243000
II. **Assets**		
(1)Non-current assets		
(a)Fixed Assets		
Tangible assets	4	920000
Intangible assets (goodwill)		8000
(b)Non-current investments		-
(2)Current assets	5	315000

	Total		1243000

Notes on Accounts

S/L No	Particulars	Amount (Rs)	Amount (Rs)
1.	**Share capital** **Authorised, Issued and paid up** 10000 equity shares of Rs.100 each fully paid up		1000000
2.	**Reserves & surplus** General reserve Profit & Loss A/C	100000 4000	104000
3.	**Current liabilities** Trade Payable Sundry creditors A Ltd B Ltd	50000 10000	60000
4.	**Tangible assets** Sundry assets A Ltd B Ltd	800000 120000	920000
5.	**Current Assets** A Ltd B Ltd	250000 65000	315000

c)Preference shares of subsidiary company	ii)when preference shares are held by holding company: When preference shares of subsidiary are held by holding company, the treatment will be same as in the case of equity shares. - The difference between the cost price and paid-up value, if any, will represent cost of control which will be added with cost of control that is derived from equity shares. - But if the subsidiary company issues these shares either at a premium or at a discount, the same will not be treated as part of cost of control / goodwill but will be incorporated with the cost of preference shares. - The preference dividend accrued to the date of acquisition will be adjusted against goodwill / cost of control. - But the dividend which has accrued from the date of acquisition to the date of preparation of accounts will, however, be considered as revenue profit and the same will be included with the share of profit of holding company in the

	liability side of the Balance Sheet.

Please refer to the following example which explains this point.

Illustration 10

The summarized Balance Sheets of A Ltd and B Ltd as on 31.12.2010 were:

Liabilities	A Ltd	B Ltd	Assets	A Ltd	B Ltd
Share capital: 40000 shares of Rs.10 each fully paid	400000		Fixed Assets	250000	140000
5000 equity shares of Rs.10 each fully paid up		50000			
5000 8% preference shares of Rs.10 each fully paid up		50000			
General Reserve (1.1.2010)	50000	30000	Investments in B Ltd	100000	
Profit & loss A/c	20000	10000			
Creditors	30000	20000	Current Assets	150000	20000
Dividend due on preference shares		5000			
	500000	160000		500000	160000

B Ltd had Rs.5000 in Profit & Loss Account as on 1.12010. The dividend in respect of preference shares for 2010 is still payable. Prepare a consolidated Balance Sheet as at 31.12.2010.

Solution

1) **Proportion of holding shares:**   Rs

    A Ltd's share in B ltd   =   80% = (i.e. 4/5)

    Minority interest   =   20% = (i.e. 1/5)

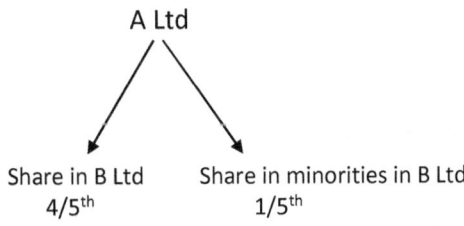

Share in B Ltd 4/5th	Share in minorities in B Ltd 1/5th

2) **Statement of capital reserve:**

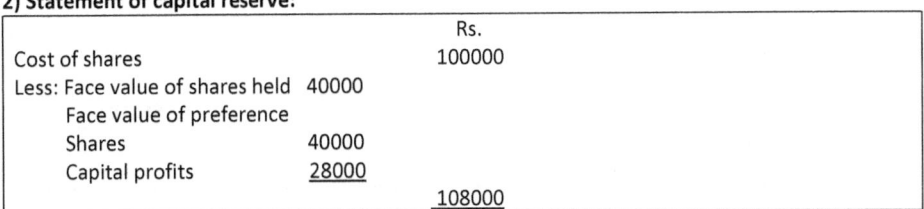

	Rs.
Cost of shares	100000
Less: Face value of shares held 40000	
Face value of preference	
Shares 40000	
Capital profits 28000	
	108000

Capital Reserve	8000

3) Statement of Capital Profits:

	Rs.
Profit & loss A/c	5000
General reserve	30000
	35000
A Ltd	Rs 35000 X 4/5 = 28000
Minority interest	Rs 35000 X 1/5 = 7000

4) Statement of Current Profits:

	Rs.
Profit & Loss A/c (Rs.10000 – Rs.5000)	5000
Less: Preference dividend (8% on Rs.50000)	4000
	1000
A Ltd	Rs 1000 X 4/5 = 800
Minority interest	Rs 1000 X 1/5 = 200

5) Statement of Minority Interest:

	Rs.
Share Capital (50000 x 1/5)	10000
Preference share capital (Rs.50000 x 1/5)	10000
Capital Profit	7000
Current profit	200
Dividend due on preference shares (Rs.4000 x 1/5)	800
-	28000

Consolidated Balance Sheet of A Ltd and its subsidiary
B Ltd as at 31st December 2010 (Rs)

Particulars	Note no.	Amount
I. **Equity and Liabilities**		
(1)Shareholder's funds		
(a) Share capital	1	400000
(b) Reserves and surplus	2	82000
(2)Minority Interest		28000
(3)Non-current liabilities		-
Long-term borrowing		
(4)Current liabilities	3	50000
Trade payables		
Total		560000
II. **Assets**		
(1)Non-current assets		

(a)Fixed Assets			
Tangible assets		4	390000
Intangible assets (goodwill)			
(b)Non-current investments			-
(2)Current assets		5	170000
	Total		560000

Notes on Accounts

S/L No	Particulars	Amount (Rs)	Amount (Rs)
1.	**Share capital**		
	Authorised, Issued and paid up		
	40000 equity shares of Rs.10 each fully paid up		400000
2.	**Reserves & surplus**		
	Capital reserve	8000	
	General reserve	50000	
	Profit & Loss A/c		
	A Ltd 20000		
	B Ltd 800		
	Pref. dividend (4000 x 4/5) 3200	24000	82000
3.	**Current liabilities**		
	Trade Payable		
	Sundry creditors		
	A Ltd	30000	
	B Ltd	20000	50000
4.	**Tangible assets**		
	Sundry assets		
	A Ltd	250000	
	B Ltd	140000	390000
5.	**Current Assets**		
	A Ltd	150000	
	B Ltd	20000	170000

d)Debentures of subsidiary company	• These are held by holding company and are disclosed under the head "investments" in the Balance Sheet of Holding Company. These are to be eliminated while preparing consolidated Balance Sheet.
	• However, if there is any difference between cost price and paid-up value of debentures, the same will be adjusted against cost of control or goodwill account if the difference exists on acquisition date. However, if the difference arises post-acquisition date it would be eliminated from statement of consolidated profit & loss.

e)Dividend	• The treatment of dividend would be comprised of:
	   - Ordinary dividend
	   - Interim dividend
	   - Proposed dividend

ei)Ordinary dividend	• If dividend has been distributed out of capital profit and has already been credited to the Profit and Loss Account of holding company, in that case, - Profit and Loss Account should be debited and - Investment account should be credited in order to make proper reconciliation for the consolidated Balance Sheet. • This signifies that the same will be adjusted against goodwill or capital reserve and will also be deducted from Profit and Loss Account. • If on the contrary, dividend has been declared and actually paid by the subsidiary company out of post-acquisition profit, which has also been received by the holding company, no adjustment is necessary for the purpose while preparing consolidated Balance Sheet.

An example to explain this follows.

Illustration 11

A Ltd acquired 4000 shares of Rs.10 each on 30.6.2010 for Rs.52000 in B Ltd. A Ltd received 10% dividend for 2009, but the dividend as received has been credited to Profit and Loss Account of A Ltd.

The summarized Balance Sheets of A Ltd and B Ltd as on 31.12.2010 were:

Liabilities	A Ltd	B Ltd	Assets	A Ltd	B Ltd
Share capital:Rs.10 each fully paid up	60000	50000	Sundry Assets	64000	96000
General Reserve (1.1.2010)	12000	10000	Investments in B Ltd (4000 shares)	52000	
Profit & loss A/c					
Balance on 1.1.2010	4000	8000			
Balance of 2010 profit	30000	20000			
Creditors	10000	8000			
	116000	96000		116000	96000

Prepare a consolidated Balance Sheet as at 31.12.2010.

Solution

1) Proportion of holding shares:

	Rs
A Ltd's share in B ltd = (4000 / 5000)=	80% = (i.e. 4/5)
Minority interest = (1000 / 5000) =	20% = (i.e. 1/5)

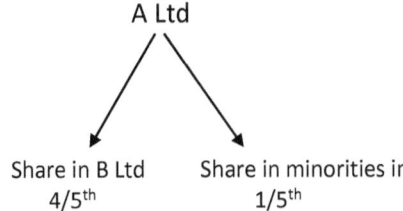

A Ltd

Share in B Ltd   Share in minorities in B Ltd
4/5th   1/5th

2) Statement of capital reserve:

	Rs.	Rs.
Cost of shares		52000
Less: Face value of shares held	40000	
Capital profits	22400	
Dividend for 2009	4000	66400
Capital Reserve		14400

3) Statement of Capital Profits:

	Rs.
Profit & loss A/c (1.1.2010)	8000
Add: Profit & loss A/c(1.1.2010 – 30.6.2010)	
Rs.20000 x ½	10000
General reserve	10000
Total	28000
A Ltd	Rs 28000 X 4/5 = 22400
Minority interest	Rs 28000 X 1/5 = 5600

4) Statement of Current Profits:

	Rs.
Profit & Loss A/c (Rs.20000 – Rs.10000)	10000
A Ltd	Rs 10000 X 4/5 = 8000
Minority interest	Rs10000 X 1/5 = 2000

5) Statement of Minority Interest:

Rs.	
Share Capital (1000 x Rs.10)	10000
Capital Profit	5600
Current profit	2000
	17600

Consolidated Balance Sheet of A Ltd and its subsidiary B Ltd as at 31st December 2010 (Rs)		
Particulars	Note no.	Amount
I. Equity and Liabilities		
(1)Shareholder's funds		
(a) Share capital	1	60000
(b) Reserves and surplus	2	64400
(2)Minority Interest		17600
(3)Non-current liabilities		
Long-term borrowing		-
(4)Current liabilities	3	18000
Trade payables		
Total		160000
II. Assets		
(1)Non-current assets		
(a)Fixed Assets		
Tangible assets	4	160000
Intangible assets (goodwill)		
(b)Non-current investments		-
(2)Current assets		-
Total		160000

Notes on Accounts

S/L No	Particulars	Amount (Rs)	Amount (Rs)
1.	Share capital		
	Authorised, Issued and paid up		
	6000 equity shares of Rs.10 each fully paid up		60000
2.	Reserves & surplus		
	Capital reserve	14400	
	General reserve	12000	
	Profit & Loss A/c		
	A Ltd		
	Balance 1.1.2010 4000		
	Add: profit for the year 30000		
	34000		
	Less: Dividend received		
	From B Ltd 4000		
	30000		
	B Ltd 8000	38000	64400
3.	Current liabilities		
	Trade Payable		
	Sundry creditors	10000	
		8000	18000

4.	A Ltd B Ltd **Tangible assets** Sundry assets A Ltd B Ltd		**64000** **96000**	**160000**

eii)Interim dividend	Interim dividend should be disbursed out of current or pose acquisition profit. The steps are as under: a) total amount of interim dividend (i.e.% dividend on subsidiary share capital) should be added to current profit b) deduct subsidiaries share of interim from minority interest c) deduct A Ltd's share of interim dividend from Profit and Loss Account of A Ltd in the liability side of the consolidated Balance Sheet.

Please refer to the illustration below.

Illustration 12

A Ltd acquired 40000 shares in B Ltd as at 1.1.2010 at a total cost of Rs.400000. The Balance Sheets as at 31.12.2010, when accounts of both companies were prepared as under:

A Ltd
Balance Sheet as at 31.12.2010 (Rs)

Liabilities	Amount	Assets	Amount
Share capital:		Land & buildings	515000
15000 equity shares of Rs.50 fully		Plant & Machinery	150000
paid up	750000	Investments	400000
Reserves & surplus		Sundry Debtors	300000
General reserve	475000	Stock-in-trade	170000
Profit & loss A/c	400000	Cash and bank	165000
Sundry creditors	75000		
	1700000		1700000

a) Includes Rs.30000 for purchases from B Ltd on which B Ltd made a profit of Rs.7500
b) Includes Rs.15000 stock at cost purchased from S Ltd part of Rs.30000 purchases as per (a) above
c) Includes interim dividend @ 16% p.a. free of tax from B Ltd

B Ltd
Balance Sheet as at 31.12.2010 (Rs)

Liabilities	Amount	Assets	Amount
Share capital:		Land & buildings	150000

50000 equity shares of Rs.5 fully paid up	250000	Plant & Machinery	135500
Reserves & surplus		Investments	-
General reserve 1.1.2010	10000	Sundry Debtors	79000
Profit & loss A/c	180000	Stock-in-trade	101000
		Cash and bank	55000
Sundry creditors	80500		
	520500		520500

Note: The Balance of Profit and Loss Account at 1.1.2010 Rs.140000; interim dividend of 16% p.a. free of tax, has been paid during the year in respect of the year ended 31.12.2010.

Prepare consolidated Balance Sheet as at 31.12.2010

Solution

1) Proportion of holding shares:

		Rs
A Ltd's share in B ltd = (4000 / 5000)=	80% = (i.e. 4/5)	
Minority interest = (1000 / 5000) =	20% = (i.e. 1/5)	

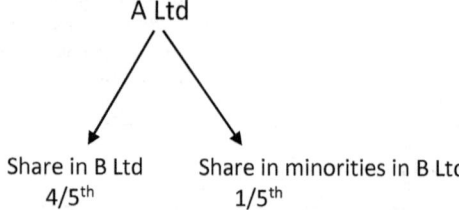

A Ltd

Share in B Ltd
4/5th

Share in minorities in B Ltd
1/5th

2) Statement of cost of control / goodwill:

		Rs.
Cost of shares		400000
Less: Face value of shares held	200000	
Capital profits	120000	
		320000
Goodwill		80000

3) Statement of Capital Profits:

	Rs.
Profit & loss A/c	140000
General reserve	10000
Total	150000
A Ltd	Rs 150000 X 4/5 = 120000
Minority interest	Rs 150000 X 1/5 = 30000

4) Statement of Current Profits:

	Rs.
Profit & Loss A/c (Rs.180000 – Rs.140000)	40000
Add: Interim dividend @16% on Rs.250000	40000
	80000

A Ltd	Rs. 80000 X 4/5 = 64000
Minority interest	Rs.80000 X 1/5 = 16000

5) Statement of Minority Interest:

	Rs.
Share Capital (1000 x Rs.5)	50000
Capital Profit	30000
Current profit	16000
	96000
Less: Interim dividend (Rs.40000 x 1/5)	8000
	88000

6) **Statement of unrealized profit on stock**

Goods purchased for Rs.30000, out of which goods remained unsold for Rs.15000
i.e. (Rs.15000 / Rs.30000) ½ portion.
So, total unrealized profit = Rs.7500 x ½ = Rs.3750.
A Ltd's share = Rs.3750 x 4/5 = Rs.3000

**Consolidated Balance Sheet of A Ltd and its subsidiary
B Ltd as at 31st December 2010 (Rs)**

Particulars	Note no.	Amount
I. **Equity and Liabilities**		
(1)Shareholder's funds		
(a) Share capital	1	750000
(b) Reserves and surplus	2	904000
(2)Minority Interest		88000
(3)Non-current liabilities		-
Long-term borrowing		
(4)Current liabilities	3	125500
Trade payables		
Total		1867500
II. **Assets**		
(1)Non-current assets		
(a)Fixed Assets		
Tangible assets	4	950500
Intangible assets (goodwill)		80000
(b)Non-current investments		-
(2)Current assets	5	837000
Total		1867500

Notes on Accounts

S/L No	Particulars	Amount (Rs)	Amount (Rs)
1.	**Share capital** **Authorised, Issued and paid up** 15000 equity shares of Rs.50 each fully paid up		750000
2.	**Reserves & surplus** General reserve	475000	
	Profit & Loss A/c		
	A Ltd 400000		
	Less: unrealized profit		
	for the year 3000		
	397000		
	Add: B Ltd 64000		
	461000		
	Less: Interim Dividend		
	From B Ltd 32000	429000	904000
3.	**Current liabilities** Creditors:		
	A Ltd	75000	
	B Ltd	80500	
		155500	
	Less: mutual indebtedness		
	Per contract	30000	125500
4.	**Tangible assets** Land & Building		
	A Ltd 515000		
	B Ltd 150000	665000	
	Plant & Machinery		
	A Ltd 150000		
	B Ltd 135500	285500	950500
5.	**Current Assets** **(1)Inventories**		
	A Ltd 170000		
	Less: unrealized profit 3000		
	167000		
	B Ltd 101000	268000	
	(2)Trade Receivables		
	A Ltd 300000		
	B Ltd 79000		
	379000		
	Less: mutual indebtedness		
	per contra 30000	349000	

(3)Cash and cash equivalents			
A Ltd	165000		
B Ltd	55000		
		220000	**837000**

eiii)Proposed dividend	• If the dividend is proposed by a subsidiary company –
	  - Profit and loss appropriation account will be debited and
	  - proposed dividend will be credited which will be shown as a current liability in the balance sheet.
	  - Proposed dividend belonging to the minority shareholders will be shown only as current liability at the time of preparing a consolidated balance sheet.
	  - But the dividend which belongs to the holding company will simply be added to either consolidated Profit & Loss Account or capital reserve depending on whether the said dividend has been proposed out of post-acquisition profits or pre acquisition profits.
	
	The treatment of proposed dividend may be summed up as under:
	• **If proposed by H:**
	To be deducted from the profit & loss (app) account of H ltd in the liability side of the consolidated Balance sheet and the same is shown under the head proposed dividend in the liability side of the consolidated balance sheet.
	
	• **If proposed by S:**
	To be deducted from the minority interest (only subsidiary portion) and the same is shown under the head proposed dividend in the liability side of the consolidated balance sheet.

Please refer example.

Illustration 13

A Ltd acquired 6000 equity shares of B Ltd of the face value of Rs 10 each at a price of Rs.85000/- on 1.4.2010. The balance sheets of the two companies as at 31.3.2010 were as follows:

Liabilities	A Ltd	B Ltd	Assets	A Ltd	B Ltd
Equity Share of Rs 10 each	500000	100000	Goodwill	150000	35000
General reserve (1.4.83)	210000	50000	Land & Building	200000	50000
Sundry Creditors	120000	46000	Plant & Machinery	250000	50000
Bills payable	40000	30000	Stock	100000	20250
Profit & Loss (1.4.83)	45000	20000	Debtors	150000	67250
Profit for the year	85000	22500	Investments	100000	

(31.3.84)					
			Bill receivable	10000	15000
			Bank	30000	25000
			Cash	10000	6000
	1000000	268500		1000000	268500

Out of the debtors and the bills receivable of H Ltd Rs 25000 and Rs 8000 respectively represented those dues from B Ltd. The stock in the hands of B Ltd includes goods purchased from A Ltd at Rs 10000 which includes profit charged by H ltd at 25% on cost. Both the companies have proposed 10% dividend for 2009-10

You are required to prepare a consolidated balance sheet of A & and subsidiary B Ltd as at 31.3.2010.

Solution:
Working Notes
1) Proportion of holding shares:
A Ltd's share in B ltd = (6000 / 10000) =   3/5
Minority interest   = (4000 / 10000) =   2/5

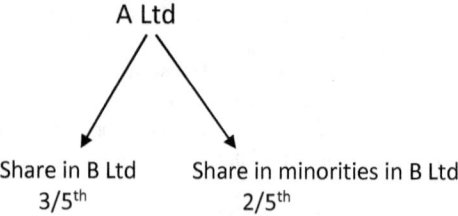

A Ltd

Share in B Ltd   Share in minorities in B Ltd
$3/5^{th}$ $2/5^{th}$

2) Statement of capital reserve:

		Rs.
Cost of shares		85000
Less: Face value of shares held	60000	
Capital profits	42000	
-		102000
Capital reserve		17000

3) Statement of Capital Profits:

	Rs.
Profit & loss A/c	50000
General reserve	20000
Total	70000

A Ltd	Rs 70000 X 3/5 = 42000
Minority interest	Rs 70000 X 2/5 = 28000

4) Statement of Current Profits:

	Rs.
Profit & Loss A/c	22500

A Ltd	Rs. 22500 X 3/5 = 13500
Minority interest	Rs.22500 X 2/5 = 9000

5) Statement of Minority Interest:

	Rs.
Share Capital (4000 x Rs.10)	40000
Capital Profit	28000
Current profit	9000
	77000
Less: proposed dividend (Rs.10000 x 2/5)	4000
	73000

6) Statement of unrealized profit on stock

Stock in the hands of B Ltd includes goods purchased for Rs.10000, from A Ltd which included profits charged by A Ltd at 25% on cost.

Rs. 10000 x 25 / 125 = Rs.2000

A Ltd's share = Rs.2000 x 3/5 = Rs.1200

Consolidated Balance Sheet of A Ltd and its subsidiary
B Ltd as at 31st March 2010 (Rs)

Particulars	Note no.	Amount
I. **Equity and Liabilities**		
(1)Shareholder's funds		
(a) Share capital	1	500000
(b) Reserves and surplus	2	319300
(2)Minority Interest (WN5)		73000
(3)Non-current liabilities		-
Long-term borrowing		
(4)Current liabilities	3	257000
Trade payables		
Total		1149300
II. **Assets**		
(1)Non-current assets		
(a)Fixed Assets		
Tangible assets	4	550000
Intangible assets (goodwill)		
(150000 + 35000)		185000
(b)Non-current investments		15000
(2)Current assets	5	399300
Total		1149300

Notes on Accounts

S/L No	Particulars	Amount (Rs)	Amount (Rs)
1.	Share capital		

	Authorised, Issued and paid up			
	50000 equity shares of Rs.10 each fully paid up			**500000**
2.	**Reserves & surplus**			
	General reserve		**210000**	
	Profit & Loss A/c			
	A Ltd (1.4.2009)	45000		
	For the year	85000		
		130000		
	Add: B Ltd	13500		
		143500		
	Less: unrealized profit			
	for the year	1200		
		142300		
	Less: Proposed Dividend			
	(Rs.500000 x 10%)	50000	**92300**	
	Capital reserve		**17000**	**319300**
3.	**Current liabilities**			
	Creditors:			
	A Ltd	120000		
	B Ltd	46000		
		166000		
	Less: mutual indebtedness			
	Per contract	25000		
			141000	
	Bills payable:			
	A Ltd	40000		
	B Ltd	30000		
		70000		
	Less: mutual indebtedness			
	Per contract	8000		
			62000	
	Proposed dividend:			
	A Ltd	50000		
	B Ltd	4000		
			54000	**257000**
4.	**Tangible assets**			
	Land & Building			
	A Ltd	200000		
	B Ltd	50000		
	Plant & Machinery		**250000**	
	A Ltd	250000		
	B Ltd	50000		
			300000	**550000**
5.	**Current Assets**			
	Inventories			
	A Ltd	100000		
	B Ltd	20250		

	120250			
Less: unrealized profit	1200		**119050**	
Trade Receivable				
A Ltd	150000			
B Ltd	67250			
	217250			
Less: mutual indebtedness			**192250**	
per contra	25000	192250		
Bills receivable				
A Ltd	10000			
B Ltd	15000			
	25000			
Less: mutual indebtedness				
per contra	8000	17000	**17000**	
Cash & cash equivalents				
Bank				
A Ltd	30000			
B Ltd	25000	55000		
Cash				
A Ltd	10000			
B Ltd	6000	16000	**71000**	**399300**

f)Revaluation of Fixed Assets	• Sometimes fixed assets of the subsidiary company are revalued at the time of acquisition of shares. If as a result of revaluation, profit or loss on fixed assets takes place, such profit or loss should be treated as capital profit or capital loss.
	• Since the capital profit cannot be utilized for the purpose of declaring dividend the same is shown in the liability side of the Balance Sheet of the subsidiary company under the head "capital reserve" or may be written off against goodwill.
	• Hence, the profit made on revaluation of fixed asset should be treated as capital profit and hence, will be distributed between holding company and minority interest according to their ratio.
	• Similarly depreciation also needs to be provided on the increased or decreased value of fixed asset against revenue profit. Hence in the event of profit on revaluation or undervaluation of assets additional provision for depreciation should be made.
	• This means that it will be deducted from the revenue / current profit and in the case of loss on revaluation or over valuation of assets provision for depreciation should be written back i.e. it will be added with the amount of revenue / current loss.

Please refer to the next illustration to provide clarity.

Illustration 14
From the following Balance Sheets of A Ltd and its subsidiary B Ltd drawn up at 31.12.2010,

prepare a Consolidated Balance Sheet as at that date, having regard to the following:

a) Reserve and Profit and Loss (Cr) of B Ltd stood at Rs.25000 and Rs.15000 respectively on the date of acquisition of its 80% shares held by A Ltd on 1.1.2010 and

b) Machinery (book value Rs.100000) and Furniture (book value Rs.20000) of B Ltd were revalued at Rs.150000 and Rs.15000 respectively for the purpose of fixing the price of its shares, there was no purchase or sale of these assets since the date of acquisition.

Balance Sheets of A Ltd and B Ltd
As at 31st December 2010 (Rs)

Liabilities	A Ltd	B Ltd	Assets	A Ltd	B Ltd
Share capital:			Machinery	100000	90000
Shares of Rs.100 each	500000	100000	Furniture	50000	17000
Reserves	200000	75000	Investments		
Profit & loss A/c	100000	25000	Shares in B Ltd		
Creditors	150000	50000	800 at Rs.200 each	160000	
			Current assets	440000	143000
Total	950000	250000		950000	250000

Solution
Working notes
1) Proportion of holding shares:

A Ltd's share in B ltd =(800 / 1000) =   4/5
Minority interest   = (200 / 1000) =   1/5

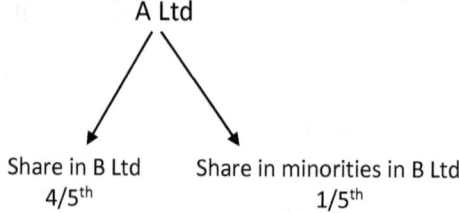

A Ltd

Share in B Ltd   Share in minorities in B Ltd
4/5th   1/5th

2) Statement of cost of control / goodwill:

		Rs.
Cost of shares		160000
Less: Face value of shares held	80000	
Capital profits	68000	
-		148000
Goodwill		12000

3) Statement of Capital Profits:

	Rs.
Profit & loss A/c	15000
General reserve	25000
Total	40000
Add: Undervaluation of machinery (150000 – 100000)	50000
	90000
Less: Overvaluation of furniture (20000 – 15000)	5000
	85000

A Ltd	Rs 85000 X 4/5 = 68000
Minority interest	Rs 85000 X 1/5 = 17000

4) Statement of Current Profits:

	Rs.
Reserve (Rs.75000 – Rs.25000)	50000
Profit & Loss A/c (Rs.25000 – Rs.15000)	10000
	60000
Less: Depreciation on Machinery undercharged	
@10% (Rs.10000 / Rs.100000 x 100) on Rs.50000	5000
	55000
Add: Depreciation on Furniture overcharged @ 15%	
(Rs.3000 / Rs.20000 x100) on Rs.5000	750
-	55750

A Ltd	Rs. 55750 X 4/5 = 44600
Minority interest	Rs.55750 X 1/5 = 11150

5) Statement of Minority Interest:

	Rs.
Share Capital (200 x Rs.10)	20000
Capital Profit	17000
Current profit	11150
	48150

**Consolidated Balance Sheet of A Ltd and its subsidiary
B Ltd as at 31st March 2010 (Rs)**

Particulars		Note no.	Amount
I.	**Equity and Liabilities**		
	(1)Shareholder's funds		
	(a) Share capital	1	**500000**
	(b) Reserves and surplus	2	**244600**
	(2)Minority Interest		**48150**
	(3)Non-current liabilities		**-**
	Long-term borrowing		
	(4)Current liabilities	3	**200000**
	Trade payables		
	Total		**1092750**
II.	**Assets**		
	(1)Non-current assets		
	(a)Fixed Assets		
	Tangible assets	4	**497750**
	Intangible assets (goodwill)		**12000**
	(b)Non-current investments		**-**
	(2)Current assets	5	**583000**
	Total		**1092750**

Notes on Accounts

S/L No	Particulars	Amount (Rs)	Amount (Rs)
1.	**Share capital** **Authorised, Issued and paid up** 5000 equity shares of Rs.100 each fully paid up		<u>500000</u>
2.	**Reserves & surplus** General reserve A Ltd 200000 B Ltd (50000 x 4/5) <u>40000</u> Profit & Loss A/c A Ltd 100000 B Ltd (44600 – 40000) <u>4600</u>	240000 <u>104600</u>	 <u>244600</u>
3.	**Current liabilities** **Trade Payables:** A Ltd B Ltd	**150000** <u>**50000**</u>	**200000**

4.	**Tangible assets**
	Plant & Machinery
	A Ltd 300000
	B Ltd 90000
	Add: under
	     valuation <u>50000</u>
	     140000
	Less: Depreciation <u>5000</u> <u>135000</u>
	Furniture & fittings
	A Ltd 50000
	B Ltd 17000
	Less: over
	     valuation <u>5000</u>
	     12000
	Add: Depreciation <u>750</u> <u>12750</u>
		435000
		
		<u>**62750**</u>
			
			<u>**497750**</u>

5.	**Current Assets** A Ltd B Ltd	**440000** <u>**143000**</u>	<u>**583000**</u>

Chapter 5 : Consolidation of holding company with one subsidiary

Learning Outcomes
- ❑ Specimen format of a consolidated Balance Sheet
- ❑ Consolidation of holding company with one subsidiary
- ❑ Consolidation of holding company and one Subsidiary showing treatment of
  - bonus issue
  - hire purchase
  - different date of acquisition
  - different reporting dates
  - Interco adjustment
  - Dividend
- ❑ Consolidation of foreign subsidiary
- ❑ Disposal of shares
- ❑ Section 212 representation

Q.5.1: Please provide a specimen format of a consolidated Balance Sheet

Consolidated Balance Sheet of Holding company and its subsidiary

Particulars	Note no.	Amount Rs
I. Equity and Liabilities		
(1)Shareholder's funds		
(a) Share capital	1	
(b) Reserves and surplus	2	
(c)Money received against share warrants		
(2)Minority Interest		
(3)Share application money pending allotment		
(4)Non-current liabilities		
(a)Long-term borrowings	3	
(b)Deferred tax liabilities (net)		
(c)Other long term liabilities		
(d)Long term provisions		
(5)Current liabilities		
(a)Short term borrowings		
(b)Trade payables	3	
(c)Other current liabilities	3	
(d)Short term provisions		
Total		
II. Assets		
(1)Non-current assets		
(a)Fixed Assets		

(i)Tangible assets	3	
(ii)Intangible assets	3	
(iii)Capital work-in-progress		
(iv)Intangible assets under development		
(b)Non-current investments		
(c)Deferred tax assets (net)		
(d) Long term loans and advances		
(e)Other non-current assets		
(2)Current assets		
(a) Current investments		
(b) Inventories	3	
(c) Trade receivables	3	
(d) Cash and cash equivalents	3	
(e) Short term loans and advances		
(f)Other current assets		
Total		

(Tutorial note: For details please refer Annexure I: Revised Schedule VI)

Notes on Accounts

S/L No	Particulars	Amount (Rs)	Amount (Rs)
1.	**Share capital**		
	Authorised		
	Xxx Equity shares of Rs.10 each	<u>XXX</u>	
	Xxx Preference shares of Rs.10 each	<u>XXX</u>	<u>XXX</u>
	Issued, subscribed and paid-up		
	Xxx Equity shares of Rs.10 each	<u>XXX</u>	
	Xxx Preference shares of Rs.10 each	<u>XXX</u>	<u>XXX</u>
2.	**Reserves and surplus**		
	General reserve	<u>XXX</u>	
	Profit and loss	XXX	
	Capital reserve on consolidation	<u>XXX</u>	<u>XXX</u>

1. **Summary of Consolidated balances**

Item	Building	Machinery	Inventories	Debtors	Bills receivable	Cash & bank	Debentures	Creditors	Bills payable
H Ltd	Xxx	Xxx	Xxx	Xxx	Xxx	Xxx	Xxx	Xxx	Xxx
S Ltd	xxx	Xxx	xxx	xxx	xxx	xxx	xxx	Xxx	xxx
Total									
Less Unrealised profit	(xxx)	(xxx)	(xxx)						
Less Mutual owings				(xxx)	(xxx)		(xxx)	(xxx)	(xxx)
Cash in transit						xxx			

Depreciation adjustment	xxx	Xxx							
Balances to consolidated Balance Sheet	xxx	xxx	xxx	xxx	xxx	xxx	xxx	xxx	Xxx

Working Notes

1. Statement of calculation of fixed assets and depreciation

	Amount Rs.	Amount Rs.
1. Book value as on (opening date)	Xxx	
2. Depreciation up to date of revaluation	Xxx	
3. Book value as on date of revaluation		Xxx
4. Revalued fixed assets		Xxx
5. Increase in value of fixed assets (4 – 3)		Xxx
6. Depreciation adjustment		Xxx

2. Statement of analysis of profits and reserves

S/L No	Particulars	Capital Profit Rs.	Revenue Profit Rs.	Revenue Reserve Rs.
1.	Opening balance of General reserve	xxx		
2.	Opening balance of Profit and Loss A/c	xxx		
3.	Reserve (in the ratio of pre-acquisition and post-acquisition period)	xxx		xxx
4.	Profit earned (in the ratio of pre-acquisition and post-acquisition period)	xxx	xxx	
5.	Less: Reserve created (in the ratio of pre-acquisition and post-acquisition period)	(xxx)	(xxx)	
6.	Less: Final dividend (equity) previous year	(xxx)		
7.	Less: Proposed Preference dividend (in the ratio of pre-acquisition and post-acquisition period)	(xxx)	(xxx)	
	Total	xxx	xxx	Xxx
	Share of minority Share of holding company			

3. Statement of calculation of goodwill / cost of control or capital reserve

Calculation of Goodwill / cost of control or Capital reserve

S/L No	Particulars	Amount Rs.	Amount Rs.
A.	Net cost of investments : - Amount paid for purchase of equity and preference shares of subsidiary Less: Dividend received out of pre-acquisition	xxx	

	profits (Equity / Preference dividend)	(xxx)	
	Less: Share of Holding co in proposed pref. Dividend of subsidiary	(xxx)	xxx
B.	Holding Company's share in net assets of subsidiary :		
	- Paid-up value of equity shares (including bonus shares) held currently	xxx	
	- Paid-up value of preference shares held	xxx	
	- Holding company's share of capital profits of subsidiary	xxx	Xxx
C.	Goodwill (A > B)/Capital reserve (B > A)		Xxx

4. Statement of calculation of minority interest

S/L No	Particulars	Amount Rs.	Amount Rs.
A.	Paid-up value of equity shares (including bonus shares) held by minority	xxx	
B.	Paid-up value of preference shares presently held by minority	xxx	
C.	Capital profit in subsidiary – share of minority	xxx	
D.	Reserve profit in subsidiary – share of minority	xxx	
E.	Revenue reserve in subsidiary – share of minority	xxx	
F.	Proposed Preference Dividend of subsidiary – share of minority	xxx	Xxx
G.	Minority interest (A + B + C + D + E + F)		Xxx

5. Statement of consolidated Profit and Loss

S/L No	Particulars	Amount Rs.	Amount Rs.
1.	Balance as per Balance Sheet of holding company		Xxx
2.	Add:		
	(a)holding company's share in revenue profit of Subs	Xxx	
	(b)holding company's share in proposed dividend of sub	Xxx	
	(c)profit on debentures held in sub(face value – cost)	xxx	Xxx
3.	Less:		
	(a)unrealised profit on stock	Xxx	
	(b)unrealised profit on plant and machinery	Xxx	
	(c)proposed equity dividend	Xxx	
	(d)proposed preference dividend	Xxx	
	(e)dividend out of pre-acquisition profit wrongly credited to profit instead of investment account	Xxx	
	(f)preliminary expenses of holding company	Xxx	
	(g)Loss on debentures held in sub (face value – cost)	xxx	(xxx)
4.	Closing balance taken to Consolidated Balance Sheet (1 + 2 – 3) = (4)		Xxx

Q.5.2: Consolidation of holding company with one subsidiary

On 31st March, 2010, the Balance Sheets of H Ltd. And S Ltd. stood as follows:
(Rs'000)

	H Ltd.	S Ltd
Liabilities		
Equity Share (Capital – Authorised)	5,000	3,000
Issue and subscribed in Equity Shares of Rs. 10 each full paid	4,000	2,400
General Reserve	928	690
Profit and Loss Account	1,305	810
Bills Payable	124	80
Sundry Creditors	487	427
Provision for Taxation	220	180
Other Provisions	65	17
	7,129	4,604
Assets:		
Plant and Machinery	2,541	2,450
Furniture and Fittings	615	298
Investment in the Equity Shares of S Ltd.	1,500	--
Stock	983	786
Debtors	700	683
Bills Receivables	120	95
Cash and Bank Balances	410	102
Sundry Advances	260	190
	7,129	4,604

Following Additional Information is available:

a) H Ltd. purchased 90 thousand Equity Shares in S Ltd. on 1st April, 2009 at which date the following balances stood in the book of S Ltd.
   General Reserve Rs. 1,500 thousand; Profit and Loss Account Rs. 633 thousand.

b) On 14th July, 2009 S Ltd. declared a dividend of 20% out of pre-acquisition profits and paid corporate dividend tax (including surcharge) at 11% H. Ltd. credited the dividend received to its Profit and Loss Account.

c) On 1st November, 2009 S Ltd. issued a 3 fully paid Equity Shares of Rs. 10 each, for every 5 shares held as bonus shares out of pre-acquisition General Reserve.

d) On 31st March, 2010, the Stock of S Ltd. included goods purchased for Rs. 50 thousand from H. Ltd., which has made a profit of 25% on Cost.

Prepare a consolidated Balance Sheet as on 31st March, 2010. (*Adapted CA Final Nov 2002*)

Solution

Consolidated Balance Sheet of H Ltd. with its subsidiary S Ltd.
as on 31st March, 2010   (Rs'000)

Particulars	Note no.	Amount
I. **Equity and Liabilities** (1)Shareholder's funds		

(a) Share capital		1	4000
(b) Reserves and surplus		2	3063
(2)Minority Interest (WN6)			1560
(3)Non-current liabilities			-
Long-term borrowing			
(4)Current liabilities			
Trade payables		3	1118
Short term provisions		4	482
	Total		10223
II. **Assets**			
(1)Non-current assets			
(a)Fixed Assets			
Tangible assets		5	5904
Intangible assets (goodwill)			-
(b)Non-current investments			-
(2)Current assets		6	4319
	Total		10223

Notes on Accounts

S/L No	Particulars	Amount (Rs'000)	Amount (Rs'000)
1.	**Share capital**		
	Authorised		5000
	Issued and paid up		
	4 lakh equity shares of Rs.10 each fully paid		4000
2.	**Reserves & surplus**		
	Capital Reserve (Note 5)	660	
	General Reserve (928 + 54)	982	
	Profit & Loss Account:		
	H Ltd 1305		
	Add: Share in S Ltd 306		
	1611		
	Less: Dividend wrongly		
	Credited 180		
	1431		
	Less: Unrealised profit 10	1421	3063
3.	**Current liabilities**		
	Trade payables		
	Bills payable H Ltd 124		
	S Ltd 80		
	Sundry creditors	204	
	H Ltd 487		
	S Ltd 427	914	1118

4.	**Short term provisions**			
	Provision for taxation			
	H Ltd	220	**400**	
	S Ltd	180		
	Other provisions			
	H Ltd	65		
	S Ltd	17	**82**	**482**
5.	**Tangible assets**			
	Plant & Machinery			
	H Ltd	2541		
	S Ltd	2450	**4991**	
	Furniture & fittings			
	H Ltd	615		
	S Ltd	298	**913**	**5904**
6.	**Current Assets**			
6.1	**Inventories**			
	H Ltd	983		
	S Ltd	786		
		1769		
	Less: unrealized			
	Profit(50x1/5)	10	**1759**	
6.2	**Trade receivable**			
	Debtors			
	H Ltd	700		
	S Ltd	683	**1383**	
	Bills receivable			
	H Ltd	120		
	S Ltd	95	**215**	
6.3	**Cash and cash equivalent**			
	H Ltd	410		
	S Ltd	102	**512**	
6.4	**Short term loans and advances**			
	Sundry advances			
	H Ltd	260		
	S Ltd	190	**450**	**4319**

Working Notes:

    1. Group structure

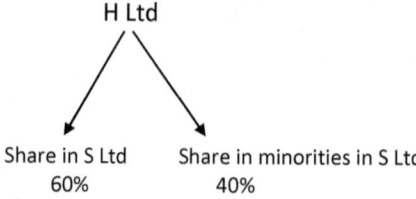

    2. S Ltd. General Reserve

	(Rs. In 000)		(Rs. In 000)
To Bonus to equity shareholders	900	By Balance b/d	1,500
(2,400/8 x 3)		By Profit and Loss A/C	
To Balance C/D	690	(Balancing Figure)	90
	1,590		1,590

    3. S Ltd. Profit and Loss Account

	(Rs. In 000)		(Rs. In 000)
To General Reserve	90	By Balance b/d	663
To Dividend paid on 14.7.2009	300	By Net Profit for the year	
Rs. 1500 x 20(Balancing figure)			600
100			
To Corporate Dividend Tax	33		
(11% of Rs. 300)			
To Balance C/D	810		-
	1,233		1233

*Out of Rs. 6, 00,000 profits for the year, Rs. 90,000 has been transferred to reserves by S Ltd.

4. Distribution of Revenue Profits

	Rs. In '000
Revenue Profit as above	600
Share of H Ltd. (60%)	360
Share of Minority shareholders (Rs.600 – Rs. 360)	240

5. Computation of Capital Profits

Item	Rs in 000	Rs in 000
General Reserve on the date of acquisition		1,500
Less: Bonus issue of shares		900
		600
Profit and Loss Account balance on the date of acquisition	633	
Less: Dividends paid	300	
Corporate tax paid	33	
	333	300
		900
Share of H Ltd. (60%)		540
Share of Minority shareholders		360

6.Computation of capital Reserve

Item	Rs in 000	Rs in 000
60% of share capital of S Ltd		1440
Add: Share of H Ltd. in the capital profits as in working note (4)		540
		1980
Less: Investments in S Ltd.	1,500	
Less: Dividends received out of pre-	180	1,320
Acquisition profits (Rs. 300/100 X 60)		660

7. Calculation of Minority Interest

	Rs'000
40% of share capital of S Ltd.	960
Add: Share of Revenue Profits (Note 3)	240
Share of Capital Profits (Note 4)	360
	1,560

Q.5.3 : Consolidation of holding company with one subsidiary

The summarized Balance Sheets of A Ltd and B Ltd are as follows: (Rs)

Balance Sheets as at 31st December 2010

	A Ltd	B Ltd
Sources of funds		
Share capital in equity shares of Rs.10 each	200000	50000
Reserves	20000	5000
Profit and Loss Account as on 1st January 2010	30000	10000
Profit for the year	8000	8000
Add: Dividends from B Ltd	4000	-
Less: Dividends paid	-	(5000)
Creditors	30000	20000

¤ Total		292000	88000
Application of funds			
Fixed Assets		200000	80000
Current Assets		32000	8000
Shares in B Ltd at cost – 3000 shares		60000	-
	Total	292000	88000

A Limited had acquired 4000 shares in B Ltd at Rs.20 each on 1st January 2010 and sold 1000 of them at the same price on 1st October 2010. The sale is cum dividend. An interim dividend of 10% was paid by B Ltd on 1st July 2000. Draft a consolidated Balance Sheet as at 31st December 2010. *(Adapted CA Final Nov 2001)*

Solution
Consolidated Balance Sheet of A Ltd and its
Subsidiary B Ltd as at 31st December 2010

Particulars	Note no.	Amount Rs.
I. **Equity and Liabilities**		
(1)Shareholder's funds		
(a) Share capital	1	200000
(b) Reserves and surplus	2	63800
(2)Minority Interest (WN5)		27200
(3)Non-current liabilities		-
Long-term borrowing		
(4)Current liabilities		
Trade payables(30000 + 20000)		50000
Total		341000
II. **Assets**		
(1)Non-current assets		
(a)Fixed Assets		
Tangible assets (200000 + 80000)		280000
Intangible assets (goodwill)(**WN4**)		21000
(b)Non-current investments		-
(2)Current assets (32000 + 8000)		40000
Total		341000

Notes on Accounts

S/L No	Particulars	Amount (Rs)	Amount (Rs)
1.	**Share capital**		
	Issued and paid up		
	20000 equity shares of Rs.10 each fully paid		200000
2.	**Reserves & surplus**		
	Reserve	20000	

	Profit & Loss Account	__43800__	__63800__

Working Notes:
1. **Group structure**

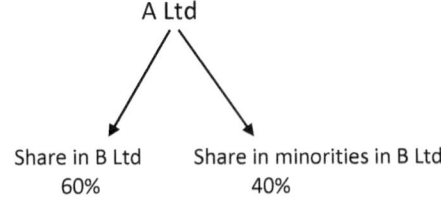

A Ltd

Share in B Ltd   Share in minorities in B Ltd
60%   40%

2.Statement of Distribution of Revenue Profits

	Rs.
Revenue Profit (Rs.8000 – Rs.5000)	3000
Share of A Ltd. (60%)	1800
Share of Minority shareholders (40%)	1200

3. Statement of Computation of Capital Profits

Item	Rs	Rs
Reserves		5000
Profit and Loss Account on the date of acquisition (1.1.2010)		10000
		15000
Share of A Ltd. (60%)		9000
Share of Minority shareholders (40%)		6000

4.Statement of Computation of cost of control / goodwill

Item	Rs	Rs
Investment in B Ltd		60000
Less: 60% of share capital of B Ltd	30000	
Add: Capital profits as in working note (3)	9000	
		39000
Goodwill		21000

5. Statement of Computation of Minority Interest

	Rs
40% of share capital of B Ltd.	20000
Add: Share of Revenue Profits (Note 2)	1200
Share of Capital Profits (Note 3)	6000
	27200

6. Statement of Computation of Profit & Loss A/c – A Ltd

	Rs
Balance as on 1.1.2010	30000
Profit for the year	8000
	38000
Add: Dividend from B Ltd	4000
	42000
Add: Share in B Ltd	1800
	43800

Q.5.4 : Consolidation of holding company with one subsidiary

The Balance Sheets of Bat Ltd and Ball Ltd as on 31.3.2010 are as follows:

Liabilities	Bat Ltd Rs.	Ball Ltd Rs.	Assets	Bat Ltd Rs.	Ball Ltd Rs.
Share capital			Investments		
(Shares of Rs.10 each)	160000	200000	Shares in Ball Ltd	196000	-
Profit and Loss Account	50000	60000	Debtors	-	120000
Creditors	-	16000	Stock	-	80000
			Cash at bank	-	70000
			Cash in hand	14000	6000
	210000	276000		210000	276000

Particulars of Bat Ltd:
1. The company was formed on1.4.2009
2. It acquired the shares of Ball Ltd as under:

Date of acquisition	No of shares	Cost Rs.
1. 4. 2009	8000	110000
31.7. 2009	6000	86000

3. The shares purchased on 31.7.2009 are ex-dividend and ex-bonus from existing holders.
4. On 31.7.2009 dividend at 10% was received from Ball Ltd and was credited to Profit and Loss Account.
5. On 31.7.2009 it received bonus shares from Ball Ltd in the ratio of one share on every four shares held.
6. Bat Ltd incurred an expenditure of Rs.500 per month on behalf of Ball Ltd and this was debited to the Profit & Loss Account of Bat Ltd, but nothing has been done in the books of Ball Ltd.
7. The balance in the Profit and Loss Account as on 31.3.2010 included Rs.36000 being the net profit made during the year.
8. Dividend proposed for 2009-10 at 10% was not provided for as yet.

Particulars of Ball Ltd
1. The balance in the Profit and Loss Account as on 31.3.2010 is after the issue of bonus shares made on 31.7.2009
2. The net profit made during the year is Rs.24000 including Rs.6000 received from insurance company in settlement of the claim towards loss of stock by fire on 30.06.2009 (Cost of

Rs.10800 included in opening stock)
3. Dividend proposed for 2009-10 at 10% was not provided for in the accounts.

Prepare a consolidated Balance Sheet of Bat Ltd as on 31.3.2010. (*Adapted CA Final : Nov 2000*)

Solution

Consolidated Balance Sheet of Bat Ltd and its Subsidiary Ball Ltd as at 31st March 2010

Particulars		Note no.	Amount Rs.
I.	**Equity and Liabilities**		
	(1)Shareholder's funds		
	(a) Share capital	1	160000
	(b) Reserves and surplus	2	47200
	(2)Minority Interest (WN5)		50800
	(3)Non-current liabilities		-
	Long-term borrowing		
	(4)Current liabilities		
	Trade payables	3	16000
	Short term provision	4	16000
	Total		**290000**
II.	**Assets**		
	(1)Non-current assets		
	(a)Fixed Assets		
	Tangible assets		-
	Intangible assets (goodwill)		
	(b)Non-current investments		-
	(2)Current assets		
	(a)Inventories		80000
	(b)Trade receivables		120000
	(c)Cash and cash		
	Equivalents (70000+20000)		90000
	Total		**290000**

Notes on Accounts

S/L No	Particulars	Amount (Rs)	Amount (Rs)
1.	**Share capital**		
	Issued and paid up		
	16000 equity shares of Rs.10 each fully paid		160000
2.	**Reserves & surplus**		
	Capital Reserve (WN4)	3040	
	Profit & Loss Account	44160	47200
3.	**Trade Payable**		

	Creditors		**16000**
4.	**Short term provision** Proposed dividend		**16000**

Working Notes:

1. **Group structure**

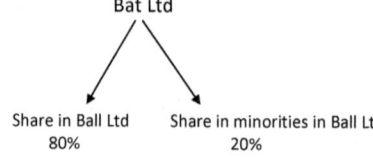

Bat Ltd

Share in Ball Ltd
80%

Share in minorities in Ball Ltd
20%

Share in Ball Ltd

$$= \frac{(8000 + 6000 + \text{bonus shares } (8000/4) = 2000)}{20000} \times 100$$

$= (16000 / 20000) \times 100$

$= 80\%$

2.Statement of Distribution of Revenue Profits

	Rs.
Revenue Profit (8/12 x 22800*)	15200
Share of Bat Ltd. (80%)	12160
Share of Minority shareholders (20%)	3040
*See W.N.3 below	

3. Statement of Computation of Capital Profits

Item	Rs	Rs
Profit and Loss Account on the date of acquisition (1.4.2009)		
(Rs.60000 – Rs.24000)		36000
Profit for the year	24000	
Add: Loss by fire	4800	
	28800	
Less: expenses not considered	6000	
	22800	
Pre-acquisition profits = 4/12 x 22800	7600	
Less: loss in pre-acquisition profits	4800	2800
		38800
Share of Bat Ltd. (80%)		31040
Share of Minority shareholders (20%)		7760

4.Statement of Computation of cost of control / goodwill

Item	Rs	Rs
Investment in Ball Ltd		196000
Less: pre-acquisition dividend		8000
		188000
Face value of investment in Ball Ltd	160000	
Add: Capital profits	31040	191040
Capital reserve		3040

5. Statement of Computation of Minority Interest

	Rs
20% of share capital of Ball Ltd.	40000
Add: Share of Revenue Profits (Note 2)	3040
Share of Capital Profits (Note 3)	7760
	50800

6. Statement of Computation of Profit & Loss A/c – Bat Ltd

	Rs
Balance	50000
Less: Pre-acquisition dividend wrongly credited	8000
	42000
Less: Proposed dividend	16000
	26000
Add: Expenses of Ball Ltd written back	6000
Share in Ball Ltd	12160
	44160

Q.5.5 : Consolidation of holding company with one Subsidiary

The Balance Sheets of Sun Ltd and Moon Ltd as on 31.3.2010 are given below: (Rs)

Liabilities	Sun Ltd	Moon Ltd	Assets	Sun Ltd	Moon Ltd
Share capital (Rs.10)	120000	100000	Fixed Assets	44000	84000
General reserve	20000	36000	Investment in Moon		
Profit & loss Account	12000	20000	Ltd	88000	
Bills payable	2000	5000	8000 shares @ Rs.11	6000	15000
Sundry creditors	4000	7000	Sundry debtors	4000	16000
Contingent liability of			Bills receivable	10000	40000
Sun Ltd: Bills discounted			Stock-in-trade	6000	13000
not yet matured Rs.2500			Cash at bank		
	158000	168000		158000	168000

Shares were purchased on 1.4.1997. When the shares were purchased General Reserve and Profit and Loss Account of Moon Ltd stood at Rs.30000 and Rs.16000 respectively. Dividends have been paid @ 10% every year after acquisition of shares, first dividend being paid out of pre-acquisition profits. No dividend has been proposed for 1999-2000 as yet and no provision need to be made in consolidated Balance Sheet. Sun Ltd has credited all dividends received to Profit and Loss Account.

On 31.3.2010, bonus shares has been declared by Moon Ltd @ 1 fully paid share for 5 held, but no effect has been given to that in the above Accounts. The bonus was declared out of profits earned prior to 1.4.2007 from General Reserve.

When the shares were purchased, agreed valuations of Fixed Assets of Moon Ltd was Rs.108000 although no effect has been given thereto in accounts.

Depreciation has been charged @ 10% p.a. on the book value as on 1.4.2007 (on straight line method), there being no addition or sale since then.

Out of current profits, Rs.2000 has been transferred to general reserve every year. Bills receivable of Sun Ltd include Rs.2000 bills accepted by Moon Ltd and bills discounted by Sun Ltd but not yet matured include Rs.1500 accepted by Moon Ltd. Sundry creditors of Sun Ltd include Rs.2000 due to Moon Ltd whereas Sundry debtors of Moon Ltd include Rs.4000 due from Sun Ltd. It is found that Sun Ltd has remitted a cheque of Rs.2000, which has not been received by Moon Ltd.

Prepare consolidated Balance Sheet as at 31.3.2010 of Sun Ltd and its subsidiary. (*Adapted CA Final May 2000*)

Solution

Consolidated Balance Sheet of Sun Ltd and its subsidiary
Moon Ltd as at 31st March 2010 (Rs)

Particulars		Note no.	Amount
I. **Equity and Liabilities**			
(1)Shareholder's funds			
(a) Share capital		1	120000
(b) Reserves and surplus		2	62080
(2)Minority Interest(WN4)			29520
(3)Non-current liabilities			-
Long-term borrowing			
(4)Current liabilities		3	14000
Trade payables			
	Total		225600
II. **Assets**			
(1)Non-current assets			
(a)Fixed Assets			
Tangible assets		4	119600
Intangible assets			
(b)Non-current investments			
(2)Current assets			
(a)Inventories		5	50000
(b)Trade receivables		6	35000
(c)Cash and cash equivalent		7	21000
	Total		225600

Notes on Accounts

S/L No	Particulars		Amount (Rs)	Amount (Rs)
1.	**Share capital** **Authorised, Issued and paid up** 12000 equity shares of Rs.10 each fully paid up			120000
2.	**Reserves & surplus** Capital reserve(WN3) General reserve Profit & Loss A/c			62080
3	**Current liabilities** Trade Payable			
	Sun Ltd	4000		
	Moon Ltd	7000		
		11000		
	Less: mutual		9000	
	Indebtedness	2000		
	Bills payable:			
	Sun Ltd	2000		
	Moon Ltd	5000		
		7000		
	Less: mutual			
	Indebtedness	2000	5000	14000
4.	**Tangible assets** Sun Ltd Moon Ltd (84000 – 12000+ 3600)			119600
5.	**Inventories** Sun Ltd Moon Ltd		10000 40000	50000
6.	**Trade receivable**			
	Sun Ltd	6000		
	Moon Ltd			
	(Rs.15000-Rs.2000 cheque			
	In transit)	13000		
		19000		
	Less: mutual			
	Indebtedness	2000	17000	
	Bills receivable			
	Sun Ltd	4000		
	Moon Ltd	16000		
		20000		
	Less: mutual			
	Indebtedness	2000		

			18000	35000
7.	**Cash and Cash equivalents**			
	Sun Ltd	6000	19000	
	Moon Ltd	13000		
	Remittance in transit		2000	21000

Working Notes:

1. **Group structure**

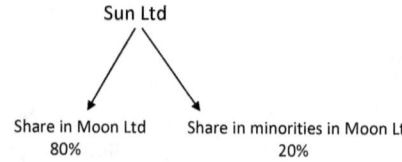

Share in Moon Ltd	Share in minorities in Moon Ltd
80%	20%

2. **Analysis of profits of Moon Ltd**

		Capital Profits	Revenue Reserve	Revenue Profits
	Rs.	Rs.	Rs.	Rs.
(a) General Reserve as on 1.4.2007	30000			
Less: Bonus issue (1/10 of Rs. 2000000)	20000	10000	-	-
(b) Increase in General Reserve (annual transfer of Rs.2000 for 3 years) (Rs. 36000 – Rs. 30000)			6000	
(c) Profit and Loss Account balance as on 1.4.2007	16000			
Less: Dividend paid for the year 2007-2008	10000	6000		
(d) Increase in Profit (Rs. 20000 – Rs. 6000)				14000
(e) Loss on revaluation ((84000 x 100 /70 i.e.120000)-108000)		(12000)		
(f) Additional depreciation written back (10% x Rs. 12000)x 3				3600
		4000	6000	17600
Sun Ltd's share (80%)		3200	4800	14080
Minority Interest (20%)		800	1200	3520

3. **Cost of Control**

	Rs.	Rs.
Cost of investments in Moon Ltd.	88000	

244

Less: Dividend of capital profits	8000	80000
Less: face value of investment (including bonus shares)		
(80000 + 80000 x 1/5)	96000	
Capital profit	3200	99200
Capital reserve		19200

4. Minority Interest

	Rs.
Equity share capital including bonus share (20000 +20000 x 1/5)]	24000
Capital profits	800
Revenue reserve	1200
Share of revenue profit	3520
	29520

5. Profit and Loss Account – Sun Ltd.

	Rs.
Balance	12000
Less: Dividend credited to investment	8000
	4000
Add: Share in Moon Ltd	14080
	18080

8. General reserve – Sun Ltd.

	Rs.
Balance	20000
Add: Share in Moon Ltd.	4800
	24800

Tutorial note:
With regards to Bills receivable of Sun Ltd it may be alternatively assumed that out of bills of Sun Ltd accepted by Moon Ltd Rs.2000, Rs.1500 have been discounted. In such case, only Rs.500 will be deducted as mutual indebtedness from bills receivable and bills payable in the balance sheet instead of Rs.2000.

Q.5.6: Consolidation of holding company with one Subsidiary

War Ltd purchased on 31st March 2009, 48000 shares in Peace Ltd at 50% premium over face value by issue of 8% debentures at 20% premium. The balance sheets of War and Peace Ltd as on 31.3.2009, the date of purchase were as under:

Liabilities	War Ltd	Peace Ltd	Assets	War Ltd	Peace Ltd
Share capital (Rs.10)	1050000	600000	Fixed Assets	650000	200000
General reserve	120000	40000	Stock-in-trade	300000	180000
Profit & loss account	80000	-	Sundry debtors	320000	200000
Sundry creditors	100000	60000	Cash in hand	60000	30000
			Preliminary expenses	20000	10000

			Profit & loss account	-	80000
	1350000	700000		1350000	700000

Particulars of War Ltd:

1. Profit made: Rs.
   2009-10   160000
   2010-11   200000
2. The above profit was made after charging depreciation of Rs.60000 and Rs.40000 respectively.
3. Out of profit shown above every year Rs.20000 had been transferred to general reserve
4. 10% dividend had been paid in both the years.
5. It has been decided to write down investment to face value of shares in 10 years and to provide for share of loss to subsidiary.

Particulars of Peace Ltd:

The company incurred losses of Rs.40000 and Rs.60000 in 2009-10 and 2010-11 after charging depreciation of 10% p.a. of the book value as on 1.4.2009.

Prepare consolidated Balance Sheet as at 31.3.2011 of War Ltd and its subsidiary. (Adapted CA Final Nov 1999)

Solution

Consolidated Balance Sheet of War Ltd and its subsidiary
Peace Ltd as at 31st March 2011 (Rs)

Particulars	Note no.	Amount
I. Equity and Liabilities		
(1)Shareholder's funds		
(a) Share capital	1	1050000
(b) Reserves and surplus	2	322000
(2)Minority Interest(WN4e)		90000
(3)Non-current liabilities		-
Long-term borrowing	3	600000
(4)Current liabilities		
Trade payables		
Total		**2062000**
II. Assets		
(1)Non-current assets		
(a)Fixed Assets		
Tangible assets	4	710000
Intangible assets (goodwill)(WN4d)		232000
(b)Non-current investments		
(2)Current assets	5	1120000
Total		**2062000**

Notes on Accounts

S/L	Particulars	Amount	Amount

No		(Rs)	(Rs)
1.	**Share capital** **Authorised, Issued and paid up** 105000 equity shares of Rs.10 each fully paid up		**1050000**
2.	**Reserves & surplus** Capital reserve(WN3) General reserve Profit & Loss A/c 62000 Less: Preliminary expenses 20000	**120000** **160000** **42000**	**322000**
3	**Non-current liabilities** **Long term borrowings** Secured loan 8% debentures		**600000**
4.	**Tangible assets** War Ltd Peace Ltd	**550000** **160000**	**710000**
5	**Current assets** War Ltd Peace Ltd	**830000** **290000**	**1120000**

Working Notes

1. **Investment in Peace Ltd (48000 shares)**

	Rs.
Face value of shares	480000
Premium (50%) over face value	240000
Cost of investment	720000

Acquired by issue of debentures at 20% premium:

	Rs	Rs.
8% debentures (nominal value =720000/120x100)	600000	
Debenture premium	120000	720000

Writing down of investment:

2009-10: 1/10 x 240000	(24000)	
2010-11: 1/10 x 240000	(24000)	(48000)
Investment as on 31.3.2011		672000

2. **Balance of Profit and Loss Account on 31st March 2011:**

Item	War Ltd Rs	Peace Ltd Rs.

Balance as on 31.3.2009	80000	(80000)
Profit / (loss)		
For 2009-10	160000	(40000)
For 2010-11	200000	(60000)
Investment written off		
For 2009-10	(24000)	
For 2010-11	(24000)	
Provision for share of loss in subsidiary		
2009-10 : 4/5 x 40000	(32000)	
2010-11 : 4/5 x 60000	(48000)	
Transfer to General Reserve		
2009-10	(20000)	
2010-11	(20000)	
Dividend		
2009-10	(105000)	
2010-11	(105000)	
	62000	(180000)

In the absence of information taxation has been ignored.

3. **Statement of assets and liabilities as at 31st March 2011**

Liabilities	War Ltd	Peace Ltd	Assets	War Ltd	Peace Ltd
Share capital	1050000	600000	Fixed Assets*	550000	160000
Capital reserve	120000	-	Investments		
(Debenture			672000		
premium)			Less: prov		
General reserve	160000	40000	for loss in		
Profit & loss			subsidiary		
Account	62000	-	80000	592000	-
8% Debentures	600000	-	Net current		
			Assets		
			(bal fig)	830000	290000
			Preliminary		
			Expenses	20000	10000
			Profit & loss		
			Account	-	180000
	1992000	640000		1992000	640000

*Statement of Fixed Assets on 31st March 2011:

	War Ltd Rs	Peace Ltd Rs.
Fixed assets on 31.3.2009	650000	200000
Less : Depreciation		
2009-10	(60000)	(20000)
2010-11	(40000)	(20000)
	550000	160000

Tutorial Note: In the absence of information about the movement in individual current assets and current liabilities, balance sheets on 31.3.2011 have been prepared on the basis on net current assets.

4. **Computation for consolidation**

   a) **Group structure**

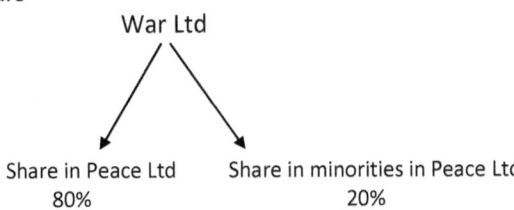

War Ltd

Share in Peace Ltd 80%   Share in minorities in Peace Ltd 20%

b)**Statement of Distribution of Revenue Profits**

	Rs.
Revenue Profit/ (loss) 2009-10 and 2010-11	(100000)
Share of War Ltd (80%)	(80000)
Share of Minority shareholders (20%)	(20000)

c)**Statement of Computation of Capital Profits**

Item	Rs	Rs
General Reserve on 31.3.2009		40000
Profit and Loss Account on 31.3.2009		(80000)
		(40000)
Share of War Ltd. (80%)		(32000)
Share of Minority shareholders (20%)		(8000)

d)**Statement of Computation of cost of control / goodwill**

Item	Rs	Rs
Investment in Peace Ltd		672000
Less: Paid up value of investments (80%)	480000	
Capital profits / (losses)	(32000)	
Preliminary expenses (4/5 x 10000)	(8000)	440000
Goodwill		232000

e)**Statement of Computation of Minority Interest**

	Rs
Share capital of Peace Ltd (20%)	120000
Add: Share of Revenue Profits (Note b)	(20000)
Share of Capital Profits (Note c)	(8000)

Preliminary expenses (1/5 x 10000)	(2000)
	90000

f) Statement of Computation of Profit & Loss A/c – War Ltd

	Rs
Balance	62000
Less: Share of loss in Peace Ltd	80000
	(18000)
Add: Provision for loss in subsidiary	80000
	62000

Q.5.7 : Consolidation of holding company and one Subsidiary showing treatment of bonus issue

On 31st March, 2004, P Ltd. acquired 1, 05,000 shares of Q Ltd. for Rs. 12,00,000. The Balance Sheet of Q Ltd. on that date was under:

Liabilities	Rs.	Assets	Rs.
1,50,000 equity shares of Rs. 10 Each fully paid	15, 00,000	Fixed Assets	10,50,000
Pre-incorporation profits	30,000	Current Assets	6,45,000
Profit and Loss Accounts	60,000		
Creditors	1, 05,000		
	16,95,000		16,95,000

On 31st March, 2010 the Balance Sheets of two companies were as follows:

Liabilities	P Ltd Rs	Q Ltd Rs	Assets	P Ltd Rs	Q Ltd Rs
Equity shares of Rs. 10 each fully paid (before bonus issue)	45,00,000	15,00,000	Fixed Assets	79,20,000	23,10,000
			1,05,000 equity shares in Q Ltd at cost	12,00,000	-
Securities Premium	9, 00,000	-			
Pre-incorporation profits	--	30,000	Current Assets	44,10,000	17,55,000
General Reserve	60,00,000	19,05,000			
Profit and Loss A/C	15,75,000	4,20,000			
Creditors	5,55,000	2,10,000			
	1,35,30,000	40,65,000		1,35,30,000	40,65,000

Directors of Q Ltd. made bonus issue on 31.3.2010 in the ratio of one equity share of Rs. 10 each fully paid for every two equity shares held on that date.
Calculate as on 31st March, 2010
   (i)   Cost of control/Capital Reserve;

(ii)   Minority Interest
(iii)   Consolidated Profit and Loss Account in each of the following cases:
         (a) Before issue of Bonus shares.
         (b) Immediately after issue of Bonus Shares.
It may be assumed that bonus shares were issued out of post-acquisition profits by using General Reserve.
Prepare a Consolidated Balance Sheet after the bonus issue.(*Adapted CA Final May 2003*)

Solution

(i)   Before issue of bonus shares

			Rs.	Rs.
(i)	Cost of control/capital reserve			
	Investment in Q Ltd.			12,00,000
	Less: Face value of investments	10, 50,000		
	Capital profits (W.N.)	63,000		11,13,000
	Cost of control			87,000
(ii)	Minority Interest			Rs.
	Share Capital			4,50,000
	Capital Profits (W.N.)			27,000
	Revenue Profits (W.N.)			6,79,500
				11,56,500
(iii)	Consolidated profit and loss account – P Ltd.			Rs.
	Balance			15,75,000
	Add: Share in revenue profits of Q Ltd. (W.N.)			15,85,500
				31,60,500

(ii)   Immediately after issue of bonus shares

		Rs.	Rs.
(i)	Cost of control/capital reserve		
	Face value of investments	15,75,000	
	(Rs. 10, 50,000+5, 25,000)		
	Capital Profits (W.N.)	63,000	16,38,000
	Less: Investment in Q Ltd.		12,00,000
	Capital reserve		4,38,000
(ii)	Minority Interest		Rs.
	Share Capital (Rs. 4,50,000 + 2,25,000)		6,75,000
	Capital Profits (W.N.)		27,000
	Revenue Profits (W.N.)		4,54,000
			11,56,500
(iii)	Consolidated Profit and Loss Account – P td.		Rs.
	Balance		15,75,000
	Add: Share in revenue profits of Q Ltd. (W.N.)		10,60,500
			26,35,500

Consolidated Balance Sheet of P Ltd. and its subsidiary Q Ltd. as on 31st March, 2010

Particulars	Note no.	Amount
I. Equity and Liabilities		
(1)Shareholder's funds		
(a) Share capital	1	4500000
(b) Reserves and surplus	2	9973500
(2)Minority Interest(WN)		1156500
(3)Non-current liabilities		-
Long-term borrowing		
(4)Current liabilities		-
Trade payables		765000
Total		16395000
II. Assets		
(1)Non-current assets		
(a)Fixed Assets		
Tangible assets (7920000 + 2310000)		10230000
Intangible assets (goodwill)		-
(b)Non-current investments		
(2)Current assets		
(4410000 + 1755000)		6165000
Total		16395000

Notes on Accounts

S/L No	Particulars	Amount (Rs)	Amount (Rs)
1.	**Share capital**		
	Authorised, Issued and paid up		
	Shares of Rs.10 each fully paid up		<u>4500000</u>
2.	**Reserves & surplus**		
	Securities Premium	900000	
	Capital reserve	438000	
	General reserve	6000000	
	Profit & Loss A/c	<u>2635500</u>	<u>9973500</u>

Working Note:
Analysis of Profits of Q Ltd.

Item	Capital profits (before and after issue of	Revenue profits before bonus Issue	Revenue profits after bonus Issue

	bonus shares)		
	Rs	Rs.	Rs.
Pre-incorporation profits	30000		
Profit & Loss a/c on 31.3.2004	60000		
	90000		
General reserve *		1905000	1905000
Less: bonus shares			750000
			1155000
Profit for period of 1st April, 2005 to			
31st March,2010 (Rs. 4,20,000 – Rs. 60,000)		360000	360000
		22650000	1515000
P Ltd's share (70%)	63000	1585500	1060500
Minority's share (30%)	27000	679500	454500

*Share of P Ltd. in General reserve has been adjusted in Consolidated Profit and Loss Account.

Q.5.8: Consolidation of holding company and one subsidiary – bonus issue , unrealised profit

---

On 31st March, 2010 the Balance Sheet of H Ltd. and its subsidiary S Ltd. stood as follows:

	H Ltd.	S Ltd.
Liabilities	Rs. in lakhs	Rs. in lakhs
Share Capital:		
Authorized	15,000	6,000
Issue and Subscribed:		
Equity Shares of Rs. 10 each, fully paid	12,000	4,800
General Reserve	2,748	1,380
Profit and Loss Account	2,715	1,620
Bills Payable	372	160
Sundry Creditors	1,461	854
Provision for Taxation	855	394
Proposed Dividend	1,200	---
	21,387	9,208

	H Ltd.	S Ltd.
Assets	Rs. in lakhs	Rs. in lakhs
Land and Buildings	2,718	---
Plant and Machinery	4,905	4,900
Furniture and Fittings	1,845	586
Investment in Shares in S Ltd.	3,000	---
Stock	3,949	1,956
Debtors	2,600	1,363
Cash and Bank Balances	1,490	204
Bills Receivables	360	199

Sundry Advances	520	---
	21,387	9,208

The following information is also provided to you:

(a) H Ltd. purchased 180 lakh shares in S Ltd. on 1st April, 2009 when the balances to General Reserve and Profit and Loss Account of S Ltd. stood at Rs. 3,000 Lakh and 1,200 lakh respectively.

(b) On 4th July, 2009 S Ltd. declared a dividend @ 20% for the year ended 31st March, 2009. H Ltd. credited the dividend received by it to its profit and loss account.

(c) On 1st January, 2010 S Ltd. issued 3 fully paid shares for every 5 shares held as bonus shares out of balances to its general reserve as on 31st March, 2009.

(d) On 31st March, 2010 all the bills payable in S Ltd's balance sheet were acceptances in favour of H Ltd. But on that date, H Ltd. held only Rs 45 lakh of these acceptances in hand, the rest having been endorsed in favour of its creditors.

(e) On 31st March, 2010 S Ltd's stock included goods which it had purchased for Rs. 100 lakh from H Ltd. which made profit @ 25% on cost.

Prepare a Consolidated Balance Sheet of H Ltd. and its subsidiary S Ltd. as at 31st March, 2010 bearing in mind the requirements of AS 21.(*Adapted CA Final: May 2004*)

Solution
Consolidated Balance sheet of H Ltd.
and its subsidiary S Ltd. as on 31st March, 2010

Particulars		Note no.	Amount (Rs lakhs)
I.	**Equity and Liabilities**		
	(1)Shareholder's funds		
	(a) Share capital	1	12000
	(b) Reserves and surplus	2	7159
	(2)Minority Interest (WN6)		3120
	(3)Non-current liabilities		-
	Long-term borrowing		
	(4)Current liabilities		
	(a)Trade payables	3	2802
	(b)Short term provisions	4	1249
	(c)Other current liabilities	5	1200
	Total		27530
II.	**Assets**		
	(1)Non-current assets		
	(a)Fixed Assets		
	Tangible assets	6	14954
	Intangible assets (goodwill)		-
	(b)Non-current investments		-
	(2)Current assets		
	(a)Inventories	7	5885
	(b)Trade receivables	8	4477

(c)Cash and cash equivalents		9	1694
(d)Short term loans and advances		10	520
	Total		27530

Notes on Accounts

S/L No	Particulars		Amount (Rs'lakhs)	Amount (Rs'lakhs)
1.	Share capital			
	Authorised			15000
	Issued and paid up			
	Equity shares of Rs.10 each fully paid			12000
2.	Reserves & surplus			
	Capital Reserve (Note 5)		1320	
	General Reserve (2784 + 108)		2892	
	Profit & Loss Account:			
	H Ltd	2715		
	Add: Share in S Ltd	612		
		3327		
	Less: Dividend wrongly Credited	360		
		2967		
	Less: Unrealised profit	20	2947	7159
	Current liabilities			
3.	Trade payables			
	Bills payable H Ltd	372		
	S Ltd	160		
		532	487	
	Less: Mutual owing	(45)		
	Sundry creditors			
	H Ltd	1461		
	S Ltd	854	2315	2802
4.	Short term provisions			
	Provision for taxation			
	H Ltd		855	
	S Ltd		394	1249
5.	Other current liabilities			
	Proposed dividend			
	H Ltd			1200
6.	Tangible assets			
	Land & buildings			
	H Ltd		2718	
	Plant & Machinery			
	H Ltd	4905		

	S Ltd	4900	9805	
	Furniture & fittings			
	H Ltd	1845		
	S Ltd	586	2431	14954
7.	**Current Assets**			
	Inventories			
	H Ltd		3949	
	S Ltd		1956	
			5905	
	Less: unrealised Profit		(20)	5885
8.	**Trade receivable**			
	Debtors			
	H Ltd	2600		
	S Ltd	1363	3963	
	Bills receivable			
	H Ltd	360		
	S Ltd	199		
		559		
	Less: Mutual owing 45		514	4477
9.	**Cash and cash equivalents**			
	H Ltd		1490	
	S Ltd		204	1694
10.	**Short term loans and advances**			
	Sundry advances			
	H Ltd			520

Working Notes:

1. S Ltd's General Reserve Account

	Rs. in Lakhs			Rs. In Lakhs
To Bonus to Equity Shareholders	1,800	By	Balance b/d	3,000
To Balance c/d	1,380	By	Profit & Loss a/c	180
	3,180			3,180

2. S Ltd's Profit and Loss Account

		Rs. in Lakhs			Rs. In Lakhs
To	General Revenue	180	By	Balance b/d	1,200
To	Dividend paid		By	Net Profit for the year*	1,200
	(20% on Rs.3,000 lakhs)	600			
	To Balance c/d	1,620			
		2,400			2,400

*Out of Rs. 1,200 lakhs profit for the year, Rs. 180 lakhs has been transferred to reserves.

3. Distribution of Revenue Profits

	Rs. In Lakhs
Revenue profits (W.N.2)	1,200
Less: Share of H Ltd. 60%	720
(General Reserve Rs. 108 + Profit and Loss account Rs.612)	
Share of Minority Shareholders (40%)	480

4. Calculation of Capital Profits

	Rs. In Lakhs
General Reserve on the date of acquisition less bonus shares (Rs.3000-Rs.1800)	1,200
Profit and Loss account on the date of acquisition less dividend paid (Rs.1200-Rs.600)	600
	1,800

H Ltd's share = 60% of Rs. 1,800 lakhs = Rs. 1,080 lakhs

Minority Interest = Rs. 1,800 – Rs. 1080 = Rs. 720 lakhs

5. Calculation of Capital Reserve

	Rs. In Lakhs
Paid up value of shares held (60% of Rs. 4,800)	2,880
Add: Share in capital profits	1,080
	3,960
Less: Cost of shares less dividend received (Rs. 3000-Rs.360)	2,640
Capital Reserve	1,320

6. Calculation of Minority Interest

	Rs. In Lakhs
40% of share capital (40% of Rs. 4,800)	1,920
Add: Share in revenue profits	480
Share in capital profits	720
	3,120

7. Unrealized profit in respect to stock

Rs.100 lakhs x 25/125 = Rs. 20 lakhs

Q.5.9: Consolidation of holding company and one subsidiary showing treatment on hire purchase

The following are the summarized Balance Sheets of PD Co Ltd and SD Co Ltd as on 31.3.10.

Liabilities	PD Ltd	SD Ltd	Assets	PD Ltd	SD Ltd
	Rs.	Rs.		Rs.	Rs.
Share capital:					
Authorized	70,00,000	30,00,000	Land & building	20,00,000	15,20,000
Issued & subscribed			Plant & Machinery	20,00,000	8,00,000
Equity shares of Rs.10			Furniture	5,00,000	1,60,000
Each fully paid	50,00,000	20,00,000	Investments	16,10,000	-
Capital Reserve	5,00,000	3,10,000	Stock	3,40,000	1,00,000
Revenue Reserve	8,50,000	75,000	Sundry debtors	3,60,000	2,00,000
Profit & Loss A/c	4,00,000	2,80,000	Bills receivable	50,000	40,000
Sundry creditors	2,50,000	2,25,000	Bank	2,40,000	80,000
Bills Payable	1,00,000	10,000			
	71,00,000	29,00,000		71,00,000	29,00,000

PD Ltd acquired 80% shares of SD Ltd on 30.9.2009 at a cost of Rs.18, 10,000. On 1.10.2009 SD Ltd declared and paid dividend on equity shares. PD Ltd appropriately adjusted its share of dividend in investment account.

On 1.4.2009, the capital reserve and profit and loss account stood in the books of SD Ltd at Rs.50, 000 and Rs.2, 75,000 respectively.

Land & Buildings standing in the books of SD Ltd at Rs.16, 00,000 on 1.4.2009, revalued at Rs.20,00, 000 on 1.10.2009. Furniture which stood in the books at Rs.2, 00,000 on 1.4.2009 revalued at Rs.1, 50,000 on 1.10.2009. In both the cases the effects have not yet been given in the books.

SD Ltd bought an item of machinery from PD Ltd on hire purchase basis. The following are the balances in respect of this machinery in the books on 31.03.2010 :

Instalment due	Rs.20,000
Instalment not due	Rs.8,000
Hire-purchase stock reserve	Rs.1,600

The above items stood included under appropriate heads in Balance Sheet.

Prepare a consolidated Balance Sheet of PD Ltd and its subsidiary SD Ltd as at 31.03.2010 complying with the requirements of AS 21. (*Adapted CA Final Nov 2004*)

Solution

Working Notes

1. Analysis of reserves and profits of SD Co Ltd as on 31.03.2010

	Pre acquisition (Capital profit)	Post- acquisition profits (1.10.2009 – 31.3.2010)		
		Capital reserve	Revenue reserve	P&L A/c
Capital reserve as on 31.3.2010	3,10,000			
Less: Balance as on 1.4.2009	50,000	50,000		
Created during the year	2,60,000	1,30,000	1,30,000	
Revenue reserve as on 31.3.2010	75,000			
Less: balance as on 1.4.2009	-			
Created during the year	75,000	37,500		37,500
Profit & Loss Account as on 31.3.2010	2,80,000			
Add: dividend paid on 1.10.2009	2,50,000			
(out of pre-acquisition profits)	-------------			
	5,30,000			
Less: balance as on 1.4.2009	2,75,000			
Earned during the year	2,55,000	1,27,500		1,27,500
Profit as on 1.4.2009	2,75,000			
Less: Dividend paid (Rs.18,10,000 –				
Rs.16.10.000) x 5/4	2,50,000			
Balance of pre-acquisition profit as on				
31.3.2010	25,000	25,000		
Revaluation reserves as on 1.10.2009:				
Profit on land and buildings (WN 2)	4,40,000			
Loss on furniture (WN 2)	(30,000)			
Difference in depreciation (for 6 moths)				
Due to revaluation :				
Short depreciation on land & building (WN3)				(10,000)
Excess depreciation on furniture (WN3)				5,000

-				
Total	7,80,000	1,30,000	37,500	1,22,500
Minority interest (20%)	1,56,000	26,000	7,500	24,500
Share of PD Ltd (80%)	6,24,000	1,04,000	30,000	98,000

2. Profit or loss on revaluation of assets in the books of SD Ltd and their book values as on 31.3.2010

Rs.

Land & buildings

Book value as on 1.4.2009	16,00,000
Depreciation at 5% p.a. for six months	
(80,000 x 100) / 16,00,0000 = 5%	40,000
	15,60,000
Revalued on 1.10.2009	20,00,000
Profit on revaluation	4,40,000
Value as per balance sheet on 31.3.2010	15,20,000

Add: Profit on revaluation	4,40,000	
Less: Short depreciation (WN3)	10,000	
Value as on 31.3.2010	19,50,000	

Furniture

Book value as on 1.4.2009	2,00,000	
Less: Depreciation @ 20% p.a. for six months		
(40,000 x100)/2,00,000 = 20%	20,000	
	1,80,000	
Revalued as on 1.10.2009	1,50,000	
Loss on revaluation	30,000	
Value as per balance sheet on 31.3.2010	1,60,000	
Less: Loss on revaluation	30,000	
Add: Excess depreciation written back (WN3)	5,000	
Value as on 31.3.2010	1,35,000	

3. Calculation of short / excess depreciation

	Building	Furniture
Revalued figure as on 1.10.2009	20,00,000	1,50,000
Rate of depreciation	5% p.a.	20% p.a.
Depreciation for six months on revalued figure		
(1.10.2009 to 31.3.2010)	50,000	15,000
Depreciation already provided	40,000	20,000
Difference (short)/excess	(10,000)	5,000

4. Calculation of cost of control

	Rs.
Share capital in SD Ltd	16,00,000
Add: capital profit	6,24,000
Less : cost of investment	16,10,000
Capital reserve	6,14,000

5. Calculation of minority interest

		Rs.
Share capital		4,00,000
Capital (pre-acquisition) profits		1,56,000
Revenue (post-acquisition) profits		
Capital reserve	26,000	
Revenue reserve	7,500	
Profit and loss	24,500	58,000
		6,14,000

6. Stock reserve (plant & machinery)

Percentage of profit on hire purchase transaction

(1600 x 100) / 8,000	=	20%
20% on Rs.20,000	=	Rs.4,000
Total unrealised profit	=	Rs. 4,000 + Rs.1,600 = Rs.5,600

7. Elimination of mutual indebtedness

Elimination of mutual indebtedness in respect of sale of machinery on hire purchase basis will be made as under in the consolidated balance sheet.

	Creditors	Debtors	Stock	Plant & Mach
	Rs.	Rs.	Rs.	Rs.
Total (PD Ltd and SD Ltd)	4,75,000	5,60,000	4,40,000	28,00,000
Less: Instalment due	20,000	20,000	-	-
Less : Instalment not due	8,000	-	8,000	-
Less : Profit on plant purchase by SD Ltd from PD Ltd on hire purchase	-	-	-	5,600
	4,47,000	5,40,000	4,32,000	27,94,400

For consolidated balance sheet purpose, the unrealised profits will be eliminated by Deducting Rs.5,600 from Plant & Machinery and from profit and loss account.

	Rs.
8. Consolidated capital reserve as on 31.3.2010	
Capital reserve of PD Ltd as on 31.3.2010	5,00,000
Add: share of post-acquisition capital reserve of SD Ltd (WN1)	1,04,000
Add: cost of control (WN4)	6,14,000
	12,18,000
9. Consolidated revenue reserve as on 31.3.2010	Rs.
Revenue reserve of PD Ltd as on 31.3.2010	8,50,000
Add: Share in post-acquisition revenue reserve of SD Ltd(WN1)	30,000
	8,80,000
10. Consolidated profit and loss account as on 31.3.2010	Rs.
Profit and loss account balance of PD Ltd as on 31.3.2010	4,00,000
Add: share in post-acquisition profit and loss account of SD Ltd	98,000
Less : Unrealised profit on hire purchase	(5,600)
	4,92,400

Note: In the question, the balance of capital reserve and profit and loss account of SD Ltd as on 1.4.2009 only has been given and not of revenue reserve. Hence, it has been assumed in the above solution that the revenue reserve is created during the year from current year's profits.

Consolidated Balance Sheet of PD Co Ltd with its subsidiary SD Co Ltd as on 31st March 2010

Particulars	Note no.	Amount (Rs)
I. **Equity and Liabilities**		
(1)Shareholder's funds		
(a) Share capital	1	5000000
(b) Reserves and surplus	2	2590400
(2)Minority Interest (WN5)		614000

(3)Non-current liabilities			-
Long-term borrowing			
(4)Current liabilities			
(a)Trade payables		3	557000
(b)Short term provisions			-
(c)Other current liabilities			-
	Total		8761400
II. **Assets**			
(1)Non-current assets			
(a)Fixed Assets			
Tangible assets		4	7379400
Intangible assets (goodwill)			-
(b)Non-current investments			-
(2)Current assets			
(a)Inventories		5	432000
(b)Trade receivables		6	630000
(c)Cash and cash equivalents		7	320000
	Total		8761400

Notes on Accounts

S/L No	Particulars		Amount (Rs)	Amount (Rs)
1.	**Share capital**			
	Authorised			7000000
	Issued and paid up			
	Equity shares of Rs.10 each fully paid			5000000
2.	**Reserves & surplus**			
	Capital Reserve (WN8)		1218000	
	Revenue Reserve (WN9)		880000	
	Profit & Loss Account (WN10)		492400	2590400
	Current liabilities			
3.	**Trade payables**			
	Sundry creditors PD Ltd	250000		
	SD Ltd	225000		
		475000		
	Less: Mutual Hire purchase			
	Indebtedness	(28000)	447000	
	Bills payable			
	PD Ltd	100000		
	SD Ltd	10000	110000	557000
4.	**Tangible assets**			
	Land & buildings			

	PD Ltd	2000000		
	SD Ltd (WN2)	1950000	**3950000**	
	Plant & Machinery			
	PD Ltd	2000000		
	SD Ltd	800000		
	2800000			
	Less: Unrealised profit on			
	Hire purchase	5600	**2794400**	
	Furniture & fittings			
	PD Ltd	500000		
	SD Ltd (WN2)	135000	**635000**	**7379400**
5.	**Current Assets**			
	Inventories			
	PD Ltd		**340000**	
	SD Ltd		**100000**	
			440000	
	Less: Hire purchase			
	Instalment not due		**8000**	**432000**
6.	**Trade receivable**			
	Sundry Debtors			
	PD Ltd	360000		
	SD Ltd	200000		
		560000		
	Less: Hire purchase			
	Instalment due	20000	**540000**	
	Bills receivable			
	PD Ltd	50000		
	SD Ltd	40000	**90000**	**630000**
7.	**Cash and cash equivalents**			
	Bank balance			
	PD Ltd		**240000**	
	SD Ltd		**80000**	**320000**

Q.5.10: Consolidation of holding company with one subsidiary with interco adjustments and treatment of dividend and bonus shares

The Balance Sheet of Golden and Silver Ltd as on 31.3.2006 are given below:

Liabilities	Golden Rs.	Silver Rs	Assets	Golden Rs.	Silver Rs.

Equity share capital	240000	240000	Fixed Assets	88000	168000
General reserve	40000	32000	Investment	180000	10000
Profit & loss Account	24000	39000	Sundry debtors	12000	30000
Bills payable	4000	10000	Bills receivable	8000	32000
Sundry creditors	8000	15000	Stock-in-trade	20000	80000
			Cash at bank	8000	16000
	316000	336000		316000	336000

Note: Contingent liability of Golden Ltd: bills discounted not yet matured at Rs.5000.

Additional information:

i)   On 1.10.2003, Golden Ltd acquired 16000 shares of Rs.10 each at the rate of Rs.11 per share.

ii) Balances to General Reserve and Profit and Loss account of Silver Ltd stood on 1.4.2003 at Rs.60000 and Rs.32000 respectively.

iii) Dividends have been paid @ 10% for each of the years 2003-04 and 2004-05. Dividend for the year 2003-04 was paid out of the pre-acquisition profits. No dividend has been proposed for the year 2005-06 as yet and no provision need to be made in consolidated Balance Sheet. Golden Ltd has credited all dividends received to Profit and Loss account.

iv) On 1.3.2006, bonus shares were issued by Silver Ltd at the rate of one fully paid share for every five held and effect has been given to that effect in the above accounts. The bonus was declared from general reserves from out of profits earned prior to 1.4.2003.

v)   On 1.10.2003, Fixed Assets was revalued at Rs.216000 but no adjustment had been made in the books.

vi) Depreciation had been charged @ 10% p.a. on the book value as on 1.4.2003 (on straight line method) there being no addition or sale since then.

vii) Out of current profits Rs.4000 has been transferred to General reserve every year.

viii) Bills receivable of Golden Ltd include Rs.4000 bills accepted by Silver Ltd. Bills discounted by Golden Ltd but not yet matured include Rs.3000 accepted by Silver Ltd.

ix) Sundry creditors of Golden Ltd include Rs.4000 due to Silver Ltd. Sundry debtors of Silver Ltd include Rs.8000 due from Golden Ltd.

x)   It is found that Golden Ltd has remitted a cheque of Rs.4000 which has not yet been received by Silver Ltd.

Prepare a consolidated Balance Sheet as at 31.3.2006 of Golden Ltd and its subsidiary. *(CA Final : Nov 2006)*

Solution
Consolidated Balance Sheet of Golden Ltd. and its subsidiary Silver Ltd.
as on 31st March, 2006

Particulars	Note no.	Amount (Rs)
I. **Equity and Liabilities** **(1)Shareholder's funds**		

(a) Share capital		1	240000
(b) Reserves and surplus		2	129600
(2)Minority Interest (WN5)			60400
(3)Non-current liabilities			-
Long-term borrowing			
(4)Current liabilities			
(a)Trade payables		3	29000
(b)Short term provisions			-
(c)Other current liabilities			-
	Total		459000

II.	**Assets**			
	(1)Non-current assets			
	(a)Fixed Assets			
	Tangible assets		4	247000
	Intangible assets (goodwill)			-
	(b)Non-current investments		5	14000
	(2)Current assets			
	(a)Inventories		6	100000
	(b)Trade receivables		7	70000
	(c)Cash and cash equivalents		8	28000
		Total		459000

Notes on Accounts

S/L No	Particulars	Amount (Rs)	Amount (Rs)
1.	**Share capital** **Issued and paid up** 24000 Equity shares of Rs.10 each fully paid		240000
2.	**Reserves & surplus** Capital reserve (WN4) General reserve (WN6) Profit & Loss Account (WN7)	53200 48000 28400	129600
3.	**Current liabilities** **Trade payables** Sundry creditors Golden Ltd 8000 Silver Ltd 15000 23000 Less: Mutual Indebtedness (4000)	19000	
	Bills payable Golden Ltd 4000 Silver Ltd 10000 14000 Less: Mutual		

	Indebtedness	(4000)	10000	29000
4.	Tangible assets			
	Golden Ltd		88000	
	Silver Ltd (168000 – 12000 + 4000)		159000	247000
5.	Non-current investment			
	Golden Ltd (180000 – (16000 shares @ Rs.11)		4000	
	Silver Ltd		10000	14000
	Current Assets			
6.	Inventories			
	Golden Ltd		20000	
	Silver Ltd		80000	100000
7.	Trade receivable			
	Debtor (12000 + 30000 – 4000) 38000			
	Less: Mutual debt 4000		34000	
	Bills Receivable (8000 + 32000) 40000			
	Less: Mutual debt 4000		36000	70000
8.	Cash and cash equivalents			
	Golden Ltd 8000			
	Silver Ltd 16000		24000	
	Add: Remittance in transit		4000	28000

Working Notes:

1. Share of Golden Ltd in Silver Ltd

	Rs.	Rs.
Share capital of Silver Ltd on 31.3.2006	240000	
Less: Issue of bonus shares (1/6 of Rs.240000)	40000	
Share capital before bonus issue		200000
No of equity shares before bonus issue (200000 / 10)		20000
No of shares held by Golden Ltd	16000	
Percentage shareholding	(16000 / 20000) =	80%
No of shares held by minority	4000	
Percentage shareholding	(4000 / 20000) =	20%

2. Statement of Analysis of profits of Silver Ltd

		Capital Profits	Revenue Reserve	Revenue Profits
	Rs.	Rs.	Rs.	Rs.
(a) General Reserve as on 31.3.2006 (after bonus issue)	32000			

Add: Bonus issue	40000		
Balance (before bonus issue)	72000		
(b) General Reserve on 1.4.2003	60000		
Less: bonus issue	40000	20000	
(c)Increase in general reserve			
(transfer of Rs.4000 p.a. for 3 years)			
(72000 – 60000) =	12000	2000	10000
(d) Profit and Loss Account			
Increase in profit after dividend			
(39000 – 12000) =	27000*	4500	22500
(e) Additional depreciation written back			
due to revaluation of fixed assets			
(12000 x 10/100 x 2.5)			3000
			-
	26500	10000	25500
Golden Ltd's share (80%)	21200	8000	20400
Minority Interest (20%)	5300	2000	5100
	26500	10000	25500

*It has been assumed that profit of Rs.27000 after payment of dividend for the year 2004-05, has been earned evenly in 3 years, (year 2003-04, 2004-05 and 2005-06)hence profit per year would be 27000/3 = Rs.9000. Half of the profit of Rs.9000 for the year 2003-04, would be pre-acquisition (capital profit) and remaining half i.e.Rs.4500 would be post-acquisition profit (revenue profit)

3. Statement of loss on revaluation

	Rs.
Value of assets on 1.4.2003 (168000 x 100/70)	240000
Less: Depreciation for 6 months (240000 x 10% x ½)	12000
Valuation of assets as on 1.10.2003	228000
Less: revalued value of assets	216000
Loss on revaluation	12000

4. Statement of Cost of Control

	Rs.	Rs.
Cost of investments in Silver Ltd.		176000
Less: Dividend out of capital profit	16000	
Less: Paid up value of investment (including bonus shares)		
(160000 +160000 x1/5)	192000	
Less: Capital profit	21200	229200
Capital reserve		53200

5. Statement of Minority Interest

	Rs.	Rs.
Equity share capital [including bonus]		
(40000 + 40000 x 20/100)		48000
Add:		
Share of capital profit	5300	
Share of revenue reserve	2000	

Share of revenue profit	5100	12400
		60400

6. Statement of Consolidated Profit and Loss Account

	Rs.	Rs.
Balance in Golden Ltd	24000	
Less: Pre-acquisition dividend credited to profit and loss		
Account (capital profit)	16000	
		8000
Add: Share in profit of Silver Ltd.		20400
		28400

7. Statement of General reserve

	Rs.
Balance in Golden Ltd	40000
Add: Share in Silver Ltd.	8000
-	48000

Q.5.11: Consolidation of holding company with one subsidiary with interco Adjustments

Astha Ltd acquired 80% of both classes of shares in Birat Ltd on 1.4.2007. The draft Balance Sheets of two companies on 31st March 2008 were as follows: (Rs'000)

Liabilities	Astha Ltd	Birat Ltd	Assets	Astha Ltd	Birat Ltd
Share capital			Plant & Machinery	2060	600
Equity shares of Rs.10			Furniture & fixtures	600	540
each fully paid up	3000	600	Investment		
14% preference shares			In equity shares of		
of Rs.100 each fully	-	400	Birat Ltd	1920	-
paid	1900	40	In preference shares		
General reserve	1600	720	of Birat Ltd	320	-
Profit & loss Account	300	320	Sundry debtors	560	316
Sundry creditors			Stock-in-trade	680	404
			Cash at bank	660	220
	6800	2080		6800	2080

Contingent liability of Astha Ltd: Claim for damages lodged by a contractor against the company pending in a law-suit – Rs.155000.

Additional information:
i)   General reserve balance of Birat Ltd was the same as on 1.4.2007

ii)	The balance in Profit and Loss account of Birat Ltd on 1.4.2007 was Rs.320000 out of which dividend of 16% p.a. on the equity capital of Rs.600000 was paid for the year 2006-07.	
iii)	Dividend in respect of preference shares of Birat Ltd for the year 2007-08 was still payable as on 31.3.2008.	
iv)	Astha Ltd credited its Profit and Loss A/c for the dividend received by it from Birat Ltd for the year 2006-07.	
v)	Sundry creditors of Astha Ltd included an amount of Rs.120000 for purchases from Birat Ltd on which the later company made a loss of Rs.10000	
vi)	Half of the above goods were still with the closing stock of Astha Ltd as at 31.3.2008.	
vii)	At the time of acquisition of Astha Ltd while determining the price to be paid for the shares in Birat Ltd it was considered that the value of plant and machinery was to be increased by 25% and that of furniture and fittings reduced to 80%. There was no transaction of purchase or sale of these assets during the year. The directors wish to give effect to these revaluations in the consolidated Balance Sheet.	
viii)	Directors of Astha Ltd are of the opinion that disclosure of its contingent liability will seriously prejudice the company's position in dispute with the contractor.	

Prepare a consolidated Balance Sheet as at 31.3.2008, assuming the rate of depreciation charged as 25% p.a. and 10% p.a. on plant and machinery and furniture and fixtures respectively. Workings should be part of the answer *(CA Final: May 2008)*

Solution

Working notes

1) Proportion of holding shares:

Astha Ltd's share in Birat ltd – both equity and preference   80%

Share of minorities in Birat Ltd = both equity and preference   20%

Astha Ltd

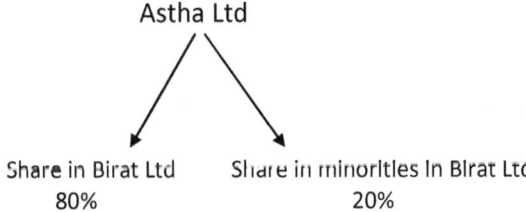

Share in Birat Ltd   Share in minorities In Birat Ltd

80%   20%

2) Statement of cost of control / goodwill:

	Rss'000	Rs'000
Investment in Astha Ltd		
In equity shares in Birat Ltd	1920.0	
Less: Dividend received for 2006-07		
(600 x 80%) x 16%	76.8	1843.2
Preference shares		320.0
		2163.2
Less: Face value of equity shares held (80%)	480.0	

Preference shares (80%)	320.0	
Share in Capital profits (W.N.1)	275.2	
		1075.2
Goodwill		1088.0

3) Statement of Capital Profits (Pre-acquisition):

	Rs'000	Rs'000
General reserve balance as on 1.04.2007		40.0
Profit & loss A/c balance as on 1.04.2007	320.0	
Less: Dividend at 16% p.a. on Rs.600000 for the year 2006-07	96.0	224.0
Total		264.0
Add: Profit on revaluation of plant & machinery (W.N.7)		200.0
		464.0
Less: Loss on revaluation of furniture (W.N.8)		120.0
		344.0
Share of Astha Ltd (Rs'000) 344.0 X 80% =		275.2
Minority interest (Rs'000) 344.0 X 20% =		68.8

4) Statement of Current Profits (post-acquisition):

	Rs'000	Rs'000
Profit during the year 2007-08 (720.0 – 224.0)	496.0	
Less: Preference dividend for the year 2007-08 @14%		
on Rs.400000	56.0	440.0
Less: Under charging of depreciation on Plant & Machinery		
due to upward revaluation (Rs.200000 x 25%)		50.0
		390.0
Add: Over charging of depreciation on Furniture & fixtures		
due to downward revaluation (Rs.120000 x 10%)		12.0
		402.0
Share of Astha Ltd= (402.0 x 80%)		321.6
Minority interest = (402.0 x 20%)		80.4

5) Statement of calculation of dividend on preference shares of Birat Ltd

	Rs'000
Dividend on preference shares (Rs.400000 x 14%)	56.0
Share of Astha Ltd (80%)	44.8
Share of Minority interest (20%)	11.2

6) Statement of Minority Interest:

	Rs'000	Rs'000
Equity Share Capital (20%)	120.0	
Preference share capital (20%)	80.0	200.0
Share of capital profit (W.N.1)		68.8
Share of revenue profit (W.N.2)		80.4
Share of preference dividend (W.N.3)		11.2

	360.4

7) Statement of value of Plant & Machinery of Birat Ltd

	Rs'000	Rs'000
Value as on 1.04.07 (600 x 100/75)	800.0	
Add: Appreciation on revaluation (25%)	200.0	
Revalued figure		1000.0
Less: Depreciation		
Already charged (800 – 600)	200.0	
Due to upward revaluation (200 x 25%)	50.0	(250.0)
		750.0

8) Statement of value of Furniture & Fixtures of Birat Ltd

	Rs'000	Rs'000
Value as on 1.04.07 (540 x 100/90)	600.0	
Less: Diminution on revaluation (20%)	120.0	
Revalued figure		480.0
Less: Depreciation		
Already charged (600 – 540)	60.0	
Written back owing to downward revaluation (120 x 10%)	(12.0)	48.0
		432.0

9) Statement of computation of consolidated Profit & Loss A/c

	Rs'000	Rs'000
Balance in Profit & Loss Account of Astha Ltd as on 1.4.07		1600.0
Add: Revenue profit from Birat Ltd (W.N.2)	321.6	
Preference dividend of Birat Ltd (W.N.3)	44.8	
Share of unrealized loss on stock (Rs.10000 x 50%)	5.0	371.4
		1971.4
Less: Dividend wrongly credited		76.8
		1894.6

10) Contingent liability:

In accordance with para 68 of AS 29, "Provisions, contingent liabilities and contingent assets", unless the possibility of an outflow in settlement is remote, an enterprise should disclose contingent liability at the Balance Sheet date along with a brief description of the nature of such contingent liability. Hence, it would be incorrect to ignore the contingent liability.

Consolidated Balance Sheet of Astha Ltd and its subsidiary
Birat Ltd as at 31st March 2008 (Rs'000)

Particulars	Note no.	Amount (Rs'000)
I. **Equity and Liabilities**		

	(1)Shareholder's funds		
	(a) Share capital	1	3000.0
	(b) Reserves and surplus	2	3794.6
	(2)Minority Interest (WN4)		360.4
	(3)Non-current liabilities		-
	Long-term borrowing		
	(4)Current liabilities		
	(a)Trade payables	3	500.0
	(b)Short term provisions		-
	(c)Other current liabilities		-
	Total		**7655.0**
II.	**Assets**		
	(1)Non-current assets		
	(a)Fixed Assets		
	Tangible assets	4	3842.0
	Intangible assets (goodwill)(WN5)		1088.0
	(b)Non-current investments		-
	(2)Current assets		
	(a)Inventories	5	1089.0
	(b)Trade receivables	6	756.0
	(c)Cash and cash equivalents	7	880.0
	Total		**7655.0**

Notes on Accounts

S/L No	Particulars	Amount (Rs'000)	Amount (Rs'000)
1.	**Share capital**		
	Issued and paid up		
	300000 Equity shares of Rs.10 each fully paid		3000.0
2.	**Reserves & surplus**		
	General reserve	1900.0	
	Profit & Loss Account (WN7)	1894.6	3794.6
	Current liabilities		
3.	**Trade payables**		
	Creditors:		
	Astha Ltd	300.0	
	Birat Ltd	320.0	
		620.0	
	Less: mutual owings	120.0	500.0
4.	**Tangible assets**		
	Plant & Machinery		
	Astha Ltd 2060.0		

	Birat Ltd (W.N.7)	750.0			
	Furniture & fittings			2810.0	
	Astha Ltd	600.0			
	Birat Ltd (W.N.8)	432.0		1032.0	3842.0
	Current Assets				
5.	**Inventories**				
	Astha Ltd			680.0	
	Virat Ltd			404.0	
				1084.0	
	Add: Unrealised loss			5.0	1089.0
6.	**Trade receivable**				
	Debtors:				
	Astha Ltd			560.0	
	Birat Ltd			316.0	
				876.0	
	Less: mutual owings			120.0	756.0
7.	**Cash and cash equivalents**				
	Astha Ltd			660.0	
	Virat Ltd			220.0	880.0

Contingent liability: Claim against damages lodged by a contractor against Astha Ltd is pending in a law suit Rs.155 (Rs'000) (W.N.9)

Q.5.12 : Consolidation of holding company and one subsidiary with different dates of acquisition

The Balance Sheet of Football Ltd. and its subsidiary Hockey Ltd. as on 31st March, 2010 are as under:

Liabilities	Football Rs.	Hockey Rs.	Assets	Football Rs.	Hockey Rs.
Equity shares of Rs. 10 each	4800000	2000000	Goodwill	450000	300000
10% Preference shares			Plant &		
of Rs.10			Machinery	1200000	500000
each	700000	380000	Motor Vehicles	950000	750000
General Reserve	550000	420000	Furniture & Fittings	650000	400000
Profit and Loss Account	1000000	600000	Investments	2600000	450000
Bank overdraft	120000	70000	Stock	450000	720000
Sundry Creditors	430000	480000	Cash at Bank	225000	210000
Bills Payable	---	160000	Debtors	930000	780000
			Bills receivable	145000	-----
	7600000	4110000		7600000	4110000

Details of acquisition of shares by Football Ltd. are as under:

Nature of shares acquisition	No. of shares acquired	Date of acquisition	Cost of
			Rs.
Preference Shares	14,250	1.4.2007	3,10,000
Equity shares	80,000	1.4.2008	9,50,000
Equity shares	70,000	1.4.2009	8,00,000

Other Information:

(i) On 1.4.2009 profit and loss account and general reserve of Hockey Ltd. had credit balances of Rs. 3,00,000 and Rs. 2,00,000 respectively.

(ii) Dividend @ 10% was paid by Hockey Ltd. for the year 2008-2009 out of its profit and loss account balance as on 1.4.2009. Football Ltd. credited its share of dividend to its profit and loss account.

(iii) Hockey Ltd. allotted bonus shares out of general reserve at the rate of 1 share for every 10 shares held. Accounting thereof has not yet been made.

(iv) Bills receivable of Football Ltd. was drawn upon Hockey Ltd.

(v) During the year 2009-2010 Football Ltd. purchased goods from Hockey Ltd. for Rs. 1,00,000 at a sale price of Rs. 1,20,000. 40 % of these goods remained unsold at the end of the year.

(vi) On 1.4.2009 motor vehicles of Hockey Ltd. were overvalued by Rs. 1,00,000. Applicable depreciation rate is 20%.

(vii) Dividends recommend for the year 2009-2010 in the holding and the subsidiary companies are 15% and 10 % respectively.

Prepare consolidated Balance Sheet as on 31st March, 2010. (*Adapted CA Final: May 2005*)

Solution

Consolidated Balance Sheet of Football Ltd. and its subsidiary Hockey Ltd.
as on 31st March, 2010

Particulars		Note no.	Amount (Rs)
I.	**Equity and Liabilities**		
	(1)Shareholder's funds		
	(a) Share capital	1	5500000
	(b) Reserves and surplus	2	1222750
	(2)Minority Interest (WN3)		986750
	(3)Non-current liabilities		-
	Long-term borrowing		
	(4)Current liabilities		
	(a)Short term borrowings	3	190000
	(b)Trade payables	4	947500
	(c)Other current liabilities	5	790000
	Total		9614500
II.	**Assets**		
	(1)Non-current assets		
	(a)Fixed Assets		
	Tangible assets	6	4370000
	Intangible assets	7	947500
	(b)Non-current investments	8	990000

(2)Current assets			
(a)Inventories		9	1162000
(b)Trade receivables		10	1710000
(c)Cash and cash equivalents		11	435000
	Total		**9614500**

Notes on Accounts

S/L No	Particulars		Amount (Rs)	Amount (Rs)
1.	**Share capital**			
	Authorised, Issued and paid up			
	480000 Equity shares of Rs.10 each fully paid		4800000	
	70000, 10% preference shares of Rs.10 each		700000	5500000
2.	**Reserves & surplus**			
	General reserve (WN5)		715000	
	Profit & Loss Account (WN4)		507750	1222750
3.	**Short term borrowings**			
	Bank overdraft			
	Football Ltd		120000	
	Hockey Ltd		70000	190000
4.	**Trade payables**			
	Sundry Creditors:			
	Football Ltd	430000		
	Hockey Ltd	480000	910000	
	Bills payable			
	Hockey Ltd	160000		
	Less: mutual owings	(145000)	15000	925000
5.	**Other current liabilities**			
	Proposed dividend			
	Equity		720000	
	Preference		70000	790000
6.	**Tangible assets**			
	Plant & Machinery			
	Football Ltd	1200000		
	Hockey Ltd	500000	1700000	
	Motor Vehicles			
	Football Ltd	950000		
	Hockey Ltd(750000-100000+20000)	670000	1620000	
	Furniture & fittings			
	Football Ltd	650000		
	Hockey Ltd	400000	1050000	4370000
7.	**Intangible assets**			

	Goodwill		
	Football Ltd	450000	
	Hockey Ltd	300000	
		750000	
	Add: goodwill on consolidation (WN2)	197500	947500
8.	**Non-current investments**		
	Investments		
	Football Ltd (2600000 – 2060000)	540000	
	Hockey Ltd	450000	990000
9.	**Inventories**		
	Football Ltd	450000	
	Hockey Ltd	720000	
		1170000	
	Less: Unrealised profit	(8000)	1162000
10.	**Trade receivable**		
	Debtors:		
	Football Ltd	930000	
	Hockey Ltd	780000	1710000
	Bills Receivable	145000	
	Less: mutual owings	(145000)	-	1710000
11.	**Cash and cash equivalents**		
	Cash at bank		
	Football Ltd	225000	
	Hockey Ltd	210000	435000

Working Notes:

1. **Analysis of profits of Hockey Ltd**

	Capital Profits	Revenue Reserve	Revenue Profits
	Rs.	Rs.	Rs.	Rs.
(a) General Reserve as on 1.4.2009	200000		
Less: Bonus issue (1/10 of Rs. 2000000)	200000	--	--
(b) Addition to General Reserve during 2009-2010 (Rs. 420000 – Rs. 200000)		220000	
(c) Profit and Loss Account balance as on 1.4.2009	300000		
Less: Dividend paid for the year 2008-2009	200000	100000	
(d) Profit for the year 2009-2010 (Rs. 600000 – Rs. 100000)			500000
(e) Adjustment for over valuation of	(100000)		

motor vehicles		
(f) Adjustment of revenue profit due to overcharged depreciation (20% on Rs. 100000)		20000
(g) Preference dividend for the year 2009-2010 @10%		(38,000)
	220000	482000
Football Ltd.'s share (3/4)	165000	361500
Minority Interest (1/4)	55000	120500
	220000	482000

(2) Cost of Control

	Rs.	Rs.
Cost of investments in Hockey Ltd.		2060000
Less: Paid up value of equity shares (including bonus shares) [80,000 + 70,000 + (10% of 1,50,000)] x Rs. 10	1650000	
Paid up value of preference shares	142500	
Pre-acquisition dividend*	70000	1862500
Cost of control/Goodwill		197500

*the dividend on 70,000 shares only (acquired on 1.4.2009) is a pre-acquisition dividend.

(3) Minority Interest

	Rs.
Equity share capital [Rs.500000 + Rs. 50,000 (Bonus)]	550000
Preference share capital (Rs. 380000 – Rs. 142500]	237500
Share of revenue reserve	55000
Share of revenue profit	120500
Proposed preference dividend	23750
	986750

(4) Profit and Loss Account – Football Ltd.

	Rs.	Rs.
Balance		1000000
Share in profit Hockey Ltd.		361500
Share in proposed preference dividend of Hockey Ltd.		14250
		1375750
Less: Pre-acquisition dividend credited to profit and loss account	70000	
Unrealized profit on stock (40% of Rs.20,000)	8000	
Proposed equity dividend	720000	
Proposed preference dividend	70000	868000
		507750

(5) General reserve – Football Ltd.

	Rs.

Balance	550000
Add: Share in Hockey Ltd.	165000
	715000

Note: No information has been given in the question regarding date of bonus issue by Hockey. It is also not mentioned whether the bonus shares are issued from pre-acquisition general reserve or post-acquisition general reserve. The above solution is given on the basis that Hockey Ltd. allotted bonus shares out of pre-acquisition general reserve.

Q.5.13:
What is the process followed in cases where the reporting dates of holding company and its subsidiary is different?

The process followed in cases where the reporting dates of holding company and its subsidiary/ies are different:

Step 1	Pass adjustments to record effects of A) Significant events B) Intra – group transactions In subsidiary companies giving effect to the different dates of reporting, so as to arrive at the carrying values as on the date of Balance Sheet of the holding company
Step 2	Calculate pre-acquisition and post – acquisition profits of subsidiary company
Step 3	Calculate goodwill / capital reserve
Step 4	Calculate minority interest
Step 5	Calculate reserves and surplus of holding company
Step 6	Prepare Consolidated Balance Sheet as usual

Q.5.14: Consolidation of holding company with subsidiary having different reporting Dates

The Balance Sheets of Aqua Ltd and Baqa Ltd as on dates of last closing of Accounts are as under:

Liabilities	Aqua Ltd 31.03.09 Rs.	Baqa Ltd 31.12.08 Rs.
Share capital (equity shares of Rs.10 each)	1100000	500000
Accumulated profits and reserves	450000	205000
15% Rs.100 non-convertible debentures	-	300000
Accounts payable	480000	280000
Other liabilities	100000	40000
Tax provision	150000	250000
	2280000	1575000

Assets	Aqua Ltd 31.03.09	Baqa Ltd 31.12.08

	Rs.	Rs.
Fixed Assets at cost	845000	526500
Less: depreciation	195000	121500
	650000	405000
Investments:		
40000 shares in Baqa Ltd	800000	
1000 debentures in Baqa Ltd	150000	
Current Assets:		
Inventories	200000	350000
Accounts receivable	250000	465000
Cash and bank	230000	355000
	2280000	1575000

The following information is also available:
1. On 8th February 2009 there was a fire at the factory of Baqa Ltd resulting in inventory worth Rs.20000 being destroyed. Baqa received 75% of the loss as insurance.
2. The same fire resulted in destruction of a machine having a written down value of Rs.100000. The insurance company admitted the company's claim to the extent of 80%. The machine was insured at its fair value of Rs.150000.
3. On 13th March 2009 Aqua sold goods costing Rs.150000 to Baqa at a mark-up of 20%. Half of these goods were resold to Aqua who in turn was able to liquidate the entire stock of such goods before closure of accounts on 31st March 2009. As on 31st March 2009 Baqa's accounts payable show Rs.60000 due to Aqua on the two transactions.
4. Aqua acquired holdings in Baqa on 1st January 2007 when the reserves and accumulated profits of Baqa Ltd stood at RS.75000.
5. Both companies have not provided for tax on current year profits. The current year taxable profits are Rs.33000 and Rs.66000 for Aqua Ltd and Baqa Ltd respectively. The tax rate is 33%.
6. The incremental profits earned by Baqa Ltd for the period January 2009 to March 2009 over that earned in the corresponding period in 2008 was Rs.56000. Except for the profits that resulted from the transactions with Aqua in the aforesaid period the entire profits have been realized in cash before 31st March 2009.

You are requested to consolidate the accounts of the two companies and prepare a consolidated Balance Sheet of Aqua Limited and its subsidiary as at 31st March 2009.
(CA Final: Nov 2009)

Solution
Consolidated Balance Sheet of Aqua Ltd and its subsidiary Baqa Ltd
As on 31st March 2009

Particulars	Note no.	Amount (Rs)
I. **Equity and Liabilities**		
(1)Shareholder's funds		

(a) Share capital	1	1100000
(b) Reserves and surplus(WN8)		517486
(2)Minority Interest (WN6)		150844
(3)Non-current liabilities		
Long-term borrowing	2	200000
(4)Current liabilities		
(a)Trade payables (WN5)		760000
(b)Short term provisions	3	432670
(c)Other current liabilities	4	140000
Total		**3301000**
II. Assets		
(1)Non-current assets		
(a)Fixed Assets		
Tangible assets (650000 + 305000)		955000
Intangible assets (WN5)		340000
(b)Non-current investments		
(2)Current assets		
(a)Inventories (WN6)		605000
(b)Trade receivables (WN7)		655000
(c)Other current assets		120000
(d)Cash and cash equivalents		
(230000 + 396000)		626000
Total		**3301000**

Notes on Accounts

S/L No	Particulars	Amount (Rs)	Amount (Rs)
1.	**Share capital**		
	Issued, subscribed and paid up		
	110000 equity shares of Rs.10 each fully paid up		1100000
2	**Long term borrowings**		
	Secured loans		200000
	15% debentures (2000 x 100)		
3.	**Short term provisions**		
	Tax provision		
	Aqua (150000 + 10890)	160890	
	Baqa 271780)	271780	432670
4.	**Other current liabilities**		
	Aqua	100000	
	Baqa	40000	140000

Working Notes

1. **Balance Sheet of Baqa Ltd with revision of balances as at 31.12.2008**

Liabilities	Rs.	Rs.
Share capital		500000
Reserves and surplus	205000	
Add: Incremental profits 1.1.09 to 31.3.09 *	56000	
Gain – excess of insurance claim over book value of machine destroyed (150000 x 80% - 100000)	20000	
Less: Provision for tax on 2008 profits (66000 x 33%)	(21780)	
Loss of destruction of goods (20000 – 20000 x 15%)	(5000)	254220
15% debentures		300000
Accounts payable	280000	
Add: Net owing to Aqua Ltd	60000	340000
Other liabilities		40000
Tax provision	250000	
Add: further provision on 2008 profits	21780	271780
Total		1706000

Assets	Rs.	Rs.
Fixed Assets	405000	
Less: WDV of machine destroyed	(100000)	305000
Inventories	350000	
Less: destroyed	(20000)	
Add: Purchase from Aqua Ltd (150000 x 120/100)	180000	
Less: Resold to Aqua (cost: 50% of 180000)	(90000)	420000
Insurance claim receivable from machine (150000 x 80%)		120000
Accounts receivable		465000
Cash and bank (WN2)		396000
Total		1706000

*Assumed as (i) including profit on sale to Aqua Ltd
        (ii) excluding gain / loss on destruction by fire
        (iii)net of tax

2. **Statement of Cash and bank of Baqa as on 31.3.2009:**

	Rs.	Rs.	Rs.
Balance as on 31.12.08			355000
Cash from operations from 1.1.09 to 31.3.09:			
Incremental profits 1.1.09 to 31.3.09 over 1.1.08 to 31.3.08:			
(assumed as including profit on sale to Aqua Ltd and excluding gain / loss on destruction by fire)		56000	
Adjustments for:			
Profit on sale to Aqua not realised in cash:			

Purchase from Aqua Ltd	180000		
Closing liability	(60000)		
Sale value	120000		
Cost of sales	(90000)	(30000)	26000
Claim for stock (20000 x 75%)			15000
Balance as on 31.3.09			396000

3. Shareholding pattern

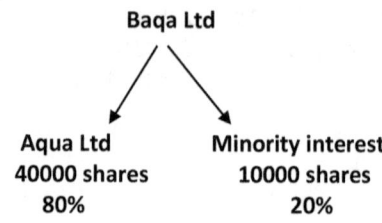

Baqa Ltd

Aqua Ltd
40000 shares
80%

Minority interest
10000 shares
20%

4. Statement of analysis of profits of Baqa Ltd

Item	Pre-acquisition Profit (Rs)	Post-acquisition Profit(Rs)	Total Rs.
Reserves and surplus (WN2)	75000	179220	254220
Aqua Ltd (80%)	60000	143376	203376
Minority interest (20%)	15000	35844	50844

5. Statement of cost of control / goodwill

Item	Rs	Rs
Cost of investment		800000(A)
Aqua Ltd's share of Baqa Ltd's net assets on date of acquisition represented by:		
i)share capital (500000 x 80%)	400000	
ii)capital profits(WN4)	60000	460000(B)
Goodwill to consolidated Balance Sheet (A – B)		340000

6. Statement of Minority interest

Item	Rs.
Share capital	100000
Share of capital profit (WN4)	15000
Share of revenue profit (WN4)	35844
To consolidated Balance Sheet	150844

7. Statement of Inter-company transactions – stock

Item	Rs.
Aggregate balance (Aqua 200000 + Baqa 420000)	620000
Less: unrealised profit on stock – (90000 x 20/120)	(15000)

To consolidated Balance Sheet	605000

8. Statement of Inter-company transactions

Item	Accounts receivable Rs.	Accounts Payable Rs.
Aqua Ltd	250000	480000
Baqa Ltd	465000	340000
Aggregate balance	715000	820000
Less: Inter-company owings	(60000)	(60000)
To consolidated Balance Sheet	655000	760000

9. Statement of reserves

Item	Rs.	Rs.
Aqua Ltd balance		450000
Less: tax provision (33000 x 33%)		(10890)
Add: Aqua Ltd post acquisition profit		143376
Less: Unrealised profit on stock (90000 x 20 /120)		(15000)
Less: Loss on cancellation of debentures		
(150000 – (1000x100)		(50000)
To consolidated Balance Sheet		517486

Q.5.15: Consolidation of holding company and one subsidiary with different reporting dates

Find below the following Balance Sheets:

Liabilities	A Ltd 31.3.2010	B Ltd 31.12.09	Assets	A Ltd 31.3.2010	B Ltd 31.12.09
Share capital (Shares of Rs.10 each)	1000000	500000	Fixed Assets Investment:	650000	405000
Reserves and surplus	450000	205000	40000 shares in B		
Secured loan:			Ltd	800000	-
13% debentures			1000 Debentures		
(Rs.100 each)	-	300000	in B Ltd	150000	-
Current liabilities:			Current Assets:		
Creditors	380000	80000	Stock	200000	350000
Other liabilities	200000	40000	Debtors	150000	265000
			Cash and bank	80000	105000
	2030000	1125000		2030000	1125000

On 5th January 2010, certain stocks of B Ltd costing Rs.20000 were completely destroyed by fire. The insurance company paid 75% of the claim. On 20th January 2010, A Ltd sold goods to B Ltd costing Rs.150000 at an invoice price of cost plus 20%. 50% of those goods were resold by B Ltd to A Ltd within 31st March 2010 (these were then sold by A Ltd to a third party before 31st March 2010). As on 31st March 2010, B Ltd owes Rs.60000 to A Ltd in respect of those goods. Pre-acquisition profits of B Ltd were Rs.75000.

Prepare consolidated Balance Sheet as on 31st March 2010 after making necessary adjustments in the Balance Sheet of B Ltd.

Solution

Consolidated Balance Sheet of A Ltd and its subsidiary B Ltd
As at 31st March 2010

Particulars	Note no.	Amount (Rs)
I. **Equity and Liabilities**		
(1)Shareholder's funds		
(a) Share capital	1	1000000
(b) Reserves and surplus		559000
(2)Minority Interest		146000
(3)Non-current liabilities		
Long-term borrowing	2	200000
(4)Current liabilities		
(a)Trade payables	3	460000
(b)Other current liabilities		240000
Total		2605000
II. **Assets**		
(1)Non-current assets		
(a)Fixed Assets		
Tangible assets (650000 + 405000)		1055000
Intangible assets		390000
(b)Non-current investments		
(2)Current assets		
(a)Inventories	4	605000
(b)Trade receivables	5	355000
(c)Cash and cash equivalents		
(80000 + 120000)		200000
Total		2605000

Notes on Accounts

S/L No	Particulars	Amount (Rs)	Amount (Rs)
1.	**Share capital**		
	Issued, subscribed and paid up		
	10000 equity shares of Rs.10 each fully paid up		<u>1000000</u>
2	**Long term borrowings**		
	Secured loans		<u>200000</u>
	13% debentures (Rs. 100 each)		

3.	Trade Payables Creditors (380000+140000) Less: mutual indebtedness	520000 60000	460000
4.	Inventories Stock in trade (200000 + 420000) Less: Unrealised profit	620000 15000	605000
5.	Trade receivables Debtors(150000 +265000) Less: Mutual indebtedness	415000 60000	355000

Working Notes

i)   **Adjustments to be made in the balance sheet items of B Ltd**

Assets	Amount Rs.
Stocks:	
As given on 31.12.2009	350000
Add: Unsold stock out of goods purchased from A Ltd	90000
	440000
Less: Loss of stock by fire	20000
	420000
Cash & bank balance:	
As given on 31.12.2009 Rs.105000	
Add: Insurance claim received Rs.15000	120000
Liabilities	
Creditors:	
As given on 31.12.2009	80000
Add: Owings to A Ltd on 31.3.2010	60000
	140000
Reserves and surplus:	
As given on 31.12.2009	205000
Less: Abnormal loss on goods destroyed	5000
	200000
Add: Profit from sale of goods purchased from A Ltd	30000
	230000

ii)   **Statement of computation of cost of control / goodwill**

Particulars	Rs	Rs
Amount paid for 40000 shares	800000	
Amount paid for 1000 debentures	150000	950000
Less: Nominal value of proportionate share capital	400000	

Nominal value of proportionate 13% debentures	100000	
Shares of pre-acquisition profits (80% of Rs.75000)	60000	560000
Goodwill to consolidated Balance Sheet		390000

iii) Statement of Minority interest

Particulars	Rs.
Paid up value of 10000 shares	100000
Add: 20% of reserves & surplus of B Ltd (20% of Rs.230000)	46000
To consolidated Balance Sheet	146000

iv) Statement of Reserves and Surplus of A Ltd

Particulars	Rs.
Balance as on 31.3.2010	450000
Add: Share of revenue reserves of B Ltd (80% of Rs.155000)	124000
	574000
Less: Unrealised profit on stock (1/6 x Rs.90000)	15000
To consolidated Balance Sheet	559000

Q.5.16: Consolidation of holding company and one subsidiary

The summarised Balance Sheets of Kush Ltd and Shuk Ltd as at 31st March 2010 are as follows:

Liabilities	Kush Ltd Rs/lakhs	Shuk Ltd Rs/lakhs	Assets	Kush Ltd Rs/Lakhs	Shuk Ltd Rs/Lakhs
Share capital			Plant at cost		
Equity shares of			Less depreciation	86.4	72.9
Rs.10 each	216.0	108.0	Furniture, fixtures &		
Share premium	32.4	-	fittings	23.4	7.2
Capital reserve on			Stock at cost	18.0	13.5
1.4.09	-	7.2	Debtors	73.8	47.6
General reserve on			Trade investment		2.7
1.4.09	13.5	9.0	Goodwill at cost	45.0	13.6
Profit & Loss A/c	70.2	21.6	Investment:		
Creditors	29.7	19.7	8.64 lakhs shares of		
			Shuk Ltd at cost	97.2	
			Balance at bank	18.0	8.0
	361.8	165.5		361.8	165.5

Additional information:

a) On 1st April 2009 Kush Ltd acquired from the shareholders of Shuk Ltd 8.64 lakhs shares of Rs.10 each in Shuk Ltd and allotted in consideration thereof 6.48 lakhs of its own shares of Rs.10 each at a premium of Rs.5 per share.

b) The consideration for the shares of Shuk Ltd was arrived at inter-alia by valuing certain assets of Shuk Ltd on 1st April 2009 as under:

I) Plant at Rs.90 lakhs

ii) Furniture, fixtures and fittings at Rs.8 lakhs

iii) No value on trade investment and goodwill

No adjustments were made in the books of accounts of Shuk Ltd in respect of the above valuation.

During 2009-10 there was no purchase or sale of these assets. It is desired that such adjustments should however be made in the consolidated accounts.

c) The figures for Plant and Furniture, fixtures and fittings at 31.3.2010 shown in the Balance Sheet are after providing depreciation for 2009-10 at the rates of 10 per cent per annum and 20 per cent per annum respectively, on the book values as at 1.04.09.

d) The profit and loss account of Shuk Ltd showed a credit balance of Rs.27 lakhs on 1.04.09. A dividend of 10% was paid in January 2010 for the year 2008-09. This dividend was credited to profit and loss account of Kush Ltd.

e) The following point was not considered in making out the accounts in the year's expenses; Rs.4500 per month were incurred by Kush Ltd on behalf of Shuk Ltd, it was by mistake debited to profit and loss account of Kush Ltd and nothing has been done in the accounts of Shuk Ltd

f) The stock of Shuk Ltd included Rs.4.5 lakhs of goods received from Kush Ltd, invoiced at cost plus 25%.

g) Debtors of Shuk Ltd include Rs.3.5 lakhs due from Kush Ltd, whereas creditors of Kush Ltd include Rs.3.1 lakhs due to Shuk Ltd, the difference being represented by a cheque in transit.

You are required to consolidate the accounts of the two companies and prepare a consolidated Balance Sheet of Kush Ltd and its subsidiary as at 31st March 2010. *(CA Final May 2010)*

Solution

Consolidated Balance Sheet of Kush Ltd and its subsidiary Shuk Ltd
As on 31.03.2010

Particulars	Note no.	Amount (Rs)
I. **Equity and Liabilities**		
(1)Shareholder's funds		
(a) Share capital	1	21600000
(b) Reserves and surplus	2	12754800
(2)Minority Interest (WN4)		2725200
(3)Non-current liabilities		
Long-term borrowing		-
(4)Current liabilities		
(a)Trade payables		4630000
(b)Other current liabilities		-
Total		41710000
II. **Assets**		
(1)Non-current assets		
(a)Fixed Assets		
Tangible assets	3	19720000

Intangible assets (Goodwill)		4500000
(b)Non-current investments		
(2)Current assets		
(a)Inventories (WN5)		3060000
(b)Trade receivables (WN6)		11790000
(c)Cash and cash equivalents	4	2640000
Total		41710000

Notes on Accounts

S/L No	Particulars	Amount (Rs)	Amount (Rs)
1.	**Share capital**		
	Issued, subscribed and paid up		
	2160000 equity shares of Rs.10 each fully paid up		21600000
2	**Reserves and surplus**		
	Capital reserve (WN3)	1712000	
	Share premium	3240000	
	General reserve (WN7)	1350000	
	Profit and loss account(WN7)	6452800	12754800
3.	**Tangible assets**		
	Plant (8640000+9000000 x90%)	16740000	
	Furniture, fixtures and fittings		
	(2340000+800000 x 80%)	2980000	19720000
4.	**Cash and cash equivalents**		
	Cash at Bank		
	(1800000 + 800000)	2600000	
	Add: cheque in transit	40000	2640000

Working Notes
1. **Group structure**
   Date of acquisition: 1.4.2009

Shuk Ltd

Kush Ltd 864000 shares 80%   Minority interest of Sukh Ltd 216000 shares 20%

Particulars	Rs.	Pre-acquisition P & L A/c	Post-acquisition P & L A/c
2. Statement of analysis of profits of Shuk Ltd with reference to the date of acquisition of shares of Shuk Ltd by Kush Ltd			
Balance		2700000	540000
Less: Dividend 2008-09 (108 lakhs)		(1080000)	
		1620000	
Plant			
Book value of Plant on 31.3.2010	7290000		
Depreciation rate of Plant	10%		
Book value of Plant on 1.4.09 (7290000 x 100/90)	8100000(A)		
Revalued amount as on 1.4.09	9000000(B)		
Revaluation surplus to be credited to Revaluation reserve (B – A)	900000		
Additional depreciation = Rs.900000 x 10% to be debited to post-acquisition profit and loss account	90000		(90000)
Furniture, fixtures and fittings			
Book value of furniture on 31.3.2010	720000		
Depreciation rate of furniture	20%		
Book value of furniture on 1.4.09 (720000 x 100/80)	900000 (A)		
Revalued amount as on 1.4.09	800000 (B)		
	100000		
Revaluation loss to be debited to pre-acquisition profit and loss (B – A)	20000	(100000)	
Excess depreciation = Rs.100000 x 20% to be credited to post-acquisition profit and loss account			20000
Purchased goodwill and trade investments			
Trade investment written off	270000		
Purchased goodwill written off	1360000		
Total asset written off – to be debited to pre-acquisition profit and loss	1630000	(1630000)	
Expenses incurred not recorded			
Expenses incurred by Kush Ltd on behalf of Shuk Ltd Rs.4500 x 12	54000		(540000
To be debited to profit and loss account of Kush Ltd			
Adjusted profit		(110000)	416000
Capital reserve		720000	
General reserve		900000	
Revaluation reserve		900000	
Total		2410000	416000
Kush Ltd	80%	1928000	332800
Minority interest	20%	482000	83200

3. Statement of cost of control / goodwill

Item	Rs	Rs
Cost of investment	9720000	
Less: pre-acquisition dividend: (1080000 x 80%)	(864000)	8856000(A)
Kush Ltd's share of Shuk Ltd's net assets on date of acquisition represented by		
i)share capital (10800000 x 80%)	8640000	
ii)capital profits(WN2)	1928000	10568000(B)
Capital reserve to consolidated Balance Sheet(B − A)		1712000

4. Statement of Minority interest

Item	Rs.
Share capital	2160000
Share of capital profit (WN2)	482000
Share of revenue profit (WN2)	83200
To consolidated Balance Sheet	2725200

5. Statement of stock

Item	Rs.
Aggregate balance (1800000 + 1350000)	3150000
Less: unrealised profit on stock − (450000 x 25/125)	90000
To consolidated Balance Sheet	3060000

6. Statement of Inter-company transactions

Item	Debtors Rs.	Creditors Rs.
Kush Ltd	7380000	2970000
Shuk Ltd	4760000	1970000
Aggregate balance	12140000	4940000
Les: Cheque in transit (350000 – 310000)	(40000)	
Less: Inter-company owings	(310000)	(310000)
To consolidated Balance Sheet	11790000	4630000

7. Statement of reserves

Item	Revenue reserve Rs.	Revenue profit Rs.
Kush Ltd balance	1350000	7020000
Add: expenses on behalf of Shuk Ltd wrongly debited to profit and loss account		54000
Less: pre-acquisition dividend from Shuk Ltd wrongly		

credited to profit and loss account		(864000)
Add: Share of post-acquisition profits from Shuk Ltd WN2		332800
Less: Unrealised profit on stock (90000 x 20 /120)		(90000)
To consolidated Balance Sheet	1350000	6452800

Q.5.17: What is the process followed in disposal of shares?

The process followed in disposal of shares is as under:

Step 1	On disposal of a subsidiary, the gain or loss on disposal is recognised in the consolidated statement of profit and loss and is calculated as the aggregate of: The difference between the proceeds of disposal of the subsidiary and the carrying amount of assets less liabilities as of the date of disposal
Step 2	The cumulative amount of any exchange differences (related to foreign subsidiaries – non-integral operations) is recognised in equity according to AS 11, The Effects of changes in foreign exchange rates.
Step 3	If a parent sells a portion of its investment in a subsidiary but stills retains a controlling interest, the consolidated financial statements at the end of the period should include assets, liabilities and operations of the subsidiary and reflect the new minority interest from the date of the transaction. The profit or loss on disposal should be transferred to profit and loss account of holding company
Step 4	If a parent sells controlling interest in the subsidiary but still retains significant influence over the entity, the remaining investment should be reflected in the balance sheet at the end of the period as a single line item using Equity method in accordance with AS 23 – Accounting of investments with associates in the consolidated financial statements. The subsequent results of operations should also be reported using the Equity method. If the disposal qualifies as discontinuing operation, presentation of the discontinuing operation would follow AS 24 Discontinuing operations
Step 5	When almost the entire subsidiary is disposed of (except for an interest which does not allow the parent to exert significant influence over the subsidiary) and If the sale of subsidiary qualifies as a discontinuing operation, presentation of discontinuing operation would follow AS 24: Discontinuing operation. The remaining interest in equity should be accounted for in accordance with AS 30 Financial instruments: recognition and measurement.

Q.5.18: Disposal of shares

From the following summarized Balance Sheets of A Ltd and its subsidiary B Ltd, prepare a consolidated Balance Sheet as on 31st December 2009

Liabilities	A Ltd Rs.	B Ltd Rs.	Assets	A Ltd Rs.	B Ltd Rs.

Share capital			Sundry assets	93000	32000
Equity shares of Rs.10	100000	20000	Shares in B Ltd. 1200		
Profit on sale of shares	3000		shares at Rs.15 each	18000	
Profit & loss A/c					
Brought forward	6000	7200			
For the year	2000	4800			
	111000	32000		111000	32000

A Ltd bought in earlier year 1600 equity shares in B Ltd @ 15 when the profit and loss account balance in B Ltd was Rs.4400. A sold 400 shares @ Rs.22.50 credited the difference between the sale proceeds and cost to Profit on sale of investment account on 30th June 2009 and crediting the balance to the investment account. Profit during the year accrued uniformly.

Solution

Consolidated Balance Sheet of A Ltd and its subsidiary B Ltd
As At 31st December 2009

Particulars		Note no.	Amount Rs
I.	**Equity and Liabilities**		
	(1)Shareholder's funds		
	(a) Share capital	1	100000
	(b) Reserves and surplus	2	15560
	(2)Minority Interest (WN3)		12800
	(3)Current liabilities		
	(a)Trade Payables		-
	Total		128360
II.	**Assets**		
	(1)Non-current Assets		
	(a)Fixed Assets		
	(i)Tangible Assets (93000 + 32000)		125000
	(ii)Intangible Assets	3	3360
	(b)Non-current Investments		
	(2)Current Assets:		
	Total		128360

Notes on Accounts

S/L No	Particulars	Amount (Rs)	Amount (Rs)
1.	**Share capital** 10000 equity shares of Rs.10 each		100000
2	**Reserves and surplus** Profit & Loss A/c (WN4)		15560

3.	Intangible Assets Goodwill (WN2)		3360

Working Notes

1. Statement of analysis of Profit of B Ltd

Item	Capital profit Rs	Revenue profit Rs
P/L Balance on the date of acquisition	4400	
Increase in balance after acquisition		2800
Profit for the year		4800
	4400	7600
Less: Minority interest (40%)	1760	3040
Share of A Ltd	2640	4560

2. Statement of cost of control / goodwill

Item	Amount Rs.	Amount Rs.
Cost of investments		18000
Less: Paid up value of shares	12000	
Share of capital profits	2640	14640
Goodwill		3360

3. Statement of Minority interest (40%)

Item	Amount Rs.	Amount Rs.
Paid up value of shares held		8000
Add: Share of revenue profits	3040	
Share of capital profits	1760	4800
To consolidated Balance Sheet		12800

4. Statement of consolidated revenue profit

Item	Amount Rs.	Amount Rs.
Balance as per Profit and Loss A/c of A Ltd		8000
Add: Profit on sale of shares (WN5)		3000
		11000
Add: Share in revenue profit of B Ltd		4560

To consolidated Balance Sheet		15560

5. Statement of Investment account

Item	Amount Rs.
Balance b/d (1600 shares @ Rs 15 each)	24000
Less: Sold 400 shares @ Rs.22.50 each and received proceeds	9000
	15000
Balance c/d (1200 shares @ Rs.15 each)	18000
Profit on sale of investments (18000 – 15000) to WN4	3000

Q.5.19:

What is the process followed in consolidation of foreign subsidiaries?

Process followed in consolidation of foreign subsidiaries is as under:

Step 1	Prepare analysis of profit of foreign subsidiary in foreign currency
Step 2	Convert the figures of foreign subsidiary into reporting currency as per AS 11 on translation of foreign branches as under: a)Pre-acquisition profits = rate prevalent on acquisition date b)Post-acquisition profits = Average rate c)Share capital = Rate prevalent on the acquisition date d)All items of assets and liabilities = Closing rate
Step 3	Calculate the amount of exchange difference and transfer to Foreign currency translation reserve. It is treated as capital and would be divided between cost of control and minority interest based on parent and minority's share.
Step 4	Follow the consolidation process thereafter.

Q.5.20: Consolidation of holding company with one foreign subsidiary

The draft balance sheets of X Ltd and its American subsidiary Y Inc as at 31st March 2010 are:

Assets	X Rs.	Y $
Fixed Assets	1800000	20000
Investments in Y Inc at cost	1600000	
Stocks	1200000	30000
Debtors	2400000	60000
Cash and bank	800000	10000
	7800000	120000

Liabilities	X Rs.	Y $
Equity share capital	3000000	30000
Profit and loss account	2000000	40000
Loan	1200000	20000

Trade creditors	600000	10000
Taxation	1000000	20000
	7800000	120000

X Ltd acquired 80% of shares in Y Inc on 1st April 2009, when the profit and loss account showed a balance of $ 23000 (before dividend). Y Inc, paid in September, 2009 dividend for2008-09 $3000. When Y Inc remitted the amount to X Ltd the exchange rate was 1 $ = Rs.43. An investment account of X Ltd, so far, only one entry had been made on the acquisition of shares.

The exchange rate prevalent on the relevant dates were

1st April 2009   1$ = Rs.40
31st March 2010 1 $ = Rs.45

There has been no movement in the Fixed Assets or share capital of Y inc during the year. Prepare the consolidated balance sheet of X Ltd and its subsidiary, Y Inc at 31st March 2010. *(Adapted: CA Final: May 1999)*

Solution

1. **Group structure**

Y Inc

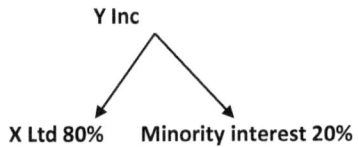

X Ltd 80%   Minority interest 20%

2. **Statement of conversion of Y Inc Balance Sheet**

Liabilities	$	Exch	Rs.	Assets	$	Exch	Rs.
Equity share capital	30000	40	1200000	Fixed Assets	20000	45	900000
				Stock	30000	45	1350000
Profit & Loss A/c				Debtors	60000	45	2700000
Pre-acquisition	20000	40	800000	Cash	10000	45	450000
Post-acquisition	20000	42.5	850000				
Loan	20000	45	900000				
Trade creditors	10000	45	450000				
Taxation	20000	45	900000				
Foreign currency translation reserve			300000				
Total	120000		5400000	Total	120000		5400000

3. **Statement of analysis of Profit and Loss of Y Inc**

Particulars	Pre-acquisition $	Post-acquisition $
Opening balance	23000	20000

Less: Dividend for 2008-09	3000	
	20000	20000

4. Statement of reconciliation of foreign currency translation reserve

Particulars	Pre-acquisition Rs.	Post-acquisition Rs.
Net assets ($)	50000*	20000
Exchange difference (45 – 40) / (45-42.5)	5	2.5
Total (250000 + 50000) = 300000	250000	50000

*(share capital 30000 + pre-acquisition profit 20000 = 50000)

5. Statement of analysis of profits and Foreign currency translation reserve of Y Inc

Particulars	Pre-acquisition Rs.	Post-acquisition Rs.	Foreign currency translation reserve Rs.
Profit and Loss Account	800000	850000	300000
Share of X Ltd (80%)	640000	680000	240000
Minority interest (20%)	160000	170000	60000

6. Statement of Minority Interest

Particulars	Amount Rs.
Share capital (Rs.1200000 x 20%)	240000
Add: Capital profit (WN5)	160000
Revenue profit (WN5)	170000
Foreign currency translation reserve	60000
	630000

7. Statement of Cost of control / capital reserve

Particulars	Amount Rs.	Amount Rs.
Cost of investment	1600000	
Less: Pre-acquisition dividend ($3000 x 43x 80%)	103200	1496800(A)
A Ltd's share of Y Inc's net assets		
- Share capital (Rs.1200000 x 80%)	960000	
- Capital profit	640000	1600000(B)
Capital reserve (B – A)		103200

8. Statement of Reserve of X Ltd

Particulars	Profit & Loss	Foreign currency translation

	Rs.	reserve Rs.
X Ltd balance	2000000	
Add: share of post-acquisition profits	680000	240000
Less: Pre-acquisition dividend	(103200)	
Reserve to Consolidated Balance Sheet	2576800	240000

Consolidated Balance Sheet of X Ltd and its subsidiary Y Inc
As at 31st March 2010

Particulars	Note no.	Amount Rs
I. **Equity and Liabilities**		
(1)Shareholder's funds		
(a) Share capital		3000000
(b) Reserves and surplus	1	2920000
(2)Minority Interest (WN6)		630000
(3)Non-current liabilities		
Long-term borrowing	2	2100000
(4)Current liabilities		
(a)Trade Payables	3	1050000
(b) Other current liabilities	4	1900000
Total		11600000
II.Assets		
(1)Non-current Assets		
(a)Fixed Assets		
(i)Tangible Assets (1800000 + 900000)		2700000
(ii)Intangible Assets		-
(b)Non-current Investments		-
(2)Current Assets:		
(a)Inventories (1200000 + 1350000)		2550000
(b)Trade Receivables (2400000 + 2700000)		5100000
(c)Cash and cash equivalents (800000 + 450000)		1250000
Total		11600000

Notes on Accounts

S/L No	Particulars	Amount (Rs)	Amount (Rs)
1.	**Reserves and surplus**		
	Capital reserve (WN7)	103200	
	Foreign Exchange translation reserve (WN8)	240000	
	Profit & Loss Account (WN8)	<u>2576800</u>	2920000
2	**Long term borrowings**		
	Loan (12000000 + 900000)		2100000

3.	Trade Payables		1050000	
	Trade Creditors (600000 + 450000)			
4.	Other current liabilities		1900000	
	Provision for taxation (1000000 + 900000)			

Chapter 6: Chain holding : Consolidation of holding company with more than one Subsidiary and Intercompany holdings

Learning Outcomes
- ❑ Concept of chain holding
- ❑ methods of treatment of pre-acquisition profit of sub-subsidiary in the consolidation process
  - direct method
  - indirect method
- ❑ consolidation of holding company and two subsidiaries
- ❑ Interco holdings (cross holdings)

6.1. What is the concept of chain holding?

In accordance with Section 2(87) of Companies Act 2013, subsidiary company or subsidiary, in relation to any other company (that is to say the holding company) means a company in which the holding company:
(i) controls the composition of the Board of Directors; or
(ii) exercises or controls more than one-half of the total share capital
either in its own or together with one or more of its subsidiary companies:
Provided that such class or classes of holding companies as may be prescribed shall not have layers of subsidiaries beyond such numbers as may be prescribed.

Example: If S Ltd is the subsidiary of H Ltd, and if SS Ltd is the subsidiary of S Ltd, then by virtue of the above section SS Ltd becomes the subsidiary of H Ltd as well.

H Ltd

S Ltd

SS Ltd

Other examples are as under:

Type I: As mentioned above Parent holds shares in subsidiary but not in sub-subsidiary.

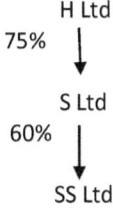

H Ltd

75%

S Ltd

60%

SS Ltd

Type II: Both holding company as well as subsidiary holds shares in sub-subsidiary.

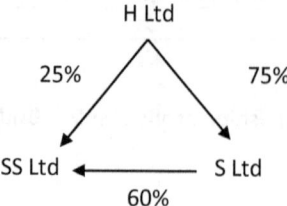

Type III : Both holding company as well as subsidiary together holds majority of the shares in sub-subsidiary.

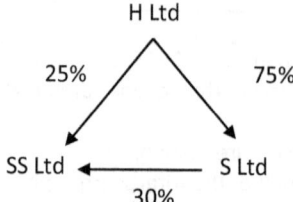

Type IV : Holding company has more than one subsidiary and all of them hold shares in the sub-subsidiary.

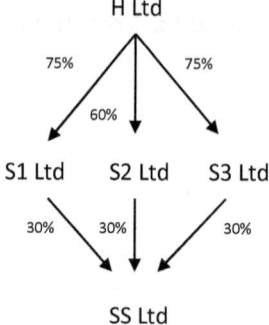

There may be many other types of chain holding.

6.2. What are the methods of treatment of pre-acquisition profit of sub-subsidiary in the consolidation process?

There are two methods in treatment of capital profits of sub-subsidiary in the consolidation process:

Direct method	Pre-acquisition profit of the sub-subsidiary should be

	a) Apportioned between minority interest and group interest and b) The group interest should be taken directly for calculation of goodwill / capital reserve. Example: H Ltd holds 60% shares of S Ltd and 20% shares of SS Ltd and S Ltd holds 60% shares of SS Ltd. Total profit of SS Ltd is Rs.100000 of which pre-acquisition profit is Rs.40000. As per this method capital profit to be apportioned as under: Rs.40000 x 20/100 = Rs.8000 to minorities of SS Ltd Rs.40000 x 80/100 = Rs.32000 to group which is considered for calculating goodwill or capital reserve. For computation of goodwill / capital reserve for the purpose of consolidation, cost of group investments is compared to their face value. Cost of investments should be arrived at after adjusting pre-acquisition profit / loss related to such investments. Hence direct method appears to be more logical.
Indirect method	Pre-acquisition profit / loss is apportioned as under : a) among minorities of the sub-subsidiaries and b) the respective group companies. From the share of the respective group companies, their minority interests are deducted and the parent company gets its indirect shares. Considering the example as above: H Ltd's direct share to SS Ltd is 20% and indirect through S Ltd is (60% x 60%) = 36%. So while computing goodwill or capital reserve the treatment would be as follows: Rs.40000 x 20/100 = Rs.8000 to minorities of SS Ltd Rs.40000 x 20/100 = Rs.8000 to H Ltd Rs.40000 x 60/100 = Rs.24000 to S Ltd. Out of S Ltd's share of Rs.24000, H Ltd will get 60% i.e. Rs.14400 which becomes the indirect share of H Ltd in capital profit of SS Ltd. Accordingly in total Rs.22400 (R.8000 + Rs.14400) is to be considered for computation of goodwill / capital reserve. This works out to 56% (20% + 36%) of Rs.40000.

Q.6.1: Chain holding – consolidation of holding company and two subsidiaries

The summarized Balance Sheets of A Ltd, B Ltd and C Ltd are given below:

Balance Sheets of A Ltd, B Ltd and C Ltd as on 31.12.2010   **(In Rs)**

Liabilities	A Ltd	B Ltd	C Ltd	Assets	A Ltd	B Ltd	C Ltd
Equity capital (Rs.10 fully paid up)	400000	200000	100000	Investments (acquired on 1.1.2010)			
Profit & Loss A/c 1.1.2010	15000	20000	8000	16000 shares in B Ltd	180000		
				7500 shares in C Ltd	80000		
Profit during	70000	38000	18000		50000		

		50000		Loan to B Ltd	200000	318000	140000
the year							
Loan from A Ltd	25000	10000	14000	Sundry assets			
Creditors							
	510000	318000	140000		510000	318000	140000

Additional information
1. Proposed dividend by each 10%
2. Stock was purchased by B Ltd from C Ltd for Rs.8000. C Ltd's cost was Rs.5000 only.
3. Loan by B Ltd carries 8% interest which has not been considered by any of the two companies.

Prepare Consolidated Balance Sheet.

Solution

1. **The group structure** is as under:

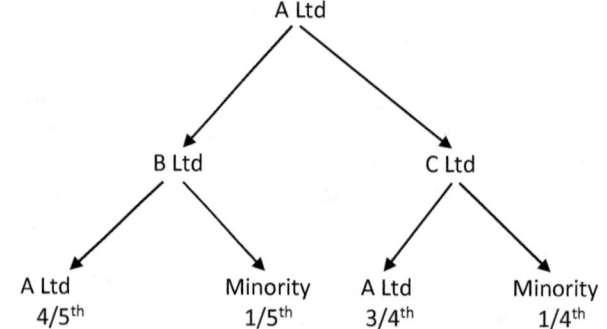

2. **Statement of capital reserve**

Particulars	B Ltd Rs	C Ltd Rs.
Profit as on 1.1.2010	20000	8000
Less: Minority interest	4000	2000
To Cost of control / goodwill (W.N.6)	16000	6000

3. **Statement of Profit & Loss A/c**

Particulars	B Ltd Rs	C Ltd Rs.
Profit during the year as per Balance Sheet	38000	18000
Less: Interest @ 8% on Rs.50000	4000	
	34000	
Less: Minority interest	6800	4500
	27200	13500
Less: Unrealised profit 4/5 x (3/4 x 3000)	-	1800
To consolidated Balance Sheet	27200	11700

4. **Statement of Share capital A/c**

Particulars	B Ltd	C Ltd

	Rs	Rs.
As per Balance Sheet	200000	100000
Less: Minority Interest	40000	25000
To Cost of control / goodwill	160000	75000

5. Statement of Minority interest

Particulars	B Ltd	C Ltd
	Rs	Rs.
Share capital	40000	25000
Capital reserve	4000	2000
Profit & Loss	6800	4500
	50800	31500
Less: proposed dividend shown separately	4000	2500
To consolidated Balance Sheet	46800	29000

6. Statement of Cost of control / goodwill

Particulars	B Ltd	C Ltd
	Rs	Rs.
Cost of investments	180000	80000
Less: paid up value of share capital (W.N.4)	160000	75000
	20000	5000
Less : Capital reserve	16000	6000
To consolidated Balance Sheet	4000	(1000)

7. Statement of Profit and Loss Account – A Ltd

Item	Amount Rs
Balance as on 1.1.2010	15000
Add: Profit during the year	70000
Add: Interest on loan	4000
	89000
Less proposed dividend	40000
To consolidated Balance Sheet	49000

Consolidated Balance Sheet of A Ltd with its subsidiaries B Ltd and C Ltd
As at 31.12.2010

Particulars	Note no.	Amount (Rs)
I. **Equity and Liabilities**		
(1)Shareholder's funds		
(a) Share capital	1	400000
(b) Reserves and surplus	2	88900
(2)Minority Interest (WN5)	3	75800
(3)Non-current liabilities		
Long-term borrowing		-

	(4)Current liabilities		
	(a)Trade payables	4	49000
	(b)Other current liabilities	5	46500
	Total		**660200**
II.	**Assets**		
	(1)Non-current assets		
	(a)Fixed Assets		
	Tangible assets	6	656200
	Intangible assets (Goodwill)(WN6)		4000
	(b)Non-current investments		
	(2)Current assets		
	(a)Inventories (WN5)		
	(b)Trade receivables (WN6)		
	(c)Cash and cash equivalents		
	Total		**660200**

Notes on Accounts

S/L No	Particulars		Amount (Rs)	Amount (Rs)
1.	**Share capital**			
	Issued, subscribed and paid up			
	40000 equity shares of Rs.10 each fully paid up			400000
2	**Reserves and surplus**			
	Capital reserve(W.N.6)		1000	
	Profit & Loss Account			
	A Ltd (W.N.7)	49000		
	B Ltd	27200		
	C Ltd	11700	87900	88900
3.	**Minority Interest (WN5)**			
	B Ltd		46800	
	C Ltd		29000	75800
4.	**Trade Payables**			
	Sundry creditors			
	A Ltd		25000	
	B Ltd		10000	
	C Ltd		14000	49000
5.	**Other current liabilities**			
	Proposed dividend			
	A Ltd		40000	
	B Ltd (minority)		4000	
	C Ltd (minority)		2500	46500

6.	Tangible assets			
	Sundry assets			
	A Ltd		**200000**	
	B Ltd	318000		
	Less: proportionate amount of			
	un-realized profit	1800	**316200**	
	C Ltd		**140000**	**656200**

Q.6.2: Chain holding: Holding company and two subsidiaries

From the following Balance Sheets of a group of companies and the other information provided, draw up the consolidated Balance Sheet as on 31.3.2010. Figures given are in Rupees Lakhs:

Liabilities	X	Y	Z	Assets	X	Y	Z
Share capital (in				Fixed Assets less			
shares of Rs.10				depreciation	130		100
each)	300	200	100	Cost of investment in Y	180	150	-
Reserves	50	40	30	Cost of investment in Z	40	-	-
Profit & loss Bal	60	50	40	Cost of investment in Z	-	-	-
Bills payable	10	-	5	Stock	50	80	20
Creditors	30	10	10	Debtors	70	20	20
Y Ltd balance	-	-	15	Bills receivable	-	10	20
Z Ltd balance	50	-	-	Z Ltd balance	-	10	-
				X Ltd balance	-	10	30
				Cash and bank balance	30	-	10
						20	
	500	300	200		500	300	200

- X Ltd holds 160000 shares and 30000 shares respectively in Y Ltd and Z Ltd ; Y Ltd holds 60000 shares in Z Ltd. These investments were made on 1.7.2009 on which date the provision was as follows:

	Y Ltd	Z Ltd
Reserves	20	10
Profit and loss account	30	16

- In December 2009, Y Ltd invoiced goods to X Ltd for Rs.40 lakhs at cost plus 25%. The closing stock of X Ltd includes such goods valued at Rs.5 lakhs
- Z Ltd sold to Y Ltd an equipment costing Rs.24 lakhs at a profit of 25% on selling price on 1.1.2010. Depreciation at 10% per annum was provided by Y Ltd on this equipment.
- Bills payables of Z Ltd represent acceptances given to Y Ltd out of which Y Ltd had discounted bills worth Rs. 3 lakhs
- Debtors of X Ltd include Rs.5 lakhs being the amount due from Y Ltd
- X Ltd proposes dividend at 10%.

Solution

Consolidated Balance Sheet of X Ltd and its
Subsidiaries Y Ltd and Z Ltd as at 31st March 2010 (Rs in lakhs)

Particulars	Note no.	Amount
I. **Equity and Liabilities**		
(1)Shareholder's funds		
(a) Share capital	1	300.00
(b) Reserves and surplus	2	151.90
(2)Minority Interest	3	79.30
(3)Non-current liabilities		
Long-term borrowing		-
(4)Current liabilities		
(a)Trade payables	4	58.00
(b)Short term provision		30.00
(c)Other current liabilities	5	25.00
Total		**644.20**
II. **Assets**		
(1)Non-current assets		
(a)Fixed Assets		
Tangible assets	6	372.20
Intangible assets (Goodwill)		
(b)Non-current investments		
(2)Current assets		
(a)Inventories	7	89.00
(b)Trade receivables	8	123.00
(c)Cash and cash equivalents		60.00
Total		**644.20**

Notes on Accounts

S/L No	Particulars	Amount (Rs/Lakhs)	Amount (Rs/Lakhs)
1.	**Share capital**		
	Issued, subscribed and paid up		
	3000000 equity shares of Rs.10 each fully paid up		<u>300.00</u>
2	**Reserves and surplus**		
	Capital reserve	13.40	
	Other reserves	81.60	
	Profit & Loss Account	<u>56.90</u>	151.90
3.	**Minority Interest**		
	Y Ltd	63.08	
	X Ltd	<u>16.22</u>	79.30
4.	**Trade Payables**		
	Sundry creditors		

	X Ltd	30.00		
	Y Ltd	10.00		
	Z Ltd 10.00			
		50.00		
	Less: Mutual indebtedness	5.00	45.00	
	Bills payable			
	X Ltd	10.00		
	Y Ltd	5.00		
		15.00		
	Less: Mutual indebtedness	2.00	**13.00**	**58.00**
5.	**Other current liabilities**			
	Current Account balances:			
	X Ltd		**50.00**	
	Z Ltd		**15.00**	
			65.00	
	Less: mutual indebtedness(10+30)		40.00	**25.00**
6.	**Tangible assets**			
	X Ltd		**130.00**	
	Y Ltd		**150.00**	
	Z Ltd		**100.00**	
			380.00	
	Less: unrealised profit		**7.80**	**372.20**
7.	**Inventories**			
	X Ltd		**50.00**	
	Y Ltd		**20.00**	
	Z Ltd		**20.00**	
			90.00	
	Less: unrealised profit		**1.00**	**89.00**
8.	**Trade Receivables**			
	Debtors			
	X Ltd	70.00		
	Y Ltd	10.00		
	Z Ltd	20.00		
		100.00		
	Less: mutual indebtedness	5.00	**95.00**	
	Bills receivables			
	Y Ltd	10.00		
	Z Ltd	20.00		
		30.00		
	Less: mutual indebtedness	2.00	**28.00**	**123.00**

Working Notes

1. **Statement of analysis of profits of Z Ltd**

Item	Capital profit	Revenue reserve	Revenue profit
Reserves on 1.7.2009	10.00		
Profit and loss A/c on 1.7.2009	16.00		
Increase in reserve		20.00	
Increase in profit			24.00
	26.00	20.00	24.00
Less: Minority interest (10%)	2.60	2.00	2.40
	23.40	18.00	21.60
Share of X Ltd	7.80	6.00	7.20
Share of Y Ltd	15.60	12.00	14.40

2. Statement of analysis of profits of Y Ltd

Item	Capital profit	Revenue reserve	Revenue profit
Reserves on 1.7.2009	20.00		
Profit and loss A/c on 1.7.2009	30.00		
Increase in reserve		20.00	
Increase in profit			20.00
	50.00	20.00	20.00
Less: Share in Z Ltd	-	12.00	14.40
	50.00	32.00	34.40
Less: Minority interest (20%)	10.00	6.40	6.88
Share of X Ltd	40.00	25.60	27.52

3. Statement of cost of control (Rs in lakhs)

Item	Amount	Amount	Amount
Investments in Y Ltd			180.00
Investments in Z Ltd			120.00
			300.00
Less: Paid up value of investments			
In Y Ltd	160.00		
In Z Ltd	90.00	250.00	
Capital profit			
In Y Ltd	40.00		
In Z Ltd	23.40	63.40	313.40
Capital reserve			13.40

4. Statement of Minority Interest (Rs in lakhs)

Item	Y Ltd	Z Ltd
Share capital	40.00	10.00
Capital profit	10.00	2.60
Revenue reserves	6.40	2.00

Revenue profit	6.88	2.40
Total	63.28	17.00
Less: unrealised profit on stock (20% of 1)	0.20	
Unrealised profit on equipment (10% of 7.8)		0.78
	63.08	16.22

5. Statement of unrealised profit on equipment sale (Rs in lakhs)

Item	Amount
Cost	24.00
Profit	8.00
Selling price	32.00
Unrealized profit = 8 – 8 x 10% x 3/12 = 8.00 – 0.20	**7.80**

6. Statement of Profit and Loss Account – X Ltd (Rs in lakhs)

Item	Amount
Balance	60.00
Less: Proposed dividend	30.00
	30.00
Share in Y Ltd	27.52
Share in Z Ltd	7.20
	64.72
Less: Unrealised profit on equipment (90% of 7.8)	7.02
	57.70
Less: Unrealised profit on stock (5 x 25/125 x 80%)	0.80
	56.90

7. Statement of reserves – X Ltd (Rs in lakhs)

Item	Amount
X Ltd	50.00
Share in Y Ltd	25.60
Share in Z Ltd	6.00
	81.60

Q.6.3: Chain holding

Following are the Balance Sheets of Mumbai Limited, Delhi Limited, Amritsar Limited and Kanpur Limited as at 31st December, 2009:

Liabilities	Mumbai Ltd.	Delhi Ltd.	Amritsar Ltd.	Kanpur Ltd.
Share Capital (Rs. 100 face value)	50,00,000	40,00,000	20,00,000	60,00,000
General Reserve	20,00,000	4,00,000	2,50,000	10,00,000
Profit and Loss Account	10,00,000	4,00,000	2,50,000	3,20,000
Sundry Creditors	3,00,000	1,00,000	50,000	80,000
	83,00,000	49,00,000	25,50,000	74,00,000
Assets				
Investments:				
30,000 shares in Delhi Ltd.	35,00,000	--	--	--
10,000 shares in Amritsar Ltd.	11,00,000	--	--	--

5,000 shares in Amritsar Ltd.	--	5,00,000	--	--
Shares in Kanpur Ltd. @ Rs. 120	36,00,000	18,00,000	6,00,000	--
Fixed Assets	--	20,00,000	15,00,000	70,00,000
Current Assets	1,00,000	6,00,000	4,50,000	4,00,000
	83,00,000	49,00,000	25,50,000	74,00,000

Balance in General Reserve Account and Profit and Loss Account, when shares were purchased in different companies were:

	Mumbai Ltd.	Delhi Ltd.	Amritsar Ltd.	Kanpur Ltd.
General Reserve	10,00,000	2,00,000	1,00,000	6,00,000
Profit and Loss Account	6,00,000	2,00,000	50,000	60,000

Required:
Prepare a consolidated Balance Sheet of the group as at 31st December, 2009 (Calculations may be rounded off to the nearest rupee).

Solution

**Consolidated Balance Sheet of Mumbai Ltd. and
its subsidiaries Delhi Ltd., Amritsar Ltd. and Kanpur Ltd.
As at 31st December, 2009**

Particulars		Note no.	Amount (Rs)
I.	**Equity and Liabilities**		
	(1)Shareholder's funds		
	(a) Share capital	1	5000000.00
	(b) Reserves and surplus	2	4032187.50
	(2)Minority Interest		3125312.50
	(3)Non-current liabilities		
	Long-term borrowing		-
	(4)Current liabilities		
	(a)Trade payables		
	Sundry creditors		530000.00
	(b)Other current liabilities		-
	Total		12687500.00
II.	**Assets**		
	(1)Non-current assets		
	(a)Fixed Assets		
	Tangible assets		10500000.00
	Intangible assets (Goodwill)		637500.00
	(b)Non-current investments		
	(2)Current assets		1550000.00
	Total		12687500.00

Notes on Accounts

S/L No	Particulars	Amount (Rs)	Amount (Rs)
1.	Share capital Issued, subscribed and paid up		

	500000 equity shares of Rs.10 each fully paid up		**5000000.00**
2	**Reserves and surplus**		
	General reserve	2551041.67	
	Profit and loss account	1481145.83	4032187.50

Working Notes:
(i) Analysis of profits of Kanpur Ltd.

	Capital Profit Rs.	Revenue Reserve Rs.	Revenue Profit Rs.
General Reserve on the date of purchase	6,00,000.00		
Profit and Loss A/c on the date of purchase of shares	60,000.00		
Increase in General Reserve		4,00,000.00	
Increase in profit			2,60,000.00
	6,60,000.00	4,00,000.00	2,60,000.00
Less: Minority Interest (1/6)	1,10,000.00	66,666.67	43,333.33
	5,50,000.00	3,33,333.33	2,16,666.67
Share of Mumbai Ltd.(1/2)	3,30,000.00	2,00,000.00	1,30,000.00
Share of Delhi Ltd.(1/4)	1,65,000.00	1,00,000.00	65,000.00
Share of Amritsar Ltd.(1/12)	55,000.00	33,333.33	21,666.67

(ii) Analysis of profits of Amritsar Ltd.

	Capital Profit Rs.	Revenue Reserve Rs.	Revenue Profit Rs.
General Reserve on the date of purchase of shares	1,00,000.00		
Profit and Loss A/c on the date of purchase of shares	50,000.00		
Increase in General Reserve		1,50,000.00	
Increase in Profit and Loss A/c			2,00,000.00
Share in Kanpur Ltd.		33,333.33	21,666.67
	1, 50,000.00	1,83,333,33	2,21,666.67
Less: Minority Interest (1/4)	37,500.00	45,833.33	55,416.67
	1,12,500.00	1,37,500.00	1,66,250.00
Share of Mumbai Ltd.	75,000	91,666.67	1,10,833.33
Share of Delhi Ltd.	37,500	45,833.33	55,416.67

(iii) Analysis of profits of Delhi Ltd.

	Capital Profit	Revenue Reserve	Revenue Profit

	Rs.	Rs.	Rs.
General Reserve on the date of purchase of shares	2,00,000.00		
Profit and Loss A/c on the date of purchase of shares	2,00,000.00		
Increase in General Reserve		2,00,000.00	
Increase in Profit and Loss A/c			2,00,000.00
Share in Kanpur Ltd.		1,00,000.00	65,000.00
Share in Amritsar Ltd.		45,833.33	55,416.67
	4,00,000.00	3,45,833.33	3,20,416.67
Less: Minority Interest(1/4)	1,00,000.00	86,458.33	80,104.17
Share of Mumbai Ltd.	3,00,000.00	2,59,375.00	2,40,312.50

(iv) Cost of control

		Rs.
Investments in		
Delhi Ltd.	35,00,000	
Amritsar Ltd.	16,00,000	
Kanpur Ltd.	60,00,000	
		1,11,00,000
Paid up value of investments in		
Delhi Ltd.	30,00,000	
Amritsar Ltd.	15,00,000	
Kanpur Ltd.	50,00,000	
Capital Profits in		(95,00,000)
Delhi Ltd.	3,00,000	
Amritsar Ltd.	1,12,500	
Kanpur Ltd.	5,50,000	(9,62,500)
Goodwill		6,37,500

(v) Minority Interest

	Rs.	Rs.
Share Capital:		
Delhi Ltd.(1/4)	10,00,000.00	
Amritsar Ltd.(1/4)	5,00,000.00	
Kanpur Ltd. (1/4)	10,00,000.00	25,00,000.00
Shares in profits & reserves (Pre and Post-Acquisitions)		
Delhi Ltd.	2,66,562.50	
Amritsar Ltd.	1,38,750.00	
Kanpur Ltd.	2,20,000.00	6,25,312.50
31,25,312.50		

(vi) General Reserve – Mumbai Ltd.

	Rs.
Balance as on 31.12.2009 (given)	20,00,000.00
Share in	
Delhi Ltd.	2,59,375.00

Amritsar Ltd.	91,666.67
Kanpur Ltd.	2,00,000.00
	25,51,041.67

(vii) Profit and Loss Account – Mumbai Ltd.

	Rs.
Balance as on 31.12.2009 (given)	10,00,000.00
Share in	
Delhi Ltd.	2,40,312.50
Amritsar Ltd.	1,10,833.33
Kanpur Ltd.	1,30,000.00
	14,81,145.83

Q.6.4: Chain holding: Unrealised profit on upstream transaction

A Limited is a holding company and B Limited and C Limited are subsidiaries of A Limited. Their balance sheets as on 31.12.2009 are given below:

	A Ltd.	B Ltd.	C Ltd.		A Ltd.	B Ltd.	C Ltd.
	Rs.	Rs.	Rs.		Rs.	Rs.	Rs.
Share Capital	1,00,000	1,00,000	60,000	Fixed Assets	20,000	60,000	43,000
Reserves	48,000	10,000	9,000	Investments			
Profit and loss				Shares in B Ltd.	95,000		
Account	16,000	12,000	9,000				
C Ltd. Balance	3,000			Shares in C Ltd.	13,000	53,000	
Sundry Creditors	7,000	5,000		Stock in Trade	12,000		
A Ltd. Balance		7,000		B Ltd. Balance	8,000		
				Sundry Debtors	26,000	21,000	32,000
A Ltd. Balance	3,000						
	1,74,000	1,34,000	78,000		1,74,000	1,34,000	78,000

The following particulars are given:
(i) The Share Capital of all companies is divided into shares of Rs. 10 each.
(ii) A Ltd. held 8,000 shares of B Ltd. and 1000 shares of C Ltd.
(iii) B Ltd. held 4,000 shares of C Ltd.
(iv) All the investments were made on 30.6.2009
(v) On 31.12.2008, the position was as shown below:

	B Ltd.	C Ltd.
	Rs.	Rs.
Reserve	8,000	7,500
Profit and Loss Account	4,000	3,000
Sundry Creditors	5,000	1,000
Fixed Assets	60,000	43,000
Stock in Trade	4,000	35,000
Sundry Debtors	48,000	33,000

(vi) 10% dividend is proposed by each company.
(vii) The whole of stock in trade of B Ltd. as on 30.6.2009 (Rs. 4,000) was later sold to A Ltd. for Rs. 4,400 and remained unsold by A Ltd. as on 31.12.2009.

(viii) Cash-in-transit from B Ltd. to A Ltd. was Rs. 1,000 as at the close of business. You are required to prepare the Consolidated Balance Sheet of the group as on 31.12.2009.

Solution

Consolidated Balance Sheet of A Ltd. and its subsidiaries B Ltd and C Ltd. as on 31st December,2009

Particulars	Note no.	Amount (Rs)
I. **Equity and Liabilities**		
(1)Shareholder's funds		
(a) Share capital		100000
(b) Reserves and surplus	1	60305
(2)Minority Interest		37820
(3)Non-current liabilities		
Long-term borrowing		-
(4)Current liabilities		
(a)Trade payables		
Sundry creditors		12000
(b)Other current liabilities		10000
Total		**220125**
II. **Assets**		
(1)Non-current assets		
(a)Fixed Assets		
Tangible assets		123000
Intangible assets (Goodwill)		5525
(b)Non-current investments		
(2)Current assets		
(a)Inventories	2	11600
(b)Trade receivables		79000
(c)Cash & cash equivalent (in transit)		1000
Total		**220125**

Notes on Accounts

S/L No	Particulars	Amount (Rs)	Amount (Rs)
1.	**Reserves and surplus**		
	Reserves	49325	
	Profit and loss account	10980	60305
2.	**Inventories**		
	Stock in Trade	12000	
	Less: Provision for Unrealized	400	11600

Working Notes:

(1) Position on 30.06.2009

	Reserves Rs.	Profit and Loss Account Rs.
B Ltd.		
Balance on 31.12.2009	10,000	12,000
Less: Balance on 31.12.2008	8,000	4,000
Increase during the year	2,000	8,000
Estimated increase for half year	1,000	4,000
Balance on 30.06.2009	9,000 (8,000 + 1,000)	8,000 (4,000 + 4,000)
C Ltd.		
Balance on 31.12.2009	9,000	9,000
Balance on 31.12.2008	7,500	3,000
Increase during the year	1,500	6,000
Estimated increase for half year	750	3,000
Balance as on 30.06.2009	8250(7,500 +750)	6,000 (3,000 + 3,000)

(ii) Analysis of Profits of C Ltd.

	Capital Profit Rs.	Revenue Reserve Rs.	Revenue Profit Rs.
Reserves on 30.06.2009	8,250		
Profit and Loss A/c on 30.06.2009	6,000		
Increase in reserves		750	
Increase in profit			3,000
	14,250	750	3,000
Less: Minority Interest (1/6)	2,375	125	500
	11,875	625	2,500
Share of A Ltd. (1/6)	2,375	125	500
Share of B Ltd. (4/6)	9,500	500	2,000

(iii) Analysis of Profits of B Ltd.

	Capital Profit Rs.	Revenue Reserve Rs.	Revenue Profit Rs.
Reserves on 30.06.2009	9,000		
Profit and Loss A/c on 30.06.2009	8,000		
Increase in reserves		1,000	
Increase in profit			4,000
Share in C Ltd.		500	2,000
	17,000	1,500	6,000
Less: Minority Interest (2/10)	3,400	300	1,200
Share of A Ltd. (8/10)	13,600	1,200	4,800

(iv) Cost of Control

	Rs.	Rs.
Investments in		
B Ltd.	95,000	

C Ltd.	66,000	1,61,000
Less: paid up value of investments in		
B Ltd.	80,000	
C Ltd.	50,000	
Capital Profits in		(1,30,000)
B Ltd.	13,600	
C Ltd.	11,875	
		(25,475)
Goodwill		5,525

(v) **Minority Interest**

	Rs.	Rs.
Share Capital:		
B Ltd.	20,000	
C Ltd.	10,000	30,000
Share in profits and reserves		
(Pre and Post-Acquisitions)		
B Ltd.	4,900	
C Ltd.	3,000	7,900
		37,900
Less: Provision for unrealized profit		
(20% of Rs. 400)		80
		37,820

(vi) **Reserves – A Ltd.**

	Rs.
Balance as on 31.12.2009 (given)	48,000
Share in	
B Ltd.	1,200
C Ltd.	125
	49,325

(vii) **Profit and Loss Account – A Ltd.**

	Rs.
Balance as on 31.12.2009 (given)	16,000
Share in	
B Ltd.	4,800
C Ltd.	500
	21,300
Less: Proposed dividend (10% of Rs. 1,00,000)	10,000
Provision for unrealized profit on stock	320
80% of (Rs. 4,400 – Rs. 4,000)	10,980

Note: The above solution has been done by direct method. Alternatively, students may follow indirect method. In indirect method, the share in pre-acquisition profits of B Ltd. in C Ltd. amounting of Rs. 9,500 will be included as capital profit while analyzing the profits of B Ltd. and will not be considered for the purpose of cost of control. Thus, in this case, the amounts of goodwill and minority interest will increase by Rs. 1,900 (2/10 of Rs. 9,500). Goodwill and minority Interest will be shown at Rs. 7,425 and Rs. 39,720 respectively in the consolidated balance sheet. Therefore, the total of the assets and liabilities side of the consolidated balance sheet will be Rs. 2,22,025.

Q.6.5: Consolidation of Parent and two subsidiaries

On 31st March, 2009 Bee Ltd. became the holding company of Cee Ltd. and Dee Ltd.by enquiring 450 lakhs fully paid shares in Cee Ltd. for Rs. 6,750 lakhs and 240 lakhs fully paid shares in Dee Ltd. for Rs. 2,160 lakhs. On that date, Cee Ltd. showed a balance of Rs. 2,550 lakhs in General Reserve and a credit balance of Rs. 900 lakhs in Profit and Loss Account. On the same date, Dee Ltd. showed a debit balance of Rs. 360 lakhs in Profit and Loss Account. While its Preliminary Expenses Account showed balance of Rs. 30 lakhs.

After one year, on 31st March, 2010 the Balance sheets of three companies stood as follows:

(All amounts in lakhs of Rupees)

Liabilities	Bee Ltd.	Cee Ltd.	Dee Ltd.
Fully paid equity shares of Rs. 10 each	27,000	7,500	3,000
General Reserve	33,000	3,150	-
Profit and loss A/c	9,000	1,200	750
15 lakh fully paid 9.5%			
Debentures of Rs. 100 each	-	-	1,500
Loan from Cee Ltd.	-	-	75
Bills Payable	-	-	150
Sundry Creditors	14,100	2,700	930
	83,100	14,550	6,405

(All amounts in lakhs of Rupees)

Assets	Bee Ltd.	Cee Ltd.	Dee Ltd.
Machinery	39,000	7,500	2,100
Furniture and Fixtures	6,000	1,500	600
Investments			
450 lakhs shares in Cee Ltd.	6,750	-	-
240 lakhs shares in Dee Ltd.	2,160	-	-
3 lakh debentures in Dee Ltd.	294	-	-
Stocks	16,500	3,000	1,500
Sundry Debtors	9,000	1,350	1,290
Cash and Bank balances	3,201	1,050	900
Loan to Dee Ltd.	-	90	-
Bills Receivable	195	60	-
Preliminary Expenses	-	-	15
	83,100	14,550	6,405

The following points relating to the above mentioned Balance Sheets are to be noted:

(i) All the bills payable appearing in Dee Ltd.'s Balance sheet were accepted in favour of Cee Ltd. out of which bills amounting to Rs. 75 lakhs were endorsed by Cee Ltd. in favour of Bee Ltd. and Bills amounting to Rs. 45 lakhs had been discounted by Cee Ltd. with its bank

(ii) On 29th March, 2010 Dee Ltd. remitted Rs. 15 lakhs by means of a cheque to Cee Ltd. to return part of the loan; Cee Ltd. received the cheque only after 31st March, 2010.

(iii) Stocks with Cee Ltd. include goods purchased from Bee Ltd. for Rs. 200 lakhs. Bee Ltd. invoiced the goods at cost plus 25%.

(iv) In August, 2009 Cee Ltd. declared and distributed dividend @ 10 % for the year ended 31st March, 2009. Bee Ltd. credited the dividend received to its Profit and Loss Account.

You are required to prepare a Consolidated Balance Sheet of Bee Ltd. and its subsidiaries Cee Ltd. and Dee Ltd. as at 31st March, 2010.(*CA Final: Nov 2005*)

Solution

Consolidated Balance Sheet of Bee Ltd. and its subsidiaries Cee Ltd. and Dee Ltd. as at 31st March, 2010

Particulars	Note no.	Amount (Rs/Lakhs)
I. **Equity and Liabilities**		
(1)Shareholder's funds		
(a) Share capital	1	27000
(b) Reserves and surplus	2	43400
(2)Minority Interest (WN2)		5487
(3)Non-current liabilities		
Long-term borrowing		
(a)Debentures		1200
(4)Current liabilities		
(a)Trade payables	3	17775
(b)Short term provision		
(c)Other current liabilities		
Total		94862
II. **Assets**		
(1)Non-current assets		
(a)Fixed Assets		
Tangible assets	4	56700
Intangible assets (Goodwill)(WN3)		246
(b)Non-current investments		
(2)Current assets		
(a)Inventories	5	20960
(b)Trade receivables	6	11790
(c)Cash and cash equivalents	7	5166
Total		94862

Notes on Accounts

S/L No	Particulars	Amount (Rs/Lakhs)	Amount (Rs/Lakhs)
1.	**Share capital**		
	Authorised, Issued, subscribed and paid up		
	270000000 equity shares of Rs.10 each fully paid up		<u>27000</u>
2	**Reserves and surplus**		
	General reserve (WN4)	33360	
	Profit & Loss Account (WN4	<u>10040</u>	<u>43400</u>

3.	**Trade Payables**			
	Sundry creditors		17730	
	Acceptances	150		
	Less: Mutual owing	105	45	17775
4.	**Tangible assets**			
	Machinery		48600	
	Furniture & fixtures		8100	56700
5.	**Inventories**			
	Stock		21000	
	Less: Unrealized profit		40	20960
6.	**Trade receivables**			
	Sundry debtors		11640	
	Loan and Advances			
	Bills receivable	255		
	Less: Mutual owing (W.N.5)	105	150	11790
7.				
	Cash and cash equivalents		5151	
	Cash and bank balances		15	5166
	Cash in transit			

Working Notes:

(1) Calculation of pre and post-acquisition profits of subsidiaries:
(Rs. in lakhs)

			Post	Acquisition
		Pre-acquisition Capital profit	General Reserve	Profit/Loss A/c
Cee Ltd.			600	
General Reserve(Cr.)		2,550		
Profit and Loss A/c(Cr.)	900			
(-) Dividend	750	150		1050
		2,700	600	1050
Holding (60%)		1,620	360	630
Subsidiary (40%)		1,080	240	420

(Rs. in lakhs)

		Post -	Acquisition
	Pre-acquisition Capital profit	Preliminary Expenses	Profit/ Loss Account
Dee Ltd.			
Profit and Loss A/c (Cr.)	(360)		1,110
Preliminary Expenses (Dr.)	(30)	15	

(-) Dividend	(390)	15	1,110
Holding (80%)	(312)	12	888
Subsidiary (20%)	(78)	3	222

2. Minority Interest (Rs. in lakhs)

Cee Ltd.				
Share Capital			3,000	
Capital Profit		1,080		
Revenue General Reserve		240		
Profit/ Loss		420	1,740	4,740
Dee Ltd.				
Share Capital			600	
Capital Profit		(78)		
Revenue Profit (Cr.)	222			
Add: Preliminary expenses written off	3	225	147	747
				5,487

(3) **Cost of Control**(Rs. in lakhs)

Cee Ltd.			
Investment	6,750		
Less: Dividend received and wrongly credited to Profit and Loss	450	6,300	
Less: Paid – up share capital (60%)	4,500		
Add: Capital Profit	1,620	6,120	180
Dee Ltd.			
Investment in Shares	2,160		
In debentures	294	2,454	
Less: Paid – up share capital (80%)	2,400		
Nominal value of debentures	300		
Capital Profit	(312)	2,388	66
Goodwill			246

(4.) **Consolidated General Reserve and Profit and Loss A/c**

	General Reserve	Profit and Loss Account
Bee Ltd.	33,000	9,000
Less: Wrong dividend credited	–	450
	33,000	8,550
Cee Ltd.	360	630
Dee Ltd. (888 + 12)	–	900
	33,360	10,080
Less: Unrealized profit on stock		40
	33,360	10,040

(5) Mutual Owing regarding bills = Rs. (150 – 45) lakhs = Rs. 105 lakhs.
(6) Unrealized Profit = [200 x (25/125)] lakhs = Rs. 40 lakhs

(7) Amount of dividend wrongly credited to Profit and Loss A/c = 60% of Rs. 750 lakhs = Rs. 450 lakhs.

Q.6.6: Consolidation of Parent and two subsidiaries

The following are the balance sheets of Arun Ltd., Brown Ltd. and Crown Ltd. as at 31.12.2009:

Liabilities	Arun Ltd. Rs.	Brown Ltd. Rs.	Crown Ltd. Rs.
Share Capital(Shares of Rs. 100 each)	6,00,000	4,00,000	2,40,000
Reserves	80,000	40,000	30,000
Profit and Loss Account	2,00,000	1,20,000	1,00,000
Sundry Creditors	80,000	1,00,000	60,000
Arun Ltd.	--	40,000	32,000
Total	9,60,000	7,00,000	4,62,000

Assets	Arun Ltd. Rs.	Brown Ltd. Rs.	Crown Ltd. Rs.
Goodwill	80,000	60,000	40,000
Fixed Assets	2,80,000	2,00,000	2,40,000
Shares in:			
Brown Ltd. (3,000 Shares)	3,60,000	--	--
Crown Ltd. (400 Shares)	60,000	--	--
Crown Ltd. (1,400 Shares)	--	2,08,000	--
Due from: Brown Ltd.	48,000	--	--
Crown Ltd.	32,000	--	--
Current Assets	1,00,000	2,32,000	1,82,000
Total	9,60,000	7,00,000	4,62,000

(i) All shares were acquired on 1.7.2009.
(ii) On 1.1.2009 the balances to the various accounts were as under:

Particulars	Arun Ltd. Rs.	Brown Ltd. Rs.	Crown Ltd. Rs.
Reserves	40,000	40,000	20,000
Profit and Loss Account	20,000	(Dr.)20,000	12,000

(iii) During 2009, Profits accrued evenly.
(iv) In August 2009, each company paid interim dividend of 10%. Arun Ltd. and Brown Ltd. have credited their profit and loss account with dividends received.
(v) During 2009, Crown Ltd. sold an equipment costing Rs. 40,000 to Brown Ltd. for Rs. 48,000 and Brown Ltd. in turn sold the same to Arun Ltd. for Rs. 52,000.
Prepare the consolidated Balance sheet as at 31.12.2009, of Arun Ltd. and its subsidiaries.(CA Final, May 2006)

Solution
Consolidated Balance Sheet of Arun Ltd. and its subsidiaries
as on 31.12.2009

Particulars	Note no.	Amount (Rs)
I. Equity and Liabilities		

(1)Shareholder's funds			
(a) Share capital		1	**600000**
(b) Reserves and surplus		2	**337271**
(2)Minority Interest (WN4)			**233729**
(3)Non-current liabilities			
Long-term borrowing			-
(4)Current liabilities			
(a)Trade payables			
Sundry creditors			**240000**
(b)Short term provisions			
	Total		**1411000**
II. **Assets**			
(1)Non-current assets			
(a)Fixed Assets			
Tangible assets			**708000**
Intangible assets		3	**181000**
(b)Non-current investments			
(2)Current assets			
(a)Cash & cash equivalent		4	**8000**
(b)Other current assets			**514000**
	Total		**1411000**

Notes on Accounts

S/L No	Particulars	Amount (Rs)	Amount (Rs)
1.	**Share capital**		
	60000 shares of Rs.100 each		**600000**
2.	**Reserves and surplus**		
	Reserves (WN8)	**83021**	
	Profit and loss account (WN8)	**254250**	**337271**
3.	**Intangible assets**		
	Goodwill (WN5)		**180000**
4.	**Cash & cash equivalents**		
	Cash in transit(WN7)		**8000**

Working Notes

1. Shareholding pattern

In Brown Ltd.	Number of shares	%age of Holding
Arun Ltd.	3,000	75%
Minority Interest	1,000	25%
In Crown Ltd.		
Arun Ltd.	400	16.667%
Brown Ltd.	1,400	58.333%
Minority Interest	600	25%

2. Analysis of appointment of profit in Crown Ltd.

(a) Calculation of Unrealized Profit in Equipment

Crown Ltd. sold equipment to Brown Ltd. at a profit of Rs. 8,000 and this would be apportioned to

	Rs.
Arun Ltd.	1,333
Brown Ltd.	4,667
Minority Interest	2,000
	8,000

Brown Ltd. sold the equipment to Arun Ltd. at a profit of Rs. 4000. This would be apportioned to:

	Rs.
Arun Ltd.	3,000
Minority Interest	1,000
	4,000

The above amounts are to be deducted from the respective share of profits.

(b) Reserves

	Rs.	
Closing balance	30,000	
Opening balance	20,000	Capital Profit
Current year Appropriation	10,000	
Apportionment of Profit from 1.1.2009 to 30.6.2009	5,000	Capital Profit
Apportionment of Profit from 1.7.2009 to 31.12.2009	5,000	Revenue Reserve

(c) Profit and Loss Account

Closing Balance	1,00,000	
Opening Balance	12,000	Capital Profit
Current year profits before interim dividend	1,12,000	
Apportionment of Profit from 1.1.2009 to 30.6.2009	56,000	
Less: Interim Dividend	24,000	
	32,000	Capital Profit
From 1.7.2009 to 31.12.2009	56,000	Revenue Profit

(d) Apportionment of profits of Crown Ltd.

	Pre-Acquisition	Post-Acquisition	
	Capital Profit	Revenue Reserve	Revenue Profit
	Rs.	Rs.	Rs.
Reserves	25,000	5,000	--
Profit and Loss A/c	44,000	--	56,000
	69,000	5,000	56,000
Arun Ltd. [16.667%]	11,500	833	9,333
Brown Ltd. [58.333%]	40,250	2,917	32,667
Minority Interest [25%]	17,250	1,250	14,000

3. Analysis of Profit of Brown Ltd.

(a) Reserves

	Rs.

Closing balance	40,000
Opening balance	40,000 (Capital Profit)
Current year Appropriation	Nil

(b) **Profit and Loss Account**

	Rs.
Closing Balance	1,20,000
Opening Balance(Dr.)	20,000
Current year Appropriation after interim dividend	1,40,000
Profit before Interim Dividend	40,000
Less: Dividend from Crown Ltd.	1,80,000
	14,000
Apportionment of Profit from 1.1.2009 to 30.6.2009	1,66,000
Less: Interim Dividend	83,000
Capital Profit	40,000
Apportionment of Profit from 1.7.2009 to 31.12.2009 (Revenue Profit)	43,000
	83,000

(c) **Apportionment of Profit of Brown Ltd.**

	Pre-Acquisition	Post-Acquisition	
	Capital Profit Rs.	Revenue Reserve Rs.	Revenue Profit Rs.
Reserves	40,000	--	--
Profit & Loss Account (Opening balance (-) 20,000 + 43,000)	23,000		83,000
Less: Unrealized Profit of Equipment from Crown Ltd.			(4,667)
Share of Post-Acquisition Profit of Crown Ltd.	--	2,917	32,667
	63,000	2,917	1,11,000
	47,250	2,188	83,250
Arun Ltd. 75%	15,750	729	27,750
Minority Interest 25%			

4. **Minority Interest**

	Brown Ltd. Rs.	Crown Ltd. Rs.
Share Capital	1,00,000	60,000
Capital Profit	15,750	17,250
Revenue: Reserves	729	1,250
Profit & Loss Account	27,750	14,000
Unrealized Profit on Equipment	(1,000)	(2,000)
	1,43,229	90,500

Total Minority Interest: Rs.1,43,229 + Rs.90,500 = Rs.2,33,729

5. Cost of Control

	Arun Ltd. in Brown Ltd. Rs.	Arun Ltd. in Crown Ltd. Rs.	Brown Ltd. in Crown Ltd. Rs.
Amount Invested	3,60,000	60,000	2,08,000
Less: Pre-acquisition dividend	30,000	4,000	14,000
Adjusted Cost of Investment (A)	3,30,000	56,000	1,94,000
Share Capital	3,00,000	40,000	1,40,000
Capital Profit (B)	47,250	11,500	40,250
Capital Reserve/Goodwill (A) – (B)	3,47,250	51,500	1,80,250
	(17,250)	4,500	13,750
Net Goodwill	Rs. 1,000		

Goodwill on Consolidation Rs. (80,000 + 60,000 + 40,000 + 1,000) = Rs.1,81,000

6. Dividend declared

	Brown Ltd. Rs.	Crown Ltd. Rs.
Dividend declared	40,000	24,000
Share of:		
Arun Ltd.	30,000	4,000
Brown Ltd.		14,000
Minority	10,000	6,000

7. Inter – Company Transactions
(a) Owings

	Dr. Arun Ltd. Rs.	Cr. Brown Ltd. Rs.	Cr. Crown Ltd. Rs.
Balance in books	80,000	40,000	32,000
Less: Inter-co. owings	72,000	40,000	32,000
Cash-in-transit	8000	NIL	NIL

(b) Fixed Assets

	Rs.
Total Fixed Assets	7,20,000
Less: Unrealized Profit on sale of equipment	12,000
Amount to be taken to consolidated Balance Sheet	7,08,000

8. Reserves and Profit and Loss Account balances in the Consolidated Balance Sheet

	Reserves Rs.	Profit and Loss A/c Rs.
Balance in Books	80,000	2,00,000
Add: Shares of Post-Acquisition Profits:		
From Brown Ltd.	2,188	83,250
From Crown Ltd.	833	9,333
Less: Pre-Acquisition dividend:		
From Brown Ltd.		(30,000)
From Crown Ltd.		(4,000)
Less: Unrealized Profit on Equipment:		
From Brown Ltd.		(3,000)

From Crown Ltd.		(1,333)
	83,021	2,54,250

Q.6.7: Consolidation of Parent and two subsidiaries

The draft Balance Sheet of 3 companies as at 31st March, 2010 is as below:
(in Rs. 000's)

Liabilities	Morning Ltd.	Evening Ltd.	Night Ltd.
Share Capital – shares of Rs. 100 each	40,000	20,000	10,000
Reserves	1,800	1,000	900
P/L A/c (1.4.09)	1,500	2,000	800
Profit for 2009-10	7,000	3,800	1,800
Loan from Morning Ltd.	-	5,000	-
Creditors	2,500	1,000	1,400
	52,800	32,800	14,900
Assets			
Investments:			
1,60,000 shares in Evening	18,000	-	-
75,000 shares in Night	8,000	-	-
Loan to Evening Ltd.	5,000	-	-
Sundry assets	21,800	32,800	14,900
	52,800	32,800	14,900

Following additional information is also available:
(a) Dividend is proposed by each company at 10%.
(b) Stock transferred by Night Ltd. to Evening Ltd. fully paid for was Rs. 8 lacks on which the former made Profit of Rs. 3 lacks. On 31st March, 2010, this was in the inventory of the latter.
(c) Loan referred to is against 8% interest. Neither Morning Ltd. nor Evening Ltd. has considered the interest.
(d) Reserves as on 1.4.2009 of Evening Ltd. and Night Ltd. were Rs. 8,00,000 and Rs. 7,50,000 respectively.
(e) Cash-in-transit from Evening Ltd. to Morning Ltd. was Rs.1,00,000 as on 31.3.2010.
(f) The shares of the subsidiaries were all acquired by Morning Ltd. on 1st April, 2009.
Prepare consolidated Balance Sheet as on 31st March, 2010. Workings should be a part of the answer. *(CA Final : Nov 2007)*

Solution

Consolidated Balance Sheet of Morning Ltd. with its subsidiaries
Evening Ltd. and Night Ltd.
As on 31st March, 2010

Particulars	Note no.	Amount Rs'000
I. **Equity and Liabilities**		
(1)Shareholder's funds		
(a) Share capital		**40000**
(b) Reserves and surplus	1	**11645**

	(2)Minority Interest	2	8005
	(3)Non-current liabilities		
	Long-term borrowing		-
	(4)Current liabilities		
	(a)Trade payables	3	4900
	(b)Short term provision		
	(c)Other current liabilities	4	4650
	Total		**69200**
II.	**Assets**		
	(1)Non-current assets		
	(a)Fixed Assets		
	Tangible assets	5	69200
	Intangible assets (Goodwill)		
	(b)Non-current investments		
	(2)Current assets		
	(a)Inventories		
	(b)Trade receivables		
	(c)Cash and cash equivalents		
	Total		**69200**

Notes on Accounts

S/L No	Particulars		Amount (Rs'000)	Amount (Rs'000)
1.	**Reserves and surplus**			
	Capital reserve (Note 5)		902.5	
	General reserve	Rs'000		
	Morning Ltd	1800		
	Evening Ltd	160		
	Night Ltd	112.5	2072.5	
	Profit & Loss Account			
	Balance on 1.04.11	1500		
	Profit during the year	7000		
	Add: Interest on loan	400		
		8900		
	Less Proposed dividend	(4000)		
		4900		
	Add: P&L A/c of Evening Ltd	2720		
	Add: P&L A/c of Night Ltd	1050	8670	11645
2.	**Minority Interest**			
	Evening Ltd		4880	
	Night Ltd		3125	8005
3.	**Trade Payables**			
	Creditors			
	Morning Ltd		2500	
	Evening Ltd		1000	

	Night Ltd		**1400**	**4900**
4.	**Other current liabilities**			
	Proposed dividend			
	Morning Ltd		**4000**	
	Evening Ltd (Minority)		**400**	
	Night Ltd (Minority)		**250**	**4650**
5.	**Tangible assets**			
	Morning Ltd		**21800**	
	Evening Ltd	32800		
	Less: Unrealised profit Night Ltd	(300)	**32500**	
	Night Ltd		**14900**	**69200**

Working Notes:
A. Morning Ltd's holding in Evening Ltd. is 1,60,000 shares out of 2,00,000 shares, i.e. 4/5th or 80% ; Minority holding 1/5th or 20%
B. Morning Ltd's holding in Night Ltd. is 75,000 shares out of 1,00,000 shares, i.e., 3/4th or 75%; Minority holding 1/4th or 25%.

Analysis of Reserves and Profits of Subsidiary Companies

	Evening Ltd. (Rs '000)	Night Ltd. (Rs '000)	Minority Interest in Evening Ltd.(1/5) (Rs '000)	Minority Interest in Night Ltd.(1/4) (Rs '000)
1. Capital Reserve (pre-acquisition reserves and profits)				
Reserves on 1.04.2009	800	750		
Profit on 1.04.2009	2,000	800		
	2,800	1,550		
Less Minority Interest	560	387.5	560	387.5
	2,240	1,162.5		
2. General Reserve				
Reserves as per Balance Sheet	1,000	900		
Less: Capital Reserve	800	750		
	200	150		
Less: Minority Interest	40	37.5	40	37.5
	160	112.5		
3. Profit and Loss Account				
Profit for the year as per Balance Sheet	3,800	1,800		
Less: Interest on Loan (5,000 x 8%)	400			
	3,400			
Less: Minority Interest	680	450	680	450
	2,720	1,350		
Less: Unrealized profit on stock transfer	---	300		
	2,720	1,050		

4. Share Capital	20,000	10,000		
As per Balance sheet	4,000	2,500		
Less: Minority Interest			4,000	2,500
Transferred for computation of	16,000	7,500		
Goodwill/Capital Reserve			5,280	3,375
Less: Proposed dividend shown			400	250
separately				
Transferred to Consolidated Balance			4,880	3,125
Sheet				

5. Computation of Cost of Control i.e. Goodwill/ Capital Reserve on consolidation

	Evening Ltd.	Night Ltd.
Cost of investments	18,000	8,000
Less: Paid up value of shares [Refer to Note 4]	16,000	7,500
	2,000	500
Less: Capital Reserve	2,240	1,162.5
	-240	-662.5
Total Capital Reserve (Rs. 240 + Rs. 662.5)	902.5	

Q.6.8: Consolidation of Parent and two subsidiaries

The Balance Sheets of three companies Angle Ltd, Bolt Ltd and Canopy Ltd as at 31st December 2009 are given below:

Liabilities	Angle Ltd	Bolt Ltd	Canopy Ltd
Share capital	1500000	1000000	600000
(equity shares of Rs.100 each)			
Reserves	200000	125000	75000
Profit & Loss A/c	500000	275000	250000
Sundry creditors	200000	250000	100000
Bills payable	-	-	50000
Angle Ltd	-	100000	80000
Total	2400000	1750000	1155000
Assets			
Goodwill	250000	580000	450000
Plant and Machinery	400000	250000	325000
Furniture and fittings	200000	150000	140000
Shares in:			
Bolt Ltd (7500 shares)	900000		
Canopy Ltd (1000 shares)	150000		
Canopy Ltd (3500 shares)	-	520000	
Stock-in-trade	100000	150000	160000
Sundry debtors	140000	70000	70000
Bills receivable	50000	20000	
Due from:			
Bolt Ltd	120000		
Canopy Ltd	80000		
Cash in hand	10000	10000	10000

Total	2400000	1750000	1155000

a) All shares were acquired on 1st July 2008
b) On 1st January 2008, the balances were:

	Angle Ltd	Bolt Ltd	Canopy Ltd
	Rs.	Rs.	Rs.
Reserves	100000	100000	50000
Profit & loss account	50000	(50000) Dr.	30000
Profit during 2008 were earned evenly			
Over the year	300000	250000	100000

c) Each company declared dividend of 10% in the year 2009 on its shares out of profits for the year 2008 ; Angle Ltd and Bolt Ltd have credited their Profit and Loss account with the dividends received
d) The increase in reserves in case of Angle Ltd, Bolt Ltd and Canopy Ltd was effected in the year 2008.
e) All the bills payable in Canopy Ltd's Balance Sheet were accepted in favour of Bolt Ltd out of which bills amounting Rs.30000 were endorsed by Bolt Ltd, in favour of Angle Ltd
f) Stock with Bolt Ltd includes goods purchased from Angle Ltd for Rs.18000. Angle Ltd invoiced the goods at cost plus 20%

Prepare consolidated Balance Sheet of the group as at 31st December 2009. Working should be part of the answer. Ignore taxation including dividend distribution tax, disclose minority interest as per AS 21.(*CA Final Nov 2008*)

Solution

Consolidated Balance Sheet of Angle Ltd. with its subsidiaries
Bolt Ltd. and Canopy Ltd.
As on 31st March, 2009

Particulars	Note no.	Amount Rs.
I. **Equity and Liabilities**		
(1)Shareholder's funds		
(a) Share capital	1	**1500000**
(b) Reserves and surplus	2	983562
(2)Minority Interest	3	624271
(3)Non-current liabilities		
Long-term borrowing		-
(4)Current liabilities		
(a)Trade payables	4	550000
Total		**3657833**
II. **Assets**		
(1)Non-current assets		
(a)Fixed Assets		
Tangible assets	5	**1465000**
Intangible assets	6	**1435833**
(b)Non-current investments		
(2)Current assets		

		7	407000
(a)Inventories		7	407000
(b)Trade receivables		8	300000
(c)Cash and cash equivalents		9	50000
	Total		3657833

Notes on Accounts

S/L No	Particulars	Amount (Rs)	Amount (Rs)
1.	**Share capital**		
	Issued, subscribed and paid up		
	150000 equity shares of Rs.10 each fully paid up		1500000
2	**Reserves and surplus**		
	Reserves (200000 + 14844 + 2083)	216927	
	Profit & Loss Account (WN4)	766635	983562
3.	**Minority Interest (WN6)**		
	Bolt Ltd	393021	
	Canopy Ltd	231250	624271
4.	**Trade Payables**		
	Sundry creditors		
	Angle Ltd 200000		
	Bolt Ltd 250000		
	Canopy Ltd 100000	550000	
	Bills payable 50000		
	Less: Mutual indebtedness (50000)	-	550000
5.	**Tangible assets**		
	Plant & Machinery		
	Angle Ltd 400000		
	Bolt Ltd 250000		
	Canopy Ltd 325000	975000	
	Furniture & fittings		
	Angle Ltd 200000		
	Bolt Ltd 150000		
	Canopy Ltd 140000	490000	1465000
6.	Intangible assets		
	Goodwill		
	Angle Ltd 250000		
	Bolt Ltd 580000		
	Canopy Ltd 450000	1280000	
	Add: Cost of control	155833	1435833
7.	**Inventories**		

	Stock-in-trade		100000	
	Angle Ltd		150000	
	Bolt Ltd		160000	
	Canopy Ltd		410000	
			(3000)	407000
	Less: Provision for unrealised profit			
8.				
	Trade Receivables			
	Sundry Debtors			
	Angle Ltd	140000		
	Bolt Ltd	70000	280000	
	Canopy Ltd	70000		
	Bills receivables			
	Angle Ltd	50000	70000	
	Bolt Ltd	20000	(50000)	300000
	Less: mutual indebtedness			
9.	**Cash and cash equivalents**			
	Angle Ltd	10000		
	Bolt Ltd	10000		
	Canopy Ltd	10000	30000	
	Cash-in-transit / dues from Bolt(WN8)		20000	50000

Disclosure of Minority Interest in accordance with AS 21
Amount of Equity attributable to minorities on the date of investment i.e.1.7.2008 (Rs)

Item	Bolt Ltd	Canopy Ltd
Share capital	250000	150000
Share in capital reserve as on 1.1.08	25000	12500
Share in capital profits as on 1.1.08	(12500)	7500
Share in capital profits for the period 1.1.08 to 30.6.08	31250	12500
	293750	182500
Total amount of equity attributable to minorities		476250

Disclosure of Minority Interest in accordance with AS 21 as on 31.12.09 (Rs)

Item	Amount
Amount of equity as on the date of investment i.e.1.7.2008	476250
Add: Movement in equity and proportionate share of profit less dividend from the date of investment up to 31.12.09	152396
	628646

Working Notes
1. Statement of ascertainment of profits for the year 2009 (Rs)

Particulars	Angle Ltd	Bolt Ltd	Canopy Ltd
Balance as on 1st January 2008	50000	(50000)	30000
Add: Profits earned during 2008	300000	250000	100000
	350000	200000	130000
Less: Dividend declared	150000	100000	60000

	200000	100000	70000
Less: Transfer to reserve	100000	25000	25000
	100000	75000	45000
Profit for the year 2009 (balancing figure)	400000	200000	205000
Balance as on 31.12.2009	500000	275000	250000

2. **Statement of undistributed profits for the year 2008 (Rs)**

Particulars	Bolt Ltd	Canopy Ltd
Profit for the year 2008	250000	100000
Less: Dividends declared	100000	60000
	150000	40000
Less: Transfer to reserves	25000	25000
	125000	15000

3. **Analysis of profits (Rs)**

Particulars		Capital profits	Revenue reserve	Revenue Profits
Canopy Ltd				
Reserves as on 1st January 2008		50000		
Transfer to reserve in the year 2008 (75000 – 50000)/2		12500	12500	
Balance as on 1st January 2008		30000		
Profit for 2008 remaining undistributed				
(100000 – 25000 – 60000)/2		7500		7500
Profit for the year 2009 (250000-30000-15000)				205000
(A)		100000	12500	212500
Minority interest (1/4th of A)		25000	3125	53125
		75000	9375	159375
Share of Angle Ltd (1/6th of A)		16667	2083	35417
Share of Bolt Ltd		58333	7292	123958
Bolt Ltd				
Reserves as on 1st January 2008		100000		
Transfer to reserve in the year 2008 (125000 – 100000)/2		12500	12500	
		(50000)		
Profit & Loss A/c – Dr. balance 1st January 2008				
Undistributed profits for 2008		62500		62500
(250000 – 25000 – 100000)/2		58333	7292	123958
Share in profits of Canopy Ltd				200000
Profit for the year 2009 (275000+50000-125000)				
(B)		183333	19792	386458
Less: Minority interest (1/4th of B)		45833	4948	96615
Share of Angle Ltd		137500	14844	289843

4. **Statement of consolidated Profit and Loss Account of Angle Ltd (Rs)**

Particulars	Amount	Amount
Profit & Loss Account balance as on 31.12.2009		500000
Add: share in revenue profits of Canopy Ltd		35417
Share of revenue profits of Bolt Ltd		289843
		825260
Less: Pre-acquisition dividend		

Angle Ltd ½ (Rs.75000 + Rs.10000)	42500	
Bolt Ltd ½ of Rs.35000	17500	60000
		765260
Less: Unrealised profit in closing stock (20/120 x 18000)		3000
		762260

5. Statement of consolidated reserves of Angle Ltd (Rs)

Particulars	Amount
Reserves as on 31.12.09	200000
Add: Share in revenue reserves of Canopy Ltd	2083
Share in revenue reserves of Bolt Ltd	14844
	216927

6. Statement of minority interest (Rs)

Particulars	Bolt Ltd	Canopy Ltd
Share capital	250000	150000
Share of capital profits	45833	25000
Share of revenue reserves	4948	3125
Share of revenue profits	96615	53125
Total	397396	231250
Grand total		628646

7. Statement of cost of control / goodwill (Rs)

Particulars	Amount	Amount
Cost of investments (900000 + 150000 +520000)		1570000
Less: Dividend attributable to pre-acquisition profits for 6 months i.e. (75000 + 45000)/2		60000
		1510000
Less: Face value of shares		
Bolt Ltd	750000	
Canopy Ltd	450000	
Capital profits		
Bolt Ltd	137500	
Canopy Ltd	16667	1354167
Goodwill		155833

8. Statement of cash-in-transit / dues from Bolt Ltd (Rs)

Particulars	Amount	Amount
1) Due to Angle Ltd:		
From Bolt Ltd	120000	
From Canopy Ltd	80000	200000
2) Due by Angle Ltd		
To Bolt Ltd	100000	
To Canopy Ltd	80000	180000
		20000

Q.6.9: Consolidation of Parent and two subsidiaries

The following information has been extracted from the books of X Ltd group (as at 31st December 2009):

Liabilities	X Ltd Rs.	Y Ltd Rs.	Z Ltd Rs.	Assets	X Ltd Rs.	Y Ltd Rs.	Z Ltd Rs.
Share capital (fully paid equity shares of Rs.10)	800000	600000	400000	Fixed Assets less depreciation	420000	376000	522000
Profit and Loss A/c	210000	190000	128000	Investment at cost	630000	400000	-
Dividend received From Y Ltd in 2008	60000			Current Assets	120000	60000	40000
From Y Ltd in 2009	60000						
From Z Ltd in 2009		36000					
Current liabilities	40000	10000	34000				
	1170000	836000	562000		1170000	836000	562000

All the companies pay dividends of 12% of paid-up share capital in March following the end of the accounting year. The receiving companies account for the dividends in their books when they are received.

X Ltd acquired 50000 equity shares of Y Ltd on 31st December 2007.

Y Ltd acquired 30000 equity shares of Z Ltd on 31st December 2008.

The detailed information of Profit and Loss Accounts is as follows:

	X Ltd Rs.	Y Ltd Rs.	Z Ltd Rs.
Balance of Profit and Loss Account on 31st December 2007 after Dividends of 12% in respect of calendar year 2007, but excluding Dividends received	86000	78000	60000
Net profit earned in 2008	120000	84000	56000
	206000	162000	116000
Less: Dividends of 12% (paid in 2009)	96000	72000	48000
	110000	90000	68000
Net profit earned in 2009 (before taking into account proposed Dividends of 12% in respect of calendar year 2009)	100000	100000	60000
	210000	190000	128000

Taking into account the transactions from 2007 to 2009 and ignoring taxation, you are required to prepare:

i)   The consolidated Balance Sheet of X Ltd group as at 31st December 2009

ii)   Cost of control

iii) Minority shareholders interest.

(Adapted CA Final: May 2007)

Solution

1) **Consolidated Balance Sheet of X Ltd. and its subsidiaries**
as on 31.12.2009

Particulars	Note no.	Amount Rs.
I. **Equity and Liabilities**		
(1)Shareholder's funds		
(a) Share capital	1	800000
(b) Reserves and surplus	2	304833
(2)Minority Interest (refer (iii))		247167
(3)Non-current liabilities		
Long-term borrowing		-
(4)Current liabilities		
(a)Trade payables	3	84000
(b)Other current liabilities	4	120000
Total		1556000
II. **Assets**		
(1)Non-current assets		
(a)Fixed Assets		
Tangible assets	5	1318000
Intangible assets	6	18000
(b)Non-current investments		
(2)Current assets		220000
Total		1556000

Notes on Accounts

S/L No	Particulars	Amount (Rs)	Amount (Rs)
1.	**Share capital**		
	Issued, subscribed and paid up		
	80000 equity shares of Rs.10 each fully paid up		800000
	Reserves and surplus		
2	Profit & Loss Account		
	Opening balance — Rs.		
	X Ltd — 206000		
	Y Ltd — 162000		
	Z Ltd — 116000	484000	
	Add Dividend recd in 2010 for 2009 — Rs.		
	X Ltd — 60000		
	Y Ltd — -		
	Z Ltd — -	60000	
		544000	

		Rs.		
	Less Dividend paid for 2010			
	X Ltd	96000		
	Y Ltd	72000		
	Z Ltd	48000		
	Less : Adjustments	(96000)	(120000)	
			424000	
	Add Dividend recd in 2011 for 2010	Rs.		
	X Ltd	60000		
	Y Ltd	36000		
	Z Ltd	-		
	Less : Adjustments	(96000)	-	
			424000	
	Add Profit for the year	Rs.		
	X Ltd	100000		
	Y Ltd	100000		
	Z Ltd	60000	260000	
			684000	
	Less: Minority Interest	Rs.		
	X Ltd	-		
	Y Ltd	39167		
	Z Ltd	32000	(71167)	
			612833	
	Less: Cost of control	Rs.		
	X Ltd	65000		
	Y Ltd	51000		
	Z Ltd	-	(116000)	
			496833	
	Less: Dividend recd out of capital profit	Rs.		
	X Ltd	60000 *		
	Y Ltd	36000 *		
	Z Ltd	-	(96000)	
			400833	
	Less: Proposed dividend	Rs.		
	X Ltd	96000		
	Y Ltd	-		
	Z Ltd	-	(96000)	
	Closing balance of profit (bal fig)			
	Share of X Ltd (bal fig)	174000		
	Share of Y Ltd (bal fig)	85833		
	Share of Z Ltd (bal fig)	45000	304833	304833
3.	**Trade Payables**			
	Sundry creditors			84000

4.	Other current liabilities Proposed dividend: X Ltd Minority interest (refer iv)		120000
5.	Tangible assets Fixed assets less depreciation	96000 24000	1318000
6.	Intangible assets Goodwill (refer ii)		18000

Notes (*)
1. X Ltd receives from Y Ltd dividend amounting to Rs.60000 for the year 2007 in the year 2008 for shares acquired in 2007. It is a capital profit, therefore it has been transferred to cost of control to reduce the cost of investment.
2. Y Ltd receives a dividend of Rs.36000 from Z Ltd for the year 2008 in the year 2009. The shares were acquired by Y Ltd on 31st December 2008. The entire amount is therefore, a capital profit and hence transferred to cost of control to reduce the cost of investment.

2) Statement of cost of control / goodwill

Particulars	Rs.	Rs.
Cost of investment in Y Ltd on 31st December 2007	630000	
Less: Dividend of the year 2007 received in 2008 out of pre-acquisition profit	60000	570000 (A)
Cost of investment in Z Ltd on 31st December 2007	400000	
Less: Dividend of the year 2008 received in 2009 out of pre-acquisition profit	36000	364000 (B)
		934000(A+B)
Less: Paid up value of shares in Y Ltd	500000	
Paid up value of shares in Z Ltd	300000	
Capital profits in Y Ltd (W.N.2)	65000	
Capital profits in Z Ltd (W.N.2)	51000	916000 (C)
Goodwill (A + B – C)		18000

3) Statement of Minority shareholders interest

Particulars	Y Ltd Rs.	Z Ltd Rs.
Share capital (Y Ltd – 1/6 and Z Ltd – ¼)	100000	100000
Capital profits (W.N.2)	13000	17000
Revenue profits(W.N.2)	26167	15000
	139167	132000
Total (Rs.139167 + Rs.132000)		271167
Less: Minority shareholders share of proposed dividend shown separately in the Balance Sheet (1/6 x Rs.72000 + ¼ x Rs.48000)		24000
Balance		247167

Working Notes

1. **Shareholding pattern**

	Number of shares	Share of holding
In Y Ltd		
X Ltd	50000	5/6
Minority interest	10000	1/6
In Z Ltd		
Y Ltd	30000	3/4
Minority interest	10000	1/4

2. **Statement of analysis of profits**

Particulars	Pre-acquisition capital profit Rs.	Post-acquisition revenue profit Rs.
Z Ltd		-
Balance on 31st December 2008 after dividend for 2008 (116000 – 48000)	68000	
Profit for the year ending 31st December 2009 before proposed dividends for 2009	-	60000
	68000	60000
Share of Y Ltd (3/4)	51000	45000
Minority interest (1/4)	17000	15000
Y Ltd		
Balance on 31st December 2007	78000	-
Profit for the year 2008 after payment of dividend for 2008 (84000 – 72000)	-	12000
Profit for the year 2009 (before payment of dividend for the year 2009)	-	100000
Revenue profit from Z Ltd	-	45000
	78000	157000
Share of X Ltd (5/6)	65000	130833
Minority interest (1/6)	13000	26167

Q.6.10: Consolidation of Parent and two subsidiaries

The following are the Balance Sheets of Ram Ltd, Shyam Ltd and Tom Ltd as on 31.03.2008:

Particulars	Ram Ltd Rs'000	Shyam Ltd Rs'000	Tom Ltd Rs'000
Liabilities			
Equity share capital (Rs.100	8000	4000	1600

each)	1600	280	-
General reserve	1360	960	-
Profit & loss Account	1280	3000	1120
Current liabilities			
Total	12240	8240	2720
Assets			
Investments:			
32000 shares in Shyam Ltd	4800	-	-
4000 shares in Tom Ltd	200	-	-
12000 shares in Tom Ltd	-	720	-
Profit and loss Account	-	-	640
Current Assets	7240	7520	2080
Total	12240	8240	2720

From the following information, prepare a consolidated Balance Sheet of Ram Ltd and its subsidiaries as on 31.03.2008:

i) Shyam Ltd has advanced Rs.800000 to Tom Ltd
ii) Current liabilities of Ram Ltd includes Rs.400000 due to Tom Ltd
iii) Shyam Ltd and Tom Ltd have not paid any dividend
iv) Ram Ltd acquired its investments on 1.4.2007 from Shyam Ltd and then amount standing to credit of General Reserve and Profit and Loss were R.280000 and Rs.520000 respectively.
v) Ram Ltd acquired investments in Tom Ltd on 1.04.2007, when the debit balance in Profit and Loss Account in books of Tom Ltd was Rs.480000.
vi) Shyam Ltd acquired its investments in Tom Ltd on 1.04.2005 and then the debit balance in profit and loss account was Rs.160000
vii) Shyam Ltd's stock includes stock worth RS.480000 which was invoiced by Ram Ltd at 20% above cost.(*CA Final Nov 2008*)

Solution
Consolidated Balance Sheet of Ram Ltd and its subsidiaries Shyam Ltd
And Tom Ltd as on 31st March 2008

Particulars		Note no.	Amount Rs'000
I.	**Equity and Liabilities**		
	(1)Shareholder's funds		
	(a) Share capital		8000
	(b) Reserves and surplus	1	3096
	(2)Minority Interest (WN7)		952
	(3)Non-current liabilities		
	Long-term borrowing		-
	(4)Current liabilities	2	4200
	Total		16248
II.	**Assets**		
	(1)Non-current assets		
	(a)Fixed Assets		

Tangible assets Intangible assets (b)Non-current investments	3	688
(2)Current assets	4	15560
Total		16248

Notes on Accounts

S/L No	Particulars	Amount (Rs'000)	Amount (Rs'000)
1.	**Reserves and surplus** General Reserve Profit & Loss Account (WN6)	1600 1496	3096
2	**Current liabilities** Ram Ltd Shyam Ltd Tom Ltd Less: Mutual indebtedness	1280 3000 1120 5400 1200	 4200
3.	**Intangible assets** Goodwill (WN5)		688
4.	**Current assets** Ram Ltd Shyam Ltd Tom Ltd Less: Mutual indebtedness Less: Unrealised profit	7240 7520 2080 16840 (1200) 15640 (80)	 550000 15560

Working Notes

1.		General Reserve of Shyam Ltd			
Particulars	Rs'000	Rs'000	Particulars	Rs'000	Rs'000
31.3.08 To Balance c/d		280	1.4.07 By Balance b/d		280
		280			280

2.		Profit & Loss A/c of Shyam Ltd			
Particulars	Rs'000	Rs'000	Particulars	Rs'000	Rs'000
31.3.08 To Balance c/d		960	1.4.07 By Balance b/d		520
			31.3.08 By profit earned during		440

			the year		
		960			960

3. Profit and Loss Account of Tom Ltd

Particulars	Rs'000	Rs'000	Particulars	Rs'000	Rs'000
1.4.05 To Balance b/d		160	31.3.06 By Balance c/d		160
		160			160
1.4.06 To Balance b/d		160	31.3.07 By Balance c/d		480
31.3.07 To loss incurred during the year (bal fig)		320			
		480			480
1.4.07 To Balance b/d		480	31.3.08 By Balance c/d		640
31.3.08 To loss incurred during the year (bal fig)		160			
		640			640

4. Statement of analysis of Profit of Tom Ltd

Item	Capital profit Rs'000	Revenue profit Rs'000
(I)From viewpoint of Shyam Ltd		
Debit balance in Profit & Loss Account as on 1.4.2005	(160)	
Loss incurred between 1.4.2005 to 31.3.2008		
(320 + 160) – W.N.2)		(480)
	(160)	(480)
Share of Shyam Ltd – 75% (carried forward to W.N.4)	(120)	(360)
(II) From viewpoint of Ram Ltd		
Debit balance in Profit & Loss Account as on 1.4.2007	(480)	
Loss incurred during the year 2007-0		(160)
	(480)	(160)
Share of Ram Ltd – 25%	(120)	(40)

2. Statement of analysis of Profit of Shyam Ltd

Item	Capital profit Rs'000	Revenue profit Rs'000
From viewpoint of Ram Ltd		
General reserve as on 1.4.07	280	
Profit & Loss Account balance as on 1.4.2007	520	
Profit earned during 2007-08 (W.N.1)		440

Brought forward Shyam Ltd's share of loss in Tom Ltd (W.N.3(I))	(120)	(360)
Share of Shyam Ltd in revenue loss of Tom Ltd for the period 1.4.05 to 31.3.07 (75% of (360-40)) being treated as capital loss from view point of Ram Ltd	(240)	240
	440	320
Share of minority interest (20%)	88	64
Balance taken to Ram Ltd (80%)	352	256

3. Statement of cost of control / goodwill

Item	Rs'000	Rs'000
Investment by Ram Ltd in		
Shyam Ltd	4800	
Tom Ltd	200	
Investment by Shyam Ltd in		
Tom Ltd	720	5720
Less: Paid up value of shares of:		
Shyam Ltd	3200	
Tom Ltd (400 + 1200)	1600	
	4800	
Capital loss of Ram Ltd in Tom Ltd (W.N.3(II))	(120)	
Capital profit of Ram Ltd in Shyam Ltd (W.N.4)	352	5032
Goodwill		688

4. Statement of Minority Interest

Item	Rs'000	Rs'000
Paid up value of shares in Shyam Ltd (20% of 4000)		800
Share of capital profit (W.N.4)	88	
Share of revenue profit (W.N.4)	64	152
		952

5. Statement of consolidated Profit and Loss A/c of Ram Ltd

Item	Rs'000	Rs'000
Profit and Loss Account balance		1360
Post-acquisition share of loss from Tom Ltd	(40)	
Post-acquisition share of profit from Shyam Ltd	256	216
		1576
Less: Unrealised profit on stock (1/4 of 480)		80
Total		1496

Q.6.11: Consolidation of Parent and two subsidiaries

From the following details prepare a consolidated Balance Sheet of Sun Ltd and its subsidiaries as on 31st March 2009: (Rs in lakhs)

Assets	Sun Ltd	Moon Ltd	Star Ltd
Fixed Assets (net)	816	312	126
Investments (at cost)			
750000 equity shares of Moon Ltd	75	-	-
240000 equity shares of Star Ltd	24	-	-
480000 equity shares of Star Ltd	-	60	-
30000 cumulative preference shares of Sun Ltd	-	-	30
4500 mortgage debentures of Sun Ltd	-	-	42
Current Assets	1059	369	336
Profit and Loss Account	288	108	63
	2262	849	597
Liabilities			
Equity share capital (Rs.10 fully paid up)	180	144	120
7.5% cumulative preference share capital (Rs.100 each fully paid)	45	36	30
Capital reserve (revaluation of fixed assets)	360	-	-
General Reserve	75	45	30
7500 8% mortgage debenture bonds of Rs.1000 each	75	-	-
Secured loans and advances:			
From banks	513	249	165
Unsecured loans:			
From Moon Ltd	-	-	36
From Star Ltd	45	-	-
Current liabilities and provisions			
Inter-company balances	27	-	-
Other liabilities	942	375	216
	2262	849	597

Other information are as follows:
   a) Moon Ltd. Subscribed for 240000 shares of Star Ltd at par at the time of first issue and further acquired 240000 shares from the market at Rs.15 each, when the Reserve and surplus account of Star Ltd. Stood at Rs.15 lakhs.
   b) Sun Ltd. Subscribed for shares of Moon Ltd and Star Ltd at par at the time of first issue of shares by both the companies.
   c) Current assets of Moon Ltd and Star Ltd include Rs.12 lakhs and Rs.18 lakhs respectively being current account balance against Sun Ltd.(*CA Final June 2009*)

Solution

Consolidated Balance Sheet of Sun Limited and its subsidiaries as on 31st March 2009

Particulars	Note no.	Amount Rs
I. **Equity and Liabilities**		
(1)Shareholder's funds		
(a) Share capital	1	19500000
(b) Reserves and surplus	2	9581250
(2)Minority Interest (WN4)		13218750
(3)Non-current liabilities		
Long-term borrowing	3	95700000
(4)Current liabilities		153300000
Total		291300000
II. **Assets**		
(1)Non-current assets		
(a)Fixed Assets		
Tangible assets	4	125400000
Intangible assets	5	300000
(b)Non-current investments		
(2)Current assets	6	165600000
Total		291300000

Notes on Accounts

S/L No	Particulars	Amount (Rs)	Amount (Rs)
1.	**Share capital**		
	1800000 equity shares of Rs.10 each	18000000	
	15000 7.5% cumulative preference shares of Rs.100 each	1500000	19500000
2	**Reserves and surplus**		
	Capital Reserve (revaluation of fixed assets)	36000000	
	Profit & Loss A/c	(26418750)	9581250
3.	**Long term borrowings**		
	Secured loan		
	8% mortgage debentures	3000000	
	Secured loan from bank	92700000	95700000
4.	**Tangible assets (net)**		
	Sun Ltd	81600000	
	Moon Ltd	31200000	
	Star Ltd	12600000	125400000

5.	Intangible assets Goodwill			300000
6.	Current assets Sun Ltd Moon Ltd Star Ltd Less: Interco owings Interco balances		105900000 36900000 33600000 176400000 8100000 2700000	 165600000

Working Notes:

S/L	Item		In Moon Ltd	In Star Ltd
1.	**Shareholding pattern** Sun Limited Moon Limited Minority Interest		**25/48** - **23/48**	**2/10** **4/10** **4/10**
2.	**Analysis of profits**	**Rs.**	**Capital** **Rs.**	**Revenue** **Rs.**
a	Star Limited Balance at acquisition Balance as per P&L A/c Less: General reserve Profit on debentures Net loss as on 31.32009 Less: Capital profit Minority interest (4/10) Share of Moon Ltd (4/10) Share of Sun Ltd (2/10)	 (6300000) 3000000 300000 (3000000) 1500000 (4500000)	 1500000 600000 600000 300000	 (4500000) (1800000) (1800000) (900000)
b	Moon Limited Profit & Loss Account as on 31.3.09 General Reserve Loss after acquisition Share of revenue loss in Star Ltd Minority interest (23/48) Sun Limited (25/48)			(10800000) 4500000 (6300000) (1800000) (8100000) (3881250) (4218750)

S/L	Item		In Moon Ltd Rs.	In Star Ltd Rs.
3.	**Goodwill / capital reserve**			
	Share capital		7500000	7200000
	Capital profit		300000	600000
			7800000	7800000
	Less: Cost of investment		7500000	8400000
	Capital reserve / (goodwill)		300000	(600000)
	Goodwill			(300000)
4.	**Minority interest**			
	Share capital		6900000	4800000
	Capital profit		-	600000
	Revenue profit		(3881250)	(1800000)
	Preference shares			
	(3600000 + 3000000)		-	6600000
	Total	13218750	3018750	10200000

5. Statement of Profit and Loss Account – Sun Ltd

Item	Amount Rs.
Balance as on 31.03.09	(28800000)
General reserve	7500000
Share of Star Limited	(900000)
Share of Moon Limited	(4218750)
Total	(26418750)

Note: In this question, inter-company balances amounting Rs.27 lakhs have been shown in the balance sheet of Sun Ltd as on 31st March 2009. However, information (c) of the question states that current assets of Moon Ltd and Star Ltd include Rs.12 lakhs and Rs.18 lakhs respectively being current account balance against Sun Ltd. The candidates may assume that Rs.30 lakhs is in addition to inter-company balance of Rs.27 lakhs. In that case, current assets and current liabilities will be reduced by Rs.30 lakhs and will be shown at Rs.1626 lakhs and Rs.1503 lakhs respectively. The total of the consolidated balance sheet will also be reduced by Rs.30 lakhs.

Q.6.12: Consolidation of Parent and two subsidiaries

Prepare the consolidated Balance Sheet as on 31st December 2009 of group of companies A Ltd, B Ltd and C Ltd. Their Balance Sheets on that date are given below:

Liabilities	A Ltd Rs.	B Ltd Rs.	C Ltd Rs.
Share capital (share of Rs.100 each)	125000	100000	60000
Reserves	18000	10000	7200
Profit & loss A/c	16000	4000	5000
Sundry creditors			
A Ltd	-	7000	-

C Ltd		3300	-	-
	Total	169300	124000	72200
Assets				
Fixed Assets		28000	55000	37400
Investment in shares:				
B Ltd		85000	-	-
C Ltd		-	53000	-
Stocks		22000	6000	-
B Ltd		8000	-	-
Debtors		26300	10000	31500
A Ltd		-	-	3300
	Total	169300	124000	72200

Other information:

i) A Ltd holds 750 shares in B Ltd and B Ltd holds 400 shares in C Ltd. These holdings were acquired on 30th June 2009.

ii) On 1st January 2009 the following balances stood in the books of B Ltd and C Ltd.

	B Ltd	C Ltd
	Rs.	Rs.
Reserves	8000	6000
P & L Account	1000	1000

iii) C Ltd sold goods costing Rs.2500 to B Ltd for Rs.3100. These goods still remain unsold. (*CA Final: study material*)

Solution

Consolidated Balance Sheet of A Ltd and its subsidiaries B Ltd and C Ltd
As on 31st December 2009

Particulars	Note no.	Amount Rs
I. **Equity and Liabilities**		
(1)Shareholder's funds		
(a) Share capital	1	125000
(b) Reserves and surplus	2	36575
(2)Minority Interest (WN4)		54600
(3)Non-current liabilities		
Long-term borrowing		-
(4)Current liabilities	3	10000
Total		226175
II. **Assets**		
(1)Non-current assets		
(a)Fixed Assets		
Tangible assets	4	120400
Intangible assets	5	9575
(b)Non-current investments		
(2)Current assets		
(a)Inventories	6	27400
(b)Trade receivables	7	67800

(c)Cash and cash equivalents		8	1000
	Total		226175

Notes on Accounts

S/L No	Particulars	Amount (Rs)	Amount (Rs)
1.	Share capital Issued and subscribed Rs.100 each fully paid up		125000
2	Reserves and surplus Reserves Profit & Loss Account	19050 17525	36575
3.	Current liabilities Sundry creditors		10000
4.	Tangible assets		120400
5.	Intangible assets Goodwill (WN3)		9575
6.	Inventories Stock Less: unrealized profit	28000 600	27400
7.	Trade Receivable Debtors		67800
8.	Cash and cash equivalent Cash in transit		1000

Working Notes

1. **Analysis of profits of C Ltd**

Particulars	Rs	Capital Profit Rs.	Revenue Reserve Rs.	Revenue Profit Rs.
Reserve on 1.1.2009		6000		
Additional reserve created in 2009		600	600	
Profit & Loss A/c on 1.1.2009		1000		
Profit for the year		2000		2000
Total		9600	600	2000
Less: Minority interest 1/3		3200	200	667

Share of B Ltd 2/3		6400	400	1333

2. Analysis of profits of B Ltd

Particulars	Rs	Capital Profit Rs.	Revenue Reserve Rs.	Revenue Profit Rs.
From C Ltd		6400*	400	1333
Reserve on 1.1.2009		8000		
Additional reserve created in 2009		1000	1000	
Profit & Loss A/c on 1.1.2009		1000		
Profit during 2009		1500		1500
Total		17900	1400	2833
Less: Minority interest ¼		4475	350	708
Share of A Ltd		13425	1050	2125
A Ltd			18000	16000
				18125
Less: Stock reserve				600
			19050	17525

Note:
(i)During 2009, Rs.1200 has been added to the Reserves of C Ltd and Rs.2000 to the reserves of B Ltd. The profit must have been earned during the whole of the year; hence, half of these Figures (i.e. up to 30.6.2009) must be considered as capital pre-acquisition and the remaining revenue.

(ii)Total unrealized profit is Rs.600 i.e.Rs.3100 less Rs.2500.

3. Statement of cost of control / goodwill

Particulars	Amount Rs.	Amount Rs.
Amount paid		
A Ltd	85000	
B Ltd	53000	
		138000
		151000
Less: Par value of shares in:		
In B Ltd	75000	
In C Ltd	40000	
Capital profits	13425	
		128425
Goodwill (to consolidated Balance Sheet)		9575

4. Statement of minority interest

Particulars	B Ltd Rs.	C Ltd Rs.

Share capital	25000	20000
Share of Capital profits	4475	3200
Share of Revenue reserve	350	200
Share of Revenue profits	708	667
Total	30533	24067
To consolidated Balance Sheet	54600	

5. Since A Ltd shows Rs.8000 against B Ltd whereas B Ltd, shows only Rs.7000 in favour of A Ltd, it must be assumed that B Ltd has remitted Rs.1000 to A Ltd ; not yet received by A Ltd. The amount is in transit.

6. If capital profit is increased by Rs.1600 cost of control will be Rs.7975. The whole of this amount may preferably be adjusted against cost of control, instead of being added to the profits of B Ltd. Consequently capital profits will increase by Rs.1600 with a corresponding reduction in Minority interest. This problem has been solved by following "indirect approach".

Q.6.13: Consolidation of Parent and two subsidiaries

The Balance Sheets of three companies A Ltd, B Ltd, C Ltd, as on 31st December 2009 are given below:

Liabilities	A Ltd Rs.	B Ltd Rs.	C Ltd Rs.
Share capital (shares of Rs.100 each)	150000	100000	60000
Reserves	20000	10000	7500
Profit & loss A/c	50000	30000	25000
Sundry creditors	20000	25000	15000
A Ltd	-	10000	8000
Total	240000	175000	115500
Assets			
Goodwill	20000	15000	10000
Fixed Assets	70000	50000	60000
Shares in B Ltd (750 shares)	90000	-	-
In C Ltd (100 shares)	15000	-	-
In C Ltd (350 shares)	-	52000	-
Due from : B Ltd	12000	-	-
C Ltd	8000	-	-
Current Assets	25000	58000	45500
Total	240000	175000	115500

All shares were acquired on 1st July 2009. On 1st Jan 2009 the balances were:

	A Ltd	B Ltd	C Ltd
Reserves	10000	10000	5000
Profit & loss A/c	5000	5000(Dr.)	3000

Profits during 2009 were earned evenly during the year.

In August 2009 each company declared and paid interim dividend on 10% p.a. for six months. A Ltd and B Ltd have credited their Profit & Loss Account with the dividends received. During 2009, C Ltd fabricated a machine costing Rs.10000 which it sold to B Ltd for Rs.12000, B Ltd then sold the machine to A Ltd for RS.13000, the transactions being completed on 3st December 2009.

Prepare the consolidated Balance Sheet of the group as on 31st December 2009.

Solution

Consolidated Balance Sheet of A Ltd and its subsidiaries B Ltd and C Ltd
As on 31st December 2009

Particulars		Note no.	Amount Rs
I.	**Equity and Liabilities**		
	(1)Shareholder's funds		
	(a) Share capital	1	150000
	(b) Reserves and surplus	2	85402
	(2)Minority Interest	3	59691
	(3)Non-current liabilities		
	Long-term borrowing		
	(4)Current liabilities	4	60000
	Total		355093
II.	**Assets**		
	(1)Non-current assets		
	(a)Fixed Assets		
	Tangible assets	5	177000
	Intangible assets	6	47593
	(b)Non-current investments		
	(2)Current assets	7	130500
	Total		355093

Notes on Accounts

S/L No	Particulars	Amount (Rs)	Amount (Rs)
1.	**Share capital**		
	Issued and subscribed		
	1500 shares of Rs.100 each fully paid up		150000
2	**Reserves and surplus**		
	Reserves		
	A Ltd	200000	
	Share in C Ltd	208	
	Share in B Ltd	548	20756
	Profit & Loss Account		64646	85402

3.	**Minority Interest**		
	B Ltd	36567	
	C Ltd	23124	59691
4.	**Current liabilities**		
	Sundry creditors		
	A Ltd	20000	
	B Ltd	25000	
	C Ltd	15000	60000
5.	**Tangible assets**		
	A Ltd	70000	
	B Ltd	50000	
	C Ltd	60000	
		180000	
	Less: unrealized profit	3000	177000
6.	**Intangible assets**		
	Goodwill	45000	
	Addition on consolidation	2593	47593
7.	**Current assets**		
	A Ltd	25000	
	B Ltd	58000	
	C Ltd	45500	
		128500	
	Add: Cash in transit	2000	130500

Working Notes

1. **Analysis of profits of C Ltd**

Particulars	Rs	Capital Profit Rs.	Revenue Reserve Rs.	Revenue Profit Rs.
General reserve on 1.1.2009		5000		
Profit & Loss A/c on 1.1.2009		3000		
Increase in reserve		1250	1250	
Profit for the year	12500			
Less: interim dividend	3000	9500		12500
Total		18750	1250	12500
Less: Minority interest 3/12		4687	312	3125
Brought forward		14063	938	9375
Share of A Ltd 2/12		3125	208	2083
Share of B Ltd		10938	730	7292

2. Analysis of profits of B Ltd

Particulars	Rs	Capital Profit Rs.	Revenue Reserve Rs.	Revenue Profit Rs.
Reserve on 1.1.2009		10000		
Profit & Loss A/c on 1.1.2009		- 5000		
Profit for the year	40000			
Less: interim dividend of C Ltd	1750			
	38250			
½	19125			19125
Less interim dividend	5000	14125		
Share in C Ltd			730	7292
Total		19125	730	26417
Less: Minority interest ¼		4781	182	6604
Brought forward		14344	548	19813

3. Statement of cost of control / goodwill

Particulars	Amount Rs.	Amount Rs.
Investments in B Ltd (90000 – 3750)		86250
Investments in C Ltd		
(15000 – 500)	14500	
(52000 – 1750)	50250	64750
		151000
Less: Paid up value of investments		
In B Ltd	75000	
In C Ltd	45000	
Capital profit in B Ltd	14344	
Capital profit in C Ltd	14063	148407
Goodwill (to consolidated Balance Sheet)		2593

4. Statement of minority interest

Particulars	B Ltd Rs.	C Ltd Rs.
Share capital	25000	15000
Capital profits	4781	4687
Revenue reserve	182	312
Revenue profits	6604	3125
To consolidated Balance Sheet	36567	23124

5. Statement of Profit & Loss Account – A Ltd

Particulars	Amount Rs.	Amount Rs.
Balance		50000
Less: Dividend credited to investment (3750 + 500)		4250
		45750

Share in B Ltd		19813
Share in C Ltd		2083
		67646
Less: Profit on Plant		3000
To consolidated Balance Sheet		64646

Q.6.14: Consolidation of Parent with two subsidiaries

The summarized Balance Sheets of the following three companies are given below: (Rs Lakhs)

Liabilities	Eagle Ltd	Garuda Ltd	Bird Ltd
Equity shares (Rs.10 each fully paid up)	60	48	40
7.5% cumulative preference shares (Rs.100 each fully paid up)	15	12	10
Capital reserve on revaluation of land, building and machinery	120		
General Reserve	25	15	10
8% 2500 Mortgage debenture bonds of Rs.1000 each	25	-	-
Secured loans and advances from banks	153	71	52
Unsecured loans:			
From Garuda Ltd	-	-	12
From Bird Ltd	15	-	-
Deposits from public	18	12	3
Current liabilities and provisions:			
Inter-company balances	9	-	-
Other liabilities and provisions	314	125	72
Total	754	283	199
Assets			
Fixed Assets (Net)	272	104	42
Investments (at cost)			
250000 equity shares of Garuda Ltd	25		
80000 equity shares of Bird Ltd	8		
160000 equity shares of Bird Ltd		20	
10000 cumulative preference shares of Eagle Ltd			10
1500 mortgage debentures of Eagle Ltd			14
Current Assets	353	123	112
Profit and Loss Account	96	36	21
Total	754	283	199

i)   Eagle Ltd subscribed for the shares of Garuda Ltd and Bird Ltd at par at the time of first issue of shares by the latter companies.

ii) Garuda Ltd subscribed for 80000 shares of Bird Ltd at par at the time of first issue and latter acquired by purchase in the market 80000 shares of Bird Ltd at Rs.15 each when Reserves and surplus of Bird Ltd stood at Rs.5 lakhs

iii) Current assets of Garuda Ltd and Bird Ltd included Rs.4 lakhs and Rs.6 lakhs respectively being the current accounts balance against Eagle Ltd. These accounts remained unreconciled.

iv) Preference dividends were in arrears for 8 years in the case of Eagle Ltd and 4 years in the case of other two companies.

Prepare the consolidated Balance Sheet with workings. *(CA Final Nov 2010)*

Solution

Consolidated Balance Sheet of Eagle Ltd and its subsidiaries Garuda Ltd and Bird Ltd as on 31st March 2010

Particulars	Note no.	Amount Rs/Lakhs
I. **Equity and Liabilities**		
(1)Shareholder's funds		
(a) Share capital	1	65.00
(b) Reserves and surplus	2	31.94
(2)Minority Interest (WN5)		44.06
(3)Non-current liabilities		
Long-term borrowing	3	319.00
(4)Current liabilities		
Other current liabilities(314+125+72)		511.00
Total		**971.00**
II. **Assets**		
(1)Non-current assets		
(a)Fixed Assets		
Tangible assets (272+104+42)		418.00
Intangible assets	4	1.00
(b)Non-current investments		-
(2)Current assets		552.00
Total		**971.00**

Notes on Accounts

S/L No	Particulars	Amount (Rs/Lakhs)	Amount (Rs/Lakhs)
1.	**Share capital**		
	Issued and subscribed		
	600000 Equity shares of Rs.10 each fully paid up	60.00	
	5000 7.5% cum preference shares of Rs.100 each fully paid up	5.00	65.00
2	**Reserves and surplus**		
	Capital Reserve per Balance Sheet	120.00	
	Less: Profit & Loss Account(WN3)	(88.06)	31.94
3.	**Long term borrowings**		
	Secured		
	8% Mortgage debentures	10.00	
	Loans & advances from banks (153 + 71 + 52)	276.00	

		286.00	
	Unsecured Public deposits (18+12+3)	33.00	319.00
4.	Intangible assets Goodwill (WN4)		1.00

Preference dividends were in arrears for eight years in Eagle Ltd and four years in subsidiaries.

Working Notes:

1. Analysis of profits of Bird Ltd

Particulars	Capital Profit Rs in lakhs	Revenue loss Rs in lakhs
Loss after adjusting reserve and profit on debenture in Eagle Ltd		10
Share of Eagle Ltd	1	3
Share of Garuda Ltd	2	6
Minority interest	2	6
	5	15

2. Analysis of profits / loss of Garuda Ltd

Particulars	Revenue loss Rs/lakhs
Loss less reserve (36-15)	21
Add: Loss in Bird Ltd	6
	27
Share of Eagle Ltd (25/48)	14.06
Minority interest	12.94

3. Analysis of profits / loss of Eagle Ltd

Particulars		Revenue loss Rs/lakhs
Loss less reserve (96-25)		71.00
Add: Loss in Garuda Ltd	14.06	
Add: Loss in Bird Ltd	3.00	17.06
		88.06

4. Statement of cost of control / goodwill

Particulars	Amount Rs/lakhs	Amount Rs/lakhs
Cost of investments in Garuda Ltd		25

Cost of investments in Bird Ltd		<u>28</u>
B Ltd		53
Less: Paid up value of shares in:		
In Garuda Ltd	25	
In Bird Ltd	24	
Capital profits in Bird Ltd	3	52
Goodwill to consolidated Balance Sheet		1

5. Statement of minority interest

Particulars	Amount Rs/Lakhs	Amount Rs/Lakhs
Share capital		
Garuda	23.00	
Bird	<u>16.00</u>	39.00
Less: loss in subsidiaries		<u>16.94</u>
		22.06
Preference shares		22.00
Total to consolidated Balance Sheet		44.06

Q.6.15: Chain holding : Consolidation of Parent and two subsidiaries

As on 30th June 2010 the draft Balance Sheets of the companies showed, the following position:

		Rock Ltd Rs.	King Ltd Rs.	Chair Ltd Rs.
Fixed Assets		135000	60000	70000
Investments at cost		<u>160000</u>	<u>150000</u>	<u>10000</u>
	(A)	<u>295000</u>	<u>210000</u>	<u>80000</u>
Current Assets:				
Stock		55240	36840	61760
Debtors		110070	69120	93880
Balance at bank		<u>131290</u>	<u>16540</u>	<u>52610</u>
	(B)	<u>296600</u>	<u>122500</u>	<u>208250</u>
Less: Current liabilities:				
Creditors		112060	73130	78190
Taxation		30000	–	22000
Proposed dividends		<u>100000</u>	<u>60000</u>	<u>40000</u>
	(C)	<u>242060</u>	<u>133130</u>	<u>140190</u>
Net current assets (B – C) = (D)		<u>54540</u>	<u>(10630)</u>	<u>68060</u>
Total (A + D)		349540	199370	148060

Financed by:			
Issued ordinary shares of Rs.10 each	200000	150000	80000
Capital reserve	50000	-	50000
Revenue reserve	99540	49370	45060
(E)	349540	199370	148060

You also obtain the following information:

i)   King Ltd acquired 6800 shares in Chair Ltd at Rs.22 per share in 2007 when the balance on capital reserve was Rs.15000 and on revenue reserve Rs.30500 consolidated.

ii)   Rock Ltd purchased 8000 shares in King Ltd in 2007 when the balance on the revenue reserve was Rs.40000. Rock Ltd purchased a further 4000 shares in King Ltd in 2008 when the balance on the revenue reserve was Rs.45000. Rock Ltd held no other investments on 30th June 2010.

iii)   Proposed dividends from subsidiary companies are included in the figure for debtors in the accounts of the parent companies.

Prepare the consolidated balance sheet of Rock Ltd and its subsidiaries in vertical form as on 30th June 2010, together with the consolidation schedules.

Solution

Consolidated Balance Sheet of Rock Limited and its subsidiaries
King Ltd and Chair Ltd as on 30th June 2010

Particulars		Note no.	Amount Rs
I.	**Equity and Liabilities**		
	(1)Shareholder's funds		
	(a) Share capital	1	200000
	(b) Reserves and surplus	2	171044
	(2)Minority Interest (WN4)		65918
	(3)Non-current liabilities		
	Long-term borrowing		-
	(4)Current liabilities		
	(a)Trade Payables(112060+73130+78190)		263380
	(b)Short term provisions	3	52000
	(c)Other current liabilities	4	118000
	Total		870342
II.	**Assets**		
	(1)Non-current Assets		
	(a)Fixed Assets		
	(i)Tangible Assets (135000 + 60000 + 70000)		265000
	(ii)Intangible assets	5	49592
	(b)Non-current Investments (W.N.(v))		10400
	(2)Current Assets:		
	(a)Inventories (55240+36840+61760)		153840
	(b)Trade Receivables (W.N.(vi))		191070
	(c)Cash and cash equivalents		200440

	Total		870342

Notes on Accounts

S/L No	Particulars	Amount (Rs)	Amount (Rs)
1.	Share capital Issued and subscribed 20000 Equity shares of Rs.10 each fully paid up		200000
2	**Reserves and surplus** Revenue Reserve (99540+16064) Capital reserve (50000 + 5440)	115604 55440	171044
3.	**Short term provisions** Provision for taxation (30000 + 22000)		52000

4.	**Other current liabilities**
	Proposed dividend
	  Minority shareholders
	  Holding company
		18000
		100000
			118000

5.	**Intangible assets** Goodwill (WN3)		49592

Working Notes

1. **Analysis of profits of Chair Ltd**

Particulars	Rs	Capital Profit Rs.	Revenue Reserve Rs.	Revenue Profit Rs.
Capital reserve in 2007		15000		
Increase in capital reserve			8000	
Revenue reserve in 2007		30500		
Increase in revenue reserve				14560
Total		45500	8000	14560
Less: Minority interest 15%		6825	1200	2184
Share of King Ltd		38675	6800	12376

2. **Analysis of profits of King Ltd**

Particulars	Rs	Capital Profit Rs.	Revenue Reserve Rs.	Revenue Profit Rs.
Revenue Reserve in 2007		40000		
Increase in revenue reserve				9370
Share in Chair Ltd			6800	12376

Total		40000	6800	21476
Less: Minority interest 20%		8000	1360	4349
Brought forward		32000	5440	17397
Less: (5000 x 4/15) for second acquisition				
Treated as capital		+1333		-1333
		33333		16064

3. Statement of cost of control / goodwill

Particulars	Amount Rs.	Amount Rs.
Cost of investment in Chair		149600
Cost of investment in King		160000
		309600
Less: Paid up value of investments		
In Chair Ltd	68000	
In King Ltd	120000	
Capital profit in Chair Ltd	38675	
Capital profit in King Ltd	33333	260008
Goodwill (to consolidated Balance Sheet)		49592

4. Statement of minority interest

Particulars	King Ltd Rs.	Chair Ltd Rs.
Share capital	30000	12000
Capital reserve	1360	1200
Revenue reserve	4349	2184
Capital profit	8000	6825
To consolidated Balance Sheet	43709	22209

5. Statement of investment

Item	Amount Rs.
King Ltd	150000
Less: Cost of Chair Limited (6800 x Rs.22)	149600
	400
Chair Ltd	10000
To consolidated Balance Sheet	10400

6. Statement of Debtors

Item	Amount Rs.
Rock Ltd	110700
Less: Dividend from King Limited	48000
	62070

King Ltd	69120	
Less: Dividend from Chair Limited	34000	35120
Chair Ltd		93880
To consolidated Balance Sheet		191070

6.3. What are intercompany holdings?

In certain situations it is possible that the subsidiary company may also hold shares in the holding company. The law would permit only if the subsidiary company had already acquired the shares when the Companies Act 1956 came into force and prior to the said date. However, the subsidiary would have no voting rights at a meeting of its holding company.

In such a scenario the following will occur:	a) The calculation of minority interest would have to be based on the fact that the subsidiary also has a claim on the profits of the holding company.
	b) The calculation for revenue and capital profits will have to be made separately, otherwise the cost of control would not be ascertained correctly.
	c) For this purpose such profits of the holding company as existed when the subsidiary company acquired the shares should be treated as capital profits.

Q.6.16: Interco holdings

You are given below the Balance Sheets of two companies A Ltd and B Ltd

Liabilities	A Ltd Rs.	B Ltd Rs.	Assets	A Ltd Rs.	B Ltd Rs.
Share capital (Rs.100 each)	500000	200000	Investment: 1600 shares in B Ltd	220000	
Profits:			1000 shares in A Ltd		150000
Capital profit	100000	80000	Sundry assets	830000	240000
Revenue profit	300000	50000			
Creditors	150000	60000			
	1050000	390000		1050000	390000

You are required to prepare a Consolidated Balance Sheet.

Solution

1. **Group structure**

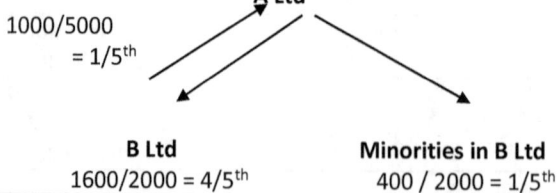

1000/5000 = 1/5th

A Ltd

B Ltd
1600/2000 = 4/5th

Minorities in B Ltd
400 / 2000 = 1/5th

2. Statement of Revenue profits

Let X = Revenue profits of A Ltd and
    Y = Revenue profits of B Ltd
Then,
X = 300000 + 4/5Y
Y = 50000 + 1/5X
Y = 50000 + 1/5 (300000 +4/5Y) substituting for X
Y = 50000 + 60000 + 4/25 Y
Y = 110000 + 4/25 Y
25Y = 2750000 + 4Y
21Y = 2750000
Y = 130952

Minority interest in revenue profits is 1/5 of Rs.130952 or Rs.26190.

Total revenue profit for A Ltd and B Ltd (Rs.300000 + Rs.50000)	= Rs.350000
Less: Minority interest as above	Rs.26190
To Consolidated Balance Sheet	Rs.323810

3. Statement of Capital profit

Let X be capital profit of A Ltd and
    Y be capital profit of B Ltd
Then,
X = 100000 +4/5Y
Y = 80000 + 1/5X
Y = 80000 + 1/5(100000 +4/5Y) (Substituting for X)
Y = 80000 + 20000 + 4/25 Y
  = 100000 + 4/25Y
25Y = 2500000 + 4Y
21Y = 2500000
Y = 119048
Minority interest @ $1/5^{th}$ would be Rs.119048 x $1/5^{th}$ = Rs.23810

	A Ltd	B Ltd
Capital profits	100000	80000
Less: transfer to make B's capital profit Rs.119048	(39048)	39048
	60952	119048
Less Minority interest		23810
Share of A Ltd (To cost of control / goodwill W.N.4)		95238

4. Statement of cost of control / goodwill

Particulars	Rs.	Rs.
Cost of investments		370000
Less: face value:		

Shares in B Ltd	160000	
Shares in A Ltd	100000	
Capital profits (Rs.119048 – R.23810)	95238	355238
		14762

5. **Statement of minority interest**

Particulars	Rs.
Shares held by outsiders (1/5 x Rs.200000)	40000
Capital profit	23810
Revenue profit	26190
	90000

Consolidated Balance Sheet of A Ltd and its subsidiary B Ltd
As on 31st December 2009

Particulars		Note no.	Amount Rs
I.	**Equity and Liabilities**		
	(1)Shareholder's funds		
	(a) Share capital	1	400000
	(b) Reserves and surplus	2	384762
	(2)Minority Interest (WN5)		90000
	(3)Non-current liabilities		
	Long-term borrowing		
	(3)Current liabilities		
	(a)Trade Payables	3	210000
	(b) Short term provisions		
	Total		1084762
II.	**Assets**		
	(1)Non-current Assets		
	(a)Fixed Assets		
	(i)Tangible Assets	4	1070000
	(ii)Intangible Assets (WN4)	5	14762
	(b)Non-current Investments		-
	(2)Current Assets:		
	(a)Inventories		-
	(b)Trade Receivables		-
	(c)Cash and cash equivalents		-
	Total		1084762

Notes on Accounts

S/L No	Particulars	Amount (Rs)	Amount (Rs)
1.	Share capital (5000 - 1000 shares held by B Ltd)		400000
2	**Reserves and surplus**		

	Capital profit (WN3)	60952	
	Revenue profit (WN3)	323810	384762
3.	**Trade Payables**		
	Creditors		
	A Ltd	150000	
	B Ltd	60000	210000
4.	**Tangible Assets**		
	Sundry assets		
	A Ltd	830000	
	B Ltd	240000	1070000
5.	**Intangible Assets**		
	Goodwill		14762

Q.6.17: Interco holdings

The following condensed Balance Sheets of H Ltd and S Ltd were prepared as on 31st December 2009:

Assets	H Ltd	S Ltd
	Rs	Rs
Goodwill	112000	40000
Plant & Machinery	95000	50400
Furniture	7000	4600
9000 ordinary shares in S Ltd	120000	-
2000 ordinary shares in H Ltd	-	24000
Stock-in-trade	48000	114000
Sundry debtors	70000	45000
Cash at bank	17000	13000
	469000	291000
Liabilities		
Share capital		
Ordinary shares of Rs.10 each	180000	100000
7.5% preference shares of Rs.10 each	150000	80000
Premium on ordinary shares	36000	-
Reserves	26000	30000
Sundry creditors	17000	61000
Profit & Loss Account	60000	20000
	469000	291000

Sundry creditors of H Ltd include Rs.15000 due to S Ltd for goods supplied since the acquisition of the shares. These goods are charged at 10% above cost. The stock of H Ltd includes goods costing Rs.33000 purchased from S Ltd.

H Ltd acquired the shares of S Ltd on 1st July 2009. As at the date of last preceding balance sheet of S Ltd viz, the 31st December 2008; the Plant and Machinery stood in the books at Rs.56000, the reserve, the reserve at Rs.30000 and the profit and loss account at Rs.8000.

The plant was revalued by H Ltd on the date of acquisition of the share of S Ltd at Rs.60000 but no adjustments were made in the books of S Ltd. On 31st December 2008, the debit balance of profit and loss account was Rs.22750 in the books of H Ltd.

Both the companies have provided depreciation on all their fixed assets at 10% per annum. You are required to prepare a consolidated balance sheet on 31st December 2009 and supporting schedule for computation.

Solution

Working Notes

(i)   Analysis of profits of S Ltd (pre-allocation)

Item	Capital profit Rs	Revenue profit Rs.
Reserves	30000	
Profit and Loss Account 1.1.2009	8000	
Profit for the year after preference dividend (12000 - 6000)	3000	3000
Profit on revaluation (60000 – 53200)	6800	
Additional depreciation		(200)
	47800	2800

(ii)   Analysis of profits of H Ltd (pre-allocation)

Item	Capital profit Rs	Revenue profit Rs.
Reserves	13000	13000
Profit and Loss Account 1.1.2009	(22750)	
Profit for the year after preference dividend (82750-11250 = 71500)	35750	35750
	26000	48750

(iii)   Statement of Capital profit of H Ltd and S Ltd (post allocation)

Let X be capital profit of H Ltd and
     Y be capital profit of S Ltd
Then, total capital profits of H Ltd = X = 26000 +9/10 Y
and total capital profits of S Ltd   = Y = 47800 + 1/9 X
X = 26000 + 9/10 (47800 + 1/9X) (substituting for Y)
X = 76689
Y = 47800 + 1/9 (76689)
Y = 56321
Minority interest in capital profits of S Ltd = Rs.5632
Share of H Ltd   (56321-5632)   = Rs.50689

(iv)   Statement of Revenue profit of H Ltd and S Ltd (post allocation)

Let a be revenue profit of H Ltd and
     b be revenue profit of S Ltd

Then, total revenue profits of H Ltd = a = 48750 +9/10 b
and total revenue profits of S Ltd   = b = 2800 + 1/9 a
a = 48750 + 9/10 (2800 + 1/9a) (substituting for b)
a = 56967
b = 2800 + 1/9 (56967)
b = 9130

(v)   Statement of capital profit

Item	H Ltd Rs	S Ltd Rs.
As per W.N i and W.N.ii	26000	47800
Adjustment as per equation	(8521)	8521
	17479	56321
Minority interest 10%		5632
Share of H Ltd		50689

(vi)   Statement of revenue profit

Item	H Ltd Rs	S Ltd Rs.
(60000 – 11250 preference dividend)	48750	2800
Adjustment	(6330)	6330
	42420	9130
Minority interest 10%		913
	8217	8217
Share of H Ltd	50637	

(vii)   Statement of cost of control/goodwill

Item	Amount Rs	Amount Rs.
H Ltd in S Ltd		
Cost of investments		120000
Less: paid up value	90000	
Capital profits (Rs.119048 – R.23810)	50689	140689
Capital reserve		20689
S Ltd in H Ltd		
Cost of investments		24000
Less: paid up value		20000
Goodwill		4000

(viii)   Statement of minority interest

Item	Amount Rs	Amount Rs.
Preference shares		80000
Dividend		6000

Equity shares	10000
Capital profit (WN5)	5632
Revenue profit (WN6)	913
Total	102545

**Consolidated Balance Sheet of H Ltd and its subsidiary S Ltd
as on 31st December 2009**

Particulars	Note no.	Amount Rs
I. **Equity and Liabilities**		
(1)Shareholder's funds		
(a) Share capital	1	310000
(b) Reserves and surplus	2	101116
(2)Minority Interest (WN8)		102545
(3)Current liabilities		
(a)Trade Payables	3	63000
(b) Other current liabilities (pref. dividend Of H Ltd)		11250
Total		**587911**
II. **Assets**		
(1)Non-current Assets		
(a)Fixed Assets		
(i)Tangible Assets	4	163600
(ii)Intangible Assets	5	135311
(b)Non-current Investments		-
(2)Current Assets:		
(a)Inventories (48000 + 114000 – 3000)		159000
(b)Trade Receivables (70000 + 45000 – 15000)		100000
(c)Cash and cash equivalents (17000 + 13000)		30000
Total		**587911**

Notes on Accounts

S/L No	Particulars	Amount (Rs)	Amount (Rs)
1.	**Share capital**		
	18000 equity shares of Rs.10 each	180000	
	Less: Held by S Ltd	(20000)	
		160000	
	15000 pref.shares of Rs.10 each fully paid up	150000	310000
2	**Reserves and surplus**		
	Reserve (WN4)	17479	

	Profit & Loss (WN5)	50637			
	Less: Stock reserve	(3000)	47637		
	Securities premium		36000	101116	
3.	**Trade Payables**				
	Sundry Creditors		78000		
	Less: Interco		(15000)	63000	
4.	**Tangible Assets**				
	Plant & Machinery				
	H Ltd	95000			
	S Ltd (50400 + 6800 – 200)	57000	152000		
	Furniture (7000 + 4600)		11600	163600	
5.	**Intangible Assets**				
	Goodwill (Per Balance Sheet)		152000		
	Add: On consolidation of S Ltd in H Ltd (WN6)		4000		
	Less: Capital reserve (WN6)		(20689)	135311	

Q.6.18: Interco holdings

Following are the draft Balance Sheets of two companies A Ltd and B Ltd as at 31.3.2010.

Liabilities	A Ltd Rs/Lakhs	B Ltd Rs/Lakhs	Assets	A Ltd Rs/Lakhs	B Ltd Rs/Lakhs
Share capital			Fixed Assets	5.00	1.50
(Rs.100 each)	6.00	3.00	Investments:		
Profits:			2400 shares in B Ltd	3.00	
Capital profit	0.80	0.85	1200 shares in A Ltd		2.00
Reserve profit	3.20	0.29	Current Assets		
Creditors	1.50	0.81	Debtors	2.00	0.80
			Stock	0.40	0.30
			Cash and bank	1.10	0.35
	11.50	4.95		11.50	4.95

The following adjustments were not yet made:
1. Stock worth Rs.5000 in B Ltd was found to be obsolete with no value.
2. A Ltd acquires an asset costing Rs.50000 on 31.3.2010. No effect has been given for both the purchase and payment.
3. During the year A Ltd sold an asset for Rs.50000 (original cost Rs.40000). The profit was included in the revenue profit.
4. Debtors of A Ltd included a sum of Rs.50000 owed by B Ltd

You are required to prepare the consolidated Balance Sheet of both the companies as on

31.3.2010 after giving effect to the above adjustments.(*Adapted CA Final Nov 1996*)

Solution

Consolidated Balance Sheet of A Ltd and its subsidiary B Ltd
as on 31.03.2010

Particulars		Note no.	Amount Rs/Lakhs
I.	**Equity and Liabilities**		
	(1)Shareholder's funds		
	(a) Share capital	1	4.80
	(b) Reserves and surplus	2	3.64
	(2)Minority Interest (WN5)		1.05
	(3)Current liabilities		
	(a)Trade Payables	3	1.81
	Total		11.30
II.	**Assets**		
	(1)Non-current Assets		
	(a)Fixed Assets		
	(i)Tangible Assets (WN8)		7.00
	(ii)Intangible Assets	4	0.40
	(b)Non-current Investments		
	(2)Current Assets:		
	(a)Inventories (0.40 + 0.25)		0.65
	(b)Trade Receivables (WN7)		2.30
	(c)Cash and cash equivalents (WN8)		0.95
	Total		11.30

Notes on Accounts

S/L No	Particulars	Amount (Rs/Lakhs)	Amount (Rs/Lakhs)
1.	**Share capital**		
	6000 shares of Rs.100 each	6.00	
	Less: Shares held by B Ltd	1.20	4.80
2	**Reserves and surplus**		
	Capital profit (WN9)	0.60	
	Revenue profit (WN9)	3.04	3.64
3.	**Trade Payables**		
	Sundry Creditors (WN7)		1.81
4.	**Intangible Assets**		
	Goodwill (WN6)		0.40

Working Notes

1. **Group structure**

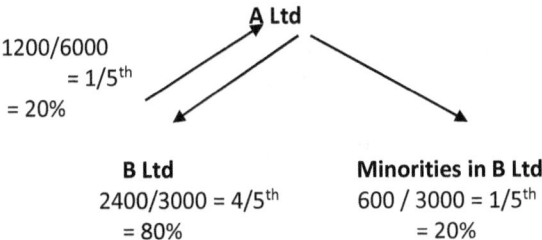

1200/6000
= 1/5th
= 20%

B Ltd	**Minorities in B Ltd**
2400/3000 = 4/5th	600 / 3000 = 1/5th
= 80%	= 20%

2. **Statement of computation of profits : In A Ltd**

Particulars	Rs in lakhs
Capital profit	0.80
Add: transfer from revenue profit regarding sale of capital asset	
(0.60 – 0.40)	0.20
Balance	1.00
Revenue profit	3.20
Less: Transfer to capital profit	(0.20)
Balance	3.00

3. **Statement of computation of profits : In B Ltd**

Particulars	Rs in lakhs
Capital profit	0.85
Revenue profit	0.29
Less: Stock written off	(0.05)
Balance	0.24

4. **Statement of analysis of profits of B Ltd**

    A. **Revenue profit**

       Let x = "A Ltd" profit and Y = "B LTD" profit

       $X = 300000 + 0.8 Y$

       $Y = 24000 + 0.2 X$

       Substituting X in Y

       $Y = 24000 + 0.2(30000 + 0.8Y)$

       $Y = 24000 + 60000 + 0.16 Y$

       $0.84 Y = 84000$

       $Y = 100000$

       Hence minority interest = 100000 x 20% = 20000

    B. **Capital profit**

       Let x = "A Ltd" profit and Y = "B LTD" profit

       $X = 100000 + 0.8 Y$

Y = 85000 +0.2 X
Substituting X in Y
Y = 85000 + 0.2(100000 +0.8Y)
Y = 85000 + 20000 +0.16 Y
0.84 Y = 105000
Y = 125000
Hence A Ltd's share = Rs.125000 x 80% = Rs.100000
Hence minority interest = 125000 x 20% = Rs.25000

5. **Statement of computation of Minority interest**

Particulars	Rs/lakhs
Paid up share capital (20%)	0.60
Capital profit (WN4)	0.25
Revenue profit (WN4)	0.20
Total	1.05

6. **Statement of computation of Cost of control / goodwill**

Particulars		Rs/lakhs
Cost of investment:		3.00 (A)
Less: A Ltd's share of Net Assets of B Ltd on acquisition date		
- Paid up share capital	2.40	
- Capital profit (WN4)	1.00	(3.40) (B)
Cancellation of B Ltd's investment in A Ltd:		
- Amount invested	2.00	
- Less: Proportionate share capital	(1.20)	0.80 (C)
Goodwill (A – B + C)		0.40

7. **Cancellation of inter-company transactions – debtors and creditors**

Item	Debtors Rs /Lakhs	Creditors Rs / Lakhs
A Ltd	2.00	1.50
B Ltd	0.80	0.81
Total	2.80	2.31
Less: Mutual indebtedness	(0.50)	(0.50)
	2.30	1.81

8. **Cancellation of inter-company transactions – fixed assets and cash**

Item	Fixed assets Rs /Lakhs	Cash/bank Rs / Lakhs
A Ltd	5.00	1.10
B Ltd	1.50	0.35
Total	6.50	1.45
Add/Less: Purchase of machinery and payment thereon	0.50	(0.50)

	7.00	0.95

9. Statement of reserves

Item	Capital profit Rs /Lakhs	Revenue profit Rs / Lakhs
Opening adjusted balance		
A Ltd (WN3)	1.00	3.00
B Ltd (WN3)	0.85	0.24
Amount transferred to minority interest (WN4 and WN5)	(0.25)	(0.20)
Capital profit transferred to cost of control (WN6)	(1.00)	
To consolidated Balance Sheet	0.60	3.04

Chapter 7 : Consolidated Profit and Loss and group Cash Flow

Learning Outcomes
- ❑ Steps followed in consolidation of Profit & Loss Account
- ❑ Steps followed in consolidation of cash flows

7.1.	What are the steps to be followed in preparation of Consolidated Profit and Loss Account?

Preparation of Consolidated Profit & Loss Account of holding company and its subsidiaries is quite straightforward.

The steps required to be followed are enumerated below for clarity.

Steps	Description
1.	*All revenue items to be added on line by line basis and intercompany adjustments need to be eliminated from the consolidated revenue items*
2.	*Unrealised profit on unsold stock sold by one of the group companies to another group company needs to be eliminated*
3.	*Share of holding company in the proposed dividend of subsidiary needs to be eliminated*
4.	*Share of holding company in the interim dividend received from subsidiary needs to be eliminated*
5.	*Share of minority in the Profits (Capital and Revenue) from Profit and Loss A/c to be transferred to Minority Interest A/c*
6.	*Share of holding company in the capital profits of subsidiary company from Profit and Loss A/c to be transferred to Capital Reserve Account*
7.	*Dividend received by holding company from subsidiary out of capital profits, wrongly credited to Profit and Loss A/c to be rectified and transferred from Profit and Loss Account to Investment Account.*

Q.7.1. Consolidated Profit and Loss Account of holding company and subsidiary

Given below are the Profit & Loss Account of H Ltd and its subsidiary Ltd for the year ended 31st March, 2010:

	H Ltd (Rs in lakhs)	S Ltd (Rs in lakhs)
Income:		
Sales and other income	5,000	1000
Increase in Stock	1,000	200
	6,000	1200

Expenses:

Raw materials consumed	800	200
Wages and salaries	800	150
Production expenses	200	100
Administrative expenses	200	100
Selling and distribution expenses	200	50
Interest	100	50
Depreciation	100	50
	2,400	700
Profit before tax	3,600	500
Profit for tax	1,200	200
Profit after tax	2,400	300
Proposed dividend	1,200	150
Balance of Profit	1,200	150

Other information:

H Ltd sold goods to S Ltd of Rs 120 lakhs at cost plus 20%. Stock of S Ltd includes such goods valuing Rs 24 lakhs. Administrative Expenses of S Ltd include Rs 5 Lakhs paid to H Ltd as consultancy fees. Selling and Distribution expenses of Y Ltd include Rs 10 lakhs paid to S Ltd as commission.

H Ltd. Holds 80% of equity share capital Rs 1000 Lakhs in S Ltd. H Ltd took credit to its Profit & Loss Account, the proportionate amount of dividend declared and paid by S Ltd for the year 2008-09.

Solution:

Consolidated Profit & Loss Account of H Ltd and its subsidiary S Ltd
For the year ended on 31st March 2010

Particulars		Note No	Rs in lakhs
I.	Revenue from operations	1	5865
II.	Total Revenue		5865
III.	Expenses		
	Cost of material purchased / consumed	3	1180
	Changes of inventories of finished goods	2	(1196)
	Employee benefit expense	4	950
	Finance cost	6	150
	Depreciation and amortization expenses	7	150
	Other expenses	5	535
	Total expenses		1769
IV.	Profit before tax (II – III)		4096
V.	Tax expenses	8	1400
VI.	Profit after tax		2696

	Profit transferred to consolidated Balance Sheet		2696
	Profit after tax		

Proposed dividend		
H Ltd	1200	
S Ltd	150	
	1350	
Less: Share of H Ltd in proposed dividend		
of S Ltd (80% of Rs.150 lakhs)	(120)	1230
Profit to be transferred to consolidated		
Balance Sheet		1466

Notes on Accounts

	Rs in lakhs	Rs in lakhs
1. Revenue from operations		
Sales and other income		
H Ltd	5000	
S Ltd	1000	
	6000	
Less: Inter-company sales	(120)	
Consultancy fees received by H Ltd from S Ltd	(5)	
Commission received by S Ltd from H Ltd	(10)	5865
2. Increase in stock		
H Ltd	1000	
S Ltd	200	
	1200	
Less: Unrealised profits RS. 24 Lakhs x (20/120)	(4)	1196
		7061
3. Cost of Material purchased / consumed		
H Ltd	800	
S Ltd	200	
	1000	
Less: Purchases by S Ltd from H Ltd	(120)	880
Direct expenses		
H Ltd	200	
S Ltd	100	300
		1180
4. Employees benefits and expenses		
Wages and salaries		
H Ltd	800	
S Ltd	150	950
5. Other expenses		
Administration expenses		
H Ltd	200	
S Ltd	100	
Less: Consultancy fees received by H Ltd from S	300	

Ltd	(5)	295
Selling and distribution expenses		
H Ltd		
S Ltd	200	
Less: Commission received from S Ltd from S	50	240
Ltd	(10)	535
6. Finance cost		
Interest:		
H Ltd	100	150
S Ltd	50	
7. Depreciation and Amortisation		
Depreciation		
H Ltd	100	150
S Ltd	50	
8. Provision for tax		
H Ltd	1200	1400
S Ltd	200	2696

Tutorial note:
It is assumed that H Ltd acquired shares in S ltd before 2008-09

Since the amount of dividend received by H Ltd for the 2008-09 is not given, it has not been deducted from sales and other income in consolidated profit & loss account and not added to consolidated opening retained earnings (which is also not given)

Q.7.2: Consolidated Profit and Loss Account

The Trial Balances of A Ltd and B Ltd as on 31st December 2011 were as under:

Particulars	A Ltd		B Ltd	
	Rs.	Rs.	Rs.	Rs.
Equity share capital (share of Rs.100 each)		1000000		200000
7 % Preference share capital (share of Rs.100 each)		-		200000
Reserves		300000		100000
6% Debenture		200000		200000
Sundry debtors / creditors	80000	90000	50000	60000
P &L A/c balance		20000		15000
Purchases / sales	500000	900000	600000	950000
Wages and salaries	100000	-	150000	
Debenture interest	12000	-	12000	
General expenses	80000	-	60000	

Preference Dividend up to 30.6.2011		3500	7000	
Stock (31.12.2011)	100000		50000	
Cash at bank	13500		6000	
Investment in B Ltd	528000			
Fixed Assets	1100000		790000	
	2513500	2513500	1725000	1725000

Investment in B Ltd were acquired on 1.4.2011 and consisted of 80% of equity capital and 50% of preference capital. Depreciation on fixed assets is written off @ 10% p.a. After acquiring control over B Ltd, A Ltd supplied to it goods at cost plus 20%, the total invoice value of such goods being Rs.60000 ; ¼ of such goods was still in stock at the end of the year.

Prepare a consolidated Profit and Loss Account for the year ended on 31st December 2011.

Solution

Consolidated Profit and Loss Statement of A Ltd and its subsidiary B Ltd for the year ended 31st March 2012

Particulars		Note No.	Rs.
I.	Revenue from operations	1	1790000
II.	Total Revenue		1790000
III.	Expenses		
	Cost of material purchased / consumed	2	1040000
	Changes of inventories of finished goods		
	Employee benefit expenses	3	250000
	Finance cost	4	24000
	Depreciation and amortisation expenses	5	189000
	Other expenses	6	140000
	Total expenses		1643000
IV.	Profit before tax (II – III)		147000
Profit transferred to consolidated Balance Sheet			
Profit after tax			147000
Preference dividend	3500		
Preference dividend payable	3500		7000
			140000
Less: Minority interest	7000		
Capital reserve (1/4 x 35000 x 80 /100)	7000		
Stock reserve ((60000 /4) x (20 / 120))	2500		
Investment account – dividend for three Months (prior to acquisition)	1750		18250
Profit to be transferred to consolidated Balance Sheet			121750

Notes to Accounts

	Rs	Rs
1. Revenue from operations		
Sales		
A Ltd	900000	
B Ltd	950000	
	1850000	
Less: Inter-company sales	(60000)	1790000
2. Cost of materials consumed / purchases		
Purchases		
A Ltd	500000	
B Ltd	600000	
	1100000	
Less: Inter-company sales	(60000)	1040000
3. Employee benefit expenses		
A Ltd	100000	
B Ltd	150000	250000
4. Finance cost		
A Ltd	12000	
B Ltd	12000	24000
5. Depreciation and Amortisation		
Depreciation		
A Ltd	110000	
S Ltd	79000	189000
6. Other expenses		
A Ltd	80000	
B Ltd	60000	140000

Consolidated Cash Flow Statement

7.2.	What are the steps to be followed in preparation of Consolidated Cash Flow Statement?

Preparation of Consolidated Cash Flow Statement of holding company and its subsidiaries is quite straightforward similar to Consolidated Profit and Loss Account.

The steps required to be followed are enumerated below for clarity.

Steps	Description
1.	*All the items of Cash flow from operating activities, investing activities and financing activities are to be added on line by line basis and*
2.	*All intercompany transactions need to be eliminated from the consolidated Cash flow statement as follows:* - *Interco sales / purchases* - *Unrealised profit on unsold stock sold by one of the group companies to another group company* - *Share of proposed dividend of holding company received from subsidiary* - *Share of interim dividend of holding company received from subsidiary*

An hypothetical example of Consolidated Cash Flow is explained in Problem 6 below.

Q.7.3: Cash flow Statement

Please find below Balance Sheets of Bengal Jute Ltd as at 31.03.2012 and 31.03.2011. You are required to prepare Cash Flow Statement for the year 2011-12.

(Rs in '000)

Balance Sheet	31.03.2013		31.03.2012	
Equity share capital	5500		4000	
General reserve	5100		4200	
Profit & Loss Account	450		400	
Share premium Account	1500			
Shareholders' funds		12550		8600
Secured loans	1800		3400	
Unsecured loans	2300		1200	
Loan funds		4100		4600
Sources of funds		16650		13200
Fixed Assets				
Gross Block	15000		12000	
Accumulated depreciation	1800		1300	
Net Block		13200		10700
Capital work-in-progress		1200		700
Investments		1700		1400
Current Assets, loans & advances				

Inventories	2510		2600	
Debtors	1090		1200	
Cash & bank balances	240		340	
Loans	1700		200	
Advance tax	850		700	
	6390		5040	
Creditors	1050		1200	
Outstanding expenses	2100		1540	
Tax provision	850		700	
Proposed dividend	2200		1600	
	6200		5040	
Net current assets		190		0
Miscellaneous expenditure		360		400
Applications		16650		13200

Other Information:
1. Fixed Assets costing Rs.120000, accumulated depreciation Rs.60000 were sold
   for Rs.70000.
2. Actual tax liability for 2011-12 was Rs.7,00,000
3. Loans represent long term loans given to group companies

4. Interest on loan funds foe 2011-12 was Rs.594500 and interest and divider income were
   Rs.442000
5. Investments costing Rs.600000 were sold for Rs.700000.

Solution		(Rs'000)
Cash flow from operating activities	Amount	Amount
Change in general reserve	900	
Change in profit & loss account	50	
Proposed dividend	2200	
Provision for tax	850	
Profit before tax		4000
Add: Depreciation	560	
Add: Miscellaneous expenses	40	
Add / (less)Loss on sale of fixed assets	(10)	
Add / (less) Loss on sale of investments	(100)	490
Fund flow from operations		4490
Add: Interest paid		594.5
Less: Interest and dividend received		(442)
Add/less working capital adjustment		
Inventories	90	
Debtors	110	
Creditors	(150)	
Outstanding expenses	560	610
Cash flow from operating activities (before tax)		5252.5
Less: Advance tax for 2012-13		850
Cash flow from operating activities (after tax)		4402.5(A)

Cash flow from financing activities		
Issue of shares		
Face value	1500	
Premium	1500	3000
Repayment of secured loans	(1600)	
Unsecured loans raised	1100	(500)
Interest payment		(594.5)
Dividend payment		(1600)
		305.5(B)
Cash flow from investing activities		
Purchase of fixed assets	(3120)	
Sale of fixed assets	70	
Capital WIP	(500)	
Fixed Assets (net)		(3550)
Purchase of investments	(900)	
Sale proceeds of investments	700	
Investments (net)		(200)
Loans		(1500)
Interest & dividend income		442
		(4808)(C)
Cash flow from operating activities		4402.5(A)
Cash flow from financing activities		305.5(B)
Cash flow from investing activities		(4808)(C)
Increase / decrease in cash and bank balance		(100)

Q.7.4: Cash flow statement

Arrange and redraft the following Cash Flow Statement in proper order keeping in mind the requirements of AS 3:

	Rs / Lakhs	Rs / Lakhs
Net Profit		60,000
Add: Sale of investments	70,000	
Depreciation on assets	11,000	
Issue of preference shares	9,000	
Loan raised	4,500	
Decrease in stock	12,000	106,500
		166,500
Less: Purchase of fixed assets	65,000	
Decrease in creditors	6,000	
Increase in debtors	8,000	
Exchange gain	8,000	
Profit on sale of investments	12,000	
Redemption of debenture	5,700	
Dividend paid	1,400	
Interest paid	945	107,045
		59,455
Add: Opening cash and cash equivalent		12,341

Closing cash and cash equivalent	71,796

Solution

Cash Flow statement	Rs /Lakhs
Cash flows from operating activities	
Net profit	60,000
Less: Exchange gain	(8000)
Less: Profit on sale of investments	(12000)
	40,000
Add: Depreciation on assets	11,000
Change in current assets and current liabilities	51,000
Less: Increase in debtors	(8,000)
Add: Decrease in stock	12,000
Less: Decrease in creditors	(6,000)
Net cash from operating activities (A)	**49,000**
Cash flows from investing activities	
Sale of investments	70,000
Purchase of fixed assets	(65,000)
Net cash from investing activities (B)	**5,000**
Cash flows from financing activities	
Issue of preference shares	9,000
Loan raised	4,500
Redemption of debentures	(5,700)
Interest paid	(945)
Dividend paid	(1,400)
Net cash from financing activities (C)	**5,455**
Net increase in cash and cash equivalents (A+B +C)	59,455
Add: Opening cash and cash equivalents	12,341
Closing cash and cash equivalents	71,796

Q.7.5: Consolidated Cash flow Statement

Consolidated Cash Flow statement (Rs in lakhs)

Particulars	X Ltd	Y Ltd	Total
Cash flow from operating activities			
Change in reserve	10	2	12
Change in P & L Account	2	1	3
Proposed dividend	18	-	18
Tax provision	20	1	21
Depreciation	5	5	10
Interest	(5)	5	-
	50	14	64
Less tax payment	(20)	(2)	(22)
	30	12	42
Working capital adjustment	(13)	12	(1)
(A)	17	24	41
Cash flow from investment activities			

Sale of fixed assets		30	0	30
Purchase of fixed assets		(30)	(20)	(50)
	(B)	0	(20)	(20)
Cash flow from Financing activities	**(C)**	(22)	10	(12)
Net cash flows (A + B + C)		(5)	14	9

Q.7.6: Consolidated Cash flow statement

Consolidated statement of profit and loss for the period ended 20X2

Rs lakhs

Sales	30,650
Cost of sales	(26,000)
Gross profit	4,650
Depreciation	(450)
Administrative and selling expenses	(910)
Interest expense	(400)
Investment income	500
Foreign exchange loss	(40)
Profit before taxation	3,350
Taxes on income	(300)
Profit	3,050

Consolidated balance sheet as at end of 20X2 (Rs lakhs)

	20X2	20X1
Assets		
Cash and cash equivalents	230	160
Accounts receivable	1,900	1,200
Inventory	1,000	1,950
Portfolio investments	2,500	2,500
Property, plant and equipment at cost	3,730	1,910
Accumulated depreciation	(1,450)	(1,060)
Property, plant and equipment net	2,280	850
Total assets	7,910	6,660
Liabilities		
Trade payables	250	1,890
Interest payable	230	100
Income taxes payable	400	1,000
Long-term debt	2200	1,040
Short-term borrowing	100	–
Total liabilities	3,180	4,030
Shareholders' equity		
Share capital	1,500	1,250
Retained earnings	3,230	1,380
Total shareholders' equity	4,730	2,630
Total liabilities and shareholders' equity	7,910	6,660

The following additional information is also relevant for the preparation of the statements of cash flows:

➢ All of the shares of a subsidiary were acquired for 590. The fair values of assets acquired and liabilities assumed were as follows: Rs lakhs

Inventories	100
Accounts receivable	100
Cash	40
Property, plant and equipment	650
Trade payables	100
Long-term debt	200

➢ 250 was raised from the issue of share capital and a further 150 was raised from long-term borrowings and 100 was raised from short-term borrowing.

➢ interest expense was 400, of which 170 was paid during the period. Also, 100 relating to interest expense of the prior period was paid during the period.

➢ dividends paid were 1,200.

➢ the liability for tax at the beginning and end of the period was 1,000 and 400 respectively. During the period, a further 200 tax was provided for. Withholding tax on dividends received amounted to 100.

➢ during the period, the group acquired property, plant and equipment with an aggregate cost of 1,250 of which 900 was acquired by means of finance leases. Cash payments of 350 were made to purchase property, plant and equipment.

➢ plant with original cost of 80 and accumulated depreciation of 60 was sold for 20.

➢ accounts receivable as at the end of 20X2 include 100 of interest receivable.

Solution

Direct method statement of cash flows	(Rs lakhs)
	20X2
Cash flows from operating activities	
Cash receipts from customers	30150
Cash paid to suppliers and employees	(27600)
Cash generated from operations	2550
Income tax paid	(900)
Net cash from operating activities	1650
Cash flows from investing activities	
Acquisition of subsidiary X, net of cash acquired (Note A)	(550)
Purchase of property, plant and equipment (Note B)	(350)
Proceeds from sale of equipment	20
Interest received	200
Dividend received	200
Net cash used in investing activities	(480)
Cash flows from financing activities	
Proceeds from issue of share capital	250
Proceeds from long-term borrowings	150
Proceeds from short term borrowings	100
Payment of finance lease liabilities	(90)
Interest paid	(270)
Dividends paid	(1,200)
Net cash used in financing activities	(1,060)

Net increase in cash and cash equivalents	**110**
Cash and cash equivalents at beginning of period (Note C)	**120**
Cash and cash equivalents at end of period (Note C)	**230**

Indirect method statement of cash flows   **(Rs lakhs)**

	20X2
Cash flows from operating activities	
Profit before taxation	3350
Adjustments for:	
Depreciation	450
Foreign exchange loss	40
Investment income	(500)
Interest expense	400
	3740
Increase in trade and other receivables	(500)
Decrease in inventories	1050
Decrease in trade payables	(1740)
Cash generated from operations	2550
Income tax paid	(900)
Net cash from operating activities	**1650**
Cash flows from investing activities	
Acquisition of subsidiary X net of cash acquired (Note A)	(550)
Purchase of property, plant and equipment (Note B)	350
Proceeds from sale of equipment	20
Interest received	200
Dividends received	200
Net cash used in investing activities	**(480)**
Cash flows from financing activities	
Proceeds from issue of share capital	250
Proceeds from long-term borrowings	150
Proceeds from short-term borrowings	100
Payment of finance lease liabilities	(90)
Interest paid	(270)
Dividends paid	(1200)
Net cash used in financing activities	**(1,060)**
Net increase in cash and cash equivalents	**110**
Cash and cash equivalents at beginning of period (Note C)	**120**
Cash and cash equivalents at end of period (Note C)	**230**

Notes to the statement of cash flows (direct method and indirect method)
A. Obtaining control of subsidiary
During the period the Group obtained control of subsidiary X. The fair values of assets acquired and liabilities assumed were as follows:

Cash	40
Inventories	100
Accounts receivable	100
Property, plant and equipment	650
Trade payables	(100)
Long-term debt	(200)
Total purchase price paid in cash	590
Less: Cash of subsidiary X acquired	(40)
Cash paid to obtain control net of cash acquired	550

B. Property, plant and equipment

During the period, the Group acquired property, plant and equipment with an aggregate cost of 1,250 of which 900 was acquired by means of finance leases. Cash payments of 350 were made to purchase property, plant and equipment.

C. Cash and cash equivalents

Cash and cash equivalents consist of cash on hand and balances with banks, and investments in money market instruments. Cash and cash equivalents included in the statement of cash flows comprise the following amounts in the balance sheet:

	20X2	20X1
Cash on hand and balances with banks	40	25
Short-term investments	190	135
Cash and cash equivalents as previously reported	230	160
Effect of exchange rate changes	–	(40)
Cash and cash equivalents as restated	230	120

Cash and cash equivalents at the end of the period include deposits with banks of 100 held by a subsidiary which are not freely remissible to the holding company because of currency exchange restrictions.
The Group has undrawn borrowing facilities of 2,000 of which 700 may be used only for future expansion.

D. Segment information

	Segment A	Segment B	Total
Cash flows from:			
Operating activities	1,790	(140)	1,650
Investing activities	(640)	160	(480)
Financing activities	(840)	(220)	(1,060)
	310	(200)	110

Alternative presentation (indirect method)

As an alternative, in an indirect method statement of cash flows, operating profit before working capital changes is sometimes presented as follows:

Revenues excluding investment income	30,650
Operating expense excluding depreciation	(26,910)
Operating profit before working capital changes	3,740

Chapter 8 : Consolidation of Parent with one subsidiary and associate and / or Joint ventures or Jointly controlled entities

Learning Outcomes
- ❑ Accounting of Associates as per AS 23
- ❑ Equity method of accounting – steps to be followed
- ❑ Accounting of Joint venture as per AS 27

    jointly controlled operations
    jointly controlled assets
    jointly controlled entities
    Proportionate consolidation method

- ❑ Consolidation of Parent , one subsidiary and one associate
- ❑ Consolidation of Parent, one subsidiary, one Jointly controlled entity and one associate
- ❑ comparative analysis of treatment of subsidiary, associate, Joint ventures and investments

8.1.Investment in associates in consolidated financial statements

An enterprise that presents consolidated financial statements should account for investments in associates in the consolidated financial statements in accordance with the accounting standard AS 23 and Ind AS 28 as explained in foregoing chapters

8.2. Accounting for Associates
Accounting Standards suggest equity method of accounting for investments in associates.

Equity method (revisited)	The following procedure should be followed:
	 a) Investment is initially recorded at cost. Subsequently, the carrying amount is increased on the basis of share of profit or decreased on the basis of share of loss in the associate.
	 b) Find out value of investments on the basis of proportionate value of net assets of the investee,
	 c) Ascertain goodwill or capital reserve arising out of the purchase consideration –
	   - if the purchase price is above the value of investments calculated in (b) above then there is goodwill and
	   - if the purchase price is less than the value of investments calculated in (b) above then there is capital reserve
	 d) Goodwill or capital reserve as ascertained in (b) above should be included in the carrying amount of the investments with a separate disclosure. On the contrary, investments are recognised at purchase price as per AS 13 without disclosing goodwill / capital reserve.

Equity method is not applicable	a) When an investment is acquired for the purpose of disposal in the near future, i.e. as short term investments and

	b) There is severe long term restriction on fund transfer by the associate to the investor. In these two cases AS 13 should be applied.

8.3. Summary of steps to be followed for Equity method of accounting for investments in associates

Step 1	Determine the date of acquisition of investment in associate
Step 2	Determine investor's share of interest in associate
Step 3	Analyse profit of associate and split between pre-acquisition and post-acquisition profits of associate with reference to date of acquisition
Step 4	Calculate investor's share of profit (both pre-acquisition and post-acquisition) of associate
Step 5	Calculate goodwill / capital reserve
Step 6	Calculate investment in associate in consolidated Balance Sheet
Step 7	Provide disclosure related to associate under consolidated Profit and Loss

8.4. Treatment of investment in joint ventures in consolidated financial statements

AS 27 identifies three broad types of joint ventures as explained in earlier chapters, and are revisited below just for recap:

- jointly controlled operations
- jointly controlled assets
- jointly controlled entities

Jointly controlled operations (JCO)	In respect of its interests in jointly controlled operations, a venturer should recognise in its separate financial statements and consequently in its consolidated financial statements: (a) the assets that it controls and the liabilities that it incurs; and (b) the expenses that it incurs and its share of the income that it earns from the joint Venture
Jointly controlled assets (JCA)	In respect of its interest in jointly controlled assets, a venture should recognize, in its separate financial statements and consequently in its consolidated financial statements: a) its share of the jointly controlled assets, classified according to the nature of the assets, b) any liabilities which it has incurred, c) its share of any liabilities incurred jointly with the other venturers in relation to the joint venture, d) any income from the sale or use of its share of the output of the joint venture, together with its share of any

	expenses incurred by the joint venture; and e) any expenses which it has incurred in respect of its interest in the joint venture.
Jointly controlled entities (JCE)	A Jointly controlled entity maintains its own accounting records and prepares and presents financial statements in the same way as other enterprises in conformity with the requirements of AS 27 applicable to that jointly controlled entity.

Separate Financial statements of a venturer	In a venturers' separate financial statements, interest in a jointly controlled entity should be accounted for as an investment in accordance with Accounting standard AS 13.
Consolidated Financial Statements of a venturer	In its consolidated financial statements, a venturer should report its interest in a jointly controlled entity using proportionate consolidation except a) an interest in a jointly controlled entity which is acquired and held exclusively with a view to its subsequent disposal in the near future and b) an interest in a jointly controlled entity which operates under severe long-term restrictions that significantly impair its ability to transfer funds to the venturer.

8.5. Summary of steps to be followed for accounting of Joint Ventures (proportionate consolidation method)

Step 1	Determine the date of acquisition of investment in joint venture (JCE)
Step 2	Determine venturer's share of interest in Jointly controlled entities (JCE)
Step 3	Analyse profit of Jointly controlled entities (JCE) and split between pre-acquisition and post-acquisition profits with reference to date of acquisition
Step 4	Calculate venturer's share of profit (both pre-acquisition and post-acquisition) of Jointly Controlled entities (JCE)
Step 5	Calculate goodwill / capital reserve
Step 6	Consolidate assets and liabilities in JCE through proportionate consolidation method in consolidated Balance Sheet
Step 7	Provide disclosure related to JCE under consolidated Profit and Loss

Q.8.1: Consolidation of Parent , one subsidiary and one associate

The draft Balance Sheet of three companies W.H, O as at 31.3.2010 is as under: (Rs'000)			
Assets	W	H	O
Fixed Assets	697	648	349
Investments 160000 shares in H	562	-	-
80000 shares in O	184	-	-

Cash at bank	101	95	80
Trade receivable	386	321	251
Inventory	495	389	287
Total	2425	1453	967

Liabilities	W	H	O
Share capital	600	200	200
(Nominal value of Re.1 per share)	-	-	-
Reserves	1050	850	478
Trade payables	375	253	189
Debentures	400	150	100
Total	2425	1453	967

You are given the following information:

a) W purchased the shares in H on 13.10.2005 when the balance in reserves was Rs.500 thousands.

b) The shares in O were purchased on 11.5.2005 when the balance in reserves was Rs.242000.

c)The following dividend have been declared but not accounted for before the accounting year end: (Rs'000)

W = 65
H = 30
O = 15

d) Included in inventories of O is inventory valued at Rs. 20000 which had been purchased from W at cost plus 2.5%.

e) Goodwill in respect of the acquisition of H has been fully written off.

f) On 31.3.2010 H made bonus issue of one share for every share held. This had not been accounted in the Balance Sheet as on 31.3.2010.

g) Included in trade payables of W is Rs.18000 to O, which is included in trade receivables of O.

Prepare consolidated Balance Sheet of was at 31.3.2010 *(CA Final: May 2010)*

Solution

Consolidated Balance Sheet of W Group as on 31st March 2010

Particulars	Note no.	Amount Rs'000
I. **Equity and Liabilities**		
(1)Shareholder's funds		
(a) Share capital		600.00
(b) Reserves and surplus	1	1355.80
(2)Minority Interest (WN4)		204.00
(3)Non-current liabilities		
Long-term borrowing	2	550.00
(4)Current liabilities		
(a)Trade Payables(375 + 253))		628.00
(b) Other current liabilities	3	71.00

		Total		3408.80
II.	**Assets**			
	(1)Non-current Assets			
	(a)Fixed Assets			
	(i)Tangible Assets (697 + 648)			1345.00
	(b)Non-current Investments (W.N.(v))		4	270.80
	(2)Current Assets:			
	(a)Inventories (495+389)			884.00
	(b)Trade Receivables (386+321)			707.00
	(c)Cash and cash equivalents		5	196.00
	(d)Other current assets		6	6.00
		Total		3408.80

Notes on Accounts

S/L No	Particulars	Amount (Rs'000)	Amount (Rs'000)
1.	**Reserves and surplus (WN8)**		
	Capital Reserve (WN6)	160.00	
	Other reserve (WN8)	1195.80	1355.80
2	**Long term borrowings**		
	Debentures (400 + 150)		550.00
3.	**Other current liabilities**		
	Proposed dividend		
	W	65.00	
	Minority Interest (Rs.30 – Rs.24)	6.00	71.00
	Holding company		
4.	**Non-current investment**		
	Investment in associate	184.00	
	(including goodwill Rs.720000)		
	Add: Accumulated reserves	86.80	270.80
	Increase in equity reserves		
	(40% x (478 15 242)) 88.40		
	Less: Unrealised profit(WN7) 1.60		
5.	**Cash and cash equivalents**		
	Cash and bank (101 + 95)		196.00
6.	**Other current assets**		
	Dividend receivable from O		6.00

Working Notes:

1. **Group structure**

H Ltd		O Ltd

W Ltd 160000 sh	Minority 40000 sh	W Ltd 40000 sh
80%	20%	40%

2. **Statement of analysis of profits of H with reference to date of acquisition (Rs'000)**

Particulars	Pre-acquisition profit	Post-acquisition profit
Balance	500.0*	350.0 (bal fig)
Less: Dividend 2009-10		(300.0)
Bonus issue@	(200.0)	-
Net	300.0	320.0
Share of W 80%	240.0	256.0
Share of Minority 20%	60.0	64.0

*Acquisition date 13.10.05

@It is assumed that bonus issue had been made out of pre-acquisition reserves.

3. **Statement of cost of control / goodwill**

Particulars	Rs'000	Rs'000
Cost of investment		562.0
Less: Paid-up value of shares including bonus		
(80% of 400)	320.0	
Share in pre-acquisition profit of H	240.0	560.0
Goodwill written off		2.0

4. **Statement of Minority interest (of H)**

Particulars	Amount Rs'000
Share capital (200000 x 20%)	40.0
Bonus issue (200000 x 20%)	40.0
Share of pre-acquisition profits (WN2)	60.0
Share of post-acquisition profits (WN2)	64.0
Total	204.0

5. **Statement of analysis of profits of O with reference to date of acquisition**

Particulars	Pre-acquisition profit	Post-acquisition profit
Balance	242000*	236000 (bal fig)
Less: Dividend 2009-10		(15000)
Net	242000	221000
Share of W 40%	96800	88400

*Acquisition date 11.05.05

6. Statement of cost of control / goodwill / capital reserve

Particulars	Amount Rs'000.	Amount Rs'000.
Cost of investment: (A)	562.0	184.0
Company W's share of net assets as on the date of Acquisition / investment represented by :		
- Share capital (200000 x 80%) and	160.0	
- Share capital (200000 x 40%)		80.0
- Bonus issue (200000 x 80%)	160.0	
- Capital profit	400.0	96.8
- Goodwill on acquisition written off(562000 – (160000+400000)	2.0	-
Total (B)	722.0	176.8
Goodwill / (capital reserve) to Consolidated B/S	(160.0)	7.2

7. Statement of Inter-company transactions between W and O

Particulars	Amount Rs'000.
Total unrealised profits (20000 x 25/125)	4.0
Extent of investing company W's interest (40% of 4000)	1.6

8. Statement of Reserves

Particulars		Amount Rs'000.
Closing balance of W Ltd		1050.0
Add: Share in post-acquisition profits of H (WN2)		256.0
Dividend from H		24.0
Less: Dividend payable 2009-10		(65.0)
		1265.0
Add: Share of profit from Associate O (88.4 - 1.6)	86.80	92.8
Share of dividend from O (15000 X 40%)	6.00	
Less: Goodwill on acquisition of H written off (WN3)		(2.0)
Total reserves to Consolidated Balance Sheet		1355.8

Q.8.2. Consolidation of Parent, one subsidiary, one Jointly controlled entity and one associate

---

Balance Sheet of four companies P Ltd , S a subsidiary, J a jointly controlled entity and A an associate as on 31.03.12 are as under: (Rs Lakhs)

Assets	% holding	P Ltd	S	J	A
Investment in S	80%	800			

Investment in J	40%		600				
Investment in A	40%		600				
Fixed Assets			1000	800	1400	1000	
Current Assets			2200	3300	3250	3650	
		TOTAL	5200	4100	4650	4650	
Liabilities							
Share capital (Re 1)			1000	400	800	800	
Retained earnings			4000	3400	3600	3600	
Creditors			200	300	250	250	
		TOTAL	5200	4100	4650	4650	

P ltd acquired shares in S many years ago, when S's retained earnings were Rs. 520 lakhs. P Ltd acquired shares in J at the beginning of the year, when J's retained earnings were Rs.400 lakhs.

P Ltd acquired shares in A on 1.4.11 when A's retained earnings were Rs.400 lakhs

The balance of goodwill related to S was written off three years ago. The value of goodwill in J remains unchanged.

Prepare consolidated Balance Sheet of P Ltd as on 31.3.09 as per AS 21, 23 and 27.

(CA Final : Nov 2009)

Solution

Working Notes

1. Computation of goodwill			Rs'lakhs	Rs'Lakhs
1.1 S (Subsidiary) - AS 21				
Cost of investment				800
Less: Paid up value of equity	80%	400	320	
Less : Share in pre-acquisition profit	80%	520	416	736
Goodwill				64
1.2 J (Jointly controlled entity) - AS 28				
Cost of investment				600
Less: Paid up value of equity	40%	800	320	
Less : Share in pre-acquisition profit	40%	400	160	480
Goodwill				120
1.3 A (Associate) - IAS 28				
Cost of investment				600
Less: Paid up value of equity	40%	800	320	
Less : Share in pre-acquisition profit	40%	400	160	480
Goodwill				120

1.4 Goodwill as per consolidated Balance Sheet		
S (Subsidiary) - AS 21		64
J (Jointly controlled entity) - AS 28		120
Less : Goodwill for subsidiary written off		-64
Goodwill as per consolidated Balance Sheet		120

2. Consolidated retained earnings		Rs'lakhs
P Ltd		4000
Share of post-acquisition profit of S	(3400-520) x 0.8	2304
Share of post-acquisition profit of J	(3600-400)x 0.4	1280
Share of post-acquisition profit of A	(3600-400)x 0.4	1280
Less: Goodwill of S written off		-64
Total consolidated retained earnings to consolidated Balance Sheet		8800

3. Minority Interest - S		
	400 X	
Share capital	0.2	80
Share in retained earnings	3400 X 0.2	680
Minority Interest to Balance Sheet		760

4. Investment in Associates - A		
Cost of investments (including goodwill Rs 120 lakhs)		600
Share of post-acquisition profit of A as above		1280
Investment in Associates to consolidated Balance Sheet		1880

Consolidated Balance Sheet of P Ltd as on 31.3.12

Particulars	Note no.	Amount Rs/Lakhs
I. Equity and Liabilities		
(1)Shareholder's funds		
(a) Share capital		1000
(b) Reserves and surplus (WN2)		8800
(2)Minority Interest (WN3)		760
(3)Non-current liabilities		
Long-term borrowing		-
(4)Current liabilities		
(a)Trade Payables(200 + 300 + 100)		600
Total		11160
II.Assets		
(1)Non-current Assets		
(a)Fixed Assets		
(i)Tangible Assets (1000+800+560)		2360

(ii)Intangible assets (WN1.4)		120
(b)Non-current Investments		-
Investment in Associates (WN4)		1880
(2)Current Assets (2200 +3300 + 1300)		6800
Total		**11160**

Q.8.3: Consolidation with Parent and one subsidiary and one jointly controlled entity

Air Ltd, a listed company, entered into an expansion programme on 1st October 2009. On that date the company purchased from Bag Ltd its investments in two Private Limited companies. The purchase was of

a) entire share capital of Cold Ltd and
b) 50% of the share capital of Dry Ltd

Both the investments were previously owned by Bag Ltd. After acquisition by Air Ltd, Dry Ltd was to be run by Air Ltd and Bag Ltd as a jointly controlled entity.

Air Ltd makes its financial statements up to 30th September each year. The terms of acquisition were:
Cold Ltd
The total consideration was based on price earnings ratio (P/E) of 12 applied to the reported profit of Rs.20 lakhs of Cold Ltd for the year 30th September 2009. The consideration was settled by Air Ltd issuing 8% debentures for Rs.140 lakhs (at par) and the balance by a new issue of Re.1. equity shares, based on its market value of Rs.2.50 each.

Dry Ltd
The market value of Dry Ltd on 1st October 2009 was mutually agreed as Rs.375 lakhs. Air Ltd satisfied its share of 50% of this amount by issuing 75 lakhs Re.1 equity shares (market value Rs.2.50 each) to Bag Ltd.

Air Ltd has not recorded in its books the acquisition o the above investments or the discharge of the consideration.

The summarized statements of financial position of the three entities at 30th September 2010 are: (Rs'0000

Particulars	Air Ltd	Cold Ltd	Dry Ltd
Assets			
Tangible assets	34260	27000	21060
Inventories	9640	7200	18640
Debtors	11200	5060	4620
Cash	-	3410	40
Total	55100	42670	44360
Liabilities			

Equity capital of Re.1 each	10000	20000	25000
Retained earnings	20800	15000	4500
Trade and other payables	17120	5270	14100
Overdraft	1540	-	-
Provision for taxes	5640	2400	700
Total	55100	42670	44360

The following information is relevant:
a) The book values of the net assets of Cold Ltd and Dry Ltd on the date of acquisition were considered to be a reasonable approximation to their fair values.
b) The current profits of Cold Ltd and Dry Ltd for the year ended 30th September 2010 were Rs.80 lakhs and Rs.20 lakhs respectively. No dividends were paid by any of the companies during the year.
c) Dry Ltd, the jointly controlled entity, is to be accounted for using proportional consolidation, in accordance with AS 27 "Interest in Joint venture".
d) Goodwill in respect of the acquisition of Dry Ltd has been impaired by Rs.10 lakhs at 30th September 2010. Gain on acquisition, if any, will be separately accounted.

Prepare the consolidated Balance Sheet of Air Ltd and its subsidiaries as at 30th September 2010. *(CA Final Nov 2010)*

Solution

Consolidated Balance Sheet of Air Ltd and its subsidiary Cold Ltd
and Jointly controlled Dry Ltd
as on 30th September 2010

Particulars	Note no.	Amount Rs'000
I. **Equity and Liabilities**		
(1)Shareholder's funds		
(a) Share capital	1	21500
(b) Reserves and surplus	2	49050
(2)Non-current liabilities		
Long-term borrowing	3	15540
(3)Current liabilities		
(a)Trade Payables(17120 + 5270+7050)		29440
(b) Short term provisions	4	8420
Total		123950
II. **Assets**		
(1)Non-current Assets		
(a)Fixed Assets		
(i)Tangible Assets (34260+27000+10530)		71790
(ii)Intangible Assets (WN4)		4000
(b)Non-current Investments		-
(2)Current Assets:		
(a)Inventories (9640+7200+9320)		26160

(b)Trade Receivables (11200+5060+2310)			18570
(c)Cash and cash equivalents		5	3430
	Total		123950

Notes on Accounts

S/L No	Particulars	Amount (Rs'000)	Amount (Rs'000)
1.	Share capital Equity capital (Rs.10000 + 40000 +7500) (Out of the above 11500 shares have been issued for consideration other than cash)		21500
2	Reserves and surplus Retained earnings (WN4) Capital reserve (WN5) Securities premium	28800 3000 17250	49050
3.	Long term borrowings 8% Debentures Overdraft	14000 1540	15540
4.	Short term provisions Provision for taxes (5640 + 2400 + 380)		8420
5.	Cash and cash equivalents Cash and bank (3410 + 20)		3430

Working Notes

1. Shareholding pattern

Particulars	Cold Ltd	Dry Ltd
Air Ltd	100%	50%
Minority	nil	

2. Statement of analysis of profit (Rs'000)

Particulars	Cold Ltd	Dry Ltd
Retained earnings as per Balance Sheet	15000	4500
Less: Current profit	8000	2000
Capital profit	7000	2500

3. Statement of apportionment of profit (Rs'000)

Particulars	Cold Ltd	Dry Ltd
Current profit	8000	2000
Air Ltd 100% / 50%	8000	1000
Minority nil	nil	

Capital profit	7000	2500
Air Ltd 100 % / 50%	7000	1250
Minority nil	Nil	

4. Statement of cost of control / capital reserve

Particulars	Cold Ltd	Dry Ltd
Cost of investment (A)	24000	18750
Share of net assets		
- share capital	20000	12500
- capital profit	7000	1250
- Total (B)	27000	13750
Goodwill / (capital reserve)	(3000)	5000
Less Goodwill impaired		1000
Goodwill / (Capital reserve) to consolidated Balance Sheet	(3000)	4000

5. Statement of retained earnings of Air Ltd

Particulars		Rs'000
Air Limited balance		20800
Add: Share of current profits of		
Cold Ltd (WN3)	8000	
Dry Ltd (WN3)	1000	
Impairment of goodwill	(1000)	8000
To consolidated Balance Sheet		**28800**

Q.8.4. Consolidation with Parent and one subsidiary and Jointly controlled entities

The Balance Sheets of three companies Sun Ltd, Moon Ltd and Light Ltd as at 31st March 2010 are given below:

Liabilities	Sun Ltd Rs.	Moon Ltd Rs.	Light Ltd Rs.	Assets	Sun Ltd Rs.	Moon Ltd Rs.	Light Ltd Rs.
Share capital (Shares of Rs.10 each)	150000	100000	60000	Fixed Assets	70000	120000	103000
				Investments			
Reserves	50000	40000	30000	(at cost)			
Profit & Loss				Shares in :			
A/c	60000	50000	40000	Moon Ltd	90000		
Sundry				Light Ltd	40000		
creditors	–	10000	8000	Light Ltd	–	50000	
				Stock in			
				trade	40000	30000	20000
				Debtors	20000	25000	30000
				Due from –			
				Moon Ltd	12000		
				Light Ltd	8000		

				Cash in hand	10000	10000	10000
	290000	235000	163000		290000	235000	163000

a) Sun Ltd held 8000 shares of Moon Ltd and 1800 shares of Light Ltd
b) Moon Ltd held 3600 shares of Light Ltd
c) All investments were made on 1st July 2009
d) The following balances were there on 1st July 2009

	Moon Ltd Rs	Light Ltd Rs.
Reserves	25000	15000
Profit and Loss A/c	20000	25000

e) Moon Ltd invoiced goods to Sun Ltd for Rs.4000 at a cost plus 25% in December 2009. The closing stock of Sun Ltd includes such goods valued at Rs.5000.

f) Light Ltd sold to Moon Ltd an equipment costing Rs.24000 at a profit of 25% on selling price on 1st January 2010. Depreciation at 10% per annum was provided by Moon Ltd on this equipment.

g) Sun Ltd proposes dividend at 10%

Prepare the consolidated Balance Sheet of the group as at 31st March 2010. Workings should be part of the answer. (*CA Final: May 2011*)

Solution

Consolidated Balance Sheet of Sun Ltd and its subsidiaries Moon Ltd and Light Ltd
As on 31st March 2010

Particulars	Note no.	Amount Rs
I. Equity and Liabilities		
(1)Shareholder's funds		
(a) Share capital	1	150000
(b) Reserves and surplus	2	172580
(2)Minority Interest	3	53620
(3)Non-current liabilities		
Long-term borrowing		-
(4)Current liabilities		
(a)Trade Payables	4	90000
(b) Other current liabilities	5	15000
Total		**481200**
II. Assets		
(1)Non-current Assets		
(a)Fixed Assets		
(i)Tangible Assets	6	285200
(ii)Intangible Assets		4000

(b)Non-current Investments			-
(2)Current Assets:			
(a)Inventories		7	89000
(b)Trade Receivables		8	75000
(c)Cash and cash equivalents		9	32000
	Total		481200

Notes on Accounts

S/L No	Particulars	Amount (Rs)	Amount (Rs)
1.	**Share Capital** Issued, subscribed and paid-up 15000 equity shares of Rs.10 each fully paid up		150000
2	**Reserves and surplus** Capital reserve (WN4) Other reserves (WN9) Profit & Loss Account (WN9)	26000 73700 72880	172580
3.	**Minority interest** Moon Ltd (WN5) Light Ltd(WN5)	41400 12220	53620
4.	**Trade Payables** Sun Ltd Moon Ltd Light Ltd	30000 35000 25000	90000
5.	**Other current liabilities** Proposed dividend		15000
6.	**Tangible Assets (WN7)** Sun Ltd Moon Ltd 120000 Less: Unrealised Profit (WN5) (7800) Light Ltd	70000 112200 103000	285200
7.	**Inventories(WN6)** Sun Ltd 40000 Less: Unrealised Profit (1000) Moon Ltd Light Ltd	39000 30000 20000	89000
8.	**Trade Receivable** Sun Ltd	20000	

	Moon Ltd	25000	
	Light Ltd	30000	75000
9.	Cash and cash equivalents		
	Sun Ltd	10000	
	Moon Ltd	10000	
	Light Ltd	10000	
	Add: Cash in transit (WN8)	2000	32000

Working Notes

1. Statement of shareholding pattern

Particulars	No of shares	Shareholding %
Moon Ltd:		
Sun Ltd	8000	80%
Minority	2000	20%
Total	10000	100%
Light Ltd:		
Sun Ltd	1800	30%
Moon Ltd	3600	60%
Minority	600	10%
Total	6000	100%

2. Statement of analysis of profits of Light Ltd

Particulars	--Pre-acquisition-- Capital profit Rs.	----------Post-acquisition------------ Revenue Reserve Rs.	Revenue Profit Rs.
Reserve on 1.7.2009	15000	-	-
Profit & Loss A/c on 1.7.2009	25000	-	-
Increase in Reserves	-	15000	-
Increase in profit	-	-	15000
Total	40000	15000	15000
Minority Interest (10%)	4000	1500	1500
	36000	13500	13500
Share of Sun Ltd (30%)	12000	4500	4500
Share of Moon Ltd (60%)	24000	9000	9000

3. Statement of analysis of profits of Moon Ltd

Particulars	--Pre-acquisition- Capital profit Rs.	----------Post-acquisition-------- Revenue Reserve Rs.	Revenue Profit Rs.
Reserve on 1.7.2011	25000		

Profit & Loss A/c on 1.7.2011	20000		
Increase in reserve		15000	
Increase in profit			30000
Moon Ltd's share from Light Ltd:			
- Undistributed profit(WN2)		9000	9000
Total	45000	24000	39000
Sun Ltd (80%)	36000	19200	31200
Minority (20%)	9000	4800	7800

4. Statement of Cost of control /goodwill /capital reserve (Rs)

Particulars	Sun Ltd in Moon Ltd (80%)	Sun Ltd in Light Ltd (30%)	Moon Ltd in Light Ltd (60%)
Cost of investment (A)	90000	40000	50000
Share of net assets			
- Share capital	80000	18000	36000
- Capital profits	36000	12000	24000
- Total (B)	116000	30000	60000
Goodwill / capital reserve (A − B)	(26000)	10000	(10000)
Total Capital reserve to consolidated Balance Sheet		(26000)	

5. Statement of Minority Interest (Rs)

Particulars	Moon Ltd 20%	Light Ltd 10%
Share capital	20000	6000
Share of capital profits	9000	4000
Share of revenue reserves	4800	1500
Share of revenue profits	7800	1500
Total	41600	13000
Less: Share of unrealised profits on		
- Stock	(200)	
- Equipment		(780)
Total Minority Interest	41400	12220
Combined Minority interest to consolidated financial statement		53620

6. Statement of inter-company transaction balances

Particulars	Rs.	Rs.
Stock		
Aggregate balance (40000 + 30000 + 20000)		90000
Less: unrealised profits on:	800	
- Sun Ltd (5000 x 25/125 x 80%)		
- Minority interest (5000 x 25/125 x 80%)	200	
		(1000)
Net to consolidated Balance Sheet		89000

7. Statement of inter-company transaction balances

Particulars	Rs.	Rs.
Equipment		
Aggregate balance (70000 + 120000 + 103000)		293000
Less: unrealised profits on:		
- Cost of machinery	24000	
- Profit element (24000 x 25/75)	8000	
- Less: depreciation provided on profit Element for 3 months @ 10% (8000 x 10% x 3/12)	200	7800
Net to consolidated Balance Sheet		285200
Share of unrealised profit : Rs.7800		
Sun Ltd (30%) : Rs.2340		
Moon Ltd (60%) : Rs.4680		
Minority interest (10%) : Rs. 780	Rs. 7800	

8. Statement of Inter-company owings (Rs)

Particulars	Sun Ltd	Moon Ltd	Light Ltd
Debit balances			
- Due from Moon Ltd	12000		
- Due from Light Ltd	8000		
Capital balances			
- Due to Sun Ltd		(10000)	(8000)
Less: Intercompany owings	(18000)	10000	8000
Cash in transit	2000	-	-

9. Statement of Reserves and Profit & Loss

Particulars	Reserves Rs.	Profit & Loss A/c Rs.
Sun Ltd balances	50000	60000
Share of post-acquisition profits:		
n) Sun Ltd from Moon Ltd	19200	31200
ii) Sun Ltd from Light Ltd	4500	4500
Total	73700	95700
Less: Share of unrealised profits on		
- Stock – Sun Ltd from Moon Ltd (5000 X 25/125 X 80%)		(800)
- Equipment – Sun Ltd from Light Ltd (7800 X 90%)		(7020)
Less : Proposed dividend		(15000)
Total to Consolidated Balance Sheet	73700	72880

Q.8.5. Consolidation of Parent, one subsidiary, one Jointly controlled entity and one associate

---

A Ltd owned 80% of B Ltd, 35% of C Ltd and 30% of D Ltd. C Ltd is a jointly controlled entity and D Ltd is an associate. Balance Sheet of all four companies as on 31.03.2014 are:

Particulars	A Ltd	B Ltd	C Ltd	D Ltd
Liabilities				
Equity share of RE.1/- each fully paid up	1,500	600	1,200	1,200
Retained earnings	6,000	5,100	5,400	5,400
Creditors	300	450	380	375
Total	7,800	6,150	6,980	6,975
Assets				
Fixed Assets	1,500	1,200	2,100	1,500
Investment in B Ltd	1,200			
Investment in C Ltd	900			
Investment in D Ltd	900			
Current Assets	3,300	4,950	4,880	5,475
Total	7,800	6,150	6,980	6,975

A Ltd acquired shares in
(i)B Ltd many years ago, when the company had retained earnings of Rs.780 lakhs
(ii)C Ltd at the beginning of the year, when the company had retained earnings of Rs.600 lakhs
(iii)D Ltd on 01.04.2013, when the company had retained earnings of Rs.600 lakhs
The balance of goodwill relating to B Ltd had been written off three years ago. The value of goodwill in C Ltd remains unchanged.
Prepare the consolidated Balance Sheet of A Ltd as on 31.03.2014 as per AS-21, AS-23 and AS-27. *(CMA Final: June 2014)*

Solution

Working Notes

1. Computation of goodwill			Rs'lakhs	Rs'Lakhs
1.1 B (Subsidiary) - AS 21				
Cost of investment				1200
Less: Paid up value of equity	80%	600	480	
Less : Share in pre-acquisition profit	80%	780	624	1104
Goodwill				96
1.2 C(Jointly controlled entity) – AS27				
Cost of investment				900
Less: Paid up value of equity	35%	1200	420	
Less : Share in pre-acquisition profit	35%	600	210	630
Goodwill				270
1.3 D (Associate) - AS 23				
Cost of investment				900

Less: Paid up value of equity	30%	1200	360	
Less : Share in pre-acquisition profit	30%	600	180	540
Goodwill				360

1.4 Goodwill as per consolidated Balance Sheet

B (Subsidiary) - AS 21	96
C(Jointly controlled entity) - AS 28	270
Less : Goodwill for subsidiary written off	-96
Goodwill as per consolidated Balance Sheet	270

2. Consolidated retained earnings | Rs'lakhs |

A Ltd		6000
Share of post-acquisition profit of B	(5100-780) x 0.80	3456
Share of post-acquisition profit of C	(5400-600) x 0.35	1680
Share of post-acquisition profit of D	(5400-600) x 0.30	1440
Less: Goodwill of S written off		-96
Total consolidated retained earnings to consolidated Balance Sheet		12480

3. Minority Interest – B

Share capital	600 X 0.2	120
Share in retained earnings	5100 X 0.2	1020
Minority Interest to Balance Sheet		1140

4. Investment in Associates – D

Cost of investments (including goodwill Rs 120 lakhs)	900
Share of post-acquisition profit of A as above	1440
Investment in Associates to consolidated Balance Sheet	2340

Consolidated Balance Sheet of P Ltd as on 31.3.12

Particulars	Note no.	Amount Rs/Lakhs
II. **Equity and Liabilities**		
(1)Shareholder's funds		
(a) Share capital		**1500**
(b) Reserves and surplus (WN2)		**12480**
(2)Minority Interest (WN3)		**1140**
(3)Non-current liabilities		
Long-term borrowing		-
(4)Current liabilities		
(a)Trade Payables(300 + 450 + 133)		**883**

		Total		16003
II.	Assets			
	(1)Non-current Assets			
	(a)Fixed Assets			
	(i)Tangible Assets (1500+1200+0.35x2100)			3435
	(ii)Intangible assets (WN1.4)			270
	(b)Non-current Investments			-
	Investment in Associates (WN4)			2340
	(2)Current Assets (3300 +4950 + 0.35x 4880)			9958
		Total		16003

Q.8.6: Please provide a comparative analysis of treatment of subsidiary, associate, Joint ventures and investments?

S/L	Particulars	Subsidiary	Joint Arrangement	Associate	Investment
1.	*Method*	Full consolidation	Proportionate Consolidation as per AS 27. However, as per Ind AS 28, equity method ; proportionate consolidation not permitted. Joint arrangement may be categorised into Joint Operations and Joint Ventures	Equity method	Cost method
2.	*Indian Accounting Standards (Ind AS)*	Ind AS 110	Ind AS 111	Ind AS 28	Ind AS 109
3.	*Accounting standard (AS)*	AS 21	AS 27	AS 23	AS 13
4.	*Shareholding pattern*	>50%	Joint operations – but 50% or less	20% - 50% but not JCE	<20 % but not Joint operations
5.	*Analysis of pre-acquisition reserve*	a)Parent b)Minority/NCI	Venturer's share	Investor's share	Not applicable
6.	*Analysis of post-acquisition reserve*	a)Parent b)Minority/NCI	Venturer's share	Investor's share	Not applicable
7.	*Cost of control/*	(a)Net cost of	(a)Net cost of	(a)Net cost of	Not

	Goodwill/ Capital reserve	investment less (b)Parent's share of net assets (a)>(b)=goodwill (a)<(b)=capital reserve	investment less (b)venturer's share of net assets (a)>(b)=goodwill (a)<(b)=capital reserve	investment less (b)investor's share of associate's net assets (a)>(b)=goodwill (a)<(b)=capital Reserve	applicable
8.	Minority interest(Non-controlling interest)	a) Minority share capital b)pre-acquisition profit/loss c)post-acquisition profit / loss	Not applicable	Not applicable	Not applicable
9.	Interco owings	Eliminate in full	Eliminate to the extent of venturers interest	Not applicable	Not applicable
10.	Unrealised profits on intra-group transactions	Eliminate in full	Eliminate to the extent of venturers interest	Eliminate to the extent of investor's interest	Not applicable
11.	Investment in associates in Consolidated Balance Sheet	Not applicable	Not applicable	Cost of investment (A) Add: share of post-acquisition profit (B) Less: share of dividends out of pre-acquisition profits, received from the associate (C) Less: share of unrealised profit on intra-group transactions (D) Add: share of net profit on revaluation of fixed assets (E) Carrying amount of investment (A+B-C-D+E) = F	Cost of investment less pre-acquisition dividend
12.	Post-acquisition reserves for consolidated balance sheet	Balance of reserves and surplus (A) Add: share of post–acquisition	Balance of reserves and surplus (A) Add: share of post–acquisition profit (B)	Balance of reserves and surplus (A) Add: share of post–acquisition	Not applicable

		profit (B) Less: Dividends out of pre-acquisition profits (C) Less: Share of unrealised profit on intra-group transactions (D) Closing balance of reserves and surplus (A+B-C-D)=(E)	profit (B) Less: Dividends out of pre-acquisition profits (C) Less: Share of unrealised profit on intra-group transactions (D) Closing balance of reserves and surplus (A+B-C-D)=(E)	

profit (B)
Less: Dividends out of pre-acquisition profits (C)
Less: Share of unrealised profit on intra - group transactions (D)
Closing balance of reserves and surplus
(A+B-C-D)=(E)

Chapter 9: Advanced problems on consolidation of financial statements

Q.9.1.

The income statements and summarised statements of changes in equity of Alpha, Beta and Gamma for the year ended 31 March 2011 are given below:

Income Statements	Alpha Rs.'000	Beta Rs.'000	Gamma Rs.'000
Revenue	4,70,000	4,34,000	2,26,000
Cost of sales	(2,56,000)	(2,18,000)	(1,76,000)
Gross profit	2,14,000	2,16,000	50,000
Distribution costs	(18,000)	(17,000)	(15,000)
Administrative expenses	(19,000)	(16,000)	(17,000)
Investment income (Note 5)	37,300	Nil	Nil
Finance cost (Note 6)	(68,000)	(65,000)	(44,000)
Profit/(loss) before tax	146,300	118,000	(26,000)
Income tax expense	(41,000)	(33,000)	Nil
Profit/(loss) for the year	105,300	85,000	(26,000)

Summarised Statements of Changes in Equity

Balance at 1 April 2010	540,000	390,000	192,000
Comprehensive income for the year	105,300	85,000	(26,000)
Dividends paid on 31 December 2010	(52,000)	(40,000)	Nil
Balance at 31 March 2011	593,300	435,000	166,000

Note 1 – purchase of shares in Beta

On 1 October 2009 Alpha purchased 75 million of the 100 million equity shares in Beta. Details of the share purchase were as follows:

– Alpha issued two new equity shares for every three shares acquired in Beta. On 1 October 2009 the market value of an Alpha share was Rs.6 and the market value of a Beta share was Rs.3·20.

– Alpha agreed to make an additional cash payment of Rs.1 for every share acquired in Beta to be paid on 30 September 2011. This payment is contingent on the profits of Beta exceeding a cumulative target in the two-year period ending 30 September 2011. The fair value of this contingent payment was Rs.55 million on 1 October 2009. The fair value had risen to Rs.58 million by 31 March 2010 and to Rs.64 million by 31 March 2011. The directors of Alpha correctly accounted for this contingent consideration in its financial statements for the year ended 31 March 2010 but no changes have been made to the carrying value of the contingent consideration since 31 March 2010.

– Alpha incurred legal and professional costs of Rs.5 million connected with the acquisition; Rs.2·4 million of these costs related to the cost of issuing shares. Alpha correctly accounted for these acquisition costs in its financial statements for the year ended 31 March 2010.

Alpha decided to value the non-controlling interest in Beta at the date of acquisition at fair value in its consolidated financial statements. The market value of a Beta share at that date was used to calculate the fair value of the non-controlling interest.

The equity of Beta as shown in its own financial statements at 1 October 2009 was Rs.300 million. At that date the property, plant and equipment (PPE) of Beta had a carrying value of

Rs.240 million and a fair value of Rs.280 million.

The estimated future useful economic life of the PPE of Beta was four years. from 1 October 2009. No disposals of PPE occurred between 1 October 2009 and 31 March 2011.

On 1 October 2009 the directors. estimated that the internally generated brand name of Beta had a fair value of Rs.30 million and a future useful economic life of 30 years.

All depreciation and amortisation is charged on a monthly basis and presented in cost of sales.

Note 2 – impairment review

On 31 March 2010 and 31 March 2011 the goodwill on consolidation of Beta was reviewed for impairment. No impairment of the goodwill was necessary as a result of the review on 31 March 2010. Beta is regarded as a single cash generating unit for impairment purposes and at 31 March 2011 its recoverable amount was estimated as Rs.550 million. Any impairment of goodwill is charged to cost of sales.

Note 3 – purchase of shares in Gamma

On 1 October 2010 Alpha purchased 40% of the equity shares of Gamma for Rs.75 million in cash. This purchase allowed Alpha to exercise a significant influence over Gamma. No material differences between the market value and the book value of the net assets of Gamma were apparent at the date of the share purchase. On 31 March 2011 an impairment review was conducted resulting in an impairment required of Rs.1·8 million.

Note 4 – inter-company sales

Beta supplies products to Alpha and Gamma. Sales of the products to Alpha and Gamma during the year ended 31 March 2011 were as follows (all sales were made at a mark-up of 33 1/3% on cost):

– Sales to Alpha Rs.18 million.

– Sales to Gamma Rs.12 million.

At 31 March 2011 and 31 March 2010 the inventories of Alpha and Gamma included the following amounts in respect of goods purchased from Beta.

	Amount in inventory at	
	31 March 2011 Rs.000	31 March 2010 Rs.000
Alpha	3,600	2,100
Gamma	2,700	Nil

Note 5 – Equity investments

At 1 April 2010 Alpha had two equity investments that it designated as fair value through other comprehensive income in accordance with Ind AS 109 *Financial Instruments*. At the date of acquisition:

Name	Original cost Rs.'000	Fair value at 31st March 2010 Rs.'000	Fair value at 31st March 2010 Rs.'000
Delta	12,000	15,000	n/a
Epsilon	11,000	14,000	15,400

On 31 January 2011 Alpha disposed of its investment in Delta for Rs.19·5 million and showed a profit on sale of Rs.4·5 million (Rs.19·5 million – Rs.15 million) as part of investment income. Apart from recording the receipt of dividend income no other entries have been made in the financial statements for the year ended 31 March 2011 regarding the

investment in Epsilon. Both investments had been correctly treated in the financial statements for the year ended 31 March 2010.

Note 6 – Convertible notes

On 1 April 2010 Alpha issued 300 million loan notes of Rs.1 per note at par. The loan notes entitled the holders to an interest payment of 5 paise per note, payable annually in arrears. The loan notes are repayable at par on 31 March 2015. As an alternative to repayment the holders. can elect to convert the notes into equity shares in Alpha. On 1 April 2010 investors. in non-convertible notes would expect an annual return of 8%. You are given the following discount factors:

Discount rate	Present value of Rs.1 payable	
	At the end of year 5	Cumulatively at the end of years. 1–5
5%	78·4 paise	Rs.4·33
8%	68·1 paise	Rs.3·99

On 1 April 2010 the directors. of Alpha recorded a loan liability of Rs.300 million and in the year ended 31 March 2011 a finance cost of Rs.15 million (300 million x 5 cents) in respect of these notes.

Note 7 – Environmental damage

During the year ended 31 March 2011 Alpha began production at three newly acquired factories. The normal production process at each factory results in environmental damage. Alpha has a policy of only rectifying such damage when legally required to do so. Details of the damage caused at the three sites up to and including 31 March 2011 are as follows:

Factory	Damage caused by 31 March 2011 (Rs.'000)	Clean-up legislation in place at 31 March 2011?
A	3000	Yes
B	1000	No
C	2000	No but legislation passed since year end with retrospective effect

No provision for environmental damage has been made in the financial statements. Any appropriate provision should be reported as part of cost of sales.

Required:

(a) Prepare the consolidated statement of Profit & Loss for Alpha for the year ended 31 March 2011;

(b) Prepare the summarised consolidated statement of changes in equity for Alpha for the year ended 31 March 2011. Your summarised statement should include a column for the non-controlling interest. Ignore deferred tax.(ACCA UK - Adapted)

Solution

(a) Consolidated statement of Profit & Loss and other comprehensive income for the year ended 31 March 2011

	Rs.'000
Revenue (W1)	886,000
Cost of sales (balancing figure)	(482,145)
Gross profit (W2)	403,855
Distribution costs (18,000 + 17,000)	(35,000)

Administrative expenses (19,000 + 16,000)	(35,000)
Investment income (W6)	2,800
Finance cost (W7)	(139,132)
Share of losses of associate (W9)	(7,000)
Profit before tax	190,523
Income tax expense (41,000 + 33,000)	(74,000)
Net profit for the year	116,523
Other comprehensive income (W10)	5,900
Comprehensive income for the year	122,423
Net profit attributable to	
Non-controlling interest (W11)	17,464
Controlling interest	99,059
Net profit for the year	116,523
Comprehensive income attributable to	
Non-controlling interest	17,464
Controlling interest	104,959
Comprehensive income for the year	122,423

(b) Consolidated statement of changes in equity for the year ended 31 March 2011

	Controlling interest	Non-controlling interest	Total
	Rs.'000	Rs.'000	Rs.'000
Balance at 1 April 2010 (W12 & W13)	602,850	101,125	703,975
Comprehensive income for the year	104,959	17,464	122,423
Equity component of convertible bonds (W14)	35,850		35,850
Dividends	(52.000)	(10,000)	(62,000)
Balance at 31 March 2011	691,659	108,589	800,248

WORKINGS
Working 1 – revenue

	Rs.000
Alpha + Beta	904,000
Sales from Alpha – Beta (see note 1)	(18,000)
	886,000

Working 2 – gross profit

	Rs.'000
Alpha + Beta	430,000
Environmental provision (3,000 + 2,000	(5,000)
Unrealised profit adjustments:	
Beta: (1/4 (3,600 – 2,100))	(375)
Gamma: (1/4 x 2,700 x 40%)	(270)
Extra depreciation (W3)	(11,000)
Change in the fair value of contingent consideration	

(Rs.64 million – Rs.58 million – see note 2)	(6,000)
Impairment of goodwill (W4)	(3,500)
	403,855

Note 1
Ind AS 28 – *Investments in associates* – requires partial elimination of unrealised profits on transactions between associates and group entities. Profits can only be included to the extent that they relate to the non-group share. This means that the group share of such profits is eliminated and an adjustment of Rs.270,000 is required to profit in this case (see working 2 above). The Ind AS does not specify exactly how such an adjustment should be reported in the consolidated statement of comprehensive income. The approach taken here is to make no adjustment to revenue whatever. Given the required adjustment to gross profit of Rs.270,000, this would alter cost of sales by an equal and opposite amount.

An alternative approach would be to reduce consolidated revenue by the group share of the revenue that relates to the inventory that is unsold by Gamma at the year-end. Given the required adjustment to gross profit of Rs.210,000, the adjustment to cost of sales follows as the balancing figure.

Note 2
The change in fair value of the contingent consideration could have been shown in other sections of the statement of comprehensive income – for example as an administration cost.

Working 3 – extra depreciation and amortisation

	Rs.000
Depreciation of PPE – ¼ x (Rs.280 million – Rs.240 million)	10,000
Amortisation of brand – 1/30 x Rs.30 million	1,000
	11,000

Working 4 – impairment of goodwill on acquisition of Beta

	Rs.'000
Carrying value of Beta in the consolidated financial statements at 31 March 2011:	
Per own financial statements	435,000
Fair value adjustments:	
PPE – (Rs.280 million – Rs.240 million) x (2·5/4)	25,000
Brand – Rs.30 million x (28·5/30)	28,500
Goodwill (W5)	65,000
	553,500
Recoverable amount	(550,000)
Impairment of goodwill	3,500

Working 5 – goodwill on acquisition of Beta

	Rs.'000	Rs.'000
Fair value of consideration given:		
Share exchange – 75,000 x 2/3 x Rs.6	300,000	
Contingent consideration	55,000	

Acquisition costs	nil	355,000 (A)
Fair value of non-controlling interest – 25,000 x Rs.3·20		80,000 (B)
Fair value of net assets of Beta at 1 October 2009: Per own financial statements	300,000	
Fair value adjustment – PPE (Rs.280 million – Rs.240 million)	40,000	
Fair value adjustment – brand	30,000	(370,000)(C)
Goodwill (A + B – C)		65,000

Working 6 – investment income

	Rs.'000
Alpha + Beta	37,300
Dividend received from Beta (75% x 40,000)	(30,000)
Profit on disposal recorded to be treated in accordance with IFRS. 9 (App B para 5.12)	(4,500)
In consolidated statement of comprehensive income	2,800

Working 7 – finance costs

	Rs.000
Alpha + Beta	133,000
Finance cost of convertible loan notes incorrectly recorded by Alpha	(15,000)
Correct finance cost of convertible loan notes (W8)	21,132
In consolidated statement of comprehensive income	139,132

Working 8 – finance costs of convertible loan notes

	Rs.000
Liability element of compound financial instrument at 1 April 2010 (15,000 x Rs.3·99) + (300,000 x Rs.0·681)	264,150
So finance cost at 8% (264,150 x 0·08)	21,132

Working 9 – share of losses of associate

	Rs.000
Loss after tax of Gamma	(26,000)
(26,000) x 40% x 6/12 equals	(5,200)
Impairment of investment	(1,800)
	(7,000)

Working 10 – other comprehensive income

	Rs.'000
Gain on revaluation of investment in Epsilon	1,400
Profit on disposal recorded to be treated in accordance with Ind AS 109	4,500
	5,900

Working 11 – *non-controlling interest in Beta*

	Rs.'000
Net profit of Beta	85,000
Unrealised profit on intercompany sales (375 + 270) (W2)	(645)
Extra depreciation and amortisation (W3)	(11,000)
Impairment of goodwill of Beta (W4)	(3,500)
	69,855
Non-controlling interest (25%)	17,464

Working 12 – consolidated equity at 1 April 2010

	Rs.'000
Alpha	540,000
Beta – post acquisition per own records (390,000 – 300,000)	90,000
Extra depreciation and amortisation (11,000 (W3) x 0·5)	(5,500)
	84,500
Group share (75%)	63,375
Unrealised profit on opening inventory (1/4 x 2,100	(525)
	602,850

Working 13 – *non-controlling interest in opening equity of Beta*

	Rs.'000	Rs.'000
Fair value of non-controlling interest at date of acquisition (W5)		80,000
Consolidated post-acquisition increase in equity from date of acquisition to start of the period (W12)	84,500	
Non-controlling interest (25%)		21,125
Total		101,125

Working 14 – *equity element of convertible bonds*

	Rs.'000
Total issue proceeds	300,000
Liability component (W8)	(264,150)
Equity component	35,850

9.2.

Alpha holds investments in Beta and Gamma. The Balance Sheets of the three entities at 30 September 2011 were as follows:

	Alpha Rs.'000	Beta Rs.'000	Gamma Rs.'000
ASSETS			
Non-current assets :			
Property, plant and equipment (Note 1)	210,000	165,000	120,000
Investments:			
– in Beta (Note 1)	180,000	Nil	Nil
– in Gamma (Note 3)	52,000	Nil	Nil
– in Sigma (Note 6)	15,000	nil	nil
	457,000	165,000	120,000

Current Assets:			
Inventories (Note 4)	65,000	36,000	29,000
Trade receivables (Note 5)	55,000	38,000	35,000
Cash and cash equivalents	12,000	7,000	9,000
Current Assets	132,000	81,000	73,000
Total Assets	589,000	246,000	193,000
EQUITY AND LIABILITIES			
Equity			
Share capital (Rs.1 shares)	180,000	100,000	60,000
Retained earnings	183,000	67,000	64,000
Other components of equity	90,000	5,000	Nil
Total equity	453,000	172,000	124,000
Non-current liabilities:			
Contingent consideration (Note 1)	20,000	Nil	Nil
Long-term borrowings (Note 8)	50,000	35,000	30,000
Deferred tax	15,000	9,000	12,000
Total non-current liabilities	85,000	44,000	42,000
Current liabilities:			
Trade and other payables	34,000	23,000	21,000
Short term borrowings	17,000	7,000	6,000
Total current liabilities	51,000	30,000	27,000
Total equity and liabilities	589,000	246,000	193,000

Note 1 – Alpha's investment in Beta

On 1 April 2010 Alpha acquired 80 million shares in Beta by means of a share exchange. Alpha issued one share for every two shares acquired in Beta. On 1 April 2010 the market value of an Alpha share was Rs.4 and the market value of a Beta share was Rs.1·80. The terms of the business combination provide for an additional cash payment to the former shareholders of Beta on 30 June 2012 based on its post-acquisition financial performance in the fiRs.t two years. since acquisition. The fair value of this additional payment was Rs.20 million on 1 April 2010. The post-acquisition performance of Beta was such that the fair value of this payment had increased to Rs.22 million by 30 September 2011. The investment in Beta and the non-current liabilities of Alpha at 30 September 2010 include Rs.20 million in respect of the additional payment due to be made on 30 June 2012.

On 1 April 2010 the individual financial statements of Beta showed the following reserves balances:
– Retained earnings Rs.41 million.
– Other components of equity Rs.3 million.

The directors. of Alpha carried out a fair value exercise to measure the identifiable assets and liabilities of Beta at 1 April 2010. The following matters. emerged:
– A property, having a carrying amount of Rs.50 million (depreciable amount Rs.30 million), had a fair value of Rs.70 million (depreciable amount Rs.33 million). The estimated future economic life of the depreciable amount of the property at 1 April 2010 was 30 years. This property was still held by Beta at 30 September 2011.
– Plant and equipment, having a carrying amount of Rs.60 million, had an estimated market value of Rs.64 million. The estimated future economic life of the plant at 1 April 2010 was four years. This plant was still held by Beta at 30 September 2011.

– Inventory, having a carrying amount of Rs.30 million, had an estimated market value of Rs.31 million. This entire inventory had been sold since 1 April 2010.

The fair value adjustments have not been reflected in the individual financial statements of Beta. In the consolidated financial statements the fair value adjustments will be regarded as temporary differences for the purposes of computing deferred tax. The rate of tax to apply to temporary differences (where required but see notes 3, 4, 6 and 7 below) is 20%.

It is the group policy to value the non-controlling interest in subsidiaries at the date of acquisition at fair value. The fair value of an equity share in Beta at 1 April 2010 can be used for this purpose.

Note 2 – Impairment reviews – Beta

On 1 April 2010 the directors of Alpha identified that Beta comprised five cash-generating units and allocated the goodwill arising on acquisition equally across each unit. No impairment of goodwill was apparent in the year ended 30 September 2010.

During the year ended 30 September 2011 four of the five cash-generating units performed very satisfactorily and no impairment of the goodwill allocated to these units had occurred. However the performance of the other unit was below expectations. During the impairment review carried out at 30 September 2011 assets (excluding goodwill) having a carrying amount in the consolidated financial statements of Rs.50 million were allocated to this unit. The recoverable amount of these assets was estimated at Rs.52 million.

Note 3 – Alpha's investment in Gamma

On 1 October 2010 Alpha paid Rs.52 million for 40% of the equity shares of Gamma. The retained earnings of Gamma on 1 October 2010 were Rs.60 million. You can ignore any deferred taxation implications of the investment by Alpha in Gamma. The investment in Gamma has not suffered any impairment since 1 October 2010.

Note 4 – Inter-company sale of inventories

The inventories of Beta and Gamma at 30 September 2011 included components purchased from Alpha during the year at a cost of Rs.16 million to Beta and Rs.10 million to Gamma. Alpha generated a gross profit margin of 25% on the supply of these components. You can ignore any deferred tax implications of the information in this note.

Note 5 – Trade receivables and payables

The trade receivables of Alpha included Rs.5 million receivable from Beta and Rs.4 million receivable from Gamma in respect of the purchase of components (see Note 4). The trade payables of Beta and Gamma included equivalent amounts payable to Alpha.

Note 6 – Alpha's investment in Sigma

Alpha's investment in Sigma does not give Alpha sole control, joint control or significant influence. The investment was purchased on 1 January 2011 for Rs.15 million. The investment was classified as fair value through other comprehensive income. The fair value of the investment in Sigma on 30 September 2011 was Rs.16 million. In the tax jurisdiction in which Alpha is located unrealised profits on the revaluation of equity investments are not subject to current tax. Any such profits are taxed only when the investment is sold.

Note 7 – Employees share option scheme

On 1 October 2009 Alpha granted 5,000 share options to 1,000 key employees. The options are due to vest on 30 September 2013 provided the employees remain in employment at 30 September 2013. On 1 October 2009 the directors. of Alpha estimated that 90% of the key employees would satisfy the vesting condition. Actual employee turnover was such that this estimate was revised to 92% on 30 September 2010 and 93% on 30 September 2011.

At 1 October 2009 the fair value of each share option was estimated to be Rs.1·20. This estimate was revised to Rs.1·25 on 30 September 2010 and Rs.1·28 on 30 September 2011. You can ignore the deferred tax implications of the information in this note.

Alpha correctly recognised this transaction in the financial statements for the year ended 30 September 2010.

However, they have made no additional adjustments in the financial statements for the year ended 30 September 2011.

Note 8 – Long-term borrowings

On 1 October 2010 Alpha issued 50 million loan notes of Rs.1 each at par. The annual interest payable on these notes is 5 cents per note, payable in arrears. The notes are redeemable at par on 30 September 2015 or convertible (at the option of the note-holders.) into equity shares on that date. On 1 October 2010 investors in loan notes with no conversion option would have required an annual rate of return of 8%. On 1 October 2010 the directors. of Alpha included Rs.50 million in long-term borrowings in respect of the loan notes. The actual interest paid of Rs.2·5 million was charged as a finance cost in Alpha's income statement for the year ended 30 September 2011.

Relevant discount factors. are as follows:

	5%	8%
Present value of Rs.1 payable at the end of year 5	78·4 cents	68·1 cents
Cumulative present value of Rs.1 payable at the end of years. 1-5	Rs.4·33	Rs.3·99

Note 9 – Modification of vehicles

On 1 January 2011 legislation was passed requiring Alpha to carry out modifications to its motor vehicles to enable harmful emissions to be reduced. The modifications should have been completed by 30 June 2011 at an estimated cost to Alpha of Rs.3 million. In fact by 30 September 2011 none of the vehicles had been modified although they continued to be used. It is likely that Alpha will be fined Rs.500,000 per month for the illegal use of the vehicles. The directors. of Alpha are uncertain exactly when they will carry out the modifications but they intend to do so sometime during the year ended 30 September 2012. They expect that a fine will become payable very shortly as legal action has commenced against Alpha.

Required:

Prepare the consolidated Balance Sheet of Alpha at 30 September 2011.
(ACCA UK - Adapted)

Solution

Consolidated statement of financial position of Alpha at 30 September 2011

	Rs.'000
ASSETS	
Non-current assets:	
Property, plant and equipment (210,000 + 165,000 + 19,850 + 2,500 (W1))	397,350
Goodwill (W2)	43,600
Investment in associate (W9)	52,600
Other investments	16,000
	509,550
Current Assets:	
Inventories (65,000 + 36,000 – 4,000 (W5))	97,000
Trade receivables (55,000 + 38,000 – 5,000 (inter-company))	88,000

Cash and cash equivalents (12,000 + 7,000)	19,000
	204,000
Total Assets	713,550
EQUITY AND LIABILITIES	
Equity attributable to equity holders. of the parent	
Share capital	180,000
Retained earnings (W5)	186,052
Other components of equity (W8)	99,785
	465,837
Non-controlling interest (W4)	39,496
Total equity	505,333
Non-current liabilities	
Long-term borrowings (45,047 (W7) + 35,000)	80,047
Deferred tax (W10)	28,670
Total non-current liabilities	108,717
Current liabilities:	
Trade and other payables (34,000 + 23,000 – 5,000 (inter-company))	52,000
Contingent consideration	22,000
Provision for fines	1,500
Short-term borrowings (17,000 + 7,000)	24,000
Total current liabilities	99,500
Total equity and liabilities	713,550

WORKINGS
Working 1 – Net assets table – Beta:

	1 April 2010 Rs.'000	Change Rs.'000	30 Sept 2011 Rs.'000
Share capital	100,000	–	100,000
Retained earnings	41,000	26,000	67,000
Other components of equity	3,000	2,000	5,000
Property adjustment – see below	20,000	(150)	19,850
Plant and equipment adjustment – see below	4,000	(1,500)	2,500
Inventory adjustment	1,000	(1,000)	Nil
Deferred tax on fair value adjustments	5,000	530	(4,470)
Net assets for the consolidation	164,000	25,880	189,880

The post-acquisition increase in net assets Rs.25·88 million (Rs.189·88 million – Rs.164 million). Rs.2 million of this increase relates to other components of equity, the balance of Rs.23·88 million relates to retained earnings.

Note re: post-acquisition depreciation adjustments:
For the property this is Rs.150,000 ((Rs.33 million – Rs.30 million) x 1·5/30). This makes the closing adjustment Rs.19·85 million (Rs.20 million – Rs.150,000).
For the plant and equipment this is Rs.1·5 million ((Rs.64 million – Rs.60 million) x 1·5/4). This makes the closing adjustment Rs.2·5 million (Rs.4 million – Rs.1·5 million).

Working 2 – Goodwill on consolidation (Beta)

	Rs.'000
Cost of investment:	
Share exchange (80 million x ½ x Rs.4)	160,000
Contingent consideration	20,000
Fair value of non-controlling interest at date of acquisition (20 million x Rs.1·80)	36,000
	216,000
Net assets at 1 April 2010 (W1)	(164,000)
Goodwill before impairment	52,000
Impairment (W3)	(8,400)
Goodwill after impairment	43,600

Working 3 – Impairment of goodwill:

	Rs.'000
Carrying value of assets in cash generating unit	50,000
Allocated goodwill (20% x Rs.52 million (W2))	10,400
	60,400
Recoverable amount of assets in cash generating unit	(52,000)
Goodwill impairment	8,400

Working 4 – Non-controlling interest in Beta:

	Rs.'000
Fair value at date of acquisition (W2)	36,000
20% of post-acquisition increase in net assets (Rs.25·88 million (W1)	5,176
	(1,680)
20% of goodwill impairment (Rs.8·4 million – (W3))	
	39,496

Working 5 – Retained earnings

	Rs.'000
Alpha	183,000
Charge for share based payment for the period (W6)	(1,410)
Additional finance cost on loan notes (3,522 – 2,500 (W7))	(1,022)
Provision for fines for illegal operation of vehicles	(1,500)
Increase in fair value of contingent consideration (Rs.22 million – Rs.20 million)	(2,000)
Beta (80% x Rs.23·88 million (W1))	19,104
Gamma (40% x (64,000 – 60,000))	1,600
Unrealised profits on sales to Beta (16,000 x 25%)	(4,000)
Unrealised profits on sales to Gamma (10,000 x 25% x 40%)	(1,000)
80% of impairment of goodwill on acquisition of Beta (Rs.8·4 million (W3) x 80%)	(6,720)
	186,052

Working 6 – Share based payment charge

	Rs.'000

Expected total cost (5,000 x 1,000 x 93% x Rs.1·20)	5,580
Amount that should be recognised to date (2/4)	2,790
Recognised in draft financial statements (5,000 x 1,000 x 92% x Rs.1·20 x ¼)	(1,380)
So additional amount to recognise	1,410

Working 7 – Convertible loan notes

	Rs.'000
Liability element (Rs.2·5 million x 3·99 + Rs.50 million x 0·681)	44,025
Equity component (balancing figure)	5,975
	50,000
Opening liability	44,025
Finance cost for the period (8%)	3,522
Actual interest paid	(2,500)
Closing liability	45047

Working 8 – Other components of equity

	Rs.'000
Alpha	90,000
Addition re: revaluation of investment in Sigma (1,000 – 20% (deferred tax) x 1,000)	800
Addition re: share based payment (W6)	1,410
Addition re: convertible loan notes (W7)	5,975
Beta (80% x Rs.2 million (W1))	1,600
	99,785

Working 9 – Investment in Gamma

	Rs.'000
Cost	52,000
Share of post-acquisition profits (W5)	1,600
Unrealised profits (W5)	(1,000)
	52,600

Working 10 – Deferred tax

	Rs.'000
Alpha + Beta	24,000
On revaluation of investment in Sigma (W8)	200
On fair value adjustments (W11)	4,470
	28,670

Working 11 – Deferred tax on fair value adjustments:
Fair value adjustments:

	1 April 2010	30 September 2011
	Rs.'000	Rs.'000
Land adjustment	20,000	19,850
Plant and equipment adjustment	4,000	2,500

Inventory adjustment	1,000	nil
Net taxable temporary differences	25,000	22,350
Related deferred tax (20%)	5,000	4,470

Q.9.3.

Alpha holds investments in two other entities, Beta and Gamma. The statements of financial position of the three entities at 31 March 2010 were as follows:

	Alpha Rs'000	Beta Rs'000	Gamma Rs'000
ASSETS			
Non-current assets:			
Property, plant and equipment (Note 1)	135,000	100000	110000
Investments (Notes 1 and 2)	139,000	15000	Nil
	274,000	115,000	110,000
Current assets:			
Inventories (Note 4)	45,000	32,000	27,000
Trade receivables (Note 6)	50,000	34,000	35,000
Cash and cash equivalents	10,000	4,000	8,000
	105,000	70,000	70,000
Total assets	379,000	185,000	180,000
EQUITY AND LIABILITIES			
Equity			
Share capital ($1 shares)	120,000	80,000	60,000
Retained earnings	163,000	44,000	55,000
Total equity	283,000	124,000	115,000
Non-current liabilities:			
Long-term borrowings	40,000	25,000	30,000
Deferred tax	20,000	8,000	10,000
Total non-current liabilities	60,000	33,000	40,000
Current liabilities:			
Trade and other payables	30,000	22,000	20,000
Short term borrowings	6,000	6,000	5,000
Total current liabilities	36,000	28,000	25,000
Total equity and liabilities	379,000	185,000	180,000

Note 1 – Alpha's investment in Beta:

On 1 April 2009 Alpha purchased 60 million shares in Beta for an immediate cash payment of Rs.100 million. The retained earnings of Beta at 1 April 2009 were Rs.35 million.

It is the group policy to value the non-controlling interest in subsidiaries at the date of acquisition at fair value. The fair value of an equity share in Beta at 1 April 2009 was estimated at Re.1·70. This fair value is considered by the directors of Alpha to be an appropriate basis for measuring the non-controlling interest in Beta on 1 April 2009.

The terms of the business combination provide for the payment of an additional Rs.15 million to the former shareholders of Beta on 31 March 2011. On 1 April 2009 Alpha's credit rating was such that it could have borrowed funds at an annual finance cost of 8%. The statement of   financial position of Alpha includes this investment at its original cost of Rs.100 million.

The directors of Alpha carried out a fair value exercise to measure the identifiable assets and liabilities of Beta at 1 April 2009. The following matters emerged:

– A property having a carrying value of Rs.40 million (depreciable amount Rs.24 million) had a fair value of Rs.60 million (depreciable amount Rs.36 million). The estimated future economic life of the depreciable amount of the property at 1 April 2009 was 30 years.

– Plant and equipment having a carrying value of Rs.51 million had a fair value of Rs.54 million. The estimated future economic life of the plant at 1 April 2009 was three years.

The fair value adjustments have not been reflected in the individual financial statements of Beta. In the consolidated financial statements the fair value adjustments will be regarded as temporary differences for the purposes of computing deferred tax. The rate of tax to apply to temporary differences is 30%.

The goodwill arising on acquisition of Beta has not suffered any impairment since 1 April 2009.

Note 2 – Alpha's investment in Gamma:

On 1 October 2009 Alpha paid Rs.39 million for 30% of the equity shares of Gamma. This investment gave Alpha significant influence over Gamma. The retained earnings of Gamma on 1 October 2009 were Rs.60 million. You can ignore any deferred taxation implications of the investment by Alpha in Gamma. The investment in Gamma has not suffered any impairment since 1 October 2009.

Note 3 – Beta's investment:

Beta's investment is a strategic equity investment in Sigma – key supplier. This investment does not give Beta control or significant influence over Sigma. Sigma is not a joint venture for Beta. The investment in Sigma is correctly classified as available for sale and on 1 April 2009 was included in the financial statements of Beta at its fair value of Rs.15 million.

The fair value of the investment in Sigma on 31 March 2010 was Rs.17 million. In the tax jurisdiction in which Beta is located unrealised profits on the revaluation of equity investments are not subject to current tax. Any such profits are taxed only when the investment is sold.

Note 4 – Inter-company sale of inventories:

The inventories of Beta and Gamma at 31 March 2010 included components purchased from Alpha during the year at a cost of Rs.10 million to Beta and Rs.12 million to Gamma. Alpha generated a gross profit margin of 25% on the supply of these components. You can ignore any deferred tax implications of the information in this note.

Note 5 – Trade receivables and payables:

The trade receivables of Alpha included Rs.5 million receivable from Beta and Rs.4 million receivable from Gamma in respect of the purchase of components (see Note 4). The trade payables of Beta and Gamma do not include any amounts payable to Alpha. This is because on 29 March 2010 Beta and Gamma paid Rs.5 million and Rs.4 million respectively to Alpha to eliminate the balances. Alpha received and recorded these payments on 2 April 2010.

Required:

Prepare the consolidated Balance Sheet of Alpha at 31 March 2010.

Solution

Consolidated Balance Sheet of Alpha at 31 March 2010

(all numbers in Rs'000 unless otherwise stated)

ASSETS	
Non-current assets:	
Property, plant and equipment (135,000 + 100,000 + 19,600 + 2,000 (W1))	256,600
Goodwill (W2)	15,760
Investment in associate (W6)	36,600
Available for sale investment	17,000
	325,960
Current assets:	
Inventories (45,000 + 32,000 – 2,500 (W4))	74,500
Trade receivables (50,000 + 34,000 – 5,000 (inter-company))	79,000
Cash and cash equivalents (10,000 + 4,000 + 5,000 (cash in transit))	19,000
	172,500
Total assets	498,460
EQUITY AND LIABILITIES	
Equity attributable to equity holders of the parent	
Share capital	120,000
Retained earnings (W4)	163,086
Other components of equity (W5)	1,050
	284,136
Non-controlling interest (W3)	36,355
Total equity	320,491
Non-current liabilities:	
Long-term borrowings (40,000 + 25,000)	65,000
Deferred tax (20,000 + 8,000 + 600 (W1) + 6,480 (W7))	35,080
Total non-current liabilities	100,080
Current liabilities:	
Trade and other payables (30,000 + 22,000)	52,000
Deferred consideration (12,860 (W2) + 1,029 (W4))	13,889
Short-term borrowings (6,000 + 6,000)	12,000
Total current liabilities	77,889
Total equity and liabilities	498,460

Workings – unless stated all figures in Rs'000

Working 1 – Net assets table – Beta

	1 April 2009	Change	31 March 2010
Share capital	80,000	-	80,000
Retained earnings:			
Per accounts of Beta	35,000	9000	44,000
Property adjustment – see below	20,000	(400)	19,600
Plant and equipment adjustment – see below	3,000	(1000)	2,000
Deferred tax on fair value adjustments	(6,900)	420	(6,480)
Revaluation of AFS investment (see below)		1400	1,400
Net assets for the consolidation	131,100	9420	140,520

The post-acquisition profits are 9,420 (140,520 – 131,100).
Of this amount 1,400 is taken to other reserves and 8,020 (9,420 – 1,400) to retained earnings.

Note re: post-acquisition depreciation adjustments:
For the property this is 400 ((36,000 – 24,000) x 1/30). This makes the closing adjustment 19,600 (20,000 – 400). For the plant and equipment this is 1,000 ((54,000 – 51,000) x 1/3). This makes the closing adjustment 2,000 (3,000 – 1,000).

Note re: revaluation of the investment:
The carrying value should be 17,000 – an increase of 2,000 from the 15,000 shown in the draft accounts of Beta. The related deferred tax is 600 (2,000 x 30%) so the net adjustment is 1,400 (2,000 – 600).

Working 2 – Goodwill on consolidation (Beta)

Cost of investment:	
Cash	100,000
Deferred consideration (15,000/(1·08)2)	12,860
Fair value of non-controlling interest at date of acquisition (20,000 x $1·70)	34,000
	146,860
Net assets at 1 April 2009 (131,100 (W1))	(131,100)
So goodwill equals	15,760

Working 3 – Non-controlling interest in Beta

Fair value at date of acquisition (W2)	34,000
25% of post-acquisition profits (9,420 (W1))	2,355
	36,355

Working 4 – Retained earnings

Alpha	163,000
Interest on deferred consideration (12,860 (W2) x 8%)	(1,029)
Beta (75% x 8,020 (W1))	6,015

Gamma (30% x (55,000 – 60,000))	(1,500)
Unrealised profits on sales to Beta (10,000 x 25%)	(2,500)
Unrealised profits on sales to Gamma (12,000 x 25% x 30%))	(900)
	163,086

Working 5 – Other components of equity

75% x 1,400 (W1) – the revaluation of the AFS investment	1,050

Working 6 – Investment in Gamma

Cost	39,000
Share of post-acquisition losses (W4)	(1,500)
Unrealised profits (W4)	(900)
	36,600

Working 7 – Deferred tax on temporary differences
Fair value adjustments:

	1 April 2009	31 March 2010
Land adjustment	20,000	19,600
Plant and equipment adjustment	3,000	2,000
Net taxable temporary differences	23,000	21,600
Related deferred tax (30%)	6,900	6,480

Q.9.4.
The statements of Profit & Los of Alpha, Beta and Gamma for the year ended 30 September 2012 are given below:

Statements of comprehensive income

	Alpha Rs'000	Beta Rs'000	Gamma Rs'000
Revenue	240,000	150,000	120,000
Cost of sales	(190,000)	(110,000)	(70,000)
Gross profit	50,000	40,000	50,000
Distribution costs	(7,000)	(6,000)	(8,000)
Administrative expenses	(10,000)	(7,000)	(8,000)
Profit from operations	33,000	27,000	34,000
Investment income	15,300	Nil	Nil
Finance cost	(8,000)	(4,900)	(7,300)
Profit before tax	40,300	22,100	26,700
Income tax expense	(10,100)	(6,000)	(6,700)
Net profit for the period	30,200	16,100	20,000
Other comprehensive income	4,000	Nil	Nil

Total comprehensive income	34,200	16,100	20,000

Note 1 – Purchase of shares in Beta
On 1 October 2011, Alpha purchased 80% of the equity shares of Beta. The purchase consideration was as follows:
– Alpha issued 32 million shares to the shareholders of Beta. The market price of an Alpha share on 1 October 2011 was Rs.2·50.
– Alpha agreed to make an additional payment of Rs.30 million to the shareholders of Beta on 30 September 2013.
This payment was contingent on the post-acquisition profits of Beta reaching a specified level in the two-year period ending on 30 September 2013. The directors of Alpha assessed that the fair value of this contingent consideration was Rs.20 million on 1 October 2011 and debited Rs.20 million to the cost of investment in Beta.
They reassessed the fair value of the contingent consideration at Rs.22 million on 30 September 2012. The increase in the fair value of the contingent consideration was caused by the better than expected performance of Beta in the post-acquisition period. The directors of Alpha made no change to the carrying value of the cost of investment in Beta as a result of this reassessment.
– Alpha incurred incremental legal and professional fees of Rs.1·5 million in connection with the acquisition of Beta and debited these costs to the cost of investment in Beta. Rs.500,000 of this amount related to the costs of issuing the Alpha shares.

Note 2 – Fair value exercise
The directors of Alpha carried out a fair value exercise on the net assets of Beta on 1 October 2011. On 1 October 2011, the equity of Beta as shown in its own financial statements was Rs.88 million. The fair values of the net assets of Beta were the same as their book values with the exception of:
– Plant and equipment that had a book value of Rs.80 million and a fair value of Rs.84 million. The estimated remaining useful economic life of this plant and equipment was two years at 1 October 2011. Depreciation of plant and equipment is charged to cost of sales.
– An intangible asset that had a fair value of Rs.6 million but was not recognised by Beta because it was internally developed. The useful life of this asset was estimated at 18 months from 1 October 2011. Amortisation of intangible assets is charged to cost of sales.
– Inventory that had a book value of Rs.3 million and a fair value of Rs.3·2 million. This entire inventory was sold in the year ended 30 September 2012.
– The fair value adjustments are temporary differences that attract deferred tax at a rate of 25%.

Note 3 – Basis of measurement of non-controlling interests. It is the policy of Alpha to measure non-controlling interests based on their fair value at the date of acquisition. The estimated fair value of the non-controlling interest in Beta at 1 October 2011 was Rs.20 million.

Note 4 – Other information regarding Beta
– On 1 October 2011, Alpha made a loan of Rs.40 million to Beta at a fixed annual interest rate of 5%. Both Alpha and Beta have correctly accounted for the interest on this loan in their individual statements of comprehensive income.
– On 31 March 2012, Beta paid a dividend of Rs.10 million to its equity shareholders.

Note 5 – Impairment review
On 30 September 2012, the directors of Alpha reviewed the goodwill on acquisition of Beta for impairment. They measured the recoverable amount of Beta (as a single cash-generating unit) at Rs.118 million at that date. Impairment of goodwill is charged to cost of sales.

Note 6 – Purchase of shares in Gamma
– On 1 January 2012, Alpha and another investor both purchased 50% of the equity capital of Gamma for a cash payment of Rs.50 million. These investments enabled the two investors to jointly control Gamma.
– On 31 March 2012, Gamma paid a dividend of Rs.10 million to its equity shareholders.
– The recoverable amount of the investment in Gamma by Alpha was estimated at Rs.50 million on 30 September 2012.
– Ignore the deferred tax implications of the investment in Gamma.

Note 7 – Inter-company sales
Alpha supplies products used by Beta and Gamma. Sales of the products to Beta and Gamma during

the year ended 30 September 2012 were as follows (all sales were made at a profit margin of 20%):
– Sales to Beta Rs.25 million.
– Sales to Gamma (all since 1 January 2012) Rs.12 million.
At 30 September 2012, the inventories of Beta and Gamma included the following amounts in respect of goods purchased from Alpha. Ignore the deferred tax implications of the inter-company sales to Beta and Gamma.

	Rs'000
Beta	5,000
Gamma	4,000

Note 8 – Share based payments
On 1 October 2011, Alpha granted 1,000 senior employees 2,500 share options each, provided they remained as employees for the two years ending 30 September 2013. On 1 October 2011, the fair value of one share option was Rs.5 and this had increased to Rs.5·40 by 30 September 2012. On 1 October 2011, the directors estimated that 950 employees would qualify for these options. At 30 September 2012, this estimate was 960 employees. Ignore the deferred tax implications of this transaction.

Note 9 – Other comprehensive income of Alpha
On 1 September 2011, Alpha entered into a contract to sell €10 million for Rs.85 million. This contract was to hedge against an expected sales receipt from a customer on 31 January 2012 that was denominated in €. On 30 September 2011, the contract was a financial asset with a fair value of Rs.1 million. Alpha designated the contract as a cash-flow hedge of the expected future sales in € and credited Rs.1 million to other comprehensive income in the year ended 30 September 2011. On 31 January 2012, the sales in € were made to the customer and the customer paid for the goods on that date. On 31 January 2012, the fair value of the contract to sell €10 million for Rs.85 million was Rs.5 million. Therefore Alpha credited a further Rs.4 million to other comprehensive income and recorded the sales revenue at €10 million, translated at the spot rate of exchange on that date.

Note 10 – Investment by Alpha in Zeta
On 1 October 2011, Alpha purchased 100,000 equity shares in Zeta for Rs.10 per share. The investment did not give Alpha control or significant influence over Zeta and was designated by Alpha as fair value through other comprehensive income. Alpha incurred transaction costs of Rs.50,000 which it recorded as part of its finance costs.
During the period Alpha received a dividend of Rs.2 per share from Zeta and at 30 September 2012 the fair value of a Zeta share was Rs.11. Alpha recorded both the dividend and the increase in fair value of its holding as investment income. Ignore the deferred tax implications of this transaction.
Required:
Prepare the consolidated statement of Profit & Loss and Other Comprehensive income for Alpha for the year ended 30 September 2012.

Solution
Consolidated statement of Profit & Loss and Other Comprehensive Income of Alpha for the year ended 30 September 2012

	Rs'000
Revenue (W1)	365,000
Cost of sales (balancing figure)	(286,050)
Gross profit (W2)	78,950
Distribution costs (7,000 + 6,000)	(13,000)
Administrative expenses (W5)	(26,000)
Investment income (W6)	200
Finance cost (W7)	(10,850)
Other income (re-classified gains on cash flow hedge)	5,000
Share of profit of joint venture (W8)	5,000
Profit before tax	39,300
Income tax expense (W10))	(14,550)
Net profit for the period	24,750
Other comprehensive income (W12)	(950)

Total comprehensive income	23,800
Net profit attributable to:	
Non-controlling interest (W13)	1,600
Controlling interest	23,150
	24,750
Total comprehensive income attributable to:	
Non-controlling interest	1,600
Controlling interest	22,200
	23,800

WORKINGS

Working 1 – Revenue	Rs'000
Alpha + Beta	390,000
Intra-group sales – to Beta	(25,000)
	365,000

Working 2 – Gross profit	Rs'000
Alpha + Beta	90,000
Unrealised profit adjustments:	
Beta: (20% x Rs.5 million)	(1,000)
Gamma: (20% x Rs.4 million x 50%)	(400)
Extra depreciation (Rs.4 million x ½))	(2,000)
Extra amortisation (Rs.6 million x 12/18)	(4,000)
Additional cost of sales of inventory	(200)
Impairment of goodwill (W3)	(3,450)
	78,950

Working 3 – Impairment of goodwill:	Rs'000
Carrying value of Beta at reporting date:	
As per own SOCE (Rs.88 million + Rs.16·1 million – Rs.10 million (the dividend))	94,100
Fair value adjustment on PPE (Rs.4 million x ½)	2,000
Fair value adjustment on intangible (Rs.6 million x 6/18)	2,000
Deferred tax on fair value adjustments (Rs.2·55 million (W4) – Rs.1·55 million (W10)	(1,000)
Goodwill on acquisition (W4)	24,350
	121,450
Recoverable amount	(118,000)
So impairment equals	3,450

Working 4 – Goodwill on acquisition of Beta	Rs'000	Rs'000
Cost of investment:		
Share exchange (32,000 x Rs.2·50)		80,000
Contingent consideration		20,000
Fair value of non-controlling interest at date of acquisition		20,000
		120,000
Equity of Gamma at date of acquisition:		
Per own records	88,000	
Fair value adjustments:		
Plant and equipment	4,000	
Intangible asset	6,000	

Inventory	200	
Deferred tax on fair value adjustments		
(25% x (Rs.4m + Rs.6m + Rs.200,000))	(2,550)	
For consolidation purposes		(95,650)
So goodwill		24,350

Working 5 – Administrative expenses	Rs'000
Alpha + Beta	17,000
Increase in fair value of contingent consideration	2,000
Beta acquisition costs	1,000
Charge for share based payment award (2,500 x 960 x Rs.5 x ½)	6,000
	26,000

Tutorial note: The above costs would, if sensibly included elsewhere in the statement, have also been awarded credit.

Working 6 – Investment income	Rs'000
Per accounts of Alpha	15,300
Dividend received from Beta	(8,000)
Interest received from Beta (40,000 x 5%)	(2,000)
Dividend received from Gamma	(5,000)
Increase in fair value of investment in Zeta	(100)
Residue in consolidated income statement	200

Working 7 – Finance cost	Rs'000
Alpha + Beta	12,900
Interest paid by Beta to Alpha (W6)	(2,000)
Transaction costs of investment in Zeta	(50)
Residue in profit and loss	10,850

Working 8 – Share of profits of Gamma	Rs'000
Share of profit (Rs.20m x 50% x 9/12)	7,500
Impairment (W9)	(2,500)
	5,000

Working 9 – Impairment of investment in Gamma	Rs'000
Cost	50,000
Share of profit (Rs.20m x 50% x 9/12)	7,500
Dividend received	(5,000)
Carrying amount	52,500
Recoverable amount	(50,000)
So impairment equals	2,500

Working 10 – Income tax expense	Rs'000
Alpha + Beta	16,100
Reversal of temporary differences on fair value adjustments (W11)	(1,550)
	14,550

Working 11 – Reversal of temporary differences	
	Rs'000
Depreciation	2,000

Amortisation	4,000
Cost of sales	200
	6,200
25% x Rs.6·2 million equals	1,550

Working 12 – Other comprehensive income	Rs'000
Gain on cash flow hedge	4,000
Reclassification of gain on cash flow hedge	(5,000)
Gain on investment at FVTOCI (100,000 x Re.1 – Rs.50,000)	50
	(950)

Working 13 – Non-controlling interest in Beta	Rs'000
Profit after tax	16,100
Fair value adjustments (W11)	(6,200)
Deferred tax on fair value adjustments (W11)	1,550
Impairment of goodwill (W3)	(3,450)
	8,000
Non-controlling interest (20%)	1,600

Q.9.5.

Alpha holds investments in two other entities, Beta and Gamma. The statements of financial position of the three entities at 31 March 2010 were as follows:

	Alpha Rs'000	Beta Rs'000	Gamma Rs'000
ASSETS			
Non-current assets:			
Property, plant and equipment (Note 1)	135,000	100,000	110,000
Investments (Notes 1 and 2)	139,000	15,000	Nil
	274,000	115,000	110,000
Current assets:			
Inventories (Note 4)	45,000	32,000	27,000
Trade receivables (Note 5)	52,000	34,000	35,000
Cash and cash equivalents	10,000	4,000	8,000
	107,000	70,000	70,000
Total assets	381,000	185,000	180,000
EQUITY AND LIABILITIES			
Equity	Rs'000	Rs'000	Rs'000
Share capital ($1 shares)	120,000	80,000	60,000
Retained earnings	163,000	44,000	55,000

Total equity	<u>283,000</u>	<u>124,000</u>	<u>115,000</u>
Non-current liabilities:			
Long-term borrowings (Note 7)	30,000	25,000	30,000
Provisions (Note 8)	12000	-	-
Deferred tax	20,000	8,000	10,000
Total non-current liabilities	62,000	33,000	40,000
Current liabilities:			
Trade and other payables	30,000	22,000	20,000
Short-term borrowings	6,000	6,000	5,000
Total current liabilities	36,000	28,000	25,000
Total equity and liabilities	381,000	185,000	180,000

Note 1 – Alpha's investment in Beta:
On 1 April 2009 Alpha purchased 60 million shares in Beta for an immediate cash payment of Rs.100 million. The retained earnings of Beta at 1 April 2009 were Rs.35 million.
It is the group policy to value the non-controlling interest in subsidiaries at the date of acquisition at fair value. The fair value of an equity share in Beta at 1 April 2009 was estimated at Rs.1·70. This fair value is considered by the directors of Alpha to be an appropriate basis for measuring the non-controlling interest in Beta on 1 April 2009.
The terms of the business combination provide for the payment of an additional $15 million to the former shareholders of Beta on 31 March 2011. On 1 April 2009 Alpha's credit rating was such that it could have borrowed funds at an annual finance cost of 8%. The statement of financial position of Alpha includes this investment at its original cost of Rs.100 million.
The directors of Alpha carried out a fair value exercise to measure the identifiable assets and liabilities of Beta at 1 April 2009. The following matters emerged:
– A property having a carrying value of Rs.40 million (depreciable amount Rs.24 million) had a fair value of Rs.60 million (depreciable amount Rs.36 million). The estimated future economic life of the depreciable amount of the property at 1 April 2009 was 30 years.
– Plant and equipment having a carrying value of Rs.51 million had a fair value of Rs.54 million. The estimated future economic life of the plant at 1 April 2009 was three years.
The fair value adjustments have not been reflected in the individual financial statements of Beta. In the consolidated financial statements the fair value adjustments will be regarded as temporary differences for the purposes of computing deferred tax. The rate of tax to apply to temporary differences is 30%.
The goodwill arising on acquisition of Beta has not suffered any impairment since 1 April 2009.
Note 2 – Alpha's investment in Gamma:
On 1 October 2009 Alpha paid Rs.39 million for 30% of the equity shares of Gamma. This investment gave Alpha significant influence over Gamma. The retained earnings of Gamma on 1 October 2009 were Rs.60 million. You can ignore any deferred taxation implications of the investment by Alpha in Gamma. The investment in Gamma has not suffered any impairment since 1 October 2009.

Note 3 – Beta's investment:

Beta's investment is a strategic equity investment in Sigma – key supplier. This investment does not give Beta control or significant influence over Sigma. Sigma is not a joint venture for Beta. The investment in Sigma is correctly classified as available for sale and on 1 April 2009 was included in the financial statements of Beta at its fair value of Rs.15 million.

The fair value of the investment in Sigma on 31 March 2010 was Rs.17 million. In the tax jurisdiction in which Beta is located unrealised profits on the revaluation of equity investments are not subject to current tax. Any such profits are taxed only when the investment is sold.

Note 4 – Inter-company sale of inventories:

The inventories of Beta and Gamma at 31 March 2010 included components purchased from Alpha during the year at a cost of Rs.10 million to Beta and Rs.12 million to Gamma. Alpha generated a gross profit margin of 25% on the supply of these components. You can ignore any deferred tax implications of the information in this note.

Note 5 – Trade receivables and payables:

The trade receivables of Alpha included $5 million receivable from Beta and Rs.4 million receivable from Gamma in respect of the purchase of components (see Note 4). The trade payables of Beta and Gamma do not include any amounts payable to Alpha. This is because on 29 March 2010 Beta and Gamma paid Rs.5 million and Rs.4 million respectively to Alpha to eliminate the balances. Alpha received and recorded these payments on 2 April 2010.

Note 6 – Lease charge

The income statement includes a charge of Rs.1.5 m being the first two of ten payments of Rs.750000 each in respect of a five-year lease of an item of plant. The payments were made On 1 April 2009 and 1 October 2009. The fair value of this plant at the date it was leased was Rs.6.0 m. Information obtained from the finance department confirms that this is a finance lease and an appropriate periodic rate of interest is 10% per annum. Alpha has treated the lease as operating lease in the above financial statements. The company depreciates plant used under finance leases on a straight line basis over the life of the lease.

Note 7 – Loan note

On 1 April 2009 Alpha issued a Rs.30 m 6 % convertible loan note at par. The loan note is Redeemable at a premium of 10% on 31 March 20133, or it may be converted into Ordinary shares on the basis of 50 shares for each Rs.100 of loan not at the option of the Holder. The interest (coupon) rate for an equivalent note without the conversion rights would have been 10%. In the draft financial statements Alpha has paid and charged Interest of Rs.1.8 m and shown the loan note at Rs.30 m on the statement of financial position.

The present value of Re.1 receivable at the end of each year, based on discount rates of 6% and 10% can be taken as :

End of year	6%	10%
1	0.94	0.91
2	0.89	0.83
3	0.84	0.75
4	0.79	0.68

Note 8 – Environmental provision

The draft financial statements contain an accumulating provision for the cost of restoring (landscaping) the site of a quarry that is being operated by Alpha. The result of an Environmental audit has concluded that the provision has been calculated on the wrong basis and is materially underprovided. A firm of environmental experts has summarised the required provision: (Rs'000)

	Current provision	Required provision
Income statement charge (y.e. 31.3.10)	1800	2450
Balance Sheet liability – as at 31.3.10	12000	21500

Required: Prepare the consolidated Balance Sheet of Alpha at 31.3.2010

Solution
Consolidated Balance Sheet of Alpha at 31 March 2010
(all numbers in Rs'000 unless otherwise stated)

ASSETS

Non-current assets:

Property, plant and equipment (135,000 + 100,000 + 19,600 + 2,000 (W1)) + 4800 (w8)	261,400
Goodwill (W2)	15,760
Investment in associate (W6)	36,600
Available for sale investment	17,000
	330,760

Current assets:

Inventories (45,000 + 32,000 – 2,500 (W4))	74,500
Trade receivables (52,000 + 34,000 – 5,000 (inter-company))	81,000
Cash and cash equivalents (10,000 + 4,000 + 5,000 (cash in transit))	19,000
	174,500
Total assets	505,260

EQUITY AND LIABILITIES

Equity attributable to equity holders of the parent

Share capital	120,000
Retained earnings (W4)	152,366
Equity element of convertible loan notes (W9)	1850
Other components of equity (W5)	1,050
	275,266
Non-controlling interest (W3)	36,355
Total equity	311,621

Non-current liabilities:

Long-term borrowings (29170 (W9) + 25,000)	54170
Provisions (W 10)	21500
Deferred tax (20,000 + 8,000 + 600 (W1) + 6,480 (W7))	35,080

Finance lease liability (W8)	3,710
Total non-current liabilities	114,460
Current liabilities:	
Trade and other payables (30,000 + 22,000)	52,000
Deferred consideration (12,860 (W2) + 1,029 (W4))	13,889
Short-term borrowings (6,000 + 6,000)	12,000
Finance lease liability (W8)	1,290
Total current liabilities	79,179
Total equity and liabilities	505,260

Workings – unless stated all figures in $'000

Working 1 – Net assets table – Beta

	1 April 2009	Change	31 March 2010
Share capital	80,000	-	80,000
Retained earnings:			
Per accounts of Beta	35,000	9000	44,000
Property adjustment – see below	20,000	(400)	19,600
Plant and equipment adjustment – see below	3,000	(1000)	2,000
Deferred tax on fair value adjustments	(6,900)	420	(6,480)
Revaluation of AFS investment (see below)		1400	1,400
Net assets for the consolidation	131,100	9420	140,520

The post-acquisition profits are 9,420 (140,520 – 131,100).
Of this amount 1,400 is taken to other reserves and 8,020 (9,420 – 1,400) to retained earnings.

Note re: post-acquisition depreciation adjustments:
For the property this is 400 ((36,000 – 24,000) x 1/30). This makes the closing adjustment 19,600 (20,000 – 400). For the plant and equipment this is 1,000 ((54,000 – 51,000) x 1/3). This makes the closing adjustment 2,000 (3,000 – 1,000).

Note re: revaluation of the investment:
The carrying value should be 17,000 – an increase of 2,000 from the 15,000 shown in the draft accounts of Beta. The related deferred tax is 600 (2,000 x 30%) so the net adjustment is 1,400 (2,000 – 600).

Working 2 – Goodwill on consolidation (Beta)

	Rs'000	Rs'000
Cost of investment:		
Cash	100,000	
Deferred consideration (15,000/(1·08)^2)	12,860	
Fair value of non-controlling interest at date of acquisition		
(20,000 x Rs.1·70)	34,000	
		146,860
Net assets at 1 April 2009 (131,100 (W1))		(131,100)
So goodwill equals		15,760

Working 3 – Non-controlling interest in Beta

Fair value at date of acquisition (W2)	34,000
25% of post-acquisition profits (9,420 (W1))	2,355
	36,355

Working 4 – Retained earnings

	Rs'000
Alpha	163,000
Interest on deferred consideration (12,860 (W2) x 8%)	(1,029)
Beta (75% x 8,020 (W1))	6,015
Gamma (30% x (55,000 – 60,000))	(1,500)
Unrealised profits on sales to Beta (10,000 x 25%)	(2,500)
Unrealised profits on sales to Gamma (12,000 x 25% x 30%))	(900)
Finance lease interest charges (W8 260 +240)	(500)
Finance lease depreciation charges (W8)	(1200)
Finance lease payments added back (W8)	1500
Interest on convertible loan notes – add back 6% interest paid (W9)	1800
Interest on convertible loan notes - interest at 10% (W9)	(2820)
Environmental provision – prior period adjustment (W10)	(8850)
Environmental provision (W10)	(650)
	152,366

Working 5 – Other components of equity

75% x 1,400 (W1) – the revaluation of the AFS investment	1,050

Working 6 – Investment in Gamma

Cost	39,000
Share of post-acquisition losses (W4)	(1,500)
Unrealised profits (W4)	(900)
	36,600

Working 7 – Deferred tax on temporary differences

Fair value adjustments:

	1 April 2009	31 March 2010
Land adjustment	20,000	19,600
Plant and equipment adjustment	3,000	2,000
Net taxable temporary differences	23,000	21,600
Related deferred tax (30%)	6,900	6,480

Working 8: Finance lease

The lease has been treated as an operating lease, it should be restated as finance lease. The Rs.1.5 m lease charge is reversed. The plant is capitalized at its fair value of Rs.6.0 m and depreciated over the five year life of the lease. The depreciation charge for this year Is Rs.1.2 m and the closing carrying value of the plant is Rs.4.8 m. At the start of the lease

Liability is Rs.6.0 m. During the current year the lease payments of Rs.1.5 m are split between their capital and interest components. A schedule of lease payments is needed to calculate this as follows:

	Opening bal	First payment	Balance	Interest @ 10%	Closing bal
1 April 2009	6000	(750)	5250	260	5510
1 Oct 2009	5510	(750)	4760	240	5000
1 April 2010	5000	(750)	4250	210	4460
1 Oct 2010	4460	(750)	3710	185	3895

This year's finance cost is Rs.260000 + Rs.240000 = Rs.500000. This Rs.500000 is charged as Interest and the balance of Rs.1000000 is treated as a repayment of capital. The year-end Lease liability of Rs.5.0 m is split between current and non-current liabilities.

Next year's cash payments total Rs.1.5 m. However, this includes Rs.210000 of interest that arises next year. Therefore the closing current liability is (Rs.1.5 m – Rs.210000) = Rs.1290000.

This is analyzed further between the accrued interest of Rs.240000 for the last six months and repayment of capital element of Rs.1050000.

Working note 9: Convertible loan note

This loan note pays 6% interest whereas market rate is 10%. The note holders will accept this low rate of interest because they have the option to convert their Loan notes into shares. The value of these options is calculated by comparing the proceeds of the loan (Rs.30 m) with the present value of cash payments on the loan discounted at the market rate of interest of 10%. The present value of the loan notes are Rs.28150000 and this is the initial value of the loan. Therefore the options are valued at Rs.1850000 and they are classified as equity.

During the life of the option Deltoid pays Rs.1.8 m p.a. in interest (6% of Rs.30 m).

However, the interest charge in the financial statements will be calculated at the market rate of 10% based on the carrying value of Rs.28150000. In the current year this is Rs. 2820000. At the end of the year the liability is Rs.29170000

Calculated as follows:

Year	Cash flow	DCF @ 10%	DCF
1	1800	0.91	1640
2	1800	0.83	1500
3	1800	0.75	1350
4	1800	0.68	1220
4	3000(10% premium on red)	0.68	2040
4	30000(capital repayment)	0.68	20400
			28150

Initial liability (from table from previous slide)	28150
Interest charged at market rate of 10%	2820
Interest paid at the nominal rate of 6%	(1800)
Closing liability	29170

Working 10: Environmental provision

The environmental provision must be restated in accordance with the new information. The closing provision increases by Rs.9500000 to Rs.21500000. The charge for the year increases by Rs.650000 to Rs.2450000. The Rs.8850000 increase in the opening provision is a prior period adjustment and it is reported in the Statement of changes in equity.

	Opening* 2009	Charge	Closing 2010
Original provision	10200	1800	12000
Revised provision	19050	2450	21500
Change in provision	8850	650	9500

* Balancing figure

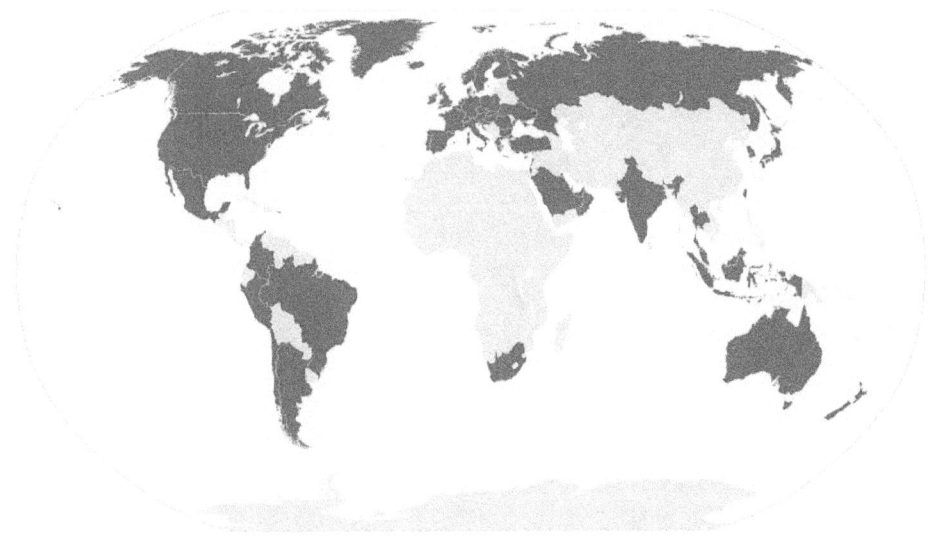

--end of volume--

www.ingramcontent.com/pod-product-compliance
Lightning Source LLC
Chambersburg PA
CBHW051848170526
45168CB00001B/28